A Special Issue of
Neuropsychological Rehabilitation

Non-Invasive Brain Stimulation: New Prospects in Cognitive Neurorehabilitation

Guest Editors

Carlo Miniussi

*University of Brescia &
IRCCS Centro San Giovanni di Dio, Italy*

and

Giuseppe Vallar

*Department of Psychology, University of Milano Bicocca
& IRCCS Italian Auxological Institute, Milan, Italy*

Psychology Press
Taylor & Francis Group
HOVE AND NEW YORK

Published in 2011 by Psychology Press Ltd
4 Park Square, Milton Park, Abingdon, Oxon, OX14 4RN, UK

www.psypress.com

Simultaneously published in the USA and Canada
by Taylor & Francis Inc
29 West 35th Street, New York, NY 10016, USA

Psychology Press is an imprint of the Taylor & Francis Group, an Informa business

British Library Cataloguing in Publication Data
A catalogue record for this book is available from the British Library

ISBN: 978-1-84872-756-4
ISSN: 0960-2011

Cover design by Hybert Design, Eton
Typeset in the UK by Techset Composition Ltd, Salisbury
Printed in the UK by Hobbs the Printers Ltd, Totton
Bound in the UK by TJ International Ltd, Padstow

This publication has been produced with paper manufactured to strict
environmental standards and with pulp derived from sustainable forests.

Contents*

---

*This book is also a special issue of the journal *Neuropsychological Rehabilitation*, and
forms issue 5 of Volume 21 (2011). The page numbers are taken from the journal and so
begin on p. 553.

NEUROPSYCHOLOGICAL REHABILITATION
2011, 21 (5), 553–559

Foreword

Brain stimulation and behavioural cognitive rehabilitation: A new tool for neurorehabilitation?

Carlo Miniussi[1,2] and Giuseppe Vallar[3,4]

[1]Department of Biomedical Sciences and Biotechnologies, National Institute of Neuroscience, University of Brescia, Italy
[2]Cognitive Neuroscience Section, IRCCS Centro San Giovanni di Dio Fatebenefratelli, Brescia, Italy
[3]Department of Psychology, University of Milano-Bicocca, Milan, Italy
[4]IRCCS Italian Auxological Institute, Milan, Italy

Keywords: Rehabilitation; Neurorehabilitation; Plasticity; Stroke; TMS; tDCS; Non-invasive brain stimulation.

This special issue of *Neuropsychological Rehabilitation* aims to present new knowledge about a recent and innovative approach that can possibly ameliorate the outcome of the rehabilitation of cognitive deficits, namely: non-invasive brain stimulation (NIBS). The issue includes a series of papers on NIBS and combined rehabilitation studies (reviews and some original contributions), highlighting the challenges, as well as the power, of this novel approach.

The old and time-honoured concept that the brain structure becomes immutable after childhood has been abandoned, based on the evidence that all areas of the brain remain plastic in adulthood and during physiological ageing, with even some evidence for neurogenesis (Berlucchi, this issue).

Correspondence should be addressed to Carlo Miniussi, Department of Biomedical Sciences and Biotechnologies, National Institute of Neuroscience, University of Brescia, Viale Europa 11, 25123, Brescia, Italy. E-mail: carlo.miniussi@cognitiveneuroscience.it

This work has been supported by a grant from the James S. McDonnell Foundation. C.M. has been supported in part by Ricerca Corrente Grants from the IRCCS Centro San Giovanni di Dio, G.V. by Ricerca Corrente Grants from the IRCCS Italian Auxological Institute, and by FAR Grants from the University of Milano-Bicocca.

This capacity of a neural system to acquire or improve skills, and to adapt to new environments through a learning process has been labelled "neuroplasticity" (e.g., Huttenlocher, 2002). Neuroplasticity refers to the ability of the nervous system to change its structure and function, as part of the processes that underlie learning and memory, to adapt to environmental changes, and to recover function after brain lesions.

In recent years, new techniques have been developed for the understanding and induction of human neuroplasticity. An important contribution has come from the introduction of NIBS (e.g., Wassermann et al., 2008). The development of NIBS techniques to induce neuroplasticity constitutes a main breakthrough in our understanding of the changes in the brain states accounting for behavioural modifiability. NIBS is also relevant to clinical neuroscience as a means to enhance plasticity, and, by implication, cognitive function in individuals with neuropsychological impairments.

Cognitive deficits are a common consequence of traumatic brain injury, stroke, epilepsy, tumours, neurodegenerative and other neurological disorders, and are a primary cause of disability worldwide (Ropper & Samuels, 2009). The rehabilitation of neuropsychological disorders of cognitive function (including aphasia; unilateral spatial neglect and other spatial disorders; amnesia; apraxia; executive deficits and disorders of attention; acalculia) is defined "cognitive rehabilitation" (e.g., Stuss, Winocur, & Robertson, 2008) and represents an expanding area of clinical care and research (Stuss, this issue). Cognitive deficits, which cause an important functional disability for the patient, and represent a burden for society, are a focus of increasing attention, also in their ethical implications. Cognitive impairment is a major public health and financial problem for society in terms of need for assistance, also due to demographic trends including the increase of average life expectancy, and the decrease of mortality in the acute phase of the disease. Cognitive disorders improve both spontaneously and after cognitive training, particularly when intensive and targeted (Cappa et al., 2005; Cicerone et al., 2005; Rohling, Faust, Beverly, & Demakis, 2009). There are many factors that determine the success of cognitive rehabilitation, which, as discussed by Stuss (this issue), should be tailored as much as possible to the neurofunctional characteristics of the patient.

The use of NIBS to study and modulate cognitive function and dysfunction in neurologically unimpaired participants and in brain-damaged patients (e.g., stroke patients and patients with neurodegenerative disorders) has recently received increased attention within the scientific community (e.g., Hummel & Cohen, 2006; Miniussi et al., 2008; Ridding & Rothwell, 2007).

Vallar and Bolognini (this issue) review studies which show evidence of improved performance through NIBS in neurologically unimpaired participants, in the domains of sensation, perception, attention, language, and executive processes. Cotelli et al. (this issue) review the neuropsychological literature concerning the effects of NIBS in aphasic stroke patients; Hesse, Sparing, and Fink (this issue) in patients with unilateral spatial neglect. Overall, the available evidence from both unimpaired participants and brain-damaged patients shows that NIBS may modulate performance, including improvement in unimpaired participants, and reduction of deficits in brain-damaged patients.

The abovementioned studies concerning cognitive deficits, such as aphasia and unilateral spatial neglect, together with the evidence that NIBS may improve motor performance in patients with hemiplegia, may elucidate the mechanisms underlying the effects of NIBS on deranged functions. The effects of NIBS aimed at improving motor performance in brain-damaged patients with hemiplegia have been most extensively investigated (Tanaka, Sandrini, & Cohen, this issue), and the underlying neurophysiological model is much simpler that those concerning cognitive functions, and their impairments. Tanaka et al. (this issue) emphasise that effects on skill acquisition induced by NIBS may differ according to the different types of stimulation protocols, and the tasks used, as well as, importantly, the interaction between the motor cortices in the two hemispheres. Under certain conditions, behavioural facilitation can be explained as a decrease in cortical inhibition of populations of neurons, as suggested by Hesse et al. (this issue) for unilateral spatial neglect (see also Cotelli et al., this issue).

NIBS has also been used for the treatment of dementia of the Alzheimer-type (AD) (Boggio et al., this issue). In these patients, NIBS may be used as a tool to assess the neuroplastic changes due to the neurodegenerative process, revealing alterations of cortical excitability. Given the limited effectiveness of pharmacological treatments for AD, non-pharmacological interventions, such as NIBS, may receive some attention in this important neurological domain. Some recent evidence appears to indicate that NIBS interventions promoting neural plasticity can induce cognitive gains, especially in subjects at risk of or with mild AD (Boggio et al., this issue).

Miniussi and Rossini (this issue) and Paulus (this issue) review the NIBS techniques used to modulate cortical activity; these include transcranial magnetic stimulation (TMS) and transcranial electrical stimulation (tES). NIBS techniques exert their effects on neuronal excitation through different mechanisms, which might also depend on a number of technical parameters that have been extensively investigated. TMS induces a current that can elicit action potentials in neurons. Conversely, tES (including transcranial direct current stimulation, tDCS) brings about a polarisation that is too weak to elicit action potentials in cortical neurons. However, tES effectively modifies the evoked cortical response to afferent stimulation (see Vallar & Bolognini, this issue), as well as the postsynaptic activity level of cortical neurons, by inducing a shift in intrinsic neuronal excitability (Paulus, this issue). Despite these differences, both stimulation techniques induce cerebral plasticity effects that are comparable in many respects: empirical evidence supports this view, as reviewed in most of the contributions in this special issue. Both TMS and tES can transiently influence behaviour by altering spontaneous neuronal activity, which may have facilitatory or inhibitory effects. Importantly, particularly for rehabilitation purposes (see also Berlucchi, this issue), NIBS effects have been shown to outlast the stimulation period, for minutes, hours, and even days (see Vallar & Bolognini, this issue). Relevant mechanisms underlying these behavioural changes include synaptic long-term potentiation and depression (LTP and LTD, see Cooke & Bliss, 2006).

Most of the contributions in this special issue also emphasise that, while NIBS approaches are valuable and have provided exciting results, the use of NIBS in conjunction with concurrent cognitive rehabilitation protocols holds promise for further advances in the treatment of neuropsychological, as well of other neurological disorders. NIBS is indeed an appealing approach to directing adaptive plasticity after structural brain damage, brain dysfunction (i.e., psychiatric disorders), or both.

It is a classical tenet of cognitive neuroscience – at least since the localisation of language functions in the left hemisphere by Paul Broca in the mid 18th century – that "mental faculties", or, using a more modern term, "cognitive functions", are localised in specific parts of the brain, that are currently conceived in terms of complex cortico-subcortical networks (Cappa & Vallar, 1992; Mesulam, 1981, 1998; Vallar, 2000). Particularly, a great deal of evidence from most areas of cognitive neuroscience (cognitive electrophysiology, functional neuroimaging, neuropsychology) suggests that it is the interaction between brain regions organised in functional networks that determines the final function, and the observed behaviour. Miniussi and Rossini (this issue) point out that the general idea behind NIBS is that inducing changes in cortical excitability leads to a recovery or reorganisation of the (dys)functional network responsible for the (impaired) cognitive function. Functions may be restored or compensated for, at least in part, by mechanisms that involve both structural and functional changes to relevant brain circuits. This view also readily accounts for the modulation of sensorimotor and cognitive function, with both reducing and enhancing of performance, or the change of physiological parameters (see Vallar & Bolognini, this issue).

Abnormalities in the interactions of the different components of a relevant neural network may play a critical role in shaping the behavioural manifestations of cognitive and sensorimotor disorders. Hence, any rehabilitation approach of a cognitive function should aim at targeting the whole spatially-distributed network responsible for the function. Activating the appropriate network and reinforcing/changing synaptic interconnections (Berlucchi, this issue) appears thus to be a critical aspect of cognitive rehabilitation. This can be achieved by combining the activation of specific networks through the behavioural techniques of cognitive rehabilitation with a potentiation, through NIBS-induce neuroplasticity, namely: combining "endogenous" (i.e., the targeted behaviour required by the rehabilitation programme) with "exogenous" (i.e., NIBS) neuromodulation. Targeting by NIBS a dysfunctional neural circuitry while it is active, due to a behavioural training, may prove to be a more powerful therapeutic tool, than the mere NIBS of a given cortical area. Notably, in behavioural paradigms inducing plasticity, when a stimulus is associated with reinforcement, its cortical representation is strengthened and enlarged (Blake, Heiser, Caywood, & Merzenich, 2006).

In the same line, combined behavioural-NIBS treatments can also result in favouring generalisation. Those neurons that respond in a similar way ("overlapping of a function") to the task goal may display increased signal-correlation. NIBS, being not focused on specific neurons (e.g., Wassermann et al., 2008), could possibly modulate more effectively the activity of the whole stimulated neural population, if (pre)activated by behavioural training.

Defining network interactions is thus a key point in order to understand brain disorders and brain reorganisation. fMRI has proven to be a useful tool for evaluating the functional status of individuals' brains, during both cognitive rehabilitation, and NIBS (see Cappa, this issue). Likewise, the structural imaging of both grey and white matter in the living human brain can be used to interpret functional data more thoroughly. fMRI, PET, ERP, and MEG methods may be also used to localise and measure the time course of the patterns of activation/deactivation of cortical regions during the performance of a task of interest. This, in turn, may help in optimising the exact timing and positioning for applying NIBS to the identified area(s) (Cappa, this issue). Moreover, information on regional treatment-related activity can be used to define the optimal effect induced by NIBS (see also Miniussi & Thut, 2010). Therefore, combining functional brain imaging data with cognitive rehabilitation is of fundamental importance in future studies.

In summary, NIBS could be used to strengthen and modify networks involved in cognitive functions, both in unimpaired participants, and in brain-damaged or brain-dysfunctional patients, in whom performance is diminished or altered. NIBS applied when the system is in a given appropriate functional state (Ruzzoli, Marzi, & Miniussi, 2010; Silvanto, Muggleton, & Walsh, 2008), also based on cognitive contingencies and affordances, may enhance, and strengthen, specific distributed functional cortico-cortical/subcortical networks, rather than inducing a non-specific arousal or activation of the neural system. This may lead to the stimulation-induced modulation of a specific cognitive function, favouring its recovery. The combination of NIBS with cognitive rehabilitation, although in its beginnings, is poised to deliver novel insights into fundamental aspects of rehabilitation, paving the way for more effective neuromodulatory therapeutic interventions.

REFERENCES

Berlucchi, G. (2011). Brain plasticity and cognitive neurorehabilitation. *Neuropsychological Rehabilitation, 21*(5), 560–578.

Blake, D. T., Heiser, M. A., Caywood, M., & Merzenich, M. M. (2006). Experience-dependent adult cortical plasticity requires cognitive association between sensation and reward. *Neuron, 52*(2), 371–381.

Boggio, P. S., Valasek, C. A., Campanhã, C., Giglio, A. C. A., Baptista, N. I., & Lapenta, O. M. et al. (2011). Non-invasive brain stimulation to assess and modulate neuroplasticity in Alzheimer's disease. *Neuropsychological Rehabilitation, 21*(5), 703–716.

Cappa, S. F. (2011). The neural basis of aphasia rehabilitation: Evidence from neuroimaging and neurostimulation. *Neuropsychological Rehabilitation, 21*(5), 742–754.

Cappa, S. F., Benke, T., Clarke, S., Rossi, B., Stemmer, B., & van Heugten, C. M. (2005). EFNS guidelines on cognitive rehabilitation: Report of an EFNS task force. *European Journal of Neurology, 12*(9), 665–680.

Cappa, S. F., & Vallar, G. (1992). Neuropsychological disorders after subcortical lesions: Implications for neural models of language and spatial attention. In G. Vallar, S. F. Cappa, & C. W. Wallesch (Eds.), *Neuropsychological disorders associated with subcortical lesions* (pp. 7–41). Oxford, UK: Oxford University Press.

Cicerone, K. D., Dahlberg, C., Malec, J. F., Langenbahn, D. M., Felicetti, T., Kneipp, S., et al. (2005). Evidence-based cognitive rehabilitation: Updated review of the literature from 1998 through 2002. *Archives of Physical Medicine and Rehabilitation, 86*(8), 1681–1692.

Cooke, S. F., & Bliss, T. V. (2006). Plasticity in the human central nervous system. *Brain, 129*(7), 1659–1673.

Cotelli, M., Fertonani, A., Miozzo, A., Rosini, S., Manenti, R., Padovani, A., et al. (2011). Anomia training and brain stimulation in chronic aphasia. *Neuropsychological Rehabilitation, 21*(5), 717–741.

Hesse, M. D., Sparing, R., & Fink, G. R. (2011). Ameliorating spatial neglect with non-invasive brain stimulation: From pathophysiological concepts to novel treatment strategies. *Neuropsychological Rehabilitation, 21*(5), 676–702.

Hummel, F. C., & Cohen, L. G. (2006). Non-invasive brain stimulation: A new strategy to improve neurorehabilitation after stroke? *Lancet Neurology, 5*(8), 708–712.

Huttenlocher, P. R. (2002). *Neural plasticity: The effects of environment on the development of the cerebral cortex.* Cambridge, MA: Harvard University Press.

Mesulam, M. M. (1981). A cortical network for directed attention and unilateral neglect. *Annals of Neurology, 10*(4), 309–325.

Mesulam, M. M. (1998). From sensation to cognition. *Brain, 121*(6), 1013–1052.

Miniussi, C., Cappa, S. F., Cohen, L. G., Floel, A., Fregni, F., Nitsche, M. A., et al. (2008). Efficacy of repetitive transcranial magnetic stimulation/transcranial direct current stimulation in cognitive neurorehabilitation. *Brain Stimulation, 1*(4), 326–336.

Miniussi, C., & Rossini, P. M. (2011). Transcranial magnetic stimulation in cognitive rehabilitation. *Neuropsychological Rehabilitation, 21*(5), 579–601.

Miniussi, C., & Thut, G. (2010). Combining TMS and EEG offers new prospects in cognitive neuroscience. *Brain Topography, 22*(4), 249–256.

Paulus, W. (2011). Transcranial electrical stimulation (tES – tDCS; tRNS, tACS) methods. *Neuropsychological Rehabilitation, 21*(5), 602–617.

Ridding, M. C., & Rothwell, J. C. (2007). Is there a future for therapeutic use of transcranial magnetic stimulation? *Nature Reviews Neuroscience, 8*(7), 559–567.

Rohling, M. L., Faust, M. E., Beverly, B., & Demakis, G. (2009). Effectiveness of cognitive rehabilitation following acquired brain injury: A meta-analytic re-examination of Cicerone et al.'s (2000, 2005) systematic reviews. *Neuropsychology, 23*(1), 20–39.

Ropper, A. H., & Samuels, M. A. (2009). *Adams & Victor's principles of neurology*. New York, NY: McGraw-Hill.

Ruzzoli, M., Marzi, C. A., & Miniussi, C. (2010). The neural mechanisms of the effects of transcranial magnetic stimulation on perception. *Journal of Neurophysiology*, *103*(6), 2982–2989.

Silvanto, J., Muggleton, N., & Walsh, V. (2008). State-dependency in brain stimulation studies of perception and cognition. *Trends in Cognitive Sciences*, *12*(12), 447–454.

Stuss, D. T. (2011). The future of cognitive neurorehabilitation. *Neuropsychological Rehabilitation*, *21*(5), 755–768.

Stuss, D. T., Winocur, G., & Robertson, I. H. (2008). *Cognitive neurorehabilitation* (2nd ed.). Cambridge, UK: Cambridge University Press.

Tanaka, S., Sandrini, M., & Cohen, L. G. (2011). Modulation of motor learning and memory formation by non-invasive cortical stimulation of the primary motor cortex. *Neuropsychological Rehabilitation*, *21*(5), 650–675.

Vallar, G. (2000). The methodological foundations of human neuropsychology: studies in brain-damaged patients. In F. Boller, J. Grafman, & G. Rizzolatti (Eds.), *Handbook of neuropsychology* (2nd ed., Vol. 1, pp. 305–344). Amsterdam, The Netherlands: Elsevier.

Vallar, G., & Bolognini, N. (2011). Behavioural facilitation following brain stimulation: Implications for neurorehabilitation. *Neuropsychological Rehabilitation*, *21*(5), 618–649.

Wassermann, E. M., Epstein, C., Ziemann, U., Walsh, V., Paus, T., & Lisanby, S. (2008). *Handbook of transcranial stimulation*. Oxford, UK: Oxford University Press.

NEUROPSYCHOLOGICAL REHABILITATION
2011, 21 (5), 560–578

Brain plasticity and cognitive neurorehabilitation

Giovanni Berlucchi[1,2]

[1]National Institute of Neuroscience–Italy
[2]Department of Neurological Sciences, Section of Physiology and
Psychology, University of Verona, Verona, Italy

Neuropsychological or cognitive rehabilitation has undergone a considerable
theoretical and practical development as a specialised field of research and
clinical application in its own right. Its possibilities of intervention have
been considerably expanded after the abandonment of a wrong belief in the
immutability of the central nervous system and the growing evidence in
favour of the existence of a considerable degree of neuroplasticity even in
the mature and aged brain. Modulation of synaptic transmission and synaptogenesis, the staple mechanism of neuroplasticity in development, maturation
and learning, is also assumed by most to underlie functional recovery in the
damaged central nervous system. In order to achieve a true scientific rationale
for neurological and neuropsychological rehabilitation, it will be necessary to
fully understand the actual overlaps and the actual differences between the
mechanisms of repair and reorganisation after brain damage and those of physiological development and normal learning.

Keywords: Synaptic plasticity; Brain damage; Functional recovery; Evolution;
Development and aging.

INTRODUCTION

There are always psychological dimensions to neurological rehabilitation,
even when the primary target for treatment is a purely sensory or motor
deficit rather than a cognitive or emotional one. The success of the rehabilitation process depends in no small part on the active participation of individual
disabled patients, on their awareness of and insight into their disabilities, and

Correspondence should be addressed to Giovanni Berlucchi, Strada Le Grazie 8, 37134
Verona, Italy. E-mail: giovanni.berlucchi@univr.it

on their attention to the rehabilitating procedures and their motivation to comply with them. Comparable brain lesions tend to cause less impairment in individuals with high intelligence and superior education than in individuals with low intelligence and poor education (Wilson, 2003), and the importance of mental powers for limiting the impact of brain damage is made clear by the concept of cognitive reserve (Stern, 2009). Many decades ago, in laying down a general frame of reference for the practice of neuropsychological rehabilitation, Zangwill (1947) affirmed that a strict scientific rationale of rehabilitation is to be sought in the understanding of the mechanisms whereby the brain adjusts itself in reaction to injury to its parts. He distinguished compensation, a reorganisation of behaviour aimed at minimising or circumventing a particular disability, from substitution, the accomplishment of a task by a new method totally different from that naturally employed by the intact brain in the performance of the same task. Compensation takes place for the most part spontaneously and without the patient's explicit intention, although a spontaneous compensatory reaction can often be enhanced by the patient's own effort. Substitution is a special form of compensation in which the new method of performing a task is developed by training over and above what patients can achieve on their own initiative. An example of compensation is the spontaneously evolving ability of hemianopic patients to adjust to the restriction of their visual field by gaze shifts which bring visual targets from the blind field into the good field. Examples of trained substitutions are communication by lip reading in the deaf and the Braille method for substituting tactual for visual discrimination and recognition in peripheral and cortical blindness.

However, more relevant to rehabilitation is the actual recovery, whether spontaneous or induced, of the function initially disturbed by the cerebral lesion. For many years the evolution of functional recovery following brain damage has been ascribed to four basic events and principles: (1) a spontaneous disappearance of the acute effects of traumatic or ischaemic lesions such as vascular and cellular inflammatory reaction, oedema, and chemical modifications of the extracellular medium; (2) a reversal of diaschisis, that is, a reversal of the temporary depression of activity in uninjured brain regions following their disconnection from the injured region; (3) the principle of vicarious function, that is, the taking over of the functions of the injured part of the brain by distant back-up areas endowed, inherently or by acquisition, with the same functional capacity; (4) the principle of redundancy, that is, the maintenance of the function of a damaged system by those parts of the same system that have escaped injury; and (5) the principle of degeneracy, that is, the performance of the same function by multiple differentiated neuronal systems either through similar mechanisms or by applying different strategies (Edelman & Gally, 2001). The taking over by the right hemisphere of language function following left hemispherectomy in children may be an instance of vicariation or degeneracy, whereas the recovery of language functions effected by spared cortical islands within damaged left regions specialised for language is an example of redundancy. A historical survey of redundancy and vicariation theories has been recently presented by Finger (2009), while approaches to the analysis of degenerate neuronal systems as a basis for recovery of neuropsychological functions have been discussed by Noppeney, Friston, and Price (2004).

Restitution of function by replacement or regeneration of lost neurons or neuronal parts has long been regarded as impossible in adult warm-blooded vertebrates, justifying Lashley's dictum that where there has been destruction of tissue, restitution of function is a problem of reorganisation of what is left undamaged (Lashley, 1938). It remains true that the mature mammalian brain cannot repair itself by full regeneration of severed connections, such as the optic nerve or the cortico-spinal pathways. This is at striking variance with the spontaneous regeneration of those same connections in the adult central nervous system of some species of cold-blooded vertebrates. However, it is now accepted that damaged but surviving neurons can re-establish at least some functional connections through processes of axonal and dendritic sprouting and synaptogenesis, perhaps akin to those occurring during the developmental growth of the brain. The as yet unproven possibility that such neuronal mechanisms are also similar or even identical to those under-lying learning in the intact brain has stimulated the proposal of rehabilitation strategies specifically aimed at favouring and sustaining the reconstitution of neural circuits through learning (Robertson & Murre, 1999). In addition, the serendipitous discovery that the adult human brain is continuously generating new neurons (Eriksson et al., 1998), albeit in very limited numbers and in very restricted cerebral regions, has suggested that lesion-induced neurogen-esis may take part in the reconstruction of damaged neural circuits. The notion that the consequences of damage to the brain tissue are not only degen-erative, but can also be at least in part reparative, has furnished new perspec-tives and new approaches to neurological and particularly neuropsychological rehabilitation. The aim of this paper is to present a selective and by no means exhaustive survey of recent work on changes in neural organisation that are thought to mediate recovery of function after brain damage, and which are shifting the focus of cognitive rehabilitation from the province of psychology to that of neuroscience.

THE BRAIN: STATIC OR DYNAMIC?

Behavioural analysis leaves no doubt that during a lifespan the nervous system must be unremittingly adapting itself to changing conditions, from learning to talk and walk by the toddler to coping with day-to-day contingencies by the healthy centenarian. The terms neural flexibility, malleability and especially plasticity are all variously used to denote the putative changes in brain organisation that may account for the diverse forms of short-lasting or enduring behavioural modifiability. Broadly stated, these include development and maturation, adaptation to novel environments, specific and unspecific kinds of learning, and compensatory adjustments in response to functional losses from aging or brain damage. The terms plasticity and neuroplasticity will be henceforth used in this broad sense.

At first sight the organisation of the nervous system seems to be more appropriate for maintaining functional stability than for enabling such varied behavioural and cognitive adaptations. Ever since Bizzozero (1894) defined neurons as perennial cellular elements, anatomists have described the brain as a basically static organ, whose main cellular components present at birth are destined to last in life as long as the brain's possessor. Modern determinations with the radiocarbon dating method have confirmed that at death the age of human neocortical neurons does indeed match that of the individual, unlike non-neural (glial) neocortical cells, some of which can be generated after birth and can therefore be younger than their owner (Bhardwaj et al., 2006). Further, incorporation of marked exogenous nucleotides into nuclear DNA has shown that in healthy human and non-human primates some neurogenesis does occur from birth to senescence, although this is normally restricted to two relatively small brain areas outside of the neocortex, the subventricular zone of the lateral ventricle and the subgranular zone of the dentate gyrus of the hippocampal formation (Eriksson et al., 1998).

Already at the end of the 19th century brain science pioneers like Cajal, Tanzi, and Lugaro conceived of neuroplasticity as a result not of the addition or subtraction of neurons to the native population, but rather of the reinforcing or weakening of neuronal synaptic interconnections within built-in network systems, or of the formation of entirely novel synaptic combinations linking pre-existing neurons into newly formed networks (Berlucchi & Buchtel, 2009). In modern times, the modifiability of existing synapses and the formation of new synapses continue to be regarded as the fundamental, if not the sole, neural basis for adaptations in behavioural and cognitive control, with the added assumption that novel synapses may also be formed by at least some of the neurons which are generated throughout postnatal life. It follows that the analytical units of choice for understanding the mechanisms of adaptive brain changes, possibly including adaptations to brain damage, are to be sought at two levels of cerebral organisation other than the neuronal level. Below the neuronal level there is the level of the synapses that are changed or formed anew by experience and in the processes of adaptation. Above the neuronal level there is the level of the functional neuronal networks which change their functioning because of the modifications of existing synapses or the formation of novel synaptic interconnections.

STRUCTURAL OR FUNCTIONAL NEUROPLASTICITY?

When considering how experience and adaptation affect different levels of cerebral organisation, a principled distinction is often made between changes in brain structure and changes in brain physiology. In theory, structural changes imply a remodelling or rearrangement of the brain physical constituents, whereas physiological changes imply a dynamic readjustment of facilitation and inhibition at select synapses, modulating conductance or resistance to impulse transmission without causing overt tissue alterations. This distinction is akin to the organic/functional dichotomy classically employed in psychiatry and medicine for setting apart those disorders that are amenable to an underlying pathology from those that are not. With regard to neuroplasticity, the structural/functional distinction has been used for arriving at more rigorous definitions of the concept by restricting it to the designation of functional brain changes that can be correlated with demonstrable structural changes (e.g., Lövdén, Bäckman, Lindenberger, Schaefer, & Schmiedek, 2010; Paillard, 1976; Will, Dalrymple-Alford, Wol, & Cassel, 2008). Yet, the material fabric of the brain is a multilayered organisation. Even those events that are regarded as exquisitely physiological in nature, such as an action potential or a momentary change in efficacy of chemical synaptic transmission, are linked with the opening and closing of structural entities such as protein membrane channels. Stated shortly, there is no physiology without anatomy, to the extent that all physiological functions are instantiated on material substrates ranging from molecules to cells to cellular ensembles.

SPINES AND SPROUTS

Universally accepted instances of structural synaptic plasticity are furnished by (1) the modifiable dendritic spines that are the targets of most synaptic, predominantly excitatory, inputs to a neuron, and (2) the branches or "sprouts" that a neuron's axon can grow in order to establish new synaptic contacts. Some spines are life-long fixtures of the neuron, but others are highly dynamic structures that may quickly appear as well as disappear. Both permanent and temporary spines are endowed with the ability to change their shape and size (the "twitching" hypothesised by Crick in 1982) due to the presence of actin filaments in their cytoplasm and their ability to synthesise proteins rapidly on demand. Changes in shape and size of dendritic spines and the attendant redistribution of post-synaptic receptors in their membrane are important modulators of efficacy of synaptic transmission, by themselves or in association with the sprouting of axon collaterals. Accordingly, the responsiveness of a neuron to its synaptic inputs is subject to a continuous regulation by the turnover and replacement processes of its dendritic spines, as well as by their momentary changes in shape and size. Moreover, a neuron's synaptic projections can be extended to previously unconnected neuronal targets by the process of axonal sprouting aimed at both old and newly formed spines.

It is now widely believed that short-term and long-term spine remodelling, including formation, elimination and shape and size changing, and axonal sprouting are principal means by which both maturation and experience can continuously organise neuronal connectivity throughout life (see reviews by Alvarez & Sabatini, 2007; Bhatt, Zhang, & Gan, 2009; Kasai, Fukuda, Watanabe, Hayashi-Takagi, & Nogucki, 2010). Spine dynamics is apparent at best in the immature brain, but it is by no means absent during adulthood, with important implications for the neuroplasticity of behavioural and cognitive control. In *in vitro* experiments on brain slices, enlargement of dendritic spines and enhanced neuronal activity have been shown to accompany the electrical manifestations of long-term potentiation (LTP) at glutamatergic synapses. By contrast, spine shrinkage, reduced spine motility, and a net loss in spine number by spine pruning are associated with long-term depression (LTD) of synaptic transmission and reduced neuronal activity (Yang & Schnaar, 2008). The LTP and LTD phenomena provide experimental support to Hebb's concept of the importance of simultaneity of neuronal firing and coincidence detection in the building up of neuronal cell assemblies, and arguably constitute the primary basic neural mechanisms of synaptic plasticity underlying learning and memory (Hebb, 1949). Benefits for learning abilities from environment enrichment and physical and mental exercise have been attributed to demonstrable constructive effects on the architecture of spine apparatus in hippocampal neurons, whereas adverse effects on learning and spine architecture and dynamics appear to be caused by sensory deprivation and stress. Conspicuous signs of spine pathology have been found in morbid brain conditions such as dementia and schizophrenia (e.g., Lewis, Glantz, Pierri, & Sweet, 2003).

Neurotrophins, the molecules that control the differentiation and survival of neurons, are also known to be involved in the modulation of synaptic transmission. The enlargement of dendritic spines associated with LTP at glutamatergic synapses relies strongly on activity-dependent protein synthesis (Tanaka et al., 2008) as well as on the action of a specific neurotrophin, the brain-derived neurotrophic factor (BDNF). BDNF plays multiple roles in neuroplasticity, from controlling neuronal connectivity during development, to acting as a powerful modulator of synaptic strength and an associative messenger for the consolidation of synaptic plasticity, to being itself influenced by experience through the epigenetic regulation of its gene (Cohen-Cory, Kidane, Shirkey, & Marshak, 2010; Cowansage, LeDoux, & Monfils, 2010).

NETWORKS AND MAPS

At the neuronal network level, analysis of neuroplasticity has been aimed at discovering changes in network activities that may account for both short-term and long-term adaptive changes in behaviour, with special attention to specific phenomena of learning and memory. In the two last decades of the 20th century many investigations have revealed that topographically organised somatosensory and motor cortical maps, as well as retinotopic maps for vision and tonotopic maps for audition, are subject to use- and lesion-dependent changes in size and organisation that are not limited to development and maturation but extend throughout life. As typical examples, skill learning with a body part leads to an increased representation of that body part in the somatosensory cortex (Buonomano & Merzenich, 1998), and the total loss of visual inputs in blindness increases the cortical representation and the functional performance of other extant sensory modalities, with invasion of the de-afferented visual cortex by touch and auditory inputs (Pascual-Leone, Amedi, Fregni, & Merabet, 2005). In amputees, somatosensory cortical regions deprived of their natural inputs from the amputated body part become reactive to inputs from other body parts. The shift in reactivity may be so prompt that it can only be accounted for by an acutely increased synaptic efficacy of already existing but normally silent connections, whereas an actual restructuring or destructuring of patterns of synaptic connections appears to be necessary for later, longer-term effects (Berlucchi & Aglioti, 1997). Various aspects of neocortical map plasticity in healthy and damaged brains have been dealt with in several recent reviews (e.g., Feldman, 2009; Mercado, 2008; Nudo, 2006; Pascual-Leone et al., 2005; Wittenberg, 2010).

Investigations of neuroplasticity at the neuronal network level outside the neocortex have preferentially selected the hippocampal formation as a target for study because of its demonstrated involvement in memory processes and because one of its components, the dentate gyrus, is the only region of the normal human brain where adult neurogenesis is an ascertained fact (Ming & Song, 2005). Across the lifespan, neural progenitor or stem cells of the dentate gyrus develop into immature neurons which integrate with perennial neurons into local circuits while undergoing maturation to granules, the main projection neurons of the gyrus. Because of unique features transiently expressed during their integration and maturation, dentate neurons born in adulthood can confer highly flexible properties to the functioning of the local networks in which they partake (Schinder & Gage, 2004). Experiments in animal models have shown that adult neurogenesis in the dentate gyrus does more than replace neurons lost because of functional wear and tear: they can indeed impart on hippocampal functional architecture a constant state of flux suitable for information acquisition and elaboration.

The unique properties of immature dentate neurons include depolarisation rather than hyperpolarisation by GABA, enhanced excitability, and facilitated LTP expression (Ge, Sailor, Ming, & Song, 2008). Based on evidence from rat models, adult-born dentate neurons have been hypothesised to make distinct contributions to learning and memory as a function of their degree of maturation; immature neurons appear to specialise in the integration of temporally adjacent events, while mature neurons specialise in event separation (Aimone, Deng, & Gage, 2010).

YOUNG BRAINS VERSUS OLD BRAINS

It is well known that special skills, such as a second language acquisition, can be learned much more easily by the immature than the mature brain. In keeping with the hypothesis that similar neural mechanisms may underlie normal learning and functional recovery alike, the growing brain also seems to possess a greater facility for compensating for damage and a greater ability for correcting dysfunctions. Pioneering work by Kennard (1942) showed in monkeys that a motor cortex lesion was followed by a better motor recovery when it was made in infancy compared to when it was made in adulthood. This and other observations have led to a generalisation known as the Kennard principle (although Kennard did not fully subscribe to it), which states that there is a negative linear relation between age at brain injury and functional outcome; other things being equal, the younger the lesioned organism, the better the outcome (Dennis, 2010). However the greater plasticity of the immature compared to the mature brain is far from absolute, as brain lesions sustained by extremely young animals can cause greater dysfunctions than similar lesions sustained at an older age. Kolb and collaborators (Kolb & Gibb, 2008; Kolb, Teskey, & Gibb, 2010) have argued that the capacity for functional recovery is not inversely related to age at injury per se, but rather it reaches an optimum when the current stage of development and maturation is most favourable to synaptogenesis and glial formation. In several species of experimental animals, such a stage of extra functional plasticity appears to occur not immediately after birth, but somewhat later in life. Damage inflicted to the brain when neural plasticity is greatest seems to be associated with the greatest long-term functional outcomes, although the assumption that plastic changes are less likely to occur as the brain ages has not been explored systematically. It is known that even senescent animals can exhibit considerable capacity for cortical reorganisation following brain damage, as well as compensatory reactions to diminished synaptic plasticity associated with old age (Burke & Barnes, 2010).

LESSONS ABOUT NEUROPLASTICITY FROM THE AGED BRAIN

The decline of cognitive functions associated with physiological aging was once thought to be caused by necrotic or apoptotic death of some neurons, particularly in the neocortex, but according to more recent evidence it is best explained by loss of synapses and neuronal connections rather than of entire neurons (Bishop, Lu, & Yankner, 2010; Marner, Nyengaard, Tang, & Pakkenberg, 2003; Pakkenberg et al., 2003; Yankner, Lu, & Loerch, 2008). Changes in neocortical structure in the aging brain consist of a volumetric reduction of both grey and white matter, and are more pronounced in anterior than posterior brain regions, reaching a maximum in the prefrontal cortex. The reduction in grey matter volume is largely accounted for by a progressive restriction and atrophy of the peripheral branches and basilar shafts of the dendritic apparatus of many cortical neurons. On the other hand, other neurons show normal or overdeveloped dendritic architectures, consistent with a maintained capacity for learning and memory (Scheibel, 2009). In normal aging, substantial neuronal losses can occur in subcortical centres such as the substantia nigra pars compacta, but they can be compensated for by a volume increase and enhancement of function of the remaining neurons (Eriksen, Stark, & Pakkenberg, 2009). A massive numerical decrease of cortical neurons and glia does occur only in Alzheimer's dementia and other neurodegenerative conditions. The two histopathological markers of Alzheimer's dementia, the intraneuronal fibrillary tangles and the extracellular amyloid plaques, whose density in the brain correlates positively with the degree of cognitive impairment, may be found in smaller numbers also in the cortex of normally functioning elderly subjects (Yankner et al., 2008).

The main lesson from the normal aging brain is that cognitive decline correlates more with reduction of white matter than with that of grey matter. Nerve fibre loss from white matter is a ubiquitous feature of normal aging. It has been calculated that the total length of myelinated fibres in the white matter of the human brain measures approximately 176,000 km at the age of 20 and 97,200 km at the age of 80 in males, and 149,000 km at the age of 20 and 82,000 km at the age of 80 in females (Marner et al., 2003). The reduction involves degeneration of axons and their sheaths, as well as a breakdown of some myelin sheaths with preservation of axons. Preserved demyelinated axons can be remyelinated, but with shorter internodal separations, and a consequent decrease of conduction speed. The parent neurons of degenerated axons can be protected against retrograde degeneration by axonal collaterals with synaptic contacts upstream of the degeneration line, thus explaining the discrepancy between preservation of neurons in the grey matter and loss of axons in the white matter (Peters & Sethares, 2003).

WHITE MATTER AND NEUROPLASTICITY

Participation of the white matter in cognitive functions and brain plasticity is suggested by several pieces of evidence. The massive post-natal myelination process of the human brain, involving an increase in thickness of myelin sheaths as well as of axonal diameters, extends into late childhood and adolescence for motor and sensory cortical areas, and into late adulthood for higher-order cortical areas (Giedd et al., 1999). The protracted growth of white matter in the first decades of life can be affected by experience, as documented by a significant increase in size of a premotor-related portion of the corpus callosum following a prolonged (29 months) and highly intensive practice with a musical instrument in children aged 5 to 7 years (Schlaug et al., 2009). The well-established finding of a larger anterior corpus callosum in professional adult musicians compared to non-musicians (Schlaug, Jäncke, Huang, Staiger, & Steinmetz, 1995) is therefore likely to depend on experience rather than on genetically determined individual differences. Increase in size of a white matter tract may be caused by a variety of factors, the most likely of which is an associated increase in axonal calibre and thickness of myelin sheaths. Learning to juggle, a complex visuo-motor skill, modifies the microstructure of the white matter underlying the intraparietal sulcus, possibly reflecting an activity-dependent modulation of myelin formation coupled with an increase in axonal diameter (Scholz, Klein, Behrens, Johansen-Berg, 2009). The velocity and the timing of exchanges of information along intra- and interhemispheric white matter tracts are crucial for the correct functioning of spatially distributed neuronal networks. To the extent that it depends on the mechanisms of long-term potentiation and long-term depression, cognitive processing is also dependent on the ability of the underlying neural networks to conduct and transmit signals at a high rate and to adhere to a precise temporal order of pre- and postsynaptic activities. Some forms of learning may require a spike timing-dependent plasticity (Caporale & Dan, 2008).

Common forms of acute brain damage, such as those due to traumatic injury, are often associated with lesions confined to the white matter. As an inevitable consequence of axon degeneration and myelin breakdown in the white matter in aging or after brain damage, the orderly integration of separate brain regions can be interfered with by the disruption of connections between distant neurons. Functional brain-imaging studies do indeed indicate that during the execution of tasks involving attention, working memory, episodic memory, and executive control, elderly subjects differ from young subjects in the spatial and temporal patterns of cortical activations (Cabeza, 2002). A reduced coordination of brain activity in old compared to young individuals is associated with poor cognitive performance, whereas a more diffuse cortical activation in the old brain compared to the young brain may represent a compensatory response allowing the maintenance of normal or near-normal levels of performance (Dennis & Cabeza, 2010). Recently, it has been shown in macaque monkeys that aging-dependent memory impairment correlates positively with myelin and axonal degenerative processes in the fornix, a white matter tract known to be implicated in memory processes (Peters, Sethares, & Moss, 2010).

CENTRAL AND PERIPHERAL NEURAL REGENERATION IN MAMMALS AND LOWER VERTEBRATES

In contrast to the inability of the mammalian brain and spinal cord to repair and heal themselves if injured, some fishes and urodele amphibians exhibit a lifelong capacity for the regeneration of damaged neuronal systems and the reconstitution of severed brain and spinal connections (Tanaka & Ferretti, 2009). This capacity is unlikely to be under direct evolutionary control, considering that cerebral and spinal lesions are highly incompatible with survival and reproduction in natural conditions (Finger & Almli, 1985). Instead, neural tissue reconstruction and self-healing, when present, are likely to depend on the reactivation by a neural lesion of growth programmes that are predicated on the possession or reacquisition of developmental properties by adult neurons (Tanaka & Ferretti, 2009). In animals where most functions are built into the brain under genetic control and are not subject to major reorganisation through experience and learning, regeneration of damaged neural systems can re-establish normal function simply by repeating embryological development (Sperry, 1951, 1956, 1963, 1968). This obviously is not be possible in animals where highly differentiated adult neurons have lost their developmental traits and cannot regain them.

Adult fishes and salamanders can regenerate cut optic nerves and recover a completely normal visual function, due to the fact that adult central regeneration replicates original embryogenesis, thus rebuilding a genetically preordained pattern of orderly connections (Sperry, 1951, 1956, 1963, 1968). By contrast, in the adult mammalian brain, a hypothetical repetition of embryological development leading to optic nerve regeneration could by no means restore the previous effects implanted by learning and experience into the visual system. The degree of brain complexity and learning capacity may be associated with inability to re-establish functional connectivity with central regeneration even in non-mammalian species.

Adult mammals are endowed with a considerable potential for the regeneration of peripheral nerves, but cut fibres of the optic nerve and other central tracts do not regenerate. Neurons in the adult mammalian brain retain some capacity for elongating their cut axons, but attempts at the reconstitution of long-distance connections is aborted by various types of inhibitory molecules of which the Nogo-A molecule, expressed by oligodendrocytes and some axons, is the first identified exponent. An additional plethora of myelin-, lesion-, and scar-related molecules, including microglia, oligodendrocyte precursors, astrocytes, meningeal cells, vascular endothelial cells, and inflammatory cells, results in an extracellular matrix highly inimical to axonal regeneration. The co-occurring axonal growth-promoting effects exerted by neurotrophins, cell adhesion molecules, and other sources, are counteracted and suppressed by the overwhelmingly inhibitory environment surrounding central nervous lesions (Benowitz & Carmichael, 2010; Yang & Schnaar, 2008). Such inhibitory control is lacking in the peripheral nervous system, where severed nerve fibres can re-grow towards distant targets under the guidance of growth-stimulating neurotrophins secreted by the Schwann cells of the myelin sheaths. Peripheral nerve regeneration can be functionally adaptive when regenerating fibres re-establish synaptic contacts with appropriate targets, but can also be maladaptive in the case of inappropriate re-connections. Instances of developmental maladaptive connectivity in the central nervous system are assumed to occur in schizophrenia and essential epilepsy, and pathological plastic brain reactions to direct damage, sensory deprivation, peripheral deafferentation, etc., may underlie neuropathic pain, spasticity, dystonia, dyskinesia and other disturbances (Kolb et al., 2010). The chances of inappropriate regeneration and maladaptive connectivity are likely to be greater in the complex mammalian brains than in the simpler brains of cold-blooded vertebrates. The complex molecular ensemble for inhibiting central tract regeneration in the mammalian brain might indeed be seen as a defence mechanism against a potentially maladaptive plasticity resulting from the impossibility to rebuild appropriate neuronal networks.

ATTEMPTS TO PROMOTE AXONOGENESIS AND NEUROGENESIS FOR THE RECONSTITUTION OF NEURONAL SYSTEMS

The idea that damaged tissue in the adult mammalian brain and spinal cord can be replaced with transplantation of neurons or other cells has been around for a long time, but only in the last two or three decades has it found a practical application in animal experiments and trials in human patients. Grafts of cells that may provide a permissive environment for central axonogenesis, such as Schwann cells or olfactory ensheathing cells, have been used for promoting axonal growth across a spinal cord transection. Elongation of central axons does occur into peripheral glial bridges, but functional synaptic reconnection is generally impeded by the adverse central glial milieu encountered after crossing the bridge. Reconnection can be helped by using molecular biology techniques in order to counteract the inhibitory signalling and to bring the phenotypic characteristics of the involved neurons back to an earlier developmental stage, more compatible with the growth processes of regeneration (Benowitz & Carmichael, 2010).

In animals, transplantation of neural precursors or neural stem cells, or even non-neural cell populations into injured brains has proven apt to alleviate deficits from experimental lesions by replacing lost neurons and neuronal circuits, and by providing missing functional molecules, such as dopamine or acetylcholine, to the host brain. Attempts at therapeutic tissue transplantations in the central nervous system of humans have been made in a limited number of patients suffering from various neurological conditions, including stroke, spinal cord injury, schizophrenia, and all the classical neurodegenerative diseases. The evidence is still insufficient to ascertain that such transplantations of exogenous tissue in the human brain or spinal cord achieve a functional recovery comparable to that obtained in animal models of neurological diseases (Dunnett, 2009; Kolb et al., 2010).

A "natural" kind of transplantation occurs when localised brain injury from stroke or trauma stimulates the production of neural progenitor cells in the subventricular zone and their migration towards the injured region as potential sources of neurons for repair. In rats, these potentially reparative reactions have been shown to occur in relation to ischaemic brain lesions (Kernie & Parent, 2010). Some of the migrated neural progenitor cells have been shown to differentiate into mature neurons which can be incorporated into functional circuits in the striatum and to a lesser extent in the penumbra surrounding a cortical lesion. Yet such neurons seem too few to allow a full reconstruction of the damaged tissue, even after stimulation with appropriate growth factors (Kolb et al., 2010). Nevertheless, attention continues to be centred on the possibility that endogenous and exogenous substitution can replace neurons lost because of acute brain damage in stroke or head trauma (Johansson, 2007; Komitova, Johansson, & Eriksson, 2006). Of great potential interest to neurological rehabilitation is the notion that in animal models the functional effectiveness of cell transplants or endogenous neurogenesis in reducing a deficit can be aided and augmented by the exposure to enriched environments or by training programmes specifically aimed at rehabilitating that particular deficit (Kolb et al., 2010). Hopes to transfer these integrated rehabilitative programmes to humans is expressed well by the phrase "learning to use a brain transplant" (Döbrössy et al., 2010).

FORMS OF HUMAN NEUROLOGICAL AND NEUROPSYCHOLOGICAL REHABILITATION INSPIRED BY ANIMAL MODELS

Much of the above evidence on structural and functional plastic changes in the normal brain has come from animal experiments. Animal models of rehabilitation of behavioural functions after brain damage have also provided invaluable information about the possible neural bases of the beneficial effects. However the application of neuropsychological rehabilitation strategies based upon animal studies to humans is problematic for various reasons. Modelling human cognitive disorders in animals and making experimental brain lesions comparable to those occurring in humans are daunting if not impossible tasks (Dobkin, 2007). Since stroke infarcts and traumatic brain lesions in humans are often confined to the white matter, making such restricted lesions in laboratory animals is difficult because they have much less white matter than humans (Kolb et al., 2010).

Nevertheless a few neurorehabilitative treatments successfully utilised with animals have been transferred as such to humans. One well-documented instance is the so-called constraint-induced therapy of upper limb hemiparesis. Classical neurophysiological experiments going back to Sherrington and Munk (see Nathan & Sears, 1960) had shown that monkeys tend to avoid the use of a deafferented upper limb even though they can move it voluntarily if somewhat imprecisely. Because of the restriction of voluntary movements to the limb on the normal side, the animal "learns" not to use the deafferented limb, thus worsening its motor disability (learned nonuse) (Taub, Uswatte, Mark, & Morris, 2006). Constraint-induced therapy consists of forcing the animal to use the deafferented limb in an intensive shaping procedure trained while the contralateral limb is mechanically restrained. Applied to stroke patients, the therapy has proven effective for rehabilitating hemiparetic arm use, and systematic correlations between recuperation of limb use and rearrangements of cortical motor maps have been found in both animals and humans (Mark, Taub, & Morris, 2006). Of relevance to neuropsychological rehabilitation is the attempt to treat some aphasic patients by restraining gestural and other nonvocal means of expression so as to leave spoken language as the sole route of communication. Also in this case, beneficial effects of the therapy have been correlated to changes in cortical organisation (Pulvermüller & Berthier, 2008). The message for neuropsychological rehabilitation from constraint-induced therapies is that the potential for functional recovery of a damaged neuronal system may be suppressed through a disuse process caused by compensation and substitution strategies. It therefore becomes critical to evaluate in each case whether rehabilitation efforts must be allocated to the potential for functional recovery of a damaged system, or concentrated on a compensatory substitution of the impaired function. Disuse or non-use is likely to be a factor of loss of function by a specialised neuronal system also in the uninjured brain, and it may explain the adverse behavioural and cerebral effects of physical and mental inactivity and impoverished environments. In turn, beneficial behavioural and cerebral effects of enriched environments as well as of physical and mental exercise can be accounted for by the repeated use of neuronal systems, or at least by their protection from disuse (Mora, Segovia, & del Arco, 2007). It remains to be seen to what extent these beneficial effects can be directly ascribed to actual learning-related brain plasticity, as contrasted with the possibility that hormonal, metabolic and neurotrophic changes caused by the treatment are instead primarily responsible for them (Sperry, 1968). Physical exercise is an important regulator of gene expression and protein synthesis of BDNF, the neurotrophin most heavily involved in brain plasticity, but other neurotrophins may also play a role (Knaepen, Goekint, Heyman, & Meeusen, 2010).

THE FUTURE OF NEUROREHABILITATION

After its beginnings as part of comprehensive rehabilitation programmes for brain-injured soldiers during and after the two world wars (Newcombe, 1969; Poppelreuter, 1917), neuropsychological or cognitive rehabilitation has undergone a considerable theoretical and practical development as a special-ised field of research and clinical application in its own right. Its possibilities of intervention have been considerably expanded after neurological thought has shifted from a therapeutic nihilism inspired by the wrong belief in an immutable central nervous system to a more optimistic outlook on the possi-bility of neuroplasticity-based treatments. It is now possible to couple tra-ditional behavioural, cognitive and psychotherapeutic interventions of neuropsychological rehabilitation (e.g., Wilson, Herbert, & Shiel, 2003) with advanced neurological treatments such as direct invasive or non-invasive brain stimulation (e.g., Wassermann et al., 2008), transplantation of stem cells and neuronal precursors, gene therapies, computer assisted learning, brain-machine interfaces, and so forth (e.g., Komitova et al., 2006). But it remains true that not a few neural lesions still cause permanent unrecoverable functional losses, and the concept of neuroplasticity itself is in need of clar-ification and qualification. Neuroplasticity is germane to development, learn-ing, and functional recovery in the central nervous system, each of which share with the others the modulation of synaptic transmission, including synaptogenesis, as a staple foundation of plasticity. From this it does not necessarily follow that plasticity of neural maturation, plasticity underlying the neural foundations of learning and memory, and plasticity leading to adaptations to neural injury are one and the same thing. In principle there may be differences in the basic mechanisms of synaptic plasticity as a func-tion of maturation, experience and presence or absence of damage, but such differences have not yet been clearly identified and qualified. In order to achieve a true scientific rationale for neurological and neuropsychological rehabilitation, it will be mandatory to achieve a full understanding of how much these domains of central nervous system organisation and activity overlap and how much they differ. Further, while the success of cognitive rehabilitation has been documented for a number of neuropsychological impairments with formalised tests in clinical and laboratory settings, evidence about long-term effects in everyday life and psychosocial functioning is still partial and in need of a detailed analysis. As in all fast developing fields, theories, models, innovative research, orthodox practice and unprejudiced open-eyed empiricism are all required to confer a systematic character onto an as yet partial therapeutic and rehabilitative endeavour.

REFERENCES

Aimone, J. B., Deng, W., & Gage, F. H. (2010). Adult neurogenesis: Integrating theories and separating functions. *Trends in Cognitive Sciences, 14,* 325–337.

Alvarez, V. A., & Sabatini, B. L. (2007). Anatomical and physiological plasticity of dendritic spines. *Annual Review of Neuroscience, 30,* 79–97.

Benowitz, L. J., & Carmichael, T. (2010). Promoting axonal rewiring to improve outcome after stroke. *Neurobiology of Disease, 37,* 259–266.

Berlucchi, G., & Aglioti, S. (1997). The body in the brain: Neural bases of corporeal awareness. *Trends in Neurosciences, 20,* 560–564.

Berlucchi, G., & Buchtel, H. A. (2009). Neuronal plasticity: Historical roots and evolution of meaning. *Experimental Brain Research, 192,* 307–319.

Bhardwaj, R. D., Curtis, M. A., Spalding, K. L., Buchholz, B. A., Fink, D., Eriksson, Y. B., Nordborg, C., Gage, F. H., Druid, H., Eriksson, P. S., & Frisén, J. (2006). Neocortical neurogenesis in humans is restricted to development. *Proceedings of the National Academy of Sciences, 103,* 12564–12568.

Bhatt, D. H., Zhang, S., & Gan, W. (2009). Dendritic spine dynamics. *Annual Review of Neuroscience, 71,* 261–282.

Bishop, N. A., Lu, T., & Yankner, B. A. (2010). Neural mechanisms of ageing and cognitive decline. *Nature, 464,* 529–535.

Bizzozero, G. (1894). Accrescimento e rigenerazione nell'organismo. *Archivio di Scienze Mediche, 18,* 1101–1137.

Buonomano, D. V., & Merzenich, M. M. (1998). Cortical plasticity: From synapses to maps. *Annual Review of Neuroscience, 21,* 149–186.

Burke, S. N., & Barnes, C. A. (2006). Neural plasticity in the ageing brain. *Nature Reviews Neuroscience, 7,* 30–40.

Burke, S. N., & Barnes, C. A. (2010). Senescent synapses and hippocampal circuit dynamics. *Trends in Neurosciences, 33,* 53–61.

Cabeza, R. (2002). Hemispheric asymmetry reduction in older adults: The HAROLD model. *Psychology and Aging, 17,* 85–100.

Caporale, N., & Dan, Y. (2008). Spike timing-dependent plasticity: A Hebbian learning rule. *Annual Review of Neuroscience, 31,* 25–46.

Cohen-Cory, S., Kidane, A. K., Shirkey, N. J., & Marshak, S. (2010). Brain-derived neurotrophic factor and the development of structural neuronal connectivity. *Developmental Neurobiology, 70,* 271–288.

Cowansage, K. K., LeDoux, J. E., & Monfils, M. H. (2010). Brain-derived neurotrophic factor: A dynamic gatekeeper of neural plasticity. *Current Molecular Pharmacology, 3,* 12–29.

Crick, F. (1982). Do dendritic spines twitch? *Trends in Neurosciences, 5,* 44–46.

Dennis, M. (2010). Margaret Kennard (1899–1975): Not a 'Principle' of brain plasticity but a founding mother of developmental neuropsychology. *Cortex, 46,* 1043–1059.

Dennis, N. A., & Cabeza, R. (2010). Age-related dedifferentiation of learning systems: An fMRI study of implicit and explicit learning. *Neurobiology of Aging,* May 12. [Epub ahead of print].

Dobkin, B. H. (2007). Curiosity and cure: Translational research strategies for neural repair-mediated rehabilitation. *Developmental Neurobiology, 67,* 1133–1147.

Döbrössy, M., Busse, M., Piroth, T., Rosser, A., Dunnett, S., & Nikkhah, G. (2010). Neurorehabilitation with neural transplantation. *Neurorehabilitation and Neural Repair, 24,* 692–701.

Dunnett, S. B. (2009). Neural transplantation. *Handbook of Clinical Neurology, 95*(55), 885–912.

Edelman, G. M., & Gally, J. A. (2001). Degeneracy and complexity in biological systems. *Proceedings of the National Academy of Sciences of the USA, 98,* 13763–13768.

Eriksen, N., Stark, A. K., & Pakkenberg, B. (2009). Age and Parkinson's disease-related neuronal death in the Substantia Nigra Pars Compacta. *Journal of Neural Transmission. Supplementa, 73*(Part 3), 203–213.

Eriksson, P. S., Perfilieva, E., Björk-Eriksson, T., Alborn, A. M., Nordborg, C., Peterson, D. A., & Gage, F. H. (1998). Neurogenesis in the adult human hippocampus. *Nature Medicine, 4,* 313–317.

Feldman, D. E. (2009). Synaptic mechanisms for plasticity in neocortex. *Annual Review of Neuroscience, 32,* 33–55.

Finger, S. (2009). Recovery of function. Redundancy and vicariation theories. *Handbook of Clinical Neurology, 95*(55), 833–841.

Finger, S., & Almli, C. R. (1985). Brain damage and neuroplasticity: Mechanisms of recovery or development? *Brain Research, 357,* 177–186.

Ge, S., Sailor, K. A., Ming, G., & Song, H. (2008). Synaptic integration and plasticity of new neurons in the adult hippocampus. *Journal of Physiology, 586,* 3759–3765.

Giedd, J. N., Blumenthal, J., Jeffries, N. O., Castellanos, F. X., Liu, H., Zijdenbos, A., Paus, T., Evans, A. C., & Rapoport, J. L. (1999). Brain development during childhood and adolescence: A longitudinal MRI study. *Nature Neuroscience, 2,* 861–863.

Hebb, D. O. (1949). *The organization of behavior: A neuropsychological theory.* New York, NY: Wiley.

Johansson, B. B. (2007). Regeneration and plasticity in the brain and spinal cord. *Journal of Cerebral Blood Flow & Metabolism, 27,* 1417–1430.

Kasai, H., Fukuda, M., Watanabe, S., Hayashi-Takagi, S., & Noguchi, J. (2010). Structural dynamics of dendritic spines in memory and cognition. *Trends in Neurosciences, 33,* 121–128.

Kennard, M. (1942). Cortical reorganization of motor function. *Archives of Neurology, 48,* 227–240.

Kernie, S. G., & Parent, J. M. (2010). Forebrain neurogenesis after focal ischemic and traumatic brain injury. *Neurobiology of Disease, 37,* 267–274.

Knaepen, K., Goekint, M., Heyman, E. M., & Meeusen, R. (2010). Neuroplasticity – exercise-induced response of peripheral brain-derived neurotrophic factor: A systematic review of experimental studies in human subjects. *Sports Medicine, 40,* 765–801.

Kolb, B., & Gibb, R. (2008). Principles of neuroplasticity and behavior. In D. T. Stuss, G. Winocur, & I. H. Robertson (Eds.), *Cognitive neurorehabilitation,* (pp. 1–21). Cambridge, UK: Cambridge University Press.

Kolb, B., Teskey, G. C., & Gibb, R. (2010). Factors influencing cerebral plasticity in the normal and injured brain. *Frontiers in Human Neuroscience, 4,* 1–12.

Komitova, M., Johansson, B. B., & Eriksson, P. S. (2006). On neural plasticity, new neurons and the postischemic milieu: An integrated view on experimental rehabilitation. *Experimental Neurology, 199,* 42–55.

Lashley, K. S. (1938). Factors limiting recovery after central nervous lesions. *Journal of Nervous and Mental Diseases, 88,* 833–855.

Lewis, D. A., Glantz, L. A., Pierri, J. N., & Sweet, R. A. (2003). Altered cortical glutamate neurotransmission in schizophrenia: Evidence from morphological studies of pyramidal neurons. *Annals of the New York Academy of Sciences, 1003,* 102–112.

Lövdén, M., Bäckman, L., Lindenberger, U., Schaefer, S., & Schmiedek, F. (2010). A theoretical framework for the study of adult cognitive plasticity. *Psychological Bulletin, 136,* 659–676.

Mark, V. W., Taub, E., & Morris, D. M. (2006). Neuroplasticity and constraint-induced movement therapy. *Europa Medicophysica, 42,* 269–284.

Marner, L., Nyengaard, J. R., Tang, Y., & Pakkenberg, B. (2003). Marked loss of myelinated nerve fibers in the human brain with age. *Journal of Comparative Neurology, 462,* 144–152.

Mercado III, E. (2008). Neural and cognitive plasticity: From maps to minds. *Psychological Bulletin, 134,* 109–137.

Ming, G., & Song, H. (2005). Adult neurogenesis in the mammalian central nervous system. *Annual Review of Neuroscience, 28,* 223–250.

Mora, F., Segovia, G., & del Arco, A. (2007). Aging, plasticity and environmental enrichment: Structural changes and neurotransmitter dynamics in several areas of the brain. *Brain Research Reviews, 55,* 78–88.

Nathan, W., & Sears, T. A. (1960). Effects of posterior root section on the activity of some muscles in man. *Journal of Neurology, Neurosurgery and Psychiatry, 23,* 10–22.

Newcombe, F. (1969). *Missile wounds of the brain: A study of psychological deficits.* London, UK: Oxford University Press.

Noppeney, U., Friston, K. J., & Price, C. J. (2004). Degenerate neuronal systems sustaining cognitive functions. *Journal of Anatomy, 205,* 433–442.

Nudo, R. J. (2006). Plasticity. *NeuroRx: Journal of the American Society for Experimental NeuroTherapeutics, 3,* 420–427.

Paillard, J. (1976). Réflexions sur l'usage du concept de plasticité en neurobiologie. *Journal de Psychologie, 1,* 33–47.

Pakkenberg, B., Pelviga, D., Marnera, L., Bundgaarda, M. J., Gundersen, H. J. G., Nyengaardb, J. R., & Regeura, L. (2003). Aging and the human neocortex. *Experimental Gerontology, 38,* 95–99.

Pascual-Leone, A., Amedi, A., Fregni, F., & Merabet, L. B. (2005). The plastic human brain cortex. *Annual Review of Neuroscience, 28,* 377–401.

Peters, A., & Sethares, C. (2003). Is there remyelination during aging of the primate central nervous system? *Journal of Comparative Neurology, 460,* 238–254.

Peters, A., Sethares, C., & Moss, M. B. (2010). How the primate fornix is affected by age. *Journal of Comparative Neurology, 518,* 3962–3980.

Poppelreuter, W. (1917). *Die psychischen Schädigungen durch Kopfschuss im Kriege, 1914/16,* Leipzig, Germany: Leopold Voss.

Pulvermüller, F., & Berthier, M. L. (2008). Aphasia therapy on a neuroscience basis. *Aphasiology, 22,* 563–599.

Robertson, I. H., & Murre, J. M. J. (1999). Rehabilitation of brain damage: Brain plasticity and principles of guided recovery. *Psychological Bulletin, 125,* 544–575.

Scheibel, A. B. (2009). *Aging of the brain: The new encyclopedia of neuroscience* (pp. 181–185). Amsterdam: Elsevier.

Schinder, A. F., & Gage, F. H. (2004). A hypothesis about the role of adult neurogenesis in hippocampal function. *Physiology, 19,* 253–261.

Schlaug, G., Forgeard, M., Zhu, L., Norton, A., Norton, A., & Winner, E. (2009). Training-induced neuroplasticity in young children. *Annals of the New York Academy of Sciences, 1169,* 205–208.

Schlaug, G., Jäncke, L., Huang, Y., Staiger, J. F., & Steinmetz, H. (1995). Increased corpus callosum size in musicians. *Neuropsychologia, 33,* 1047–1055.

Scholz, J., Klein, M. C., Behrens, T. E. J., & Johansen-Berg, H. (2009). Training induces changes in white-matter architecture. *Nature Neuroscience, 12,* 1370–1371.

Sperry, R. W. (1951). Mechanisms of neural maturation. In S. Stevens (Ed.), *Handbook of experimental psychology* (pp. 236–280). New York, NY: Wiley.

Sperry, R. W. (1956). The eye and the brain. *Scientific American, 194,* 48–52.

Sperry, R. W. (1963). Chemoaffinity in the orderly growth of nerve fiber patterns and connections. *Proceedings of the National Academy of Sciences, 50,* 703–710.

Sperry, R. W. (1968). Plasticity of neural maturation. *Developmental Biology Supplement, 2,* 306–327.

Stern, Y. (2009). Cognitive reserve. *Neuropsychologia, 47,* 2015–2028.

Tanaka, E. M., & Ferretti, P. (2009). Considering the evolution of regeneration in the central nervous system. *Nature Reviews Neuroscience, 10,* 713–723.

Tanaka, J., Horiike, Y., Matsuzaki, M., Miyazaki, T., Ellis-Davies, G. C. R., & Kasai, H. (2008). Protein synthesis and neurotrophin-dependent structural plasticity of single dendritic spines. *Science, 319,* 1683–1687.

Taub, E., Uswatte, G., Mark, V. W., & Morris, D. M. (2006). The learned nonuse phenomenon: Implications for rehabilitation. *Europa Medicophysica, 42,* 241–256.

Wassermann, E. M., Epstein, C. M., Ziemann, U., Walsh, V., Paus, T., & Lisanby, S. H. (2008). *The oxford handbook of transcranial stimulation.* New York, NY: Oxford University Press.

Will, B., Dalrymple-Alford, J., Wol, V. M., & Cassel, J.-C. (2008). The concept of brain plasticity: Paillard's systemic analysis and emphasis on structure and function (followed by the translation of a seminal paper by Paillard on plasticity). *Behavioural Brain Research, 192,* 2–7, (translation: 192, 7–11).

Wilson, B. A. (2003). Treatment and recovery from brain damage. In L. Nadel (Ed.), *Encyclopedia of cognitive sciences* (pp. 410–416). London, New York and Tokyo: Nature Publishing Group.

Wilson, B. A., Herbert, C. M., & Shiel, A. (2003). *Behavioural approaches in neuropsychological rehabilitation: Optimising rehabilitation procedures.* Hove, UK: Psychology Press.

Wittenberg, G. F. (2010). Experience, cortical remapping, and recovery in brain disease. *Neurobiology of Disease, 27,* 252–258.

Yang, L. J., & Schnaar, R. L. (2008). Axon regeneration inhibitors. *Neurological Research, 30,* 1047–1052.

Yankner, B. A., Lu, T., & Loerch, P. (2008). The aging brain. *Annual Review of Pathology and Mechanisms of Dieases, 3,* 41–66.

Zangwill, O. L. (1947). Psychological aspects of rehabilitation in cases of brain injury. *British Journal of Psychology, General Section, 37,* 60–69.

NEUROPSYCHOLOGICAL REHABILITATION
2011, 21 (5), 579–601

Transcranial magnetic stimulation in cognitive rehabilitation

Carlo Miniussi[1,2] and Paolo Maria Rossini[3,4]

[1]Dept of Biomedical Sciences and Biotechnologies, National Institute of Neuroscience, University of Brescia, Brescia, Italy
[2]Cognitive Neuroscience Section, IRCCS San Giovanni di Dio Fatebenefratelli, Brescia, Italy
[3]IRCCS San Raffaele-Pisana and Casa di Cura San Raffaele-Cassino, Italy
[4]Neurology, University Campus Biomedico di Roma, Rome, Italy

Repetitive transcranial magnetic stimulation (rTMS) can generate an increase or a decrease of neuronal excitability, which can modulate cognition and behaviour. Transcranial magnetic stimulation-induced cortical changes have been shown to result in neural plasticity. Thus, TMS provides an important opportunity to gain more insight into the mechanisms responsible for the remarkable flexibility of the central nervous system. The aim of this review was to cover the topics that could be useful when using TMS in the cognitive rehabilitation field after brain damage. The basic TMS principles are introduced, together with the clinical application for diagnosis and prognosis, the biological aspects, and the use in cognitive neuroscience studies. Finally, several hypotheses are discussed to explain the likely mechanisms induced by TMS that favour the recovery of a function after brain damage and cause the adult brain to undergo plasticity. The possibility of non-invasively interacting with the functioning of the brain and its plasticity mechanisms – a possibility that may eventually lead to cognitive and behavioural modifications – opens new and exciting scenarios in the cognitive neurorehabilitation field.

Keywords: rTMS; Plasticity; Cognition; Neurorehabilitation; Stroke; Non-invasive brain stimulation.

Correspondence should be addressed to Carlo Miniussi, Dept of Biomedical Sciences and Biotechnologies, School of Medicine, University of Brescia, Viale Europa 1125123 Brescia, Italy. E-mail: carlo.miniussi@cognitiveneuroscience.it

The writing of this paper was supported by the James S. McDonnell Foundation (to CM).

INTRODUCTION

Recently, non-invasive brain stimulation techniques, such as transcranial magnetic stimulation (TMS), have been developed. These techniques interact with spontaneous brain activity and related sensory-motor and higher order cognitive abilities. Transcranial magnetic stimulation uses a coil to deliver a brief ($\sim$200 to 300 μs) and powerful (0.2 to 4.0 T) magnetic pulse to the scalp. The stimulation-induced effects of TMS depend on several technical parameters, including the intensity and number of stimulations (i.e., frequency), the coil orientation, and the focality and depth of stimulation. The effects also depend on a number of variables related to the stimulated subject, including age, eventual pharmacological treatments and the state of the subject (Miniussi, Ruzzoli, & Walsh, 2010; Rossini, Rossini, & Ferreri, 2010; Silvanto, Muggleton, & Walsh, 2008).

When a strong, transient magnetic field is delivered through a coil in close proximity with the scalp, there is a transitory electric current in the cortical surface under the coil, which causes the depolarisation of cell membranes (Barker, Freeston, Jalinous, & Jarratt, 1987; Barker, Jalinous, & Freeston, 1985) and a transynaptic depolarisation or hyperpolarisation of a population of cortical neurons. Because the electrical field induced by TMS is markedly reduced as the distance from the stimulating coil increases, the cortex ($\sim$2 cm below the scalp) is the target of this method. TMS originated in the mid-1980s, when Barker and colleagues (1985) built the first magnetic stimulator, which was able to excite cortical neurons from the scalp surface. TMS was originally introduced in clinical neurophysiology for the evaluation of the functional state of the corticospinal pathway (Barker et al., 1985, 1987), and TMS initially involved the delivery of single magnetic pulses. When TMS was directed over the primary motor cortex, the discharges induced the activation of the corticospinal tract, which produced a peripheral motor response known as the motor evoked potential (MEP). Since the discovery of TMS, this technique has been used to investigate the state of cortical excitability, the excitability of the cortico-cortical or corticospinal pathway (e.g., Rothwell, Day, Thompson, Dick, & Marsden, 1987), the role of a given brain region in a particular cognitive function and the timing of its activity (e.g., Walsh & Pascual-Leone, 2003), and the pathophysiology of various disorders (e.g., Fregni & Pascual-Leone, 2006; Kobayashi & Pascual-Leone, 2003; Rossini & Rossi, 2007).

In the mid-1990s, technological advances allowed the delivery of rhythmic trains of magnetic pulses in a rapid sequence up to a 100-Hz repetition rate, which was referred to as repetitive TMS (rTMS). Studies have shown that rTMS interacts with cortical activity more effectively than TMS. Therefore, new applications began evaluating the potential benefits of rTMS in the treatment of psychiatric disorders (see George et al., 2009 for a review). In recent years, rTMS has been rapidly developed as a potential therapeutic tool in many other clinical fields (e.g., Couturier, 2005; Gershon, Dannon, & Grunhaus, 2003; Hoffman et al., 2005; Hummel & Cohen, 2006; Mally & Stone, 2007; Ridding & Rothwell, 2007; Wassermann & Lisanby, 2001).

Concerning the use of rTMS, there is a general consensus that low-frequency rTMS consists of continuous trains below 1 Hz, and high-frequency rTMS consists of intermittent trains above 5 Hz (Rossi et al., 2009). The cut-off between high and low frequencies, however, is not arbitrary. This cut-off is empirically based on direct and indirect measures of brain activity as well as behaviour. Therefore, treating low- and high-frequency rTMS as separate phenomena is essential because the application of these two kinds of stimulation for several minutes might produce distinct effects on brain activity. Converging evidence has indicated that rTMS below 1 Hz reduces cortical excitability both locally and in functionally related regions, whereas rTMS trains above 5 Hz seem to have the opposite effect. Namely, high-frequency stimulation has been shown to produce an increase in the MEP amplitude (Maeda, Keenan, Tormos, Topka, & Pascual-Leone, 2000), whereas low-frequency stimulation produced a decrease in the MEP amplitude (Chen et al., 1997; Maeda et al., 2000). Therefore, rTMS allows for transient modulation of neural excitability, and the effect is dependent on the stimulation frequency and intensity (Thut and Pascal-Leone 2010). Importantly, these effects have been shown to outlast the stimulation period itself. Hebbian mechanisms for synaptic plasticity might be the key for the TMS-induced facilitation. Hebb (1949) postulated that an increase in synaptic efficacy arises when two neurons, the presynaptic and the postsynaptic cells, are activated simultaneously. In this respect, we know that it is possible to induce learning by the repetitive use of a function, which activates specific cortical circuitry. Thus, the same principles may make it possible to induce plasticity by the repetitive use of brain stimulation. Repetitive brain stimulation could generate a prolonged depolarising response and facilitate activity-dependent communications, which would strengthen the circuitry.

Given these premises, there is currently a growing interest in applying TMS as a tentative therapeutic approach in the cognitive rehabilitation field (Rossi & Rossini 2004). For example, TMS could be used to re-establish cognitive performance in stroke patients (see Miniussi et al., 2008 for a review) and patients suffering from progressive neurodegenerative diseases (Cotelli, Calabria, et al., 2011; Finocchiaro et al., 2006). The aim of this review was to cover the basic principles about TMS that could be useful for cognitive rehabilitation in neurological patients. Interested readers are referred to exhaustive reviews on other TMS-related topics (e.g., George et al., 2009; Hallett, 2000; Rossini & Rossi, 2007; Sandrini, Umilta, & Rusconi, 2011; Wassermann et al., 2008).

BASIC PRINCIPLES

The primary property of magnetic stimulation is its ability to penetrate all body structures, which allows for the stimulation of regions well below layers of bone (e.g., the brain tissue under the skull). The electric field induced in the tissue generally causes cell membranes to depolarise. If the depolarisation of the membrane overcomes its threshold, an action potential is generated. The locus of activation in the brain appears to be the area where the induced electrical field is maximal (Krings et al., 1997), and this location depends on the stimulating coil characteristics. Focal activation is achieved using a double 70-mm diameter coil with two loops in which the current flows in opposite directions. Also termed the figure-eight coil, it is the one that is most commonly used. With this coil, the induced electric field peaks under the intersection of the coil windings in an area of ~2 cm^2 (Thickbroom, Sammut, & Mastaglia, 1998; Thielscher & Kammer, 2004). Different coil types are presently available, and each one has its own advantages and disadvantages. For example, large coils cannot produce very focal stimulation. A large volume of neural tissue may be activated by a large coil, but these devices can penetrate relatively deep in the brain (e.g., see the H coil, Roth, Zangen, & Hallett, 2002; Zangen, Roth, Voller, & Hallett, 2005). In contrast, small coils produce more focal stimulation but do not penetrate deep into the brain. Indeed, the depth of penetration depends on the coil size, the coil geometry, the intensity of the applied stimulus and individual anatomical factors (e.g., the distance between the cortex and the scalp).

TMS studies on humans were initially focused on the motor system because the effects of TMS on the motor system are easily discernible from peripheral muscles. In the motor cortex, the activation of pyramidal neurons by TMS has been suggested to predominantly occur via interneurons in the superficial cortical layers (Di Lazzaro et al., 2007; Nakamura, Kitagawa, Kawaguchi, & Tsuji, 1996; Rossini, Caramia, & Zarola, 1987). Using TMS, studies have shown that it is possible to evaluate the state of motor cortex excitability by measuring what is known as the motor threshold. The motor threshold, which reflects the global excitability of the corticospinal motor pathway, has been defined as the intensity of TMS that produces an identifiable MEP of ~50 μV in at least five out of ten TMS pulses (Rossini et al., 1994). Although threshold in human adults is largely independent of age, gender and hemisphere, it varies with different target muscles (Rossini et al., 1987; Rossini, Desiato, & Caramia, 1992). Differences in the excitability threshold are dependent on the cortical muscle representation (Rothwell et al., 1987). In the upper limbs, for example, the threshold is lowest for the hand muscles and highest for the proximal arm muscles.

Two variables of the MEP that are important in the study of the motor system are amplitude and latency. The amplitude may have a high degree of inter-trial and intra-individual variability, especially during stimulating sessions that are only slightly supra-threshold. With increasing stimulus intensity, MEPs increase in amplitude and become less variable in shape. Interestingly, a similar increase in amplitude and decrease in shape variability can be achieved by voluntary (even minimal) contraction of the target muscle. Nevertheless it should be noted that amplitude is never maximal, unless particular techniques of stimulation are used (e.g., triple stimulation techniques, see Rossi et al., 2009). Latency reflects the total motor conduction time from cortex to the target muscle. Latency of the MEP is determined by the fibre diameter, the myelin sheath thickness and the number of synapses that the impulse must cross. There are also several additional factors influencing the amplitude and latency of MEPs. Indeed, a slight voluntary contraction of the target muscle increased excitability and shortened the MEP's onset latency and amplitude (Barker et al., 1987; Di Lazzaro et al., 1998; Rossini et al., 1987; Rothwell et al., 1987). This finding suggested that all of these measures are sensitive to changes in the cortical state, and they can be utilised to evaluate changes (increases or decreases) in the excitability of the motor cortex that are induced by different types of protocols. Therefore, TMS can be used on the motor cortex of conscious human subjects as a non-invasive technique to study neuroplasticity. Several paradigms have been developed, and TMS can be applied one stimulus at a time (single-pulse TMS), in pairs of stimuli separated by a variable and programmable interval (paired-pulse TMS), or in patterned stimulation (for a precise classification see Rossi et al., 2009).

Single-pulse TMS applied on the scalp overlying the primary motor cortex (M1) allows for routine evaluations of the excitability and conductivity of corticospinal motor pathways. This approach has primarily been applied in studies of movement physiology in healthy subjects, in patients with neurological disorders and in post-lesion follow-up studies of plastic cerebral reorganisation.

Under certain technical circumstances, paired-pulse techniques have been shown to provide measures of intracortical facilitation and inhibition as well as cortico-cortical interactions, which are important when evaluating changes in system state or functionality (Nakamura, Kitagawa, Kawaguchi, & Tsuji, 1997; Sommer, Tergau, Wischer, & Paulus, 2001). Moreover, plastic modifications of intracortical excitability can be achieved by pairing a peripheral nerve stimulus to a single TMS stimulus of the motor cortex (i.e., paired associative stimulation – PAS; Classen et al., 2004; Mariorenzi, Zarola, Caramia, Paradiso, & Rossini, 1991; Stefan, Kunesch, Benecke, Cohen, & Classen, 2002).

When multiple stimuli of TMS are delivered in trains, one can differentiate conventional and patterned protocols of repetitive stimulation. For conventional protocols, there is agreement on the term rTMS. When the motor system is targeted with a repetitive rhythmic stimulation for several minutes, rTMS effects have been fairly consistent and appear to cause long-lasting neurophysiological effects. As previously reported, continuous low-frequency rTMS above threshold reduced cortical excitability, which was measured by a decrease in MEP amplitude. Sequences of intermittent high frequency, however, appeared to facilitate cortical excitability and induce an increase in MEP amplitude (Fitzgerald, Fountain, & Daskalakis, 2006).

Patterned rTMS refers to a repetitive application of short rTMS bursts at a high inner frequency, which are separated by short pauses of no stimulation. To date, theta burst stimulation (TBS) is the most commonly used method of patterned rTMS. In TBS, short bursts of 50-Hz rTMS are repeated as a continuous or intermittent train at a rate in the theta range (5 Hz). The excitatory and inhibitory effects of this type of stimulation can be manipulated by continuous or intermittent delivery of these theta bursts over time (Huang, Edwards, Rounis, Bhatia, & Rothwell, 2005). This experimental approach demonstrated that a short, low-intensity TBS protocol transiently modified the excitability of the motor cortex, which outlasted the period of actual TMS for up to one hour. The TBS protocol has now been used to modulate motor thresholds (Huang et al., 2005), visual cortex excitability (Silvanto, Muggleton, Cowey, & Walsh, 2007 even if they used a modified protocol, i.e., 8 pulses at 40 Hz, separated by 1800 ms for 50 sec), and cognitive functions (Vallesi, Shallice, & Walsh, 2007; Waterston & Pack, 2010). Recently, quadripulse stimulation (QPS), which is able to induce long-term changes in cortical excitability, has been added to the patterned rTMS procedures (Hamada et al., 2008). In addition, QPS might also be used to induce symptomatic relief of several types of neurological symptoms (Hamada & Ugawa, 2010).

CLINICAL APPLICATION OF TMS FOR DIAGNOSIS AND PROGNOSIS IN THE MOTOR SYSTEM

The high reproducibility in standardised conditions makes MEPs efficacious for evaluating corticospinal tract functionality, even in a sub-clinical involvement of the central motor pathways (Rossini & Rossi, 1998). Characteristics of MEPs rely on the number of neurons recruited and the integrity of the direct corticospinal tract. Thus, in patients with spinal cord disorders, MEPs may be useful in diagnostic procedures to demonstrate the site of spinal cord lesion and monitor the disease progression. The ability of TMS to predict the quality of motor recovery in stroke patients has yielded contradictory results, which were likely caused by variability in the clinical pictures of recruited patients. Most authors agree, however, that the evoked potentials measured in the acute stage have predictive value (Binkofski et al., 1996; Cicinelli, Traversa, & Rossini, 1997). For instance, the absence of a response to TMS in the first 48 hours after a stroke has been shown to be predictive of an absent or a very poor functional hand motor recovery (Binkofski et al., 1996; Cicinelli et al., 1997; Nardone & Tezzon, 2002; Pennisi et al., 1999). Follow-up of stroke patients undergoing neurorehabilitation of the upper limb showed an increase in the number of cortical sites where an MEP of the paretic hand could be elicited, which suggested a cortical reorganisation of the area representing the hand (Liepert et al., 1998, 2000; Miltner, Bauder, Sommer, Dettmers, & Taub, 1999; Traversa, Cicinelli, Bassi, Rossini, & Bernardi, 1997; Wittenberg et al., 2003). Therefore, TMS may provide fruitful information regarding the final functional outcome on the motor system (see Rossini, Calautti, Pauri, & Baron, 2003).

Presently, a peripheral "functional" marker (i.e., MEP) is present over the motor cortex, which can be used to directly measure the state of the cortex. In addition, other induced responses can also be recorded (e.g., the primary visual cortices can be localised for inducing the perception of contralateral visual phosphenes, and a visual phosphene induction threshold can be set) (Kammer & Baumann, 2010). The combination of TMS with simultaneous electroencephalography (EEG) might allow direct measurements of the state of all cortical areas. Similar to the way that MEPs recorded from muscles after TMS over motor cortex are markers of the state of the motor system, TMS-evoked potentials recorded over the scalp might be quantifiable markers of the cerebral neurophysiological state in "silent areas". Therefore, an integration of TMS and EEG might provide real-time information on the excitability of the cortex as well as the link between functional activity and behaviour modifications (Komssi & Kahkonen, 2006; Miniussi & Thut, 2010). TMS EEG coregistration has only recently become feasible because of technical developments (Ilmoniemi et al., 1997; Virtanen, Ruohonen, Naatanen, & Ilmoniemi, 1999), and a great deal of work remains to be done.

BIOLOGICAL ASPECTS

Studies have shown that 1-Hz cortical inhibitory effects on a stimulated area were dependent on both GABA and NMDA receptor system activity (Fitzgerald et al., 2005), whereas high-frequency stimulation might rely on the same system but have opposite effects. Moreover, these effects can be altered by drugs that specifically interact with neurotransmission in the GABA and NMDA receptor systems (Ziemann, Chen, Cohen, & Hallett, 1998; Ziemann, Hallett, & Cohen, 1998). Therefore, both long-term depression (LTD) and long-term potentiation (LTP) have been postulated as likely mechanisms to explain the persistent effects of rTMS on cortical activity (Cooke & Bliss, 2006; Thickbroom, 2007). For instance, one study showed that rTMS (from 1 to 10 Hz) to the auditory cortex of gerbils resulted in a frequency-dependent LTD-like suppression or LTP-like enhancement of auditory cortex activity congruent with the stimulation frequency (Wang, Wang, & Scheich, 1996). Recently, studies have proposed that genetic factors might also influence the response to TMS plasticity protocols, and particular attention has been paid to the brain-derived neurotrophic factor (BDNF) gene. The mature form of BDNF is a neurotrophin that plays a pivotal role in neurodevelopment because it regulates and promotes synaptic plasticity mechanisms (Egan et al., 2003). Single-pulse TMS has been used to demonstrate that the BDNF genotype was associated with changes in the excitability of the primary motor cortex, which occurred after practising a motor task (Kleim et al., 2006). In addition, the response of healthy subjects to three different plasticity-inducing protocols in the motor cortex was associated with the polymorphism of the BDNF gene that they carried (Cheeran et al., 2008). In addition, experiments in rats showed that the administration of BDNF after stroke improved recovery (Schabitz et al., 2004). Interestingly, the physiological consequences of the BDNF polymorphism might not be manifested in the basal state, but they may become evident in response to a behaviourally driven increase in neural activity. Thus, genetic variations in patients could produce significant differences in the brain stimulation protocols (Bocchio-Chiavetto et al., 2008).

TMS IN THE FIELD OF COGNITIVE NEUROSCIENCE

The use of TMS in the field of cognitive neuroscience depends mainly on its ability to transiently interact with the stimulated neural network rather than its ability to modulate cortical excitability. Therefore, rTMS can be used with two distinct approaches: on-line stimulation and off-line stimulation. Interaction with on-going cognitive processing when TMS or rTMS is applied during the performance of a task is called on-line TMS (Sandrini et al., 2011). In this case, it is generally assumed that an alteration of cortical activity within a specific targeted area can significantly impair performance (Walsh & Pascual-Leone, 2003; but see Miniussi et al., 2010). Moreover, the effects induced by on-line stimulation are generally short-lived, probably on the order of a few hundred milliseconds to a few seconds. Therefore, the idea that increasing excitability via high-frequency stimulation will lead to a behaviourally measurable modification is barely applicable. Both facilitation and inhibition, which are timing, site and task specific, have been reported irrespective of the frequency of stimulation (Boroojerdi et al., 2001; Cappa, Sandrini, Rossini, Sosta, & Miniussi, 2002; Harris, Benito, Ruzzoli, & Miniussi, 2008; Kirschen, Davis-Ratner, Jerde, Schraedley-Desmond, & Desmond, 2006; Kohler, Paus, Buckner, & Milner, 2004; Luber et al., 2007; Mottaghy et al., 1999; Sparing et al., 2001).

In the case of off-line stimulation, rTMS is applied for several minutes before the subject is tested on a task. In this case, rTMS affects the modulation of cortical excitability (increase vs. decrease) and aims to change the cognitive performance. Studies, however, have not always confirmed the idea of a strict and unequivocal association between both behavioural improvements and excitation and disruptions and inhibition (Andoh et al., 2006; Drager, Breitenstein, Helmke, Kamping, & Knecht, 2004; Hilgetag, Theoret, & Pascual-Leone, 2001; Kim et al., 2005; Waterston & Pack, 2010). Nevertheless, modification of the activity of a neural network by rTMS carries important behavioural implications for neurorehabilitation, which will be considered later.

A lot of evidence has suggested that the effects induced by several off-line rTMS approaches were site specific, but not site limited (Bestmann et al., 2008). Thus, the long-term consequences induced by sustained repetitive brain stimulation were most likely due to activity changes in a given network of cortical and subcortical areas rather than a local inhibition or excitation of an individual brain area (Selimbeyoglu & Parvizi, 2010). In other words, brain stimulation can modulate the ongoing properties of a neuronal network by amplification or reduction of its activity. Because the brain operates through flexible and interactive distributed networks (primarily for cognition and behaviour), we can expect that the modification of a node of the network would affect the entire network. Moreover, the stimulated area cannot be considered to be isolated from its own functions or the functional status induced by the state of the subject (Harris et al., 2008; Pasley, Allen, & Freeman, 2009; Ruzzoli, Marzi, & Miniussi, 2010; Silvanto et al., 2008). These aspects suggest that the functional effects induced in one area could be co-opted into different functions depending on the mode of activation or which of its interconnected networks was activated (e.g., Harris, Clifford, & Miniussi, 2008; Selimbeyoglu & Parvizi, 2010; Silvanto, Cowey, Lavie, & Walsh, 2005).

In general, two of the great advantages of TMS are that it can be used in a large group of subjects, and the location of the coil can be precisely controlled with the neuronavigation approach. The manipulation with rTMS can be meaningful if the coil positioning can be accurately localised on an individual basis, particularly in those functions where interindividual differences are particularly relevant (Manenti et al., 2010). Therefore in some cases it is very important to guide the positioning of the coil over the target area by neuronavigation systems with single subject functional magnetic resonance imaging (Sack et al., 2009).

Another advantage is that TMS can be applied at different time points during the execution of a cognitive task. Thus, TMS can provide valuable information about when a brain region is involved in a cognitive task. Ultimately, TMS could be used to map the flow of information across different brain regions during the execution of a complex cognitive task.

Occasionally, some technical aspects of rTMS (e.g., its spatial resolution, the noise produced and the possibility of a general arousal induction) have hindered precise interpretation of the observed functional effects. Thus, a control condition must be used to strengthen the results of rTMS experiments. Several approaches could be used to ensure that changes in performance are specifically attributed to the effects of TMS on the target site. One common approach has been the use of sham (i.e., placebo) stimulation as a baseline condition. Although all parameters were the same as actual stimulation, no effective magnetic stimulation should reach the brain in the sham condition (Rossi et al., 2007; please note that tilting the coil by 180° is not a sham condition). Another approach involves stimulating contralateral homologous (i.e., homotopic) or vertex areas while the subject performs the same task with auditory and somatosensory perceptions being the same. This allows for a comparison of rTMS effects at different brain sites, but only one has functional relevance. In addition, subject behaviour can also be observed across several distinct tasks. Following stimulation at one site, however, only one task is functionally related to the stimulated site.

All of these technical/control aspects are very important in experiments that involve cognition because the functional effects that can be induced after stimulation of a cortical area can take on different functions depending on which of its interconnected networks is engaged in a given task (Sack & Linden, 2003). In addition, there are ethical implications of TMS application because attempting to modify "natural" cerebral abilities raises concerns, which share some similarities with the problems connected with neuro-doping.

TMS AND COGNITIVE NEUROREHABILITATION

Several studies in normal subjects have suggested that TMS may lead to enhanced cognitive performance (Vallar & Bolognini, this issue). In healthy subjects, most of these effects were transient (in the range of minutes), but repeated TMS in follow-up sessions, in concert with learning and plasticity processes, may prolong the facilitating effects beyond the end of the stimulation period and provide important opportunities for long-lasting positive effects (Miniussi et al., 2008). Some preliminary data have shown improved picture naming or word repetition performance in vascular aphasia (Cotelli, Fertonani, et al., this issue; Kakuda, Abo, Kaito, Watanabe, & Senoo, 2010; Martin et al., 2004; Naeser et al., 2010; Naeser, Martin, Nicholas, Baker, Seekins, Helm-Estabrooks et al., 2005; Naeser, Martin, Nicholas, Baker, Seekins, Kobayashi et al., 2005), primary progressive aphasia (Finocchiaro et al., 2006) and Alzheimer's disease (Cotelli, Calabria, et al., 2011). Repetitive TMS can also be used to improve performance in sensory extinction (Oliveri et al., 1999, 2000) and unilateral neglect (Brighina et al., 2003; Shindo et al., 2006) associated with stroke.

The general idea behind brain stimulation is that inducing changes in cortical excitability leads to a recovery or reorganisation of the functional network responsible for the impaired cognitive function. Function may be restored or compensated by mechanisms that involve both structural and functional changes of the brain circuits. In addition, the restored function might be based on the same general rules that were valid during the development of the nervous system or during learning-dependent plasticity. Even if adaptation of the adult brain relies on functional plasticity rather than growth or maturation, there are several potential mechanisms to explain restored functioning. Indeed, there could be a gradual readjustment of an intact but functionally suppressed area (initially due to diaschisis but then due to a steady reduction in synaptic strength). Following a lesion, a reduction of the excitability of cortical neurons within the affected area might induce a depression/depotentiation of the cognitive circuit underlying the function, which would result in an impaired function carried on by a "non-specialised area". Recovery of a function might be due to:

1. An enhancement of cortical excitability by focal brain stimulation of a given network might change this maladaptive pattern through a specific potentiation-like phenomenon, which would enable synaptic plasticity and promote recovery of the degraded function. A similar mechanism might work in Alzheimer's patients because neuronal death is not an all-or-none phenomenon. Even in severely affected areas, studies have shown evidence of plastic changes in surviving neurons (Backman et al., 1999; Becker et al., 1996). In Alzheimer's patients, it has been shown that rTMS can induce a partial recovery of language abilities (Cotelli, Calabria, et al., 2011; Finocchiaro et al., 2006), which may be due to a strengthening of the synaptic activity of the surviving neurons in the stimulated network. Following the loss of a part of the neural population, a reduction of excitability of cortical neurons within the affected area might induce a depression/depotentiation of the cognitive circuit underling the function, resulting in an impaired function. The same phenomena can be present in stroke patients. After a lesion of an area adjacent or connected, areas become "silent" due to diaschisis, therefore lesion-induced effects are a weakening of the synaptic activity resulting in silent synapses. TMS might induce a gradual readjustment of an intact but "functionally" suppressed area due to a steady reduction in synaptic strength. Therefore, these data supported the idea that brain stimulation-induced changes in synaptic strength are an essential step towards recovery of function. Indeed, improving the performance of a specific system within the functional network leads to more effective processing.
2. Recruitment or rebalance of compensatory networks may be used to accomplish the impaired function. These networks may include

perilesional areas and/or contralateral homologue cortical regions, which might have similar anatomical structure and can therefore carry out the impaired functions. This type of compensatory function has been promoted by specific cognitive rehabilitative interventions, such as brain stimulation, which aim to exploit the preserved abilities to compensate for the deficit.

3. Early intervention might even favour the restoration of neural function by regeneration of damaged neurons or partially lost connections. We know that BDNF promotes synaptic plasticity mechanisms and is essential for neuronal cell survival and differentiation. Indeed, studies in rats with a cerebral infarct have shown that BDNF was significantly increased after rTMS treatment, which suggested that TMS was able to promote BDNF expression in the cerebral cortex (Zhang, Mei, Liu, & Yu, 2007) and promote neuronal cell survival.

4. In addition, a number of investigations have also suggested that the rhythmic aspects of transcranial stimulation can exert positive effects on cognitive performance. Interestingly, the modification of cortical oscillatory activity through the use of rhythmic repetitive stimulation (Barr et al., 2009; Klimesch, Sauseng, & Gerloff, 2003) may readjust pathological patterns of brain activity. This would allow an opportunity to induce new oscillatory patterns, which could adequately modulate the neural response of a network (i.e., entrainment) (Thut & Miniussi, 2009).

All of these mechanisms are likely to be the same ones that favour the naturally occurring recovery of a function after brain damage and cause the adult brain to undergo plasticity. Interestingly, lesion-induced plasticity has been suggested to be stronger when it occurs shortly after the occurrence of the damaging event (Clarkson & Carmichael, 2009), and this plasticity becomes weaker as more time passes (Carmichael, 2006). Therefore, brain stimulation might create more time for plasticity to occur, which would favour functional compensation.

In behavioural paradigms, inducing plasticity when a stimulus is cognitively associated with reinforcement allows its cortical representation to be strengthened and enlarged (Blake, Heiser, Caywood, & Merzenich, 2006). Several experiments have shown that plasticity changes were not caused by sensory experience alone; they also require learning and reward to be associated with the sensory experience (Blake et al., 2006). This finding suggested that a simple stimulation of the brain by TMS, which was not associated with a focused cognitive rehabilitation procedure that could be fully experienced by the patient, might prove to induce weak and transient effects. Moreover, BDNF synaptic modulation is also activity-dependent, and therefore activity could control the synapse specificity of neurotrophin regulation-supported recovery (Lu, 2003).

All in all, these considerations advocate that TMS leads to the stimulation-induced modulation of network activity rather than simple excitation or inhibition of the target area (McIntyre, Savasta, Walter, & Vitek, 2004). Therefore, TMS could be used to achieve a strengthening or modification of a network that is specific for a diminished cognitive function. Studies have suggested that the best way to perpetrate this strengthening is to stimulate the area and activate the network supporting the specific function (Barbay et al., 2006). This approach can be achieved by combining exogenously induced plasticity (i.e., brain stimulation) with a specific training-induced plasticity (i.e., cognitive training). In part, this approach resembles the one used to improve motor performance in patients with hemiplegia (for discussion on this issue see Fregni & Pascual-Leone, 2007; Hummel & Cohen, 2006; Nowak, Grefkes, Ameli, & Fink, 2009; Talelli & Rothwell, 2006). If brain stimulation is applied when the system is in a given functional state, it will enhance and strengthen the specific distributed functional cortico-cortical (or subcortical) network that is active rather than inducing a non-specific arousal or activation of the system.

Many additional aspects need to be considered in future studies, such as the timing of rTMS application after stroke, the duration of the rehabilitation protocol, the type of frequency and the ideal area that should be stimulated. For example, studies have not determined if the facilitation of the affected area (Meinzer et al., 2008; but see also Kleim et al., 2003; Nudo, Wise, SiFuentes, & Milliken, 1996; Plautz et al., 2003) or the inhibition of the unaffected contralateral hemisphere (Kakuda et al., 2010; Martin et al., 2004) is more effective in improving the hampered function (see the interhemispheric competition model, Ward & Cohen, 2004). In addition, some researchers studying the motor cortex have suggested that the stimulation of both areas would be the most effective strategy (Takeuchi, Tada, Toshima, Matsuo, & Ikoma, 2009). Because motor cortex is a primary area, it has a similar functional representation on both hemispheres. Cognitive functions that do not rely on primary areas and are unilaterally localised, however, might not follow the same logic. In addition, the parameters that induce a clear result in a normal system may lead to an opposite pattern of results in a pathological system that has a different homeostasis (for a review on variability in inducing cortical plasticity in normal subjects see Ridding & Ziemann, 2010). Furthermore, cortical stimulation in future applications might include combined rTMS and transcranial electrical stimulation (see Paulus, this issue) to induce modifications of cortical responsiveness.

SAFETY

According to recently published safety guidelines, the risk of TMS use should be assessed carefully, and its dosage should generally be limited (Rossi et al.,

2009). Since the introduction of TMS, many thousands of subjects have been examined with TMS or rTMS to assess motor or cognitive functions of the central nervous system. There is now a considerable volume of data supporting the safety of magnetic stimulation. The main area of concern has been the triggering of kindling activity, which can induce seizures. Of course, stroke is a factor that may increase the possibility of inducing seizures since it affects cortical excitability. Therefore, rTMS trains that are usually safe for healthy volunteers might potentially increase the risk of seizures in these patients. In stroke patients the current density distributions can be modified in magnitude and direction by the altered structure, potentially altering the population of stimulated neural elements (Rossi et al., 2009). This needs to be considered when assessing the safety of rTMS treatment and rigorous monitoring is critical. In addition, patients will likely be taking medications, and interactions between rTMS and concomitant treatments should be considered (Rossi et al., 2009) because several neuroleptics and antidepressants also increase seizure risk. Seizure induction, however, has rarely been reported following rTMS, and animal studies have shown that there is no clear evidence that rTMS leads to increased seizure susceptibility (Akamatsu et al., 2001; Ebert & Ziemann, 1999; Fleischmann, Hirschmann, Dolberg, Dannon, & Grunhaus, 1999; Fleischmann, Prolov, Abarbanel, & Belmaker, 1995; Godlevsky et al., 2006; Post, Muller, Engelmann, & Keck, 1999), structural alterations (Counter, Borg, & Olofsson, 1993; de Sauvage, Lagroye, Billaudel, & Veyret, 2008; Liebetanz, Nitsche, & Paulus, 2003; Post et al., 1999; Sgro, Ghatak, Stanton, Emerson, & Blair, 1991) or off-line impairment of cognitive functions (Post et al., 1999), even after long-term treatments. Researchers who are interested in using TMS are indeed encouraged to read the comprehensive document that has recently been created by a large panel of international experts (Rossi et al., 2009).

CONCLUSIONS

Further investigations are needed to determine whether TMS can be used to ameliorate deficits in the cognitive domain with long-lasting effects. An important aspect is that TMS cannot be considered the treatment by itself but it should give us the opportunity, when the associated with a focused cognitive rehabilitation, to reduce the treatment time and potentiate the final effects. Indeed, it will represent a challenging field of research for years to come. There are several aspects that should be considered to control all of the variables that could hamper a neurorehabilitation protocol. Protocol that should consider the full involvement and motivation by the patient. Perhaps the most important consideration should be that the goal of the treatment may not be to restore the function of damaged components. Indeed, the goal could be exploitation of the preserved abilities to compensate for the deficit and/or to speed-up progressive ("plastic") recruitment of new neural networks, which might re-establish lost or degraded functions. Therefore, it is important to determine precisely the anatomo-functional state of each individual subject and establish the location and extension of the damaged area, its neurophysiological state (e.g., by means of TMS EEG co-registration methods) and the state of the perilesional cortex. Because the mechanisms of recovery from stroke could be strictly related to the type of damage, the potential cognitive strategy to be used in combination with brain stimulation could be chosen based on the preserved regions. In addition, brain stimulation is applied to an ongoing brain activity, which is determined by both lesion-induced plasticity mechanisms and new behavioural learning mechanisms. All of these matters should be evaluated in the context of the internal milieu of the central nervous system, which will try to maintain a balance (likely through homeostatic plasticity). In terms of maintaining balance in the CNS, there may also be negative plasticity that contributes to the deficits and/or symptoms interfering with normal functions (e.g., spasticity or abnormal reflexes). Thus, the goal of rehabilitative interventions should be to try to favour positive neuroplastic changes. Natural recovery mechanisms must also be considered as important components of stroke rehabilitation studies because natural effects can also contribute to enhanced physical, psychological and social functioning. In the search for more effective and long-lasting effects of neurorehabilitation, spontaneous recovery should be included in neurorehabilitation studies as an important variable that can be eventually potentiated by brain stimulation. In addition, spontaneous recovery in search of a new balance might induce maladaptive neural plasticity that could be avoided with the adequate guidance of a well-designed rehabilitation protocol.

REFERENCES

Akamatsu, N., Fueta, Y., Endo, Y., Matsunaga, K., Uozumi, T., & Tsuji, S. (2001). Decreased susceptibility to pentylenetetrazol-induced seizures after low-frequency transcranial magnetic stimulation in rats. *Neuroscience Letters, 310*(2–3), 153–156.

Andoh, J., Artiges, E., Pallier, C., Riviere, D., Mangin, J. F., Cachia, A., et al. (2006). Modulation of language areas with functional MR image-guided magnetic stimulation. *Neuroimage, 29*(2), 619–627.

Backman, L., Andersson, J. L., Nyberg, L., Winblad, B., Nordberg, A., & Almkvist, O. (1999). Brain regions associated with episodic retrieval in normal aging and Alzheimer's disease. *Neurology, 52*(9), 1861–1870.

Barbay, S., Plautz, E. J., Friel, K. M., Frost, S. B., Dancause, N., Stowe, A. M., et al. (2006). Behavioral and neurophysiological effects of delayed training following a small ischemic infarct in primary motor cortex of squirrel monkeys. *Experimental Brain Research, 169*(1), 106–116.

Barker, A. T., Freeston, I. L., Jalinous, R., & Jarratt, J. A. (1987). Magnetic stimulation of the human brain and peripheral nervous system: An introduction and the results of an initial clinical evaluation. *Neurosurgery, 20*(1), 100–109.

Barker, A. T., Jalinous, R., & Freeston, I. L. (1985). Non-invasive magnetic stimulation of human motor cortex. *Lancet, 1*(8437), 1106–1107.

Barr, M. S., Farzan, F., Rusjan, P. M., Chen, R., Fitzgerald, P. B., & Daskalakis, Z. J. (2009). Potentiation of gamma oscillatory activity through repetitive transcranial magnetic stimulation of the dorsolateral prefrontal cortex. *Neuropsychopharmacology, 34*(11), 2359–2367.

Becker, J. T., Mintun, M. A., Aleva, K., Wiseman, M. B., Nichols, T., & DeKosky, S. T. (1996). Compensatory reallocation of brain resources supporting verbal episodic memory in Alzheimer's disease. *Neurology, 46*(3), 692–700.

Bestmann, S., Ruff, C. C., Blankenburg, F., Weiskopf, N., Driver, J., & Rothwell, J. C. (2008). Mapping causal interregional influences with concurrent TMS-fMRI. *Experimental Brain Research, 191*(4), 383–402.

Binkofski, F., Seitz, R. J., Arnold, S., Classen, J., Benecke, R., & Freund, H. J. (1996). Thalamic metabolism and corticospinal tract integrity determine motor recovery in stroke. *Annals of Neurology, 39*(4), 460–470.

Blake, D. T., Heiser, M. A., Caywood, M., & Merzenich, M. M. (2006). Experience-dependent adult cortical plasticity requires cognitive association between sensation and reward. *Neuron, 52*(2), 371–381.

Bocchio-Chiavetto, L., Miniussi, C., Zanardini, R., Gazzoli, A., Bignotti, S., Specchia, C., et al. (2008). 5-HTTLPR and BDNF Val66Met polymorphisms and response to rTMS treatment in drug resistant depression. *Neuroscience Letters, 437*(2), 130–134.

Boroojerdi, B., Phipps, M., Kopylev, L., Wharton, C. M., Cohen, L. G., & Grafman, J. (2001). Enhancing analogic reasoning with rTMS over the left prefrontal cortex. *Neurology, 56*(4), 526–528.

Brighina, F., Bisiach, E., Oliveri, M., Piazza, A., La Bua, V., Daniele, O., et al. (2003). 1 Hz repetitive transcranial magnetic stimulation of the unaffected hemisphere ameliorates contralesional visuospatial neglect in humans. *Neuroscience Letters, 336*(2), 131–133.

Cappa, S. F., Sandrini, M., Rossini, P. M., Sosta, K., & Miniussi, C. (2002). The role of the left frontal lobe in action naming: rTMS evidence. *Neurology, 59*(5), 720–723.

Carmichael, S. T. (2006). Cellular and molecular mechanisms of neural repair after stroke: Making waves. *Annals of Neurology, 59*(5), 735–742.

Cheeran, B., Talelli, P., Mori, F., Koch, G., Suppa, A., Edwards, M., et al. (2008). A common polymorphism in the brain-derived neurotrophic factor gene (BDNF) modulates human cortical plasticity and the response to rTMS. *Journal of Physiology, 586*(Pt 23), 5717–5725.

Chen, R., Classen, J., Gerloff, C., Celnik, P., Wassermann, E. M., Ha, M., et al. (1997). Depression of motor cortex excitability by low-frequency transcranial magnetic stimulation. *Neurology, 48*(5), 1398–1403.

Cicinelli, P., Traversa, R., & Rossini, P. M. (1997). Post-stroke reorganization of brain motor output to the hand: A 2–4 month follow-up with focal magnetic transcranial stimulation. *Electroencephalography and Clinical Neurophysiology, 105*(6), 438–450.

Clarkson, A. N., & Carmichael, S. T. (2009). Cortical excitability and post-stroke recovery. *Biochemical Society Transactions, 37*(Pt 6), 1412–1414.

Classen, J., Wolters, A., Stefan, K., Wycislo, M., Sandbrink, F., Schmidt, A., et al. (2004). Paired associative stimulation. *Supplemental Clinical Neurophysiology, 57,* 563–569.

Cooke, S. F., & Bliss, T. V. (2006). Plasticity in the human central nervous system. *Brain, 129*(Pt 7), 1659–1673.

Cotelli, M., Calabria, M., Manenti, R., Rosini, S., Zanetti, O., Cappa, S. F., et al. (2011). Improved language performance in Alzheimer disease following brain stimulation.

Journal of Neurology Neurosurgery and Psychiatry. Advance online publication. doi:10.1136/jnnp.2009.197848

Cotelli, M., Fertonani, A., Miozzo, A., Rosini, S., Manenti, R., Padovani, A., et al. (2011). Anomia training and brain stimulation in chronic aphasia. *Neuropsychological Rehabilitation*, *21*(5), 717–741.

Counter, S. A., Borg, E., & Olofsson, A. (1993). Oto-traumatic effects of computer simulated magnetic coil impulse noise: Analysis of mechanisms. *Acta Otolaryngology*, *113*(6), 699–705.

Couturier, J. L. (2005). Efficacy of rapid-rate repetitive transcranial magnetic stimulation in the treatment of depression: A systematic review and meta-analysis. *Journal of Psychiatry Neuroscience*, *30*(2), 83–90.

de Sauvage, R. C., Lagroye, I., Billaudel, B., & Veyret, B. (2008). Evaluation of the potential genotoxic effects of rTMS on the rat brain and current density mapping. *Clinical Neurophysiology*, *119*(2), 482–491.

Di Lazzaro, V., Restuccia, D., Oliviero, A., Profice, P., Ferrara, L., Insola, A., et al. (1998). Effects of voluntary contraction on descending volleys evoked by transcranial stimulation in conscious humans. *Journal of Physiology*, *508*(Pt 2), 625–633.

Di Lazzaro, V., Thickbroom, G. W., Pilato, F., Profice, P., Dileone, M., Mazzone, P., et al. (2007). Direct demonstration of the effects of repetitive paired-pulse transcranial magnetic stimulation at I-wave periodicity. *Clinical Neurophysiology*, *118*(6), 1193–1197.

Drager, B., Breitenstein, C., Helmke, U., Kamping, S., & Knecht, S. (2004). Specific and non-specific effects of transcranial magnetic stimulation on picture-word verification. *European Journal of Neuroscience*, *20*(6), 1681–1687.

Ebert, U., & Ziemann, U. (1999). Altered seizure susceptibility after high-frequency transcranial magnetic stimulation in rats. *Neuroscience Letters*, *273*(3), 155–158.

Egan, M. F., Kojima, M., Callicott, J. H., Goldberg, T. E., Kolachana, B. S., Bertolino, A., et al. (2003). The BDNF val66met polymorphism affects activity-dependent secretion of BDNF and human memory and hippocampal function. *Cell*, *112*(2), 257–269.

Finocchiaro, C., Maimone, M., Brighina, F., Piccoli, T., Giglia, G., & Fierro, B. (2006). A case study of Primary Progressive Aphasia: Improvement on verbs after rTMS treatment. *Neurocase*, *12*(6), 317–321.

Fitzgerald, P. B., Benitez, J., Oxley, T., Daskalakis, J. Z., de Castella, A. R., & Kulkarni, J. (2005). A study of the effects of lorazepam and dextromethorphan on the response to cortical 1 Hz repetitive transcranial magnetic stimulation. *Neuroreport*, *16*(13), 1525–1528.

Fitzgerald, P. B., Fountain, S., & Daskalakis, Z. J. (2006). A comprehensive review of the effects of rTMS on motor cortical excitability and inhibition. *Clinical Neurophysiology*, *117*(12), 2584–2596.

Fleischmann, A., Hirschmann, S., Dolberg, O. T., Dannon, P. N., & Grunhaus, L. (1999). Chronic treatment with repetitive transcranial magnetic stimulation inhibits seizure induction by electroconvulsive shock in rats. *Biological Psychiatry*, *45*(6), 759–763.

Fleischmann, A., Prolov, K., Abarbanel, J., & Belmaker, R. H. (1995). The effect of transcranial magnetic stimulation of rat brain on behavioral models of depression. *Brain Research*, *699*(1), 130–132.

Fregni, F., & Pascual-Leone, A. (2006). Hand motor recovery after stroke: Tuning the orchestra to improve hand motor function. *Cognitive Behavioural Neurology*, *19*(1), 21–33.

Fregni, F., & Pascual-Leone, A. (2007). Technology insight: non-invasive brain stimulation in neurology-perspectives on the therapeutic potential of rTMS and tDCS. *Nature Clinical Practice Neurology*, *3*(7), 383–393.

George, M. S., Padberg, F., Schlaepfer, T. E., O'Reardon, J. P., Fitzgerald, P. B., Nahas, Z. H., et al. (2009). Controversy: Repetitive transcranial magnetic stimulation or transcranial direct current stimulation shows efficacy in treating psychiatric diseases (depression, mania, schizophrenia, obsessive–compulsive disorder, panic, posttraumatic stress disorder). *Brain Stimulation, 2*(1), 14–21.

Gershon, A. A., Dannon, P. N., & Grunhaus, L. (2003). Transcranial magnetic stimulation in the treatment of depression. *American Journal of Psychiatry, 160*(5), 835–845.

Godlevsky, L. S., Kobolev, E. V., van Luijtelaar, E. L., Coenen, A. M., Stepanenko, K. I., & Smirnov, I. V. (2006). Influence of transcranial magnetic stimulation on spike-wave discharges in a genetic model of absence epilepsy. *Indian Journal of Experimental Biology, 44*(12), 949–954.

Hallett, M. (2000). Transcranial magnetic stimulation and the human brain. *Nature, 406*(6792), 147–150.

Hamada, M., Terao, Y., Hanajima, R., Shirota, Y., Nakatani-Enomoto, S., Furubayashi, T., et al. (2008). Bidirectional long-term motor cortical plasticity and metaplasticity induced by quadripulse transcranial magnetic stimulation. *Journal of Physiology, 586*(16), 3927–3947.

Hamada, M., & Ugawa, Y. (2010). Quadripulse stimulation: A new patterned rTMS. *Restor Neurology Neuroscience, 28*(4), 419–424.

Harris, I. M., Benito, C. T., Ruzzoli, M., & Miniussi, C. (2008). Effects of right parietal transcranial magnetic stimulation on object identification and orientation judgments. *Journal of Cognitive Neuroscience, 20*(5), 916–926.

Harris, J. A., Clifford, C. W., & Miniussi, C. (2008). The functional effect of transcranial magnetic stimulation: Signal suppression or neural noise generation? *Journal of Cognitive Neuroscience, 20*(4), 734–740.

Hebb, D. O. (1949). *The Organization of Behavior: A Neuropsychological Theory.* New York: Wiley.

Hilgetag, C. C., Theoret, H., & Pascual-Leone, A. (2001). Enhanced visual spatial attention ipsilateral to rTMS-induced 'virtual lesions' of human parietal cortex. *Nature Neuroscience, 4*(9), 953–957.

Hoffman, R. E., Gueorguieva, R., Hawkins, K. A., Varanko, M., Boutros, N. N., Wu, Y. T., et al. (2005). Temporoparietal transcranial magnetic stimulation for auditory hallucinations: Safety, efficacy and moderators in a fifty patient sample. *Biological Psychiatry, 58*(2), 97–104.

Huang, Y. Z., Edwards, M. J., Rounis, E., Bhatia, K. P., & Rothwell, J. C. (2005). Theta burst stimulation of the human motor cortex. *Neuron, 45*(2), 201–206.

Hummel, F. C., & Cohen, L. G. (2006). Non-invasive brain stimulation: A new strategy to improve neurorehabilitation after stroke? *Lancet Neurology, 5*(8), 708–712.

Ilmoniemi, R. J., Virtanen, J., Ruohonen, J., Karhu, J., Aronen, H. J., Naatanen, R., et al. (1997). Neuronal responses to magnetic stimulation reveal cortical reactivity and connectivity. *Neuroreport, 8*(16), 3537–3540.

Kakuda, W., Abo, M., Kaito, N., Watanabe, M., & Senoo, A. (2010). Functional MRI-based therapeutic rTMS strategy for aphasic stroke patients: A case series pilot study. *International Journal of Neuroscience, 120*(1), 60–66.

Kammer, T., & Baumann, L. W. (2010). Phosphene thresholds evoked with single and double TMS pulses. *Clinical Neurophysiology, 121*(3), 376–379.

Kim, Y. H., Min, S. J., Ko, M. H., Park, J. W., Jang, S. H., & Lee, P. K. (2005). Facilitating visuospatial attention for the contralateral hemifield by repetitive TMS on the posterior parietal cortex. *NeuroscienceLetters, 382*(3), 280–285.

Kirschen, M. P., Davis-Ratner, M. S., Jerde, T. E., Schraedley-Desmond, P., & Desmond, J. E. (2006). Enhancement of phonological memory following transcranial magnetic stimulation (TMS). *Behav Neurology, 17*(3–4), 187–194.

Kleim, J. A., Bruneau, R., VandenBerg, P., MacDonald, E., Mulrooney, R., & Pocock, D. (2003). Motor cortex stimulation enhances motor recovery and reduces peri-infarct dysfunction following ischemic insult. *Neurology Research, 25*(8), 789–793.

Kleim, J. A., Chan, S., Pringle, E., Schallert, K., Procaccio, V., Jimenez, R., et al. (2006). BDNF val66met polymorphism is associated with modified experience-dependent plasticity in human motor cortex. *Nature Neuroscience, 9*(6), 735–737.

Klimesch, W., Sauseng, P., & Gerloff, C. (2003). Enhancing Cognitive performance with repetitive transcranial magnetic stimulation at human individual alpha frequency. *European Journal of Neuroscience, 17*(5), 1129–1133.

Kobayashi, M., & Pascual-Leone, A. (2003). Transcranial magnetic stimulation in neurology. *Lancet Neurology, 2*(3), 145–156.

Kohler, S., Paus, T., Buckner, R. L., & Milner, B. (2004). Effects of left inferior prefrontal stimulation on episodic memory formation: A two-stage fMRI-rTMS study. *Journal of Cognitive Neuroscience, 16*(2), 178–188.

Komssi, S., & Kahkonen, S. (2006). The novelty value of the combined use of electroencephalography and transcranial magnetic stimulation for neuroscience research. *Brain Research Reviews, 52*(1), 183–192.

Krings, T., Buchbinder, B. R., Butler, W. E., Chiappa, K. H., Jiang, H. J., Rosen, B. R., et al. (1997). Stereotactic transcranial magnetic stimulation: Correlation with direct electrical cortical stimulation. *Neurosurgery, 41*(6), 1319–1325, discussion 1325–1316.

Liebetanz, D., Nitsche, M. A., & Paulus, W. (2003). Pharmacology of transcranial direct current stimulation: Missing effect of riluzole. *Supplemental Clinical Neurophysiology, 56,* 282–287.

Liepert, J., Bauder, H., Wolfgang, H. R., Miltner, W. H., Taub, E., & Weiller, C. (2000). Treatment-induced cortical reorganization after stroke in humans. *Stroke, 31*(6), 1210–1216.

Liepert, J., Miltner, W. H., Bauder, H., Sommer, M., Dettmers, C., Taub, E., et al. (1998). Motor cortex plasticity during constraint-induced movement therapy in stroke patients. *Neuroscience Letters, 250*(1), 5–8.

Lu, B. (2003). BDNF and activity-dependent synaptic modulation. *Learn Memory, 10*(2), 86–98.

Luber, B., Kinnunen, L. H., Rakitin, B. C., Ellsasser, R., Stern, Y., & Lisanby, S. H. (2007). Facilitation of performance in a working memory task with rTMS stimulation of the precuneus: frequency- and time-dependent effects. *Brain Research, 1128*(1), 120–129.

Maeda, F., Keenan, J. P., Tormos, J. M., Topka, H., & Pascual-Leone, A. (2000). Modulation of corticospinal excitability by repetitive transcranial magnetic stimulation. *Clinical Neurophysiology, 111*(5), 800–805.

Mally, J., & Stone, T. W. (2007). New advances in the rehabilitation of CNS diseases applying rTMS. *Expert Reviews in Neurotherapy, 7*(2), 165–177.

Manenti, R., Tettamanti, M., Cotelli, M., Miniussi, C., & Cappa, S. F. (2010). The neural bases of word encoding and retrieval: A fMRI-guided transcranial magnetic stimulation study. *Brain Topography, 22*(4), 318–332.

Mariorenzi, R., Zarola, F., Caramia, M. D., Paradiso, C., & Rossini, P. M. (1991). Non-invasive evaluation of central motor tract excitability changes following peripheral nerve stimulation in healthy humans. *Electroencephalography and Clinical Neurophysiology, 81*(2), 90–101.

Martin, P. I., Naeser, M. A., Theoret, H., Tormos, J. M., Nicholas, M., Kurland, J., et al. (2004). Transcranial magnetic stimulation as a complementary treatment for aphasia. *Seminars in Speech Language, 25*(2), 181–191.

McIntyre, C. C., Savasta, M., Walter, B. L., & Vitek, J. L. (2004). How does deep brain stimulation work? Present understanding and future questions. *Journal of Clinical Neurophysiology, 21*(1), 40–50.

Meinzer, M., Flaisch, T., Breitenstein, C., Wienbruch, C., Elbert, T., & Rockstroh, B. (2008). Functional re-recruitment of dysfunctional brain areas predicts language recovery in chronic aphasia. *Neuroimage, 39*(4), 2038–2046.

Miltner, W. H., Bauder, H., Sommer, M., Dettmers, C., & Taub, E. (1999). Effects of constraint-induced movement therapy on patients with chronic motor deficits after stroke: A replication. *Stroke, 30*(3), 586–592.

Miniussi, C., Cappa, S. F., Cohen, L. G., Floel, A., Fregni, F., Nitsche, M. A., et al. (2008). Efficacy of repetitive transcranial magnetic stimulation/transcranial direct current stimulation in cognitive neurorehabilitation. *Brain Stimulation, 1*(4), 326–336.

Miniussi, C., Ruzzoli, M., & Walsh, V. (2010). The mechanism of transcranial magnetic stimulation in cognition. *Cortex, 46*(1), 128–130.

Miniussi, C., & Thut, G. (2010). Combining TMS and EEG offers new prospects in cognitive neuroscience. *Brain Topogr, 22*(4), 249–256.

Mottaghy, F. M., Hungs, M., Brugmann, M., Sparing, R., Boroojerdi, B., Foltys, H., et al. (1999). Facilitation of picture naming after repetitive transcranial magnetic stimulation. *Neurology, 53*(8), 1806–1812.

Naeser, M. A., Martin, P. I., Lundgren, K., Klein, R., Kaplan, J., Treglia, E., et al. (2010). Improved language in a chronic nonfluent aphasia patient after treatment with CPAP and TMS. *Cognitive and Behavioral Neurology, 23*(1), 29–38.

Naeser, M. A., Martin, P. I., Nicholas, M., Baker, E. H., Seekins, H., Helm-Estabrooks, N., et al. (2005). Improved naming after TMS treatments in a chronic, global aphasia patient: Case report. *Neurocase, 11*(3), 182–193.

Naeser, M. A., Martin, P. I., Nicholas, M., Baker, E. H., Seekins, H., Kobayashi, M., et al. (2005). Improved picture naming in chronic aphasia after TMS to part of right Broca's area: An open-protocol study. *Brain and Language, 93*(1), 95–105.

Nakamura, H., Kitagawa, H., Kawaguchi, Y., & Tsuji, H. (1996). Direct and indirect activation of human corticospinal neurons by transcranial magnetic and electrical stimulation. *Neuroscience Letters, 210*(1), 45–48.

Nakamura, H., Kitagawa, H., Kawaguchi, Y., & Tsuji, H. (1997). Intracortical facilitation and inhibition after transcranial magnetic stimulation in conscious humans. *Journal of Physiology, 498*(Pt 3), 817–823.

Nardone, R., & Tezzon, F. (2002). Inhibitory and excitatory circuits of cerebral cortex after ischaemic stroke: Prognostic value of the transcranial magnetic stimulation. *Electromyography and Clinical Neurophysiology, 42*(3), 131–136.

Nowak, D. A., Grefkes, C., Ameli, M., & Fink, G. R. (2009). Interhemispheric competition after stroke: Brain stimulation to enhance recovery of function of the affected hand. *Neurorehabilitation and Neural Repair, 23*(7), 641–656.

Nudo, R. J., Wise, B. M., SiFuentes, F., & Milliken, G. W. (1996). Neural substrates for the effects of rehabilitative training on motor recovery after ischemic infarct. *Science, 272*(5269), 1791–1794.

Oliveri, M., Rossini, P. M., Filippi, M. M., Traversa, R., Cicinelli, P., Palmieri, M. G., et al. (2000). Time-dependent activation of parieto-frontal networks for directing attention to tactile space. A study with paired transcranial magnetic stimulation pulses in right-brain-damaged patients with extinction. *Brain, 123*(Pt 9), 1939–1947.

Oliveri, M., Rossini, P. M., Traversa, R., Cicinelli, P., Filippi, M. M., Pasqualetti, P., et al. (1999). Left frontal transcranial magnetic stimulation reduces contralesional extinction in patients with unilateral right brain damage. *Brain, 122*(Pt 9), 1731–1739.

Pasley, B. N., Allen, E. A., & Freeman, R. D. (2009). State-dependent variability of neuronal responses to transcranial magnetic stimulation of the visual cortex. *Neuron, 62*(2), 291–303.

Paulus, W. (2011). Transcranial electrical stimulation (tES – tDCS; tRNS, tACS) methods. *Neuropsychological Rehabilitation, 21*(5), 602–617.

Pennisi, G., Rapisarda, G., Bella, R., Calabrese, V., Maertens De Noordhout, A., & Delwaide, P. J. (1999). Absence of response to early transcranial magnetic stimulation in ischemic stroke patients: Prognostic value for hand motor recovery. *Stroke, 30*(12), 2666–2670.

Plautz, E. J., Barbay, S., Frost, S. B., Friel, K. M., Dancause, N., Zoubina, E. V., et al. (2003). Post-infarct cortical plasticity and behavioral recovery using concurrent cortical stimulation and rehabilitative training: A feasibility study in primates. *Neurology Research, 25*(8), 801–810.

Post, A., Muller, M. B., Engelmann, M., & Keck, M. E. (1999). Repetitive transcranial magnetic stimulation in rats: Evidence for a neuroprotective effect *in vitro* and *in vivo*. *European Journal of Neuroscience*, *11*(9), 3247–3254.

Ridding, M. C., & Rothwell, J. C. (2007). Is there a future for therapeutic use of transcranial magnetic stimulation? *Nature Reviews Neuroscience*, *8*(7), 559–567.

Ridding, M. C., & Ziemann, U. (2010). Determinants of the induction of cortical plasticity by non-invasive brain stimulation in healthy subjects. *Journal of Physiology*, *588*(Pt 13), 2291–2304.

Rossi, S., Ferro, M., Cincotta, M., Ulivelli, M., Bartalini, S., Miniussi, C., et al. (2007). A real electro-magnetic placebo (REMP) device for sham transcranial magnetic stimulation (TMS). *Clinical Neurophysiology*, *118*(3), 709–716.

Rossi, S., Hallett, M., Rossini, P. M., Pascual-Leone, A., & Safety of T. M. S. C. G (2009). Safety, ethical considerations, and application guidelines for the use of transcranial magnetic stimulation in clinical practice and research. *Clinical Neurophysiol*, *120*(12), 2008–2039.

Rossi, S., Rossini, P. M. (2004). TMS in cognitive plasticity and the potential for rehabilitation. *Trends in Cognitive Science*, *8*(6), 273–279.

Rossini, P. M., Barker, A. T., Berardelli, A., Caramia, M. D., Caruso, G., Cracco, R. Q., et al. (1994). Non-invasive electrical and magnetic stimulation of the brain, spinal cord and roots: Basic principles and procedures for routine clinical application. Report of an IFCN committee. *Electroencephalography and Clinical Neurophysiology*, *91*(2), 79–92.

Rossini, P. M., Calautti, C., Pauri, F., & Baron, J. C. (2003). Post-stroke plastic reorganisation in the adult brain. *Lancet Neurology*, *2*(8), 493–502.

Rossini, P. M., Caramia, M., & Zarola, F. (1987). Central motor tract propagation in man: Studies with non-invasive, unifocal, scalp stimulation. *Brain Research*, *415*(2), 211–225.

Rossini, P. M., Desiato, M. T., & Caramia, M. D. (1992). Age-related changes of motor evoked potentials in healthy humans: Non-invasive evaluation of central and peripheral motor tracts excitability and conductivity. *Brain Research*, *593*(1), 14–19.

Rossini, P. M., & Rossi, S. (1998). Clinical applications of motor evoked potentials. *Electroencephalography and Clinical Neurophysiology*, *106*(3), 180–194.

Rossini, P. M., & Rossi, S. (2007). Transcranial magnetic stimulation: Diagnostic, therapeutic, and research potential. *Neurology*, *68*(7), 484–488.

Rossini, P. M., Rossini, L., & Ferreri, F. (2010). Brain-behavior relations: Transcranial magnetic stimulation. *IEEE Engineering in Medicine and Biology Magazine*, *29*(1), 84–95.

Roth, Y., Zangen, A., & Hallett, M. (2002). A coil design for transcranial magnetic stimulation of deep brain regions. *Journal of Clinical Neurophysiology*, *19*(4), 361–370.

Rothwell, J. C., Day, B. L., Thompson, P. D., Dick, J. P., & Marsden, C. D. (1987). Some experiences of techniques for stimulation of the human cerebral motor cortex through the scalp. *Neurosurgery*, *20*(1), 156–163.

Ruzzoli, M., Marzi, C. A., & Miniussi, C. (2010). The neural mechanisms of the effects of transcranial magnetic stimulation on perception. *Journal of Neurophysiology*, *103*(6), 2982–2989.

Sack, A. T., & Linden, D. E. (2003). Combining transcranial magnetic stimulation and functional imaging in Cognitive brain research: possibilities and limitations. *Brain Research Reviews*, *43*(1), 41–56.

Sack, A. T., Kadosh, R. C., Schuhmann, T., Moerel, M., Walsh, V., & Goebel, R. (2009). Optimizing functional accuracy of TMS in cognitive studies: A comparison of methods. *Journal of Cognitive Neuroscience*, *21,* 207–221.

Sandrini, M., Umilta, C., & Rusconi, E. (2011). The use of transcranial magnetic stimulation in Cognitive neuroscience: A new synthesis of methodological issues. *Neuroscience and Biobehavioral Reviews*, *5*(3), 516–536.

Schabitz, W. R., Berger, C., Kollmar, R., Seitz, M., Tanay, E., Kiessling, M., et al. (2004). Effect of brain-derived neurotrophic factor treatment and forced arm use on functional motor recovery after small cortical ischemia. *Stroke, 35*(4), 992–997.

Selimbeyoglu, A., & Parvizi, J. (2010). Electrical stimulation of the human brain: Perceptual and behavioral phenomena reported in the old and new literature. *Frontiers in Human Neuroscience, 4,* 46.

Sgro, J. A., Ghatak, N. R., Stanton, P. C., Emerson, R. G., & Blair, R. (1991). Repetitive high magnetic field stimulation: The effect upon rat brain. *Electroencephalography and Clinical Neurophysiology Supplement, 43,* 180–185.

Shindo, K., Sugiyama, K., Huabao, L., Nishijima, K., Kondo, T., & Izumi, S. (2006). Long-term effect of low-frequency repetitive transcranial magnetic stimulation over the unaffected posterior parietal cortex in patients with unilateral spatial neglect. *Journal of Rehabilitation Medicine, 38*(1), 65–67.

Silvanto, J., Cowey, A., Lavie, N., & Walsh, V. (2005). Striate cortex (V1) activity gates awareness of motion. *Nature Neuroscience, 8*(2), 143–144.

Silvanto, J., Muggleton, N. G., Cowey, A., & Walsh, V. (2007). Neural activation state determines behavioral susceptibility to modified theta burst transcranial magnetic stimulation. *European Journal of Neuroscience, 26*(2), 523–528.

Silvanto, J., Muggleton, N., & Walsh, V. (2008). State-dependency in brain stimulation studies of perception and cognition. *Trends in Cognitive Science, 12*(12), 447–454.

Sommer, M., Tergau, F., Wischer, S., & Paulus, W. (2001). Paired-pulse repetitive transcranial magnetic stimulation of the human motor cortex. *Experimental Brain Research, 139*(4), 465–472.

Sparing, R., Mottaghy, F. M., Hungs, M., Brugmann, M., Foltys, H., Huber, W., et al. (2001). Repetitive transcranial magnetic stimulation effects on language function depend on the stimulation parameters. *Journal of Clinical Neurophysiology, 18*(4), 326–330.

Stefan, K., Kunesch, E., Benecke, R., Cohen, L. G., & Classen, J. (2002). Mechanisms of enhancement of human motor cortex excitability induced by interventional paired associative stimulation. *Journal of Physiology, 543*(Pt 2), 699–708.

Takeuchi, N., Tada, T., Toshima, M., Matsuo, Y., & Ikoma, K. (2009). Repetitive transcranial magnetic stimulation over bilateral hemispheres enhances motor function and training effect of paretic hand in patients after stroke. *Journal of Rehabilitation Medicine, 41*(13), 1049–1054.

Talelli, P., & Rothwell, J. (2006). Does brain stimulation after stroke have a future? *Current Opinion in Neurology, 19*(6), 543–550.

Thickbroom, G. W. (2007). Transcranial magnetic stimulation and synaptic plasticity: Experimental framework and human models. *Expimental Brain Research, 180*(4), 583–593.

Thickbroom, G. W., Sammut, R., & Mastaglia, F. L. (1998). Magnetic stimulation mapping of motor cortex: Factors contributing to map area. *Electroencephalography and Clinical Neurophysiology, 109*(2), 79–84.

Thielscher, A., & Kammer, T. (2004). Electric field properties of two commercial figure-8 coils in TMS: Calculation of focality and efficiency. *Clinical Neurophysiology, 115*(7), 1697–1708.

Thut, G., & Miniussi, C. (2009). New insights into rhythmic brain activity from TMS-EEG studies. *Trends in Cognitive Science, 13*(4), 182–189.

Thut, G., & Pascual Leone, A. (2010). A review of combined TMS-EEG studies to characterize lasting effects of repetitive TMS and assess their usefulness in cognitive and clinical neuroscience. *Brain Topography, 22,* 4.

Traversa, R., Cicinelli, P., Bassi, A., Rossini, P. M., & Bernardi, G. (1997). Mapping of motor cortical reorganization after stroke. A brain stimulation study with focal magnetic pulses. *Stroke, 28*(1), 110–117.

Vallar, G., & Bolognini, N. (2011). Behavioural facilitation following brain stimulation: Implications for neurorehabilitation. *Neuropsychological Rehabilitation*, *21*(5), 618–649.

Vallesi, A., Shallice, T., & Walsh, V. (2007). Role of the prefrontal cortex in the foreperiod effect: TMS evidence for dual mechanisms in temporal preparation. *Cerebral Cortex*, *17*(2), 466–474.

Virtanen, J., Ruohonen, J., Naatanen, R., & Ilmoniemi, R. J. (1999). Instrumentation for the measurement of electric brain responses to transcranial magnetic stimulation. *Medical and Biological Engineering and Computing*, *37*(3), 322–326.

Walsh, V., & Pascual-Leone, A. (2003). *Transcranial Magnetic Stimulation: A Neurochronometrics of Mind*. Cambridge, MA: Mit Press.

Wang, H., Wang, X., & Scheich, H. (1996). LTD and LTP induced by transcranial magnetic stimulation in auditory cortex. *Neuroreport*, *7*(2), 521–525.

Ward, N. S., & Cohen, L. G. (2004). Mechanisms underlying recovery of motor function after stroke. *Archives in Neurology*, *61*(12), 1844–1848.

Wassermann, E. M., Epstein, C., Ziemann, U., Walsh, V., Paus, T., & Lisanby, S. (2008). *Handbook of Transcranial Stimulation*. Oxford, UK: Oxford University Press.

Wassermann, E. M., & Lisanby, S. H. (2001). Therapeutic application of repetitive transcranial magnetic stimulation: A review. *Clinical Neurophysiology*, *112*(8), 1367–1377.

Waterston, M. L., & Pack, C. C. (2010). Improved discrimination of visual stimuli following repetitive transcranial magnetic stimulation. *Public Library of Science: One*, *5*(4), e10354.

Wittenberg, G. F., Chen, R., Ishii, K., Bushara, K. O., Eckloff, S., Croarkin, E., et al. (2003). Constraint-induced therapy in stroke: Magnetic-stimulation motor maps and cerebral activation. *Neurorehabilitation and Neural Repair*, *17*(1), 48–57.

Zangen, A., Roth, Y., Voller, B., & Hallett, M. (2005). Transcranial magnetic stimulation of deep brain regions: Evidence for efficacy of the H-coil. *Clinical Neurophysiology*, *116*(4), 775–779.

Zhang, X., Mei, Y., Liu, C., & Yu, S. (2007). Effect of transcranial magnetic stimulation on the expression of c-Fos and brain-derived neurotrophic factor of the cerebral cortex in rats with cerebral infarct. *Journal of Huazhong University Science, Technology and Medical Science*, *27*(4), 415–418.

Ziemann, U., Chen, R., Cohen, L. G., & Hallett, M. (1998). Dextromethorphan decreases the excitability of the human motor cortex. *Neurology*, *51*(5), 1320–1324.

Ziemann, U., Hallett, M., & Cohen, L. G. (1998). Mechanisms of deafferentation-induced plasticity in human motor cortex. *Journal of Neuroscience*, *18*(17), 7000–7007.

NEUROPSYCHOLOGICAL REHABILITATION
2011, 21 (5), 602–617

Transcranial electrical stimulation (tES – tDCS; tRNS, tACS) methods

Walter Paulus

Department of Clinical Neurophysiology, University Medical Faculty Göttingen, Göttingen, Germany

Weak transcranial direct current stimulation (tDCS) with a homogenous DC field at intensities of around 1 mA induces long-lasting changes in the brain. tDCS can be used to manipulate brain excitability via membrane polarisation: cathodal stimulation hyperpolarises, while anodal stimulation depolarises the resting membrane potential, whereby the induced after-effects depend on polarity, duration and intensity of the stimulation. A variety of other parameters influence tDCS effects; co-application of neuropharmacologically active drugs may most impressively prolong or even reverse stimulation effects. Transcranial alternating stimulation (tACS) and random noise stimulation (tRNS) are used to interfere with ongoing neuronal oscillations and also finally produce neuroplastic effects if applied with appropriate parameters.

Keywords: Transcranial direct current stimulation (tDCS); Transcranial alternating current stimulation (tACS); Transcranial random noise stimulation (tRNS); Transcranial magnetic stimulation (TMS); Rehabilitation; Plasticity.

INTRODUCTION

Two methods of non-invasive electromagnetic stimulation of the human brain have dominated the last decades: transcranial magnetic stimulation (TMS), which activates axons via short-pulsed stimulation and leads thereby to new action potentials; and transcranial electric stimulation, predominantly

Correspondence should be addressed to Walter Paulus, Department of Clinical Neurophysiology, University Medical Faculty Göttingen, Robert Koch Str. 4037075 Göttingen, Germany E-mail: wpaulus@med.uni-goettingen.de

I thank José Casadiego Bastidas for the calculations. Funded by the German Ministry of Education and Research, BMBF 01GQ0810 and the Rose Foundation.

by tDCS, which can be used to manipulate the membrane potential of neurons and modulate spontaneous firing rates, but is insufficient on its own to discharge resting neurons or axons. Using diametrically opposite stimulation techniques such as high constant magnetic fields does not seem to influence cortical excitability (Schlamann et al., 2010), nor can short-pulsed electric transcranial stimulation be pursued regularly, since it induces significant skin pain (Merton & Morton, 1980). Despite their very different modes of action, however, prolonged application of both rTMS and tDCS can cause after-effects on the excitability of neurons and networks that outlast the stimulus by minutes or even hours. There have been a number of recent advances in both methods: theta burst stimulation (TBS) is a rapid TMS method of achieving long-term effects allowing lower intensities and duration of stimulation, it is only mentioned in the present context because of interesting parallels concerning the total stimulation duration and sign of after-effects; transcranial random noise stimulation (tRNS) is a highly effective method of avoiding directional sensitivity of standard tDCS; sinusoidally varying transcranial stimulation (transcranial alternating current stimulation: tACS) may be able to interact with ongoing rhythms in the cortex. Other, usually older, methods such as Limoge current have been tried in the past, but are more complicated in their stimulation parameters and less well validated (overview in Zaghi, Acar, Hultgren, Boggio, & Fregni, 2010).

tDCS

Technique

Transcranial electrical stimulation methods have a very long tradition. As early as about 1800, when Volta invented his electric pile, researchers began to investigate the application of direct current (DC) in a variety of neurological diseases. In, by modern standards not well-documented, case reports, it was claimed that chronic stroke could benefit from direct current application (Hellwag & Jacobi, 1802). Numerous investigations soon followed in the 19th century. These early efforts were given up mainly because of the lack of sufficiently reliable evaluation methods. When effects of direct current application were measured by transcranial magnetic stimulation at the motor cortex (Priori, Berardelli, Rona, Accornero, & Manfredi, 1998) tDCS became reliable in terms of parameters such as stimulation intensity and duration and validation of its plastic after-effects (Nitsche, Nitsche, et al., 2003; Nitsche & Paulus 2000; 2001) (overview in Nitsche et al., 2008). In order to achieve after-effects, it appears to be necessary to stimulate for at least three minutes with the intensity of at least 0.6 mA (Nitsche & Paulus, 2000). Not surprisingly, the direction of electrode polarisation is decisive in the direction of the after-effects. If the anode is placed above the motor cortex, transcranial magnetic stimulation will result in a larger motor evoked potential (MEP). If the cathode is placed at the motor cortex, MEP size will be reduced. Both electrodes introduce a uniform steady state extracellular electric field responsible for plastic effects in neural tissue (Bikson et al., 2004). Originally it seemed to be that the longer the stimulation lasted, the longer the after-effects would last. So, for instance, when applying tDCS with a duration of 5–13 minutes anodally, after-effects increase proportionately, with a duration of about 1–2 hours (Nitsche & Paulus, 2001). Cathodal stimulation turned out to be somewhat more efficient than anodal stimulation with an after-effect duration of 1 hour after 9 minutes tDCS (Nitsche, Nitsche, et al., 2003). Most recent data, however, have shown that there is an upper limit for sustaining the excitatory after-effects from anodal tDCS. The application of 26 minutes of continuous anodal tDCS finally resulted in inhibition (Monte-Silva et al., 2011). Following application of cathodal tDCS continuously for 18 minutes, after-effects did not switch into excitation, and turned out not to be as impressively prolonged as with time increments of shorter durations (Monte-Silva, Kuo, Liebetanz, Paulus, & Nitsche, 2010). We expect a similar pattern with ever longer cathodal tDCS, since we recently obtained other evidence for the reversal of theta burst after-effects with prolonged duration (Gamboa, Antal, Moliadze, & Paulus, 2010). Most likely, this effect is related to calcium homeostasis (Wankerl, Weise, Gentner, Rumpf, & Classen, 2010). In a complex theta burst design targeting the L-type voltage gated calcium channel (L-VGCC) and involving the antagonist nimodipine, the N-Methyl-D-aspartic acid (NMDA) receptor antagonist dextromethorphan and a comparison between rest and activated conditions, the authors argued that calcium dynamics determine the polarity of LTP/ LTD-like changes *in vivo*. L-VGCCs were suggested to act as molecular switches mediating metaplasticity induced by endogenous neuronal activation. Of particular relevance to neurorehabilitation is the finding of increased tDCS efficacy with repetitive stimulation over days (Reis et al., 2009). Thus in the near future the most efficient stimulation protocols may turn out to be repetitive daily stimulations, further optimised with repetitive tDCS applications. So far not much attention has been put on the importance of intervals. With 5 Hz rTMS it could be shown that an uninterrupted stimulation turned out to be inhibitory, only the introduction of intervals seems to be responsible for the otherwise generally accepted facilitatory features of 5 Hz rTMS (Rothkegel, Sommer, & Paulus, 2010). Since, as already mentioned, pure prolongation of tDCS duration will lead to a reversal of the sign of stimulation after-effects, one way of optimising the relation between stimulation parameters and induced plasticity is the introduction of intervals. Here it appears that, for example, 13 minute intervals with a break of 13 to 20 minutes leads to longer plastic after-effects than uninterrupted stimulation or intervals of three hours (Monte-Silva et al., 2011).

tDCS applied with 1 mA needs larger electrodes than those used for electroencephalography in order to avoid skin burns. Even when using electrode sizes of 35 cm^2, current application starts to become painful (Furubayashi et al., 2008) at 3 mA. This can also be seen as a natural safety protection against higher intensities, although the method itself is regarded as safe as demonstrated by animal experiments (Liebetanz et al., 2009). In order to provide a more physiological comparability and better safety criteria, other parameters have been used (see overview in Liebetanz et al., 2009; Nitsche, Liebetanz, et al., 2003):

Current density

The current density is defined as the electric current per unit of cross-sectional area, and if this current density is flowing homogeneously through an area A, then the current density J can be written as:

$$J = \frac{I}{A},$$ (1)

where I is the electric current (Heald & Marion, 1995).

In the case of an electrode, the cross-sectional area A is given by the active area of the electrode (McCreery, Agnew, Yuen, & Bullara, 1990).

Total charge

Given the fact that the electric current I is the amount of charge that is flowing through a cross-sectional area A per unit of time (Heald and Marion, 1995), it is possible to calculate the charge Q that flowed in terms of the electric current as:

$$Q = \int_{t_1}^{t_2} I(t)dt,$$ (2)

where t_1 and t_2 are the limits of the interval in which the flow of charge is studied (Figure 1).

Having n electric impulses (Figure 2), of intensity and duration I_p and τ, respectively, it can be demonstrated that the total charge is given by the product among the intensity, the duration and the amount of pulses.

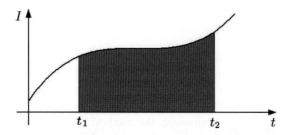

Figure 1. Example of a curve *Current vs Time*. The shaded area represents the charge that flowed during the interval [t₁, t₂].

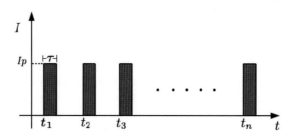

Figure 2. Scheme of a sequence of electric pulses.

Proof:
The charge, Equation (2), takes the form:

$$Q_t = I_p \left[\int_{t_1}^{t_1+\tau} dt + \int_{t_2}^{t_2+\tau} dt + \cdots + \int_{t_n}^{t_n+\tau} dt \right], \tag{3}$$

$$Q_t = I_p[t_1 + \tau - t_1 + t_2 + \tau - t_2 + \cdots + t_n + \tau - t_n]. \tag{4}$$

Perfoming the algebraic sum among all the terms, is easy to see that the term τ appears n-times in the Equation (4). Thus, the total charge corresponding to the n pulses is:

$$Q_t = n\tau I_p. \tag{5}$$

In the present context, as shown by (Nitsche, Liebetanz, et al., 2003), the total charge refers to the stimulated area. Hence, the total charge is given then by:

$$\sigma_t = \frac{n\tau I_p}{A}, \tag{6}$$

where A, is the active area of the electrode (McCreery et al., 1990).

Charge density

Similarly, as with the total charge, it can be demonstrated that for pulses, the charge density for each pulse is given by:

$$\sigma = \frac{\tau I_p}{A},$$ (7)

Electrode size itself can be varied. Larger electrodes may be used as reference electrodes, for instance on the forehead, whereas smaller electrodes may allow a selective stimulation of thenar and hypothenar muscles (Nitsche, Doemkes, Karakose, Antal, & Liebetanz, 2007). Since tDCS induces a polarisation of brain tissue the position of the reference electrode is critical (Miranda, Lomarev, & Hallett, 2006). Originally we only found a stimulation effect with the reference electrode on the forehead and not at other localisations on the skull (Nitsche & Paulus, 2000). Most studies at the motor cortex have been performed so far with a contralateral reference electrode, although application of extra-cephalic return electrodes, e.g., at the deltoid muscle, is possible (Priori et al., 2008). However, this set up needs higher stimulation intensities proportional to increasing inter-electrode distance (Moliadze, Antal, & Paulus, 2010b). Complex calculation models are under way (Wagner et al., 2007) to determine the optimal electrode position for targeting a certain area, taking into account different current flow routes in the cerebrospinal fluid of normal subjects and stroke patients (Datta et al., 2009). Also, diffusion tensor-imaged MRI weighting is integrated in these models in order to take into account the 10 times better conductivity of fibre tracts along the tract as compared to a perpendicular current flow.

Pharmacological effects

tDCS effects can be modified, abolished, prolonged or even reversed by co-application of drugs acting on the central nervous system. Thus drug co-application allows to control for final tDCS outcome in a most important way. It may be even more important in the context of drugs being applied for stroke treatment, such as those reducing spasticity or treating depression. First it was shown that neuroplastic after-effects are NMDA-receptor dependent (Liebetanz, Nitsche, Tergau, & Paulus, 2002), whereas acute effects are not (Nitsche et al., 2003a). Anodal after-effects can be selectively suppressed by both the sodium channel blocker carbamazepine and the calcium channel blocker flunarizine (Nitsche, Fricke, et al., 2003). Most important to neuro-rehabilitation seems to be the possibility of selectively prolonging anodal but not cathodal after-effects by a factor of about 20 into the next day by co-application of either d-cycloserine (Nitsche, Jaussi, et al., 2004) or amphetamine (Nitsche, Grundey, et al., 2004). In contrast, a low dose of a dopamine D2 receptor antagonist selectively prolongs cathodal inhibition effects by a similar amount into the 24-hours range (Nitsche et al., 2006). The application of 100 mg l-dopa which roughly doubles the dopamine concentration in the brain (overview in Paulus & Trenkwalder, 2006) has a most interesting effect. Anodal after-effects are converted into inhibition, whereas cathodal inhibition remains. Whereas under tDCS and a placebo drug after-effects vanish after 30–90 minutes, under tDCS and l-dopa inhibitory after-effects are now prolonged by a factor of 30 lasting until the following evening. As a control we added a paired associative stimulation protocol (PAS 25) (Kuo, Paulus, & Nitsche, 2008). In this case excitation was maintained and not converted into inhibition, it showed however a similarly impressive prolongation by about a factor of 30. Here we argued that synapse-specific plasticity, as induced by PAS, is boosted by this dose of l-dopa whereas synapse-unspecific plasticity, as induced by tDCS, is suppressed. This effect however only holds true for the 100 mg dose; with low (25 mg) or high (200 mg) doses of l-dopa facilitatory as well as inhibitory plastic after-effects were abolished. This clear non-linear, dosage-dependent effect of dopamine on both facilitatory and inhibitory plasticity supports the assumption of the importance of a specific dosage of dopamine optimally suited to improve plasticity (Monte-Silva, Liebetanz, Grundey, Paulus, & Nitsche, 2010). This might be important for the therapeutic application, especially for rehabilitative purposes.

Other drugs of relevance for boosting tDCS after-effects are rivastigmine, which increases the acetylcholine content of the CNS and provides results similar to 100 mg of l-dopa (Kuo, Grosch Fregni, Paulus, & Nitsche, 2007), and the serotonin re-uptake inhibitor citalopram, which converts cathodal inhibitory after-effects into excitation and prolongs standard tDCS after-effects into the 24-hours range (Nitsche et al., 2009).

tDCS under-activation

The effects described so far used mainly MEP measurements. Intracortical excitability parameters such as short latency intracortical inhibition (SICI) or facilitation (SCF) (overview in context with pharmacological alterations in Paulus et al., 2008) were also influenced both during and after tDCS (Nitsche et al., 2005). tDCS after-effects however only provide this clear-cut picture if tDCS is applied during muscle relaxation. In cases of mental challenge, after-effects show a tendency to be reversed; in cases of active movement during tDCS, application excitation switches into inhibition and cathodal inhibition tends to increase further (Antal, Terney, Poreisz, & Paulus, 2007). Also, homeostatic priming is able to reverse both tDCS and rTMS effects (Lang et al., 2004; Siebner et al., 2004). Understanding of these complex relations is far from complete. It is however of particular importance for neurorehabilitation since, in general, preconditioning by activation may reverse or significantly alter rTMS (Ziemann, Ilic, Pauli, Meintzschel, & Ruge, 2004), theta burst (Gentner, Wankerl, Reinsberger, Zeller, & Classen, 2008) or tDCS after-effects (Nitsche, Roth, et al., 2007) as measured in terms of MEP size. However, the effect on learning is obviously dissociated from the MEP after-effects since all positive learning effects, either with tDCS (Nitsche, Schauenburg, et al., 2003), tRNS (Terney, Chaieb, Moliadze, Antal, & Paulus, 2008) or tACS (Antal et al., 2008; Moliadze, Antal, & Paulus, 2010a), were obtained during stimulation. A further frequency-specific dissociation occurred between MEP size increase and effect on implicit learning with tACS at high frequencies (see below) (Moliadze et al., 2010a).

Recently it could be shown by the aid of multichannel EEG recordings through functional connectivity and graph theoretical analysis that tDCS induces changes in brain synchronisation and topological functional organis-ation. In this study functional connectivity patterns significantly increased within premotor, motor, and sensorimotor areas of the stimulated hemisphere during motor activity in the 60–90 Hz frequency range. Additionally, tDCS induced significant intrahemispheric and interhemispheric connectivity changes in all the studied frequency bands (Polania, Nitsche, & Paulus, 2011).

On the basis of fMRI data it was shown that nodal minimum path lengths significantly increased in the left somatomotor (SM1) cortex after anodal tDCS whereas functional coupling significantly increased between premotor and superior parietal areas with the left SM1. Also, the nodal connectivity degree in the left posterior cingulate cortex (PCC) area as well as in the right dorsolateral prefrontal cortex (right DLPFC) significantly increased (Polania, Paulus, Antal, & Nitsche, 2011).

Apart from TMS evaluation methods, tDCS effects were also localised by quantifying cerebral blood flow during an H_2O PET investigation (Lang et al., 2005). Other methods which have been used for evaluating tDCS after-effects are evoked potentials (Accornero, Li Voli, La Riccia, & Gregori, 2007; Antal, Kincses, Nitsche, Bartfai, & Paulus, 2004), EEG (Ardolino, Bossi, Barbieri, & Priori, 2005), psychophysics (Antal, Nitsche, & Paulus, 2001; Antal & Paulus, 2008), phosphenes (Antal, Kincses, et al., 2004; Lang et al., 2007), visuomotor learning paradigms (Antal, Nitsche, et al., 2004), fMRI (Antal, Polania, Schmidt-Samoa, Dechent, & Paulus, 2011), a variety of clinical studies (cf. other chapters in this issue), cognitive performance in normal subjects, such as naming facilitation (Fertonani, Rosini, Cotelli, Rossini, & Miniussi, 2010), and cognitive neurorehabilitation (Miniussi et al., 2008).

In particular, tDCS was shown to improve neurorehabilitation in stroke patients (Hummel et al., 2005) and is now the subject of a large European trial in stroke (Christian Gerloff, personal communication). Many more ongoing trials are registered, e.g., on the National Institutes of Health homepage under clinical trials. Other applications on a behavioural level have been published, e.g., for Alzheimer's disease (Ferrucci et al., 2008).

tDCS induces behavioural effects as shown by an implicit motor learning paradigm (Nitsche, Schauenburg, et al., 2003) and a probabilistic classification learning task (Kincses, Antal, Nitsche, Bartfai, & Paulus, 2004). Although tDCS is much easier to blind in clinical studies as compared to rTMS, awareness of a prickling skin sensation starts at an intensity of about 500 µA (Ambrus, Paulus, & Antal, 2010). Blinding options can be achieved in the placebo group with a short stimulation and the electric current being switched off after some 20 seconds. An alternative can be the use of short electric pulses without a DC offset. tDCS is usually faded in for seconds in order to avoid retinal phosphenes when a forehead reference point close to the eyes is used. Apart from easier blinding, another advantage of tDCS compared to rTMS studies seems to be the robustness against brain-derived neurotrophic factor (BDNF) polymorphisms (Antal et al., 2010), which, in theta burst stimulation, impedes plasticity in the Met allele carriers (Cheeran et al., 2008). In the mouse model, the BDNF dependency however seems to be higher (Fritsch et al., 2010). The role polymorphisms will play in the context of neurorehabilitation needs to be investigated.

tRNS

Alternating current is no longer sensitive to the direction of current flow. In order to screen for most efficient frequencies in a physiological range, we used a random noise frequency pattern (tRNS: transcranial random noise stimulation) (Terney et al., 2008) with a potential to desynchronise (pathological) rhythms. A frequency spectrum between 0.1 Hz and 640 Hz was chosen to screen for whether or not any plastic after-effects could be seen. This tRNS paradigm includes a normally distributed random level of current generated for every sample at a sampling rate of 1280 samples per second with no overall DC offset. In the frequency spectrum all coefficients had a similar size with a "white noise" characteristic. All other parameters were taken over from the established tDCS studies. A consistent excitability increase lasting at least 60 minutes, through both physiological measures and behavioural tasks, was induced by 10 minutes of tRNS stimulation (Terney et al., 2008). Unexpectedly higher frequencies (100–640 Hz) and not frequencies in the EEG range were responsible for generating this excitability increase. This effect may either be attributed to the repeated opening of Na channels or to a higher sensitivity of neuronal networks to field modulation than the average single neuron threshold (Francis, Gluckman, & Schiff, 2003) (see tACS at 140 Hz below). During tRNS and finger tapping, a reduction of the blood-oxygen-level dependence (BOLD) response in the motor cortex can be seen on the fMRI (Chaieb et al., 2009). While tRNS appears to possess at least the same therapeutic potential as anodal tDCS, it is easier to blind than tDCS (Ambrus et al., 2010) with the 50% perception threshold for tDCS at 400 μA while this threshold was at 1200 μA in the case of tRNS.

tACS

Sinusoidally applied transcranial alternating current stimulation (tACS) allows manipulation of intrinsic cortical oscillations with externally applied electrical frequencies. Of course, any combination of any frequency is possible, the more frequencies are involved the closer the results may approach tRNS effects. A combination with tDCS has been shown to be effective for boosting memory (Marshall, Helghadottir, Molle, & Born, 2006), although without control experiments it cannot be decided if the tDCS or the tACS effect is responsible for the memory improvement. A later study on the motor cortex argues in favour of a tDCS effect for motor cortex plasticity (Groppa et al., 2010). More complex stimulation protocols, such as Limoge's current, have been reviewed recently (Zaghi et al., 2010). TACS after-effects induced with a single frequency and close to efficacy intensity threshold (Antal et al., 2008b) were confined to an improvement of motor learning which was only seen with 10 Hz, a frequency imminent in the motor cortex (Castro-Alamancos, Rigas, & Tawara-Hirata, 2007). Since other tACS frequencies between 5 Hz and 40 Hz failed to induce any measurable efficacy, this finding appeared disappointing at first glance. However, because the intensity was limited to 400 μA in order to avoid retinal phosphenes with higher amplitudes (Antal et al., 2008b), the results are not directly comparable with the tDCS effects which were obtained at 1 mA (Nitsche, Liebetanz, et al., 2003). This higher sensitivity of the retina to electric stimulation is also the reason why tDCS intensity is ramped up over seconds to avoid phosphene sensations. Other evidence for the influence of tACS on the motor cortex with 20 Hz is slowed voluntary movement (Pogosyan, Gaynor, Eusebio, & Brown, 2009). Also it was possible to increase alpha power by stimulating with a tACS frequency in the individual EEG range (Zaehle, Rach, & Herrmann, 2010).

A second paper using tACS at Oz reports trying to circumvent the induction of retinal phosphenes by a different reference electrode remote from the eye (Kanai, Chaieb Antal, Walsh, & Paulus, 2008). The closer one or both tACS electrodes are to the retina the more likely retinal stimulation occurs. Stimulation of the visual cortex at Oz with a reference at Cz seemed to be able to elicit directly cortical phosphenes in a frequency-dependent way, with a peak slightly lower in darkness than in brightness. Phosphene threshold was at 250 μA; stimulation effects were explored up to 1 mA. This finding was however challenged by arguing that even remote electrodes may be able to stimulate the retina by far field potentials (Schutter & Hortensius 2009; Schwiedrzik 2009). Separation of retinal and cortical phosphenes is not easy (Paulus 2010). However, while it is clear that tACS at the visual cortex influences TMS-induced phosphenes (Kanai, Pulus, & Walsh, 2010), more studies are necessary for a clearer separation. tACS seems likely to open a new era of directly interfering with cortical rhythms and is expected to synchronise actively cortical rhythms, although at present interference with phosphenes in the frequency range of about 10 to 40 Hz is a problem.

This problem does not occur if tACS is used in the so-called ripple frequency range (Moliadze et al., 2010a). Ripples are short hippocampal oscillations in the frequency range between 100 and 250 Hz associated with memory encoding. If in the resting condition tACS is applied for 10 minutes at 140 Hz with 1 mA at the motor cortex, an hour-long MEP increase by TMS has been documented. Stimulation at 80 Hz remained without an effect, while 250 Hz clearly had a smaller efficacy. With activation, tACS after-effects are abolished or even reversed as those seen with tDCS (Antal et al., 2007). However, this reduction of MEP size with activation was least with 140 Hz or, in other words, this frequency turned out to be most resistant against the decrease of MEP size under activation. Motor learning under an implicit motor learning paradigm (Nitsche, Schauenburg, et al., 2003) was however better with 250 than with 140 Hz, a finding that demands further investigation.

CONCLUSION

In summary, an almost infinite spectrum of stimulation possibilities arises with the use of transcranial electrical stimulation techniques. For future applications it will be a most challenging task to unveil their individual physiological mechanisms, one such investigation is already under way, e.g., in the Bikson group (Bikson, Radman, & Datta, 2006; Radman, Su, An, Parra, & Bikson, 2007). Most importantly, it can be demonstrated that also in symmetrical dendritic arborisations, superimposed electrical direct current fields can alter membrane potential (Radman, Ramos, Brumberg, & Bikson, 2009). Nevertheless, it will ultimately be of importance to pursue the simplest solutions in order to best facilitate the finding of targeted cortical excitability manipulations in the context of neurorehabilitation. Possible applications focus on facilitating the impaired functions of lesioned areas as well as suppressing maladaptive plasticity. Further areas concern the ability of electrical fields to foster neuronal growth. It has been shown that nerve growth can be enhanced and directed by an electric field (McCaig, Rajnicek, Song, & Shao, 2005).

REFERENCES

Accornero, N., Li Voti, P., La Riccia, M., & Gregori, B. (2007). Visual evoked potentials modulation during direct current cortical polarization. *Experimental Brain Research, 178,* 261–266.

Ambrus, G. G., Paulus, W., & Antal, A. (2010). Cutaneous perception thresholds of electrical stimulation methods: Comparison of tDCS and tRNS. *Clinical Neurophysiology, 121,* 1908–1914.

Antal, A., Boros, K., Poreisz, C., Chaieb, L., Terney, D., & Paulus, W. (2008). Comparatively weak after-effects of transcranial alternating current stimulation (tACS) on cortical excitability in humans. *Brain Stimulation, 1,* 97–105.

Antal, A., Chaieb, L., Moliadze, V., Monte-Silva, K., Poreisz, C., et al. (2010). Brain-derived neurotrophic factor (BDNF) gene polymorphisms shape cortical plasticity in humans. *Brain Stimulation, 3,* 230–237.

Antal, A., Kincses, T. Z., Nitsche, M. A., Bartfai, O., & Paulus, W. (2004). Excitability changes induced in the human primary visual cortex by transcranial direct current stimulation: Direct electrophysiological evidence. *Investigative Ophthalmology & Visual Science, 45,* 702–707.

Antal, A., Nitsche, M. A., Kincses, T. Z., Kruse, W., Hoffmann, K. P., & Paulus, W. (2004). Facilitation of visuo-motor learning by transcranial direct current stimulation of the motor and extrastriate visual areas in humans. *European Journal of Neuroscience, 19,* 2888–2892.

Antal, A., Nitsche, M. A., & Paulus, W. (2001). External modulation of visual perception in humans. *Neuroreport, 12,* 3553–3555.

Antal, A., & Paulus, W. (2008). Transcranial direct current stimulation and visual perception. *Perception, 37,* 367–374.

Antal, A., Polania, R., Schmidt-Samoa, C., Dechent, P., & Paulus, W. (2011). Transcranial direct current stimulation over the primary motor cortex during fMRI. *Neuroimage, 55*(2), 590–596.

Antal, A., Terney, D., Poreisz, C., & Paulus, W. (2007). Towards unravelling task-related modulations of neuroplastic changes induced in the human motor cortex. *European Journal of Neuroscience, 26,* 2687–2691.

Ardolino, G., Bossi, B., Barbieri, S., & Priori, A. (2005). Non-synaptic mechanisms underlie the after-effects of cathodal transcutaneous direct current stimulation of the human brain. *Journal of Physiology, 568,* 653–663.

Bikson, M., Inoue, M., Akiyama, H., Deans, J. K., Fox, J. E., et al. (2004). Effects of uniform extracellular DC electric fields on excitability in rat hippocampal slices *in vitro. Journal of Physiology, 557,* 175–190.

Bikson, M., Radman, T., & Datta, A. (2006). Rational modulation of neuronal processing with applied electric fields. *Conference Proceedings IEEE English Medical Biological Society, 1,* 1616–1619.

Castro-Alamancos, M. A, Rigas, P., & Tawara-Hirata, Y. (2007). Resonance (approximately 10 Hz) of excitatory networks in motor cortex: Effects of voltage-dependent ion channel blockers. *Journal of Physiology, 578,* 173–191.

Chaieb, L., Kovacs, G., Cziraki, C., Greenlee, M., Paulus, W., & Antal, A. (2009). Short-duration transcranial random noise stimulation induces blood oxygenation level dependent response attenuation in the human motor cortex. *Experimental Brain Research, 198,* 439–444.

Cheeran, B., Talelli, P., Mori, F., Koch, G., Suppa, A., et al. (2008). A common polymorphism in the brain-derived neurotrophic factor gene (BDNF) modulates human cortical plasticity and the response to rTMS. *Journal of Physiology, 586,* 5717–5725.

Datta, A., Bansal, V., Diaz, J., Patel, J., Reato, D., & Bikson, M. (2009). Gyri-precise head model of transcranial direct current stimulation: Improved spatial focality using a ring electrode versus conventional rectangular pad. *Brain Stimulation, 2,* 201–207.

Ferrucci, R., Mameli, F., Guidi, I., Mrakic-Sposta, S., Vergari, M., et al. (2008). Transcranial direct current stimulation improves recognition memory in Alzheimer disease. *Neurology, 71,* 493–498.

Fertonani, A., Rosini, S., Cotelli, M., Rossini, P. M., & Miniussi, C. (2010). Naming facilitation induced by transcranial direct current stimulation. *Behavioural Brain Research, 208,* 311–318.

Francis, J. T., Gluckman, B. J., & Schiff, S. J. (2003). Sensitivity of neurons to weak electric fields. *Journal of Neuroscience, 23,* 7255–7261.

Fritsch, B., Reis, J., Martinowich, K., Schambra, H. M., Ji, Y., et al. (2010). Direct current stimulation promotes BDNF-dependent synaptic plasticity, potential implications for motor learning. *Neuron, 66,* 198–204.

Furubayashi, T., Terao, Y., Arai, N., Okabe, S., Mochizuki, H., et al. (2008). Short and long duration transcranial direct current stimulation (tDCS) over the human hand motor area. *Experimental Brain Research, 185,* 279–286.

Gamboa, O. L., Antal, A., Moliadze, V., & Paulus, W. (2010). Simply longer is not better: Reversal of theta burst after-effect with prolonged stimulation. *Experimental Brain Research, 204,* 181–187.

Gentner, R., Wankerl, K., Reinsberger, C., Zeller, D., & Classen, J. (2008). Depression of human corticospinal excitability induced by magnetic theta-burst stimulation: Evidence of rapid polarity-reversing metaplasticity. *Cerebral Cortex, 18,* 2046–2053.

Groppa, S., Bergmann, T. O., Siems, C., Molle, M., Marshall, L., & Siebner, H. R. (2010). Slow-oscillatory transcranial direct current stimulation can induce bidirectional shifts in motor cortical excitability in awake humans. *Neuroscience, 166,* 1219–1225.

Heald, M., & Marion, J. (1995). *Classical electromagnetic radiation* (3rd ed.). Fort Worth, TX: Saunders College Publishing.

Hellwag, C. F., & Jacobi, M. (1802). *Erfahrungen über die Heilkräfte des Galvanismus und Betrachtungen über desselben chemische und physiologische Wirkungen.* Hamburg, Germany: Friedrich Perthes.

Hummel, F., Celnik, P., Giraux, P., Floel, A., Wu, W. H., et al. (2005). Effects of non-invasive cortical stimulation on skilled motor function in chronic stroke. *Brain, 128,* 490–499.

Kanai, R., Chaieb, L., Antal, A., Walsh, V., & Paulus, W. (2008). Frequency-dependent electrical stimulation of the visual cortex. *Current Biology, 18,* 1839–1843.

Kanai, R., Paulus, W., & Walsh, V. (2010). Transcranial alternating current stimulation (tACS) modulates cortical excitability as assessed by TMS-induced phosphene thresholds. *Clinical Neurophysiology, 121,* 1551–1554.

Kincses, T. Z., Antal, A., Nitsche, M. A., Bartfai, O., & Paulus, W. (2004). Facilitation of probabilistic classification learning by transcranial direct current stimulation of the prefrontal cortex in the human. *Neuropsychologia, 42,* 113–117.

Kuo, M. F., Grosch, J., Fregni, F., Paulus, W., & Nitsche, M. A. (2007). Focusing effect of acetylcholine on neuroplasticity in the human motor cortex. *Journal of Neuroscience, 27,* 14442–14447.

Kuo, M. F., Paulus, W., & Nitsche, M. A. (2008). Boosting focally-induced brain plasticity by dopamine. *Cerebral Cortex, 18,* 648–651.

Lang, N., Siebner, H. R., Chadaide, Z., Boros, K., Nitsche, M. A., et al. (2007). Bidirectional modulation of primary visual cortex excitability: A combined tDCS and rTMS study. *Investigative Ophthalmology & Visual Science, 48,* 5782–5787.

Lang, N., Siebner, H. R., Ernst, D., Nitsche, M. A., Paulus, W., et al. (2004). Preconditioning with transcranial direct current stimulation sensitizes the motor cortex to rapid-rate transcranial magnetic stimulation and controls the direction of after-effects. *Biological Psychiatry, 56,* 634–639.

Lang, N., Siebner, H. R., Ward, N. S., Lee, L., Nitsche, M. A., et al. (2005). How does transcranial DC stimulation of the primary motor cortex alter regional neuronal activity in the human brain? *European Journal of Neuroscience, 22,* 495–504.

Liebetanz, D., Koch, R., Mayenfels, S., Konig, F., Paulus, W., & Nitsche, M. A. (2009). Safety limits of cathodal transcranial direct current stimulation in rats. *Clinical Neurophysiology, 120,* 1161–1167.

Liebetanz, D., Nitsche, M. A., Tergau, F., & Paulus, W. (2002). Pharmacological approach to the mechanisms of transcranial DC-stimulation-induced after-effects of human motor cortex excitability. *Brain, 125,* 2238–2247.

Marshall, L., Helgadottir, H., Molle, M., & Born, J. (2006). Boosting slow oscillations during sleep potentiates memory. *Nature, 444,* 610–613.

McCaig, C. D., Rajnicek, A. M., Song, B., & Zhao, M. (2005). Controlling cell behavior electrically: Current views and future potential. *Physiology Review, 85,* 943–978.

McCreery, D. B., Agnew, W. F., Yuen, T. G. H., & Bullara, L. (1990). Charge density and charge per phase as cofactors in neural injury induced by electrical stimulation. *IEEE Transactions on Biomedical Engineering, 37*(10), 996–1001.

Merton, P. A., & Morton, H. B. (1980). Stimulation of the cerebral cortex in the intact human subject. *Nature, 285,* 227.

Miniussi, C., Cappa, S. F., Cohen, L. G., Floel, A., Fregni, F., et al. (2008). Efficacy of repetitive transcranial magnetic stimulation/transcranial direct current stimulation in cognitive neurorehabititation. *Brain Stimulation, 1,* 326–336.

Miranda, P. C., Lomarev, M., & Hallett, M. (2006). Modeling the current distribution during transcranial direct current stimulation. *Clinical Neurophysiology, 117,* 1623–1629.

Moliadze, V., Antal, A., & Paulus, W. (2010a). Boosting brain excitability by transcranial high frequency stimulation in the ripple range. *Journal of Physiology, 588,* 4891–4904.

Moliadze, V., Antal, A., & Paulus, W. (2010b). Electrode-distance dependent after-effects of transcranial direct and random noise stimulation with extracephalic reference electrodes. *Clinical Neurophysiology, 121,* 2165–2171.

Monte-Silva, K., Hessenthaler, S., Kuo, M. F., Liebetanz, D., Paulus, W., & Nitsche, M. (2011). *Induction of l-LTP-like plasticity in the human motor cortex by repeated non-invasive brain stimulation.* Manuscript submitted for publication.

Monte-Silva, K. K., Kuo, M. F., Liebetanz, D., Paulus, W., & Nitsche, M. A. (2010). Shaping the optimal repetition interval for cathodal transcranial direct current stimulation (tDCS). *Journal of Neurophysiology, 103,* 1735–1740.

Monte-Silva, K. K., Liebetanz, D., Grundey, J., Paulus, W., & Nitsche, M. A. (2010). Dosage-dependent non-linear effect of l-dopa on human motor cortex plasticity. *Journal of Physiology, 588,* 3415–3424.

Nitsche, M. A., Cohen, L. G., Wassermann, E. M., Priori, A., Lang, N., et al. (2008). Transcranial direct current stimulation: State of the art 2008. *Brain Stimulation, 1,* 206–223.

Nitsche, M. A., Doemkes, S., Karakose, T., Antal, A., Liebetanz, D., et al. (2007). Shaping the effects of transcranial direct current stimulation of the human motor cortex. *Journal of Neurophysiology, 97,* 3109–3017.

Nitsche, M. A., Fricke, K., Henschke, U., Schlitterlau, A., Liebetanz, D., et al. (2003). Pharmacological modulation of cortical excitability shifts induced by transcranial direct current stimulation in humans. *Journal of Physiology, 553,* 293–301.

Nitsche, M. A., Grundey, J., Liebetanz, D., Lang, N., Tergau, F., & Paulus, W. (2004). Catecholaminergic consolidation of motor cortical neuroplasticity in humans. *Cerebral Cortex, 14,* 1240–1245.

Nitsche, M. A., Jaussi, W., Liebetanz, D., Lang, N., Tergau, F., & Paulus, W. (2004). Consolidation of human motor cortical neuroplasticity by D-cycloserine. *Neuropsychopharmacology, 29,* 1573–1578.

Nitsche, M. A., Kuo, M. F., Karrasch, R., Wachter, B., Liebetanz, D., & Paulus, W. (2009). Serotonin affects transcranial direct current-induced neuroplasticity in humans. *Biological Psychiatry, 66,* 503–508.

Nitsche, M. A., Lampe, C., Antal, A., Liebetanz, D., Lang, N., et al. (2006). Dopaminergic modulation of long-lasting direct current-induced cortical excitability changes in the human motor cortex. *European Journal of Neuroscience, 23,* 1651–1657.

Nitsche, M. A., Liebetanz, D., Lang, N., Antal, A., Tergau, F, & Paulus, W. (2003). Safety criteria for transcranial direct current stimulation (tDCS) in humans. *Clinical Neurophysiology, 114,* 2220–2222; author reply 2–3.

Nitsche, M. A., Nitsche, M. S., Klein, C. C., Tergau, F., Rothwell, J. C., & Paulus, W. (2003). Level of action of cathodal DC polarisation induced inhibition of the human motor cortex. *Clinical Neurophysiology, 114,* 600–604.

Nitsche, M. A., & Paulus, W. (2000). Excitability changes induced in the human motor cortex by weak transcranial direct current stimulation. *Journal of Physiology, 527*(3), 633–639.

Nitsche, M. A., & Paulus, W. (2001). Sustained excitability elevations induced by transcranial DC motor cortex stimulation in humans. *Neurology, 57,* 1899–1901.

Nitsche, M. A., Roth, A., Kuo, M. F., Fischer, A. K., Liebetanz, D., et al. (2007). Timing-dependent modulation of associative plasticity by general network excitability in the human motor cortex. *Journal of Neuroscience, 27,* 3807–3812.

Nitsche, M. A., Schauenburg, A., Lang, N., Liebetanz, D., Exner, C., et al. (2003). Facilitation of implicit motor learning by weak transcranial direct current stimulation of the primary motor cortex in the human. *Journal of Cognitive Neuroscience, 15,* 619–626.

Nitsche, M. A., Seeber, A., Frommann, K., Klein, C. C., Rochford, C., et al. (2005). Modulating parameters of excitability during and after transcranial direct current stimulation of the human motor cortex. *Journal of Physiology, 568,* 291–303.

Paulus, W. (2010). On the difficulties of separating retinal from cortical origins of phosphenes when using transcranial alternating current stimulation (tACS). *Clinical Neurophysiology, 121,* 987–991.

Paulus, W., Classen, J., Cohen, L. G., Large, C. H., Di Lazzaro, V., et al. (2008). State of the art: Pharmacologic effects on cortical excitability measures tested by transcranial magnetic stimulation. *Brain Stimulation, 1,* 151–163.

Paulus, W., & Trenkwalder, C. (2006). Less is more: Pathophysiology of dopaminergic-therapy-related augmentation in restless legs syndrome. *Lancet Neurology, 5,* 878–886.

Pogosyan, A., Gaynor, L. D., Eusebio, A., & Brown, P. (2009). Boosting cortical activity at Beta-band frequencies slows movement in humans. *Current Biology, 19,* 1637–1641.

Polania, R., Nitsche, M. A., & Paulus, W. (2011). Modulating functional connectivity patterns and topological functional organization of the human brain with transcranial direct current stimulation. *Human Brain Mapping, 32*(8), 1236–1249.

Polania, R., Paulus, W., Antal, A., & Nitsche, M. A. (2011). Introducing graph theory to track for neuroplastic alterations in the resting human brain: A transcranial direct current stimulation study. *NeuroImage, 54,* 2287–2296.

Priori, A., Berardelli, A., Rona, S., Accornero, N., & Manfredi, M. (1998). Polarization of the human motor cortex through the scalp. *Neuroreport, 9,* 2257–2260.

Priori, A., Mameli, F., Cogiamanian, F., Marceglia, S., Tiriticco, M., et al. (2008). Lie-specific involvement of dorsolateral prefrontal cortex in deception. *Cerebral Cortex, 18,* 451–455.

Radman, T., Ramos, R. L., Brumberg, J., & Bikson, M. (2009). Role of cortical cell type and morphology in subthreshold and suprathreshold uniform electric field stimulation. *Brain Stimulation, 2,* 215–228.

Radman, T., Su, Y., An, J. H., Parra, L. C., & Bikson, M. (2007). Spike timing amplifies the effect of electric fields on neurons: Implications for endogenous field effects. *Journal of Neuroscience, 27,* 3030–3036.

Reis, J., Schambra, H. M., Cohen, L. G., Buch, E. R., Fritsch, B., et al. (2009). Noninvasive cortical stimulation enhances motor skill acquisition over multiple days through an effect on consolidation. *Proceedings of the National Academy of Sciences of the United States of America, 106,* 1590–1595.

Rothkegel, H., Sommer, M., & Paulus, W. (2010). Breaks during 5Hz rTMS are essential for facilitatory after effects. *Clinical Neurophysiology, 121,* 426–430.

Schlamann, M., Voight, M. A., Maderwald, S., Bitz, A. K., Kraff, O., Ladd, S. C., et al. (2010). Exposure to high-field MRI does not affect cognitive function. *Journal of Magnetic Resonance Imaging, 31,* 1061–1066.

Schutter, D. J., & Hortensius, R. (2009). Retinal origin of phosphenes to transcranial alternating current stimulation. *Clinical Neurophysiology, 12,* 987–991.

Schwiedrzik, C. M. (2009). Retina or visual cortex? The site of phosphene induction by transcranial alternating current stimulation. *Frontiers in Integrated Neuroscience, 3,* 6.

Siebner, H. R., Lang, N., Rizzo, V., Nitsche, M. A., Paulus, W., et al. (2004). Preconditioning of low-frequency repetitive transcranial magnetic stimulation with transcranial direct current stimulation: Evidence for homeostatic plasticity in the human motor cortex. *Journal of Neuroscience, 24,* 3379–3385.

Terney, D., Chaieb, L., Moliadze, V., Antal, A., & Paulus, W. (2008). Increasing human brain excitability by transcranial high-frequency random noise stimulation. *Journal of Neuroscience, 28,* 14147–14155.

Wagner, T., Fregni, F., Fecteau, S., Grodzinsky, A., Zahn, M., & Pascual-Leone, A. (2007). Transcranial direct current stimulation: A computer-based human model study. *NeuroImage, 35,* 1113–1124.

Wankerl, K., Weise, D., Gentner, R., Rumpf, J. J., & Classen, J. (2010). L-type voltage-gated Ca2+ channels: A single molecular switch for long-term potentiation/long-term depression-like plasticity and activity-dependent metaplasticity in humans. *Journal of Neuroscience, 30,* 6197–6204.

Zaehle, T., Rach, S., & Herrmann, C. S. (2010). Transcranial alternating current stimulation enhances individual alpha activity in human EEG. *PLOS One, 5,* 13766.

Zaghi, S., Acar, M., Hultgren, B., Boggio, P. S., & Fregni, F. (2010). Noninvasive brain stimulation with low-intensity electrical currents: Putative mechanisms of action for direct and alternating current stimulation. *Neuroscientist, 16,* 285–307.

Ziemann, U., Ilic, T. V., Pauli, C., Meintzschel, F., & Ruge, D. (2004). Learning modifies subsequent induction of long-term potentiation-like and long-term depression-like plasticity in human motor cortex. *Journal of Neuroscience, 24,* 1666–1672.

NEUROPSYCHOLOGICAL REHABILITATION
2011, 21 (5), 618–649

Behavioural facilitation following brain stimulation: Implications for neurorehabilitation

Giuseppe Vallar and Nadia Bolognini

Department of Psychology, University of Milano-Bicocca, and IRCCS
Auxological Institute, Milan, Italy

Studies showing facilitation of behavioural performance by transcranial
magnetic stimulation (TMS), and transcranial direct current stimulation
(tDCS) in sensory and perceptual domains, spatial attention, working
memory, and executive and emotional tasks are reviewed. In these domains
the performance of neurologically unimpaired participants may be modulated,
with behavioural facilitation or interference, by TMS, and by tDCS. The
mapping of the frequency-dependent effects of TMS, and of the polarity-
dependent effects of tDCS on behaviour does not systematically and mechanistically result in an increase or decrease of behavioural performance. Factors
such as the parameters of the cerebral stimulation (localisation, duration, intensity), and the features of the task (complexity, phase of training) contribute to
determine the final net effect on the participants' performance. Non-invasive
brain stimulation (NIBS), which modulates learning, and appears to have,
under some conditions, long lasting effects, is a promising tool to be used in
the rehabilitation of a variety of neurological and cognitive disorders, that
typically involve repeated behavioural training sessions.

Keywords: TMS; tDCS; Behavioural facilitation; Cognition; Learning.

INTRODUCTION

In recent years, techniques involving brain stimulation have been increasingly
used in order to investigate the neural correlates of behaviour, by temporarily

Correspondence should be addressed to Giuseppe Vallar MD, Department of Psychology,
University of Milano-Bicocca, Piazza dell'Ateneo Nuovo 1, 20126-Milan, Italy.

This work has been supported in part by University of Milano-Bicocca FAR and MIUR PRIN
Grants to GV and NB.

altering the activity of cerebral neurons (Bolognini & Vallar, 2010; Wasser-mann et al., 2008). So far, the more widely used approach has been the one of temporarily disrupting the activity of focal brain cortical areas, and of connected regions, by transcranial magnetic stimulation (TMS, reviewed in Miniussi and Rossini, this issue), bringing about the so-called "virtual" lesions (Pascual-Leone, Walsh, & Rothwell, 2000; Walsh & Cowey, 1998, 2000). The lesion-like effects of TMS have been interpreted in terms of adding "neural noise" (see Ruzzoli, Marzi, & Miniussi, 2010, for a discussion of effects on perceptual processes; Siebner, Hartwigsen, Kassuba, & Rothwell, 2009, for a discussion of the distinction between "virtual lesion", brought about by a high intensity TMS pulse, and "noisy input" added by smaller stimulation intensities; Walsh & Pascual-Leone, 2003). However, TMS may also cause behavioural changes, that are not characterised by a decrease of performance (namely, a "lesion" effect, a negative change), involving instead a variation, a positive change, an increase of performance level in the task of interest (see Harris, Benito, Ruzzoli, & Miniussi, 2008, for an empirical study; Miniussi, Ruzzoli, & Walsh, 2010; Ziemann, 2010).

When using TMS in a repetitive mode (i.e., repetitive rTMS), stimulation frequency seems to be the key parameter that determines the direction of the effects. From a physiological standpoint, a slow (i.e., < 1 Hz) temporal rate of rTMS tends to accentuate inhibitory effects, whereas at faster rates of repetition (i.e., > 1 Hz), facilitatory effects come to the fore (see Fitzgerald, Fountain, & Daskalakis, 2006, for a review on motor cortical excitability and inhibition). The relative predominance of TMS-induced behavioural facilitation or suppression is also dependent on the initial activation state of cortical neurons, namely, "state-dependency": this is critical, since the neural impact of any external stimulus represents an interaction with the ongoing brain activity at the time of stimulation (Silvanto, Muggleton, & Walsh, 2008; Silvanto & Pascual-Leone, 2008).

The possibility of inducing negative and positive behavioural changes applies even more to transcranial direct current stimulation (tDCS), which, in a polarity-dependent fashion, may increase (in the case of anodal tDCS), or reduce (in the case of cathodal tDCS) neuronal excitability (see review in Paulus, this issue).

Comparing the two techniques (Gandiga, Hummel, & Cohen, 2006; Zimerman & Hummel, 2010), TMS affords greater spatial and temporal resolution than tDCS. The spatial resolution of TMS is highly dependent upon the shape of the stimulating coil, and can be in the order of a few millimetres (e.g., when using figure-eight coils with circular components of 45 mm). In contrast, tDCS is usually applied through electrodes with a size of $25-35$ cm^2. These differences in precision may lend themselves to different applications for TMS and tDCS, depending on whether the manipulation of a particular cognitive operation is more readily accomplished by focused or distributed activity.

The possibility of modifying behaviour through non-invasive brain stimulation (NIBS), with an increased level of performance, represents a relevant case of "cosmetic neurology". The term was originally introduced by Anjan Chatterjee (2004), with reference to the possibility of modulation, aiming at positive changes, of "movement, mentation, and mood", and to the ethical concerns about these potential "quality of life" interventions. Chatterjee (2004) considered mainly pharmacological treatments, but also made a brief comment on using rTMS in the treatment of depression (see López-Ibor, López-Ibor, & Pastrana, 2008, for review).

The studies considered in this review illustrate a variety of modulations of human performance, with an increase of accuracy, decrease of response latencies, or both, produced by NIBS. These effects are temporary, and usually short-lasting, typically in the range of minutes, but may pave the way to paradigms aimed at assessing more long-lasting changes, and stable increases of performance level. Seen in this perspective, these investigations may be considered a precursor of possible neurological treatments, through NIBS, aimed at restoring performance made defective by brain dysfunction or damage (see reviews by Cotelli et al.; Hesse et al., both in this issue), and at improving it in "healthy", neurologically unimpaired, individuals.

There is now definite evidence that brain stimulation may facilitate behaviour in healthy participants (see recent reviews in Utz, Dimova, Oppen-länder, & Kerkhoff, 2010; Zimerman & Hummel, 2010), affecting plasticity (see for reviews Kolb, Teskey, & Gibb, 2010, and Berlucchi, this issue). In this review we shall consider the domains of perceptual processes, cross-modal integration, language, executive functions, and emotions, as well as possible implications for neuropsychological rehabilitation.

SENSORY AND PERCEPTUAL PROCESSING

There is definite evidence that perceptual processes can be transiently modulated by NIBS in healthy humans.

Visual processing

tDCS paradigms have been specifically used to convincingly demonstrate enhanced cortical excitability in visual areas (Antal & Paulus, 2008, for review). tDCS delivered to the occipital cortex (including V1) can modulate in a polarity-dependent way the visual evoked potentials (VEPs) that characterise the occipital activation in response to visual stimulation. Investigating the effects of tDCS on VEPs is of relevance in order to explore this putative modulation at an electrophysiological level, relating such findings with behavioural effects. It should be noted that, unlike TMS, the temporal resolution of tDCS is limited, in that the stimulation cannot be time-locked with a relevant stimulus. By contrast the duration of the induced effects is long, in the range of minutes. Therefore, the combination of tDCS and electrophysiological indexes offers an interesting method to modify, and trace, cortical excitability.

In one study (Antal, Kincses, Nitsche, Bartfai, & Paulus, 2004), VEPs evoked by sinusoidal luminance grating in an on/off mode were recorded before, immediately after, and 10, 20, and 30 minutes after the delivery of 5, 10, or 15 minutes of anodal or cathodal tDCS (1 mA intensity) to the primary visual cortex. Cathodal tDCS decreases, and anodal tDCS increases the amplitude (latencies are unaffected) of the N70 (the earliest VEP peak of cortical origin). Overall, the effects of cathodal stimulation occur immediately, and last longer (10 minutes), after the end of 10 and 15 minutes of stimulation. As for anodal tDCS, the increase of the N70 amplitude emerges only 10 minutes after the end of 15 minutes of tDCS. A trend towards an increased P100 amplitude (a component probably produced by different neuronal populations than the N70) after cathodal stimulation was also found. Overall, these results suggest differential effects of tDCS on different neuronal populations, which are located in different cortical layers and generate the N70 and P100 components, hence suggesting selective modulatory effects by tDCS on different stages of visual processing. The effects of cathodal stimulation are greater for low-contrast stimuli as compared to high-contrast stimuli, and appear overall somewhat stronger than those of anodal stimulation. A plausible account for this latter finding is that, when an external stimulus activates the visual areas maximally, the sub-threshold excitability shifts induced by tDCS may be physiologically irrelevant as for producing a clear change in the VEPs (Antal, Nitsche, & Paulus, 2006). Finally, the effectiveness of the tDCS stimulation appears related to its duration, with longer stimulation periods being more effective in modulating VEPs (Antal, Kincses, Nitsche, Bartfai, & Paulus, 2004, 5 vs. 10 vs. 15 min).

Accornero, Li Voti, La Riccia, and Gregori (2007) found that cathodal stimulation (1 mA for 3 or 10 minutes) increases the amplitude of the P100, which is decreased by anodal tDCS. These VEP changes persist for a few minutes after the termination of the polarisation, longer with 10 vs. 3 minutes of tDCS. This finding differs in part from the abovementioned results by Antal, Kincses, Nitsche, Bartfai, & Paulus (2004), who found only a mild facilitation effect on the P100 by cathodal polarisation, with anodal polarisation being ineffective. In both studies (Accornero et al., 2007; Antal, Kincses, Nitsche, Bartfai, and Paulus, 2004) the observed effects are somewhat larger with low-contrast stimuli. These discrepant results might reflect differences in the stimuli used to elicit VEPs (Accornero et al., 2007, pattern-reversal checkerboard patterns; Antal, Kincses, Nitsche, Bartfai, & Paulus 2004, sinusoidal luminance gratings), and the position of the reference electrode (Cz vs. anterior or back neck base). These contrasting findings point out the role of methodological differences (stimuli parameters, the montage of the electrodes) in shaping the effects of tDCS (Antal & Paulus, 2008).

tDCS (1 mA, 10 minutes) delivered to the visual cortex can also affect the beta (15.625–31.25 Hz), and gamma (31.25–65.2 Hz) frequency powers in VEPs in a polarity-specific way, namely, with a decrement following cathodal stimulation, and a marginal increase following anodal stimulation (Antal, Varga, Kincses, Nitsche, & Paulus, 2004). The modulation by cathodal tDCS is present immediately and 10 to 20 minutes after the end of stimulation. An increment of the beta and gamma frequency ranges of the cortical electrical activity in humans is closely related in time to the N70 peak of the VEP elicited by elementary visual stimuli (Bodis-Wollner, Davis, Tzelepi, & Bezerianos, 2001). Since gamma activity is related to perceptual, attentional and memory processes, these findings hint at the possibility of using tDCS for modulating these higher-order activities (Herrmann, Munk, & Engel, 2004). Hence, tDCS may offer a tool whereby certain oscillatory activities and related neuronal connections within the brain could be strategically strengthened or weakened, possibly providing the opportunity to compensate focal cortical dysfunctions.

A reliable index of the tDCS-induced excitability changes in visual responses is obtained by measuring the perception of visual phosphenes, elicited by TMS of the occipital cortex. The phosphene threshold (PT: the lowest intensity of TMS at which phosphenes are detectable) is a measure of the level of excitability of visual areas (Kammer, Puls, Erb, & Grodd, 2005). Fierro et al. (2005) showed that, following a period of light deprivation, which determines a reduction of PT, 1 Hz rTMS (900 pulses) delivered during the last 15 minutes of deprivation prolongs the light deprivation-induced cortical hyper-excitability state, as indexed by the longer time needed to recover the baseline PT after light re-exposure. This effect might represent an rTMS-induced potentiation of the impact of light deprivation on cortical excitability. Conversely, 15 minutes of 10 Hz rTMS (delivered in trains of 50 pulses, separated by 45 second intervals) exhibit the opposite effect, by decreasing sensitivity in the visual cortex (Fierro et al., 2005). Noteworthy, without light deprivation, 1 Hz rTMS over the visual cortex leads to a decrease of its excitability (Boroojerdi, Prager, Muellbacher, & Cohen, 2000). Taken together, these pieces of evidence suggest that the effects of rTMS depend also on the functional state of the visual cortex.

Cathodal tDCS (1 mA, for 10 minutes) over the occipital cortex (including V1) results in an increase of the PT for stationary and moving phosphenes, induced by TMS stimulation of V1 (stationary phosphenes), and of the motion sensitive visual areas (moving phosphenes: area MT or V5, see Born & Bradley, 2005, for a review). By contrast, anodal tDCS (1 mA, for 10 minutes) of the occipital cortex (including V1) reduces the PT (Antal, Kincses, Nitsche, & Paulus, 2003a, b). These tDCS-induced excitability shifts last for about 10 minutes. Finally, anodal tDCS (1 mA for 15 minutes) delivered over the occipital cortex (electrodes placed in O1 or O2, according to the International 10-20 EEG System) of healthy participants transiently increases contrast sensitivity, as assessed by automatic threshold perimetry, compared with sham stimulation, while cathodal stimulation has no effects (Kraft et al., 2010).

With respect to perceptual facilitation following TMS, evidence in the visual domain is scarce. However, it should be noted that in most studies, TMS has been applied with the aim of causing a transient and reversible disruption of cortical activity, in order to study brain–behaviour relationships (Bolognini & Ro, 2010). In a recent study (Waterston & Pack, 2010), both continuous theta-burst (cTBS) TMS, delivered as five bursts of three 50-Hz pulses every second for 40 seconds, for a total of 600 pulses, and 1 Hz rTMS (1200 pulses), delivered to V1, improve performance in visual psychophysical tasks. Coarse discrimination performance (i.e., healthy participants indicate whether Gabor patterns appear to be vertical or horizontal, with stimuli being presented at single or multiple locations) improves across the visual field, with effects lasting over 60 minutes post-TMS. By contrast, no consistent effect is found in an orientation discrimination task (participants indicate whether the Gabor pattern, presented at 6° to the right of the fixation, is oriented to the left or to the right of the vertical axis). These results suggest that cTBS and rTMS can improve performance on visual psychophysical tasks, but the magnitude and the direction of the effects are task-dependent. This evidence also illustrates the point that a decrease in neuronal excitability (as it should be induced by low-frequency rTMS or cTBS) does not necessarily translate into diminished performance.

Harris et al. (2008) applied short trains of 12 Hz rTMS to the posterior inferior parietal lobe, around the intraparietal sulcus, a region belonging to the dorsal visual stream (Milner & Goodale, 2006), while healthy participants performed an object identification task (picture–word verification, and categorising objects), or an object orientation judgement task (picture–arrow verification, and deciding the rotation of an object). This protocol produces an impairment of orientation judgements, but also improves performance in object identification. This pattern of results supports the view that the posterior parietal cortex (PPC) is critical for processing the spatial attributes of objects, but not their identity (see Gangopadhyay, Madary, & Spicer, 2010, for review). Furthermore, the facilitatory effects of parietal rTMS on object identification have been interpreted as indicating an indirect role of this region in the process of object recognition: according to the authors, the parietal TMS-induced interference may possibly speed up the recognition process, removing potentially conflicting spatial reference frames (Harris et al., 2008, p. 925).

rTMS may also be able to improve visual detection by interfering with cortical suppression. Discrimination of brief moving stimuli is paradoxically more difficult for larger rather than for smaller items (i.e., "spatial suppression", which reflects the receptive field property of centre–surround antagonism). Following 15 minutes of 1 Hz rTMS of the visual motion area MT/V5, there is an improvement of motion discrimination for large stimuli, presumably by weakening surround suppression strength. This effect is selective for stimuli presented in the contralateral hemi-field (Tadin, Silvanto, Pascual-Leone, & Battelli, 2011).

The behavioural effects of tDCS on visual functions have been explored by using a variety of paradigms, with results broadly matching the physiological effects discussed earlier. For instance, tDCS can affect, in a polarity-specific way, static and dynamic contrast sensitivities (sCS, and dCS, respectively), evaluated before anodal or cathodal tDCS over the occipital cortex (including V1), during, immediately after, and at a 10 minute delay. Significant sCS and dCS losses occur during, and immediately (0 minutes) after cathodal stimulation (1 mA current intensity, for 7 minutes) while anodal stimulation is functionally ineffective; 10 minutes after the end of tDCS, performance returns to the baseline (Antal, Nitsche, & Paulus, 2001). Again, the lack of effects of anodal stimulation may reflect a sort of ceiling effect: in healthy participants the visual system is likely to be already optimally tuned, and visual perception cannot be further improved by anodal tDCS.

As for the visual perception of motion, cathodal stimulation of left MT/V5 (1 mA for 7 minutes, electrode placed approximately 3–4 cm above the mastoid–inion line and 6–7 cm left of the midline in the sagittal plane, reference electrode at Cz) improves performance (reducing the motion perception threshold), in a task where healthy participants are required to identify the direction of coherent motion among randomly moving dots; anodal stimulation is ineffective (Antal, Nitsche, Kruse, Kincses, Hoffman, & Paulus 2004, experiment IIA). However, when the task is one of identifying the direction of coherently moving dots presented without distracters (experiment IIB), accuracy is decreased by cathodal MT/V5 stimulation, and increased by anodal MT/V5 stimulation. An account for these apparently paradoxical effects is in terms of the state of activation of the MT/V5 region at the time of the tDCS delivery. The complexity of the task could induce a kind of "noisy" activation state of the encoding neuronal network. Specifically, the coherent motion with distracters (i.e., randomly moving dots) represents a "noisy" activation state, with cathodal tDCS of V5 enhancing performance by reducing noise. Conversely, coherent motion without distracters is a "noise-free" condition, where cathodal tDCS acts by decreasing the activation of the relevant neural network, with the behavioural result of decreasing the level of performance. Taking this view, the complexity of the visual task interacts with the physiological state of the cortex to determine the behavioural outcome of the polarity-dependent tDCS effect; consequently, both polarities (cathodal and anodal) may be used to change the signal-to-noise ratio, with the final goal of improving performance, depending on the characteristics of the task (Antal & Paulus, 2008).

tDCS also affects visual adaptation mechanisms. Both cathodal and anodal stimulations of MT/V5 (1 mA intensity, for 15 minutes) reduce the duration of the perceived motion after-effect (MAE), without affecting the participants' performance in a luminance-change-detection task, used to determine attentional load during adaptation. Stimulation of the occipital cortex (V1, active electrode placed at Oz, reference at Cz) does not impact on the MAE (Antal, Varga, Nitsche, et al., 2004).

tDCS might affect the interaction between different neural representations of different motion directions in MT/V5 (Antal, Varga, Nitsche, et al., 2004). It has been shown that there is a mutual inhibition between different motion directions, and adaptation results in an imbalance of these interactions, which in turn leads to an illusory motion percept (Mather & Harris, 1998). In this context, modulation of the neural excitability with tDCS might result in an attenuated expression of the adaptation-induced imbalance, and, consequently, in weakened MAEs.

Similarly, cathodal stimulation of the right temporo-parietal cortex (active electrode at P6–P8, and reference at Cz) but not of the occipital cortex (V1, electrodes at Oz–Cz), may reduce the magnitude of facial adaptation, namely, the phenomenon whereby the prolonged adaptation to a face biases the perception of a subsequent one; anodal and sham stimulations are ineffective (Varga et al., 2007).

Finally, because of the large size of the stimulating electrode (5 x 7 cm), it is interesting to observe such a selective effect, specific for V5/MT stimulation (see also Antal, Nitsche, Kruse, et al., 2004; Antal, Varga, Nitsche, et al., 2004), but not for V1. Yet, computer-based modelling studies of tDCS indicate that maximum current density magnitudes are located beneath the electrodes, at the cortical level (Wagner et al., 2007).

The tDCS-induced changes of neural responsivity in the stimulated cortical regions might interfere with the cellular mechanisms underlying the processes of neural adaptation and plasticity. In line with this proposal, in humans both anodal and cathodal stimulation of the motor cortex decreases the magnitude of training-induced transient motor cortex plasticity, as assessed by thumb movements (Rosenkranz, Nitsche, Tergau, & Paulus, 2000).

Visuomotor processing

The relationship between the tDCS effects and the phase of the visuomotor task (namely: early vs. late) is of particular interest for its potential clinical applications. Performance in visuo-motor tasks requires the transfer of visual data to motor performance, and depends on visual perception and higher order processing, mainly during the learning phase. When the task (tracking the position of a moving dot using a manipulandum) is learned (i.e., with a 70–80% level of tracking accuracy), performance is improved during, and immediately after, cathodal tDCS of MT/V5 (7 minutes, with an intensity of 1 mA), while anodal stimulation is ineffective. After 30 minutes the participants' performance is back to the baseline level. The cathodal effect is specific for MT/V5 stimulation, not occurring when the occipital (primary visual cortex, V1, Oz–Cz montage) and the primary motor (M1, active electrode at C3) cortices are targeted (Antal, Nitsche, Kruse, et al., 2004, experiment I). A different pattern of results emerges, however, when tDCS is delivered in the early learning phase of the same task: the accuracy of the tracking movements is increased by anodal tDCS of both MT/V5 and M1, while cathodal stimulation does not affect performance level, and both cathodal and anodal stimulations of the occipital cortex are ineffective (Antal, Nitsche, Kincses, et al., 2004). Noteworthy, the anodal effect is short-lived, as learning improves, compared with the no stimulation condition: it is present only in the first block of the learning trials (50), lasting about 5 minutes from the beginning of the stimulation, which continues throughout the second block. The finding that the anodal facilitation is restricted to the early learning phase of the task suggests specific effects of anodal vs. cathodal tDCS on the activity of the relevant neural networks. As long as the task becomes over-learned, cortical excitability reaches an activation state that seems to no longer require the excitatory tuning provided by anodal tDCS. Rather, under this condition, learning may benefit from inhibition (see also Antal & Paulus, 2008, for discussion).

Overall, the physiological and behavioural effects induced by NIBS on visual functions mirror those observed in the motor system (Nitsche & Paulus, 2000; 2001, see also Cohen, Sandrini, & Tanaka, this volume), although they appear somewhat less consistent, possibly due to neurophysiological differences among the different cortical areas, the different geometry of the polarising dipole used, and the initial state of neuronal populations and of state-dependent responses to brain stimulation (Antal & Paulus, 2008; Silvanto & Pascual-Leone, 2008). The polarity-specific effects of tDCS, and the frequency-specific effects of TMS, in terms of enhancement or degradation of visual perception, depend on the dynamic interplay of different factors, including the experimental paradigms, the strength and type of the visual stimulation, and the phase of the task during which tDCS is delivered.

Somatosensory processing

TMS has been used in healthy participants to document inter-hemispheric influences behaviourally, with TMS over the right parietal cortex enhancing processing of touch in the ipsilateral right hand (Seyal, Ro, & Rafal, 1995). To explore the neural bases of this effect, TMS was combined with concurrent functional magnetic resonance imaging (fMRI). 10 Hz rTMS (5 pulses) was delivered, at a high or low intensity, over the right parietal cortex, during two sensory contexts: either without any other stimulation, or while participants received median nerve stimulation to the right wrist, which projects to the left primary somatosensory cortex (S1). TMS to the right parietal cortex affects the blood oxygenation level-dependent signal in left S1, with high- vs. low-intensity TMS increasing the left S1 signal during right somatosensory input, but decreasing it in its absence. This state-dependent modulation of left S1 by parietal TMS over the contralateral hemisphere is accompanied by a related pattern of TMS-induced influences in the thalamus. Hence, TMS applied over the parietal cortex of one hemisphere can affect responses in S1 of the other hemisphere. These remote effects of right parietal TMS apply in a manner that depends on concurrent somatosensory input to the right hand (ipsilateral to the side of the TMS), and may relate to cortico-thalamic circuitry, as well as to trans-callosal connections. Overall, the use of concurrent TMS–fMRI can show causal influences of local TMS on brain activity in remote but interconnected regions in the contralateral hemisphere, that can vary in a state-dependent manner.

Ishikawa et al. (2007) found that cTBS for 40 seconds (a burst of 3 TMS pulses at 50 Hz, repeated at 5 Hz) over the left sensorimotor cortex changes the amplitude of later components of the somatosensory evoked potentials (SEPs), particularly the parietal component P25/N33, evoked from the contralateral, but not ipsilateral, median nerve. These effects depend on the scalp position of the cTBS: following cTBS over M1, the P25/N33 component is facilitated for about 50 minutes; however, cTBS at the same intensity over a point 2 cm posterior to left M1 suppresses the P25/N33 component for at least 10 minutes. A related study (Katayama & Rothwell, 2007) shows that intermittent TBS (iTBS consisting in a 2 second train of TBS repeated every 10 seconds for a total of 190 seconds, 600 pulses) over S1 (coil positioned over C3), facilitates the N20–P25 and P25–N33 amplitudes, with the maximal effect appearing 15 minutes after the stimulation; no effects over M1 are found. These components involve generators in the central sulcus and in the somatosensory cortex (Allison et al., 1989; Allison, McCarthy, Wood, & Jones, 1991; Allison, Wood, McCarthy, & Spencer, 1991). Taken together, these two studies (Ishikawa et al., 2007; Katayama & Rothwell, 2007) indicate that a short period of TBS can affect processing in somatosensory cortex.

Considering the behavioural effects, 5 Hz rTMS (a train consisting in 50 single pulses of 5 Hz lasting 10 seconds with an inter-train interval of 5 seconds) delivered over the cortical representation of the right index finger of S1 can induce a lowering of the two-point tactile discrimination threshold of this finger. The perceptual improvement induced by rTMS is linearly correlated with an enlargement of the right index finger representation in S1, as revealed by fMRI, hence showing a close link between cortical and perceptual changes (Tegenthoff et al., 2005). Moreover, it has been shown that the combination of rTMS (25 trains of TMS pulses, with one train consisting in 50 single pulses of 5 Hz lasting 10 seconds, with an inter-train interval of 5 seconds) over left S1, coupled with right index finger tactile coactivation, boosts tactile discrimination ability in that finger (Ragert et al., 2003). Tactile coactivation is a task-free, passive stimulation protocol, independent of cognitive factors such as attention or reinforcement. The basic idea is to coactivate a large number of receptive fields on the tip of the index finger in a Hebbian manner, in order to strengthen their mutual interconnectedness (Godde, Spengler, & Dinse, 1996). The addition of rTMS induces a further improvement of discrimination thresholds, in comparison to the coactivation-induced perceptual changes alone. The individual improvement after rTMS and tactile coactivation depends on the effectiveness of the coactivation protocol when applied alone: those participants who exhibit little gain in tactile performance after coactivation alone, show the largest improvement, suggesting that the combined application is particularly effective for poor learners.

As far as pain sensation is concerned, cTBS results in a greater diminution of pain ratings and N2–P2 amplitudes on the hand contralateral to the site of motor cortex stimulation, compared to the sham condition (Csifcsak, Nitsche, et al., 2009; Poreisz, Csifcsak, et al., 2008, for behavioural data). Various types of TBS paradigms (continuous, intermittent, intermediate) on S1 reduce the amplitude of the N2 component of laser evoked potentials (LEPs), with no analgesic effects (Poreisz, Antal, et al., 2008).

In addition, tDCS of different cortical areas may bring about specific effects. When delivered over the S1, cathodal tDCS (1 mA for 9 minutes) results in a reduction of the N20 component of the SEPs, lasting up to 60 minutes, after contralateral (with respect to the side of tDCS) median nerve stimulation; no effect emerges after anodal tDCS; the N30 and the low and high frequency components of the SEPs are unaffected (Dieckhöfer et al., 2006). Similarly, cathodal, but not anodal, tDCS (1 mA, for 15 minutes) of S1 diminishes the amplitude of the N20 component of LEPs when the contralateral hand is laser-stimulated, in order to induce pain (Antal et al., 2008). The contribution of S1 to pain processing has been under extensive debate (Shibasaki, 2004). A possible mechanism is that the antinociceptive effect is obtained by the indirect inhibition of the secondary somatosensory cortex (S2), and the anterior cingulate cortex (ACC) through S1 stimulation. In line with the proposal, the N20 component of LEPs is generated bilaterally in the operculo-insular region, and in the ACC (Garcia-Larrea, Frot, & Valeriani, 2003).

The electrophysiological effects of tDCS (1 mA for 10 minutes) over the sensorimotor cortex have been investigated centring the active electrode over the M1 hand area, as determined by a single pulse TMS (Matsunaga, Nitsche, Tsuji, & Rothwell, 2004). The amplitudes of P25/N33, N33/P40 (parietal components), and P22/N30 (frontal component) following stimulation of the contralateral median nerve increase for at least 60 minutes after the termination of anodal tDCS. Instead, P14/N20, N20/P25 (parietal components), and N18/P22 (frontal component) are unaffected. Cathodal stimulation at the same intensity has no effect on SEPs from either arm. It appears that the cortical areas most likely to be polarised by tDCS are those on the surface of the brain, directly under the stimulating electrodes, where the applied voltage is greatest. Indeed, tDCS has little effect on the N20 component, which is generated at some depth from the cortical surface in area 3b (Allison et al., 1989; Allison, McCarthy et al., 1991), where cells may experience a smaller voltage gradient from the applied tDCS.

Finally, cathodal tDCS (1 mA for 10 minutes) over M1 (stimulating electrode at C3) reduces the amplitude of the N2 and P2 components of LEPs, while anodal tDCS exhibits no definite effects, with neither stimulations affecting the laser energy values necessary to induce moderate pain (Csifcsak, Antal, et al., 2009).

As for the behavioural effects of tDCS on somatosensory processing, a 7 minute cathodal (1 mA) stimulation of S1 impairs tactile discrimination of vibratory stimuli in the contralateral index finger, with anodal stimulation being ineffective (Rogalewski, Breitenstein, Nitsche, Paulus, & Knecht, 2004). Conversely, an improvement of spatial tactile discrimination (as assessed by a grating orientation task) in the contralateral index finger, lasting up to 40 minutes, is induced by 20 minutes of anodal tDCS (the effects of cathodal stimulation were not assessed, see Ragert, Vandermeeren, Camus, & Cohen, 2008). tDCS delivered to S1 may have beneficial effects on the perception of laser-induced pain: cathodal stimulation (1 mA intensity, 15 minutes duration) diminishes pain (assessed in terms of pain intensity ratings) in the hand contralateral to the side of the tDCS, with anodal tDCS being ineffective; the amplitude of the N2 component is also reduced (Antal et al., 2008). This antinociceptive effect of cathodal stimulation makes tDCS protocols applicable to patients with chronic pain of central origin.

For M1 stimulation, cathodal tDCS (15 minutes at a 1 mA current intensity) may temporarily alter sensitivity (measured by quantitative behavioural somatosensory testing), in a variety of A-fibre-mediated somatosensory modalities. Specifically, a functional loss has been found in the contralateral hand for non-painful cold and mechanical detection thresholds, and in mechanical pain threshold (but no effects for mechanical pain sensitivity and pressure pain threshold); anodal tDCS exerts no modulation. These findings suggests a short-term suppression of lemniscal or suprathalamic sensory pathways, or both, following cathodal tDCS of M1 (Bachmann et al., 2010). In another study, cathodal tDCS (1 mA current intensity, delivered for 10 minutes) of M1 diminishes laser-induced mild pain sensation in the hand contralateral to the side of the stimulation, while anodal M1 tDCS reduces the threshold for warm sensation only, with changes being measured on numeric analogue scales (Csifcsak, Antal, et al., 2009). Anodal tDCS of M1 (2 mA for 5 minutes) increases perceptual thresholds, as well as the threshold for a painful sensation, evoked by peripheral electrical stimulation of the contralateral index finger; conversely, anodal stimulation of the dorsolateral prefrontal cortex (DLPFC) increases pain threshold only; sham and occipital stimulations are ineffective, and the effects of cathodal tDCS were not explored (Boggio, Zaghi, Lopes, & Fregni, 2008). This evidence indicates that anodal tDCS of both M1 and DLFPC modulates pain perception, with possibly different mechanisms: anodal M1 stimulation may result in an analgesic effect by influencing the sensory components of pain (i.e., a change in both perception and pain thresholds), whereas DLPFC stimulation may act by affecting the affective-emotional components of the pain sensation (i.e., a change of the pain threshold only), especially the unpleasantness associated with pain.

In sum, the available evidence shows facilitatory effects on somatosensory processing by both TMS and tDCS. Overall, the effects of high frequency rTMS and anodal tDCS appear to be facilitatory, at the electrophysiological and behavioural levels, while cathodal tCDS may interfere with somatosensory processing. In the case of the pain sensation the pattern appears to be more complex.

Auditory processing

Concerning the auditory modality, the effects of NIBS remain largely unexplored in healthy individuals. One recent study shows that 20 minutes of 2 mA cathodal tDCS of the left inferior frontal areas, and of the right superior temporal areas, decreases pitch matching ability; the effects of anodal tDCS were not explored (Loui, Hohmann, & Schlaug, 2010). It is worth mentioning, however, that anodal tDCS of the left temporo-parietal area reduces tinnitus in patients showing this symptom, as 10-Hz rTMS does (Plewnia, Bartels, & Gerloff, 2003), with a putative lesion-like effect (see also Langguth et al., 2003, using 1-Hz TMS in a single patient study). This study illustrates that a stimulation that increases neuronal excitability, such as anodal tDCS, may exhibit the behavioural effect of reducing an (unpleasant) sensation (Fregni et al., 2006). The putative mechanism here could be one of excitation of a cerebral region, which, in turn, exerts inhibitory effects on other (dysfunctional) regions where the symptom of interest arises (in the case of tinnitus, the auditory cortex).

Conclusions

To sum up, the available evidence in healthy participants shows a range of facilitatory effects on sensory and perceptual processes. NIBS paradigms could prove to be beneficial for the treatment of impaired sensory processing in brain-damaged patients (visual field disorders, somatosensory deficits), and pathological changes of cortical excitability in sensory areas, such as in migraine (Brighina, Palermo, & Fierro, 2009) and tinnitus (Been, Ngo, Miller, & Fitzgerald, 2007; Kleinjung, Steffens, Londero, & Langguth, 2007). NIBS could be used for inducing a modification of neuroplastic processes in clinical settings, and as a diagnostic tool for assessing pathological changes in cortical excitability, particularly when combined with electrophysiological measures. Finally, the pharmacological prolongation of the excitability-diminishing effects of cathodal tDCS (see Nitsche et al., 2006), makes this technique applicable in patients suffering from diseases characterised by enhanced cortical excitability, such as migraine and epilepsy (Nitsche & Paulus, 2009). Also, patients suffering from chronic pain may benefit from the antinociceptive effect of tDCS (O'Connell, Wand, Marston, Spencer, & Desouza, 2010). Further studies of all types of stimulation are needed.

SPATIAL ATTENTION, SPATIAL WORKING MEMORY, AND CROSS-MODAL PROCESSING

Most TMS studies have reported interference with spatial attention and cross-modal processing (see, for example, the review by Stewart, Ellison, Walsh, & Cowey, 2001). In a number of investigations, however, facilitatory effects of high frequency rTMS and of single or double pulse TMS have been reported. rTMS (20 Hz, with three 5 second trains) delivered to the left prefrontal cortex (stimulation sites were localised with reference to the international 10–20 EEG system) may reduce latencies both in a go/no go choice reaction time task and of the P300 component, while stimulation of the right prefrontal cortex does not affect these behavioural and electrophysiological measures (Evers, Böckermann, & Nyhuis, 2001). Single pulse TMS delivered to the left premotor cortex may facilitate motor responses in a reaction time task (Koski, Molnar-Szakacs, & Iacoboni, 2005). Single pulse TMS delivered to the DLPFC may facilitate contralateral express saccades (Müri et al., 1999). Contralateral memory-guided saccades may be facilitated by double pulse TMS over the frontal eye fields, with control occipital stimulation being ineffective (Wipfli et al., 2001). High frequency rTMS, titrated at human individual EEG alpha frequency (IAF; the average alpha frequency being 10 Hz for young adults), and administered before the task, improves the performance of healthy participants in a mental rotation test. Specifically, stimulation (IAF + 1 Hz) of both the right posterior parietal cortex (PPC, P6), and of the mesial frontal cortex (Fz) improves performance, while both IAF-3 Hz and 20 Hz frequencies are ineffective (Klimesch, Sauseng, & Gerloff, 2003).

A recent study reports hemispheric differences in the facilitatory effects of rTMS in a spatial working memory task. A 5 Hz rTMS (30 pulses) delivered to the right PPC of healthy participants during the retention phase of a task involving matching the position of the target with that of the probe brings about a decrease of response time. Conversely, TMS of the left PPC has no detectable effects, and a control attentional task (matching the side of the target with that of the probe) is unaffected by TMS of either hemisphere (Yamanaka, Yamagata, Tomioka, Kawasaki, & Mimura, 2010).

The DC polarisation of the human right PPC may enhance spatial orienting across different sensory modalities (Bolognini, Olgiati, Rossetti, & Maravita, 2010). Specifically, in a simple reaction time task, anodal tDCS (2 mA, for 15 minutes) of the right PPC (active electrode at P4) decreases response latency to unimodal visual and auditory stimuli, as well as to bimodal audio-visual stimuli; the modulation is specific for stimuli contralateral to the side of the tDCS, with control stimulation of the occipital cortex being ineffective. These findings suggest an involvement of the right PPC in spatial attention, independent of stimulus modality (auditory vs. visual). Moreover, a dissociation of the tDCS effects was found with respect to the processing of cross-modal blue visual stimuli, which are not detected by the human collicular pathway (Leh, Ptito, Schönwiesner, Chakravarty, & Mullen, 2010), vs. cross-modal red visual stimuli, which are detected by both the superior colliculus, and the PPC. The tDCS-induced facilitation is stronger for blue audiovisual stimuli, mostly integrated at a cortical level, whereas responses to red audiovisual stimuli, which are likely to involve a subcortical level of processing, are less susceptible to the polarisation of the PPC.

In a recent study in healthy participants (Bolognini, Fregni, Casati, Olgiati, & Vallar, 2010), anodal tDCS (2 mA, 30 minutes) delivered to the right PPC (active electrode at P4) is effective in facilitating the participants' performance in a variety of tasks involving the orientation of spatial attention and visual search, including: bimodal exploration training, visual exploration, and visuo-spatial orienting. The enhancing effects of right PPC stimulation are specific for tasks assessing visuo-spatial attention and search, and do not extend to working memory for sequences of visually presented numbers and alertness. Finally, left PPC (active electrode at P3) stimulation is largely ineffective, in line with current views which assign to the right hemisphere a major role in spatial attention throughout the whole of peripersonal space (Bisiach & Vallar, 2000; Mesulam, 2002).

Figure 1A shows the greater reduction of response latencies in the second training block of a bimodal audiovisual exploratory task during right anodal PPC tDCS, as compared to a sham condition, which, in a second experiment, does not differ from left PPC anodal tDCS (Figure 1B). Noteworthy, the effect of right PPC tDCS occurs in the early phase of training (see Antal, Nitsche, Kincses, et al., 2004, for related evidence). Figure 2 shows that right, but not left, anodal PPC tDCS reduces latencies in a visual search task.

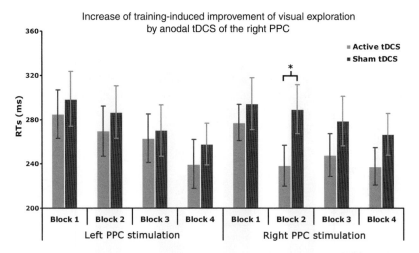

Figure 1. Response latencies (ms) in a task requiring the detection of visual targets presented in a 2 x 2 m panel. The visual stimulus is associated with an auditory stimulus, delivered in the same position, in a cross-modal condition. Each audiovisual stimulus is presented for 100 msec. Left and right posterior parietal cortex (PPC) stimulation, and their sham conditions are shown by training block, each including 96 audiovisual trials. The asterisk indicates a significant difference between sham and right PPC tDCS in Block 2. Error bars: SE.

Cross modal processing has also been assessed using the "sound-induced flash illusion", whereby multiple beeps cause the perceptual "fission" of a single flash (Shams, Kamitani, & Shimojo, 2000). Anodal tDCS of the right temporal cortex (active electrode at T4), and cathodal tDCS (2 mA, for 8 minutes) of the occipital cortex (including V1, active electrode at O2) increase the fission illusion, while anodal occipital and cathodal temporal stimulations decrease the illusory effects, and sham and PPC (P4) tDCS are ineffective (Bolognini, Rossetti, Casati, Mancini, & Vallar, 2011).

Finally, 1 Hz rTMS for 15 minutes delivered to a left anterior temporal lobe (ATL) site (half-way between T3 and F7) improves the ability of healthy young adults to guess the number of elements of a large set (about 100), revealing "savant-like numerosity skills" (Snyder, 2009; Snyder, Bahramali, Hawker, & Mitchell, 2006)

Conclusions

To summarise, a number of studies show that TMS (high frequency rTMS, single and double pulse TMS) and anodal tDCS may facilitate spatial attention, working memory and cross-modal integration (but see also the "release" of the intriguing "savant" effect, discussed above). These enhancing effects occur at different cortical sites, depending on the processes involved.

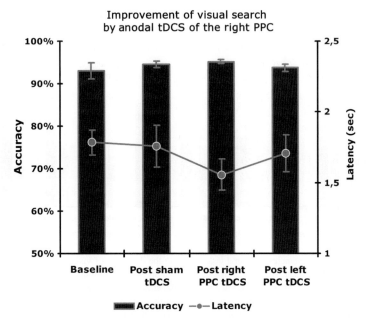

Figure 2. Accuracy and response latencies by stimulation condition (baseline, sham, left PPC tDCS, right PPC tDCS) in a visual search task (the EF test), in which participants are required to search for a single target (i.e., the green letter "F"), intermingled among distracters (i.e., the green letters "E"). Error bars: SE.

Accordingly, these stimulations may be of possible use in the rehabilitation of disorders of spatial attention, such as unilateral spatial neglect (Hesse et al., this volume), in association with traditional behavioural treatments (Fortis et al., 2010; Pizzamiglio, Guariglia, Antonucci, & Zoccolotti, 2006).

LANGUAGE

Performance in linguistic tasks may be facilitated by both TMS and tDCS in healthy participants. As for TMS (see a review in Devlin & Watkins, 2007), Töpper et al. (1998) found that supra motor threshold TMS over Wernicke's area facilitates picture naming, when the stimulation precedes the stimulus by 500 or 1000 msec; control TMS of the motor cortex and of the right temporal lobe is ineffective. Similar results were obtained by Mottaghy et al. (1999), using rTMS, with trains of 20 Hz with a 2 second duration (Mottaghy, Sparing, & Töpper, 2006; see also Sparing et al., 2001, for evidence of effects of 20 Hz but not of 1 Hz rTMS stimulation of Wernicke's, but not of Broca's area). Stoeckel, Gough, Watkins, and Devlin (2009), using single pulse TMS, found that stimulation of the left supramarginal gyrus at 180 msec post-stimulus onset (but not at other intervals, ranging from 120 to 300 msec) facilitates phonological and semantic (homophone and synonym) judgements on written words, but not visual judgements. Trains of 20 Hz rTMS delivered to the left DLPFC facilitate action naming, while right-sided and sham stimulations are ineffective, and object naming is unaffected (Cappa, Sandrini, Rossini, Sosta, & Miniussi, 2002). Experiments manipulating visual adaptation (Cattaneo, Rota, Walsh, Vecchi, & Silvanto, 2009), and priming (Cattaneo, Rota, Vecchi, & Silvanto, 2008), in the processing of letters, show that the facilitation effects brought about by single pulse TMS are related to the cortical activation state, with preferential facilitatory effects on less active neural populations.

In addition, low frequency rTMS (1 Hz) may facilitate performance in a picture word-verification task: in addition to non-specific effects, premotor stimulation (Broca's area) has been reported to reduce response latencies, while temporal stimulation (Wernicke's area) increases latencies (Dräger, Breitenstein, Helmke, Kamping, & Knecht, 2004).

As for tDCS, a number of recent studies has shown facilitation effects on linguistic performance. Verbal fluency increases during tDCS delivered to the left DLPFC (active electrode at F3), with a 2 mA, but not a 1 mA intensity, for 20 minutes; cathodal and sham polarisations are ineffective (Iyer et al., 2005). Learning of the association between novel words (i.e., nonwords) and pictures, and the translation of the new words in the corresponding items in the participants' native language, is facilitated by 1 mA tDCS, delivered for 20 minutes to a site corresponding to a superior-posterior temporal region, including Wernicke's area (electrode position CP5), compared with sham and cathodal stimulation (Flöel, Rösser, Michka, Knecht, & Breitenstein, 2008). Naming of pictures after learning of the association between them and new words is facilitated by anodal tDCS (1 mA for 20 minutes) delivered to the CP5 site, compared with a right occipito-parietal (O2) site, and sham tDCS, which are both ineffective (Fiori et al., 2011). Anodal tDCS (2 mA intensity) delivered for 7 minutes to the left posterior perisylvian region, including Wernicke's area (CP5) reduces latencies in a visual naming task, compared with cathodal, sham, and anodal stimulation of the right hemispheric homologue areas (CP6) (Sparing, Dafotakis, Meister, Thirugnanasambandam, & Fink, 2008). Also, anodal stimulation delivered to the left DLPFC (2 mA for 8 or 10 minutes) reduces latencies in picture naming, while both sham and cathodal stimulations are ineffective, and no effects of either of them on an attentional task are found (Fertonani, Rosini, Cotelli, Rossini, & Miniussi, 2010).

Conclusions

In sum, there is definite evidence that both TMS and tDCS may facilitate linguistic performance. In most, although not all (Dräger et al., 2004), studies it is high frequency rTMS and single pulse TMS that exhibit enhancing effects. As for tDCS, the anodal stimulation appears to display facilitation effects. Finally, the state of cortical activation prior to stimulation is a relevant factor.

EXECUTIVE PROCESSES

The enhancing and modulatory effects of TMS and tDCS extend to some executive processes, whose main neural underpinnings include the DLPFC, particularly in the left hemisphere.

Analogical, but not literal, reasoning is enhanced by rTMS (5 Hz, three trains of 10 second duration) delivered to the left DLPFC, compared to sham stimulation; rTMS of the right DLPFC is ineffective, while rTMS of the left motor cortex brings about non-specific facilitatory effects (Boroojerdi et al., 2001).

The anodal and cathodal tDCS stimulation (1 mA intensity for 15 minutes) of the left DLPFC enhances planning performance (Dockery, Hueckel-Weng, Birbaumer, & Plewnia, 2009), as assessed by the Tower of London task, a widely used test for the assessment of this ability (Shallice, 1982). Specifically, cathodal tCDS, normalised for sham tDCS, improves performance during the early stages of training and learning, while anodal tDCS is effective in later sessions. Importantly, the behavioural gain is maintained at 6- and 12-month follow up assessments. These polarity effects, and their interactions with the learning stages, are tentatively explained in terms of reduction of noisy neuronal activity during the early phase of learning by cathodal stimulation, and by the enhancement of specific active neuronal connections during the later training phase; in this particular learning cognitive task, cathodal tDCS may act as a "neuronal noise reducer" or "filter" (Dockery et al., 2009).

It is worth noting here that in the studies by Antal and co-workers, discussed earlier, anodal tDCS facilitates learning in an early stage (Antal, Nitsche, Kincses, et al., 2004), while cathodal tDCS exhibits enhancing effects when the visuomotor task is learned (Antal, Nitsche, Kruse, et al., 2004). These differential effects of anodal vs. cathodal tDCS in the different stages of learning suggest a complex pattern of interactions between the polarity of the tDCS, the learning task used, and its stage.

The DC stimulation of the left DLPFC also affects the performance of healthy participants in the Remote Associative Test (RAT) (Cerruti & Schlaug, 2009). The RAT is a complex verbal task where participants are presented with three words (e.g., *child-scan-wash*), and are requested to find a common linguistic associate, which forms a compound noun or a two-word phrase (in the example, *brain*). The task is regarded as involving some executive processes, since many words complete one or two, but not all three words, and appears to be related with creative thought (Ansburg & Hill, 2003). Anodal tDCS of the left DLPF (intensity of 1 mA for 20 minutes; F3) improves performance in the RAT task, as compared with the sham condition (the comparison with the cathodal stimulation approaches the significance level for multiple comparisons) (Cerruti & Schlaug, 2009). In another experiment, a hemispheric asymmetry was found: anodal tDCS improves the participants' performance in the RAT test, when delivered to the left DLPFC (F3), but not to the right DLPFC (F4). A further control condition is provided by a verbal fluency test, where the participants' performance is improved by none of the three stimulation conditions (anodal, cathodal, sham), with identical stimulation parameters (1 mA, F3, see also Iyer et al., 2005, for related converging evidence, showing that fluency is improved by anodal left tDCS at the F3 position with 2 mA intensity, but not with 1 mA).

The role of the left DLPFC is also suggested by a study using a probabilistic guessing task (Hecht, Walsh, & Lavidor, 2010). Anodal tDCS of the left DLPFC (2 mA intensity for about 22 minutes, associated with cathodal stimulation of the right DLPFC) reduces responses latencies across blocks of trials, while left cathodal associated with right anodal stimulation is ineffective.

Anodal tDCS of the left or right DLPFC (2 mA intensity for less than 15 minutes, with cathodal stimulation of the right or left DLPFC, respectively) decreases risk-taking behaviour, as assessed by the Balloon Analog Risk Task (BART, see Lejuez et al., 2002). In the BART, participants accumulate money in a temporary bank, by inflating a computerised balloon, through repeated trials; when participants stop inflating, the money is transferred to a permanent bank, but, if the balloon explodes (and this may happen at any time), the money is definitely lost. Sham and unilateral anodal DLPFC tDCS are ineffective (Fecteau, Pascual-Leone, et al., 2007). Using another task assessing risk-taking behaviour (namely, the Risk Task, a decision making task involving gambling, with participants being required to guess the colour of the box hiding the winning token), Fecteau, Knoch, et al. (2007) found, in healthy young adult participants, that right anodal associated with left cathodal tDCS (2 mA intensity for less than 10 minutes) increases low-risk responses, as compared with both sham and left anodal associated with right cathodal stimulations. Interestingly, in older adult participants, the effect is different, with left anodal-right cathodal tDCS (2 mA intensity for 10 minutes) bringing about an increase of high-risk prospects (Boggio et al., 2010).

One recent study (Stone & Tesche, 2009) investigated the switching between processing global vs. local features, using a task (Navon, 1977), that may include both executive (the switching) and spatial attentional components. Cathodal tDCS (2 mA intensity for 20 minutes) of the left PPC (P3) brings about an overall interference with switching during the stimulation, both local-to-global, and global-to-local. Conversely, anodal tDCS interferes with switching to global processing only, both during stimulation and at a 20 minute delay. These results are interpreted in terms of an overall interference by left PPC cathodal stimulation with local, global, and switching processes (Fink et al., 1997). The effects of anodal stimulation appear to be more selective, confined to the shift to global processing, that may be accounted for in terms of enhancement of the predominantly left hemisphere-based local processing (Fink et al., 1996; Yamaguchi, Yamagata, & Kobayashi, 2000).

Finally, dual tDCS (1.6 mA intensity for 5 minutes), with cathodal stimulation of the left ATL (approximately half way between T7 and FT7), and anodal stimulation of the right ATL (half way between T8 and FT8) facilitates the participants' performance in a problem solving task, compared with the reversed montage (anodal left ATL, cathodal right ATL) and sham stimulation (Chi & Snyder, 2011). These findings are interpreted in the context of a contribution of the right ATL to insight, revealed by inhibition of the left ATL, coupled with right-sided excitatory stimulation.

Conclusions

The available evidence indicates that NIBS delivered to the DLPFC modulates executive processes. The relationship between the parameters of the stimulation and the behavioural effects appears less definite than in the case of language (where, in most studies, excitatory stimulation leads to an improving of performance), probably due to the greater complexity of the task used, and of the assessed functions. Recent investigations point to a possible role of the right ATL in some problem solving tasks, in the context of an inter-hemispheric inhibitory/excitatory balance of neural activity.

EMOTIONAL PROCESSES

A few studies have investigated the modulation of emotional factors through tDCS. Anodal tDCS of the left DLPFC (2 mA intensity for 5 minutes) diminishes the participants' rating of unpleasantness and of discomfort/pain for aversive images, while sham stimulation and tDCS delivered to the occipital and motor cortices are ineffective (Boggio, Zaghi, & Fregni, 2009). In a task assessing the recognition of facial expressions, healthy women are more accurate than men; with anodal tDCS of the left temporal cortex (T3, and cathodal stimulation of the right temporal cortex on T4, with a 2 mA intensity, and an 8 minute stimulation) women are more accurate, and men less accurate, when responding to sad faces, as compared to a sham condition (Boggio, Rocha, da Silva, & Fregni, 2008).

In a study assessing the delayed free recall of pleasant, unpleasant, and neutral stimuli, the memory performance of healthy participants improves after left cathodal/right anodal tDCS (delivered to the temporo-parietal cortex, with 1 mA intensity for 20 minutes) for pleasant pictures, and after left anodal/right cathodal tDCS for unpleasant items. The results are interpreted as indicating hemispheric differences in the processing of emotional stimuli, with lateralised cortical neural networks being modulated by tDCS (Penolazzi et al., 2010).

Conclusions

In the case of emotional processes, results show facilitation of performance when memory paradigms are used, such as recognition or recall, while for other paradigms, such as rating emotional features of the stimulus, the term "modulation" is perhaps more appropriate. Nevertheless, the limited available evidence definitely shows that tDCS affects processes with emotion-related components, with potential clinical implications.

GENERAL CONCLUSIONS

The available evidence concerning sensory, perceptual, and attentional processes, and working memory, executive, and emotional processes indicates that NIBS may facilitate the performance of healthy participants in a variety of experimental conditions. In the studies considered in this review, the duration of the effects is typically confined to the time period of the stimulation in the case of TMS, but may span up to about 60 minutes in some electrophysiological experiments using tDCS (Dieckhöfer et al., 2006; Matsunaga et al., 2004), and TBS (Waterston & Pack, 2010). Furthermore, some studies have shown an enhancing effect in training paradigms (Antal, Nitsche, Kincses, et al., 2004; Antal, Nitsche, Kruse, et al., 2004c; Bolognini, Fregni, et al., 2010; Dockery et al., 2009), and the few follow-up assessments of the behavioural improvement appear promising (Dockery et al., 2009). Accordingly, these techniques seem appropriate for being utilised in long-term behavioural modulation paradigms, and in rehabilitation settings, which are characterised by repeated training sessions. This conclusion appears particularly appropriate for tDCS, since the apparatus is much less complex and expensive, and the technique can be used in a variety of conditions, including home-based treatments.

From a neurophysiological standpoint, the effects of anodal tDCS, of high-frequency rTMS and TBS delivered intermittently, are typically excitatory, by depolarising cortical neurons in the underlying cerebral cortex, while those of cathodal tDCS, low-frequency rTMS, and cTBS are inhibitory, through a process of hyperpolarisation (see Paulus, this issue). This excitatory/inhibitory neurophysiological dimension, however, does not mechanistically map onto the observed behavioural effects, with excitatory stimulation systematically resulting in a behavioural enhancement, and inhibitory stimulation in a reduction of performance in the task of interest. Relevant factors include not only the site and size of the stimulated area and its parameters (duration, intensity, frequency), but also the type of task, the state of cortical activation at the time of the stimulation, and the stage of learning when a training paradigm is used.

It appears that, particularly when participants perform complex tasks, assessing cognitive abilities, such as executive processing, the relationships between the polarity of the tDCS, and the frequency of TMS, on the one hand, and the behavioural effects, on the other hand, become less straightforward (see, for instance, the effects of TMS and tDCS stimulations on language vs. executive processing reviewed above).

There is evidence indicating that the direction of the behavioural effects of NIBS, as well as the NIBS-induced plasticity, critically depend on the pre-existing level of excitability (Lang et al., 2004; Silvanto et al., 2008; Silvanto & Pascual-Leone, 2008), suggesting "the existence of a homeostatic mechanism... that stabilises cortical excitability within a physiologically useful range" (Siebner et al., 2004, p. 3379, data from the human motor cortex). Therefore, the application of NIBS before and during the task of interest may result in different functional states.

With respect to the issue of the size of the stimulated area, the focality of the stimulation is a relevant issue in the investigation of the neural basis of cognition: currently, TMS represents the gold standard option, as it is focal enough to map cortical functions within a centimetre or so. However, in light of therapeutic applications, targeting larger areas of the cortex might represent a better approach. In fact, many models of the effect of focal brain lesions, such as a stroke, postulate that behavioural effects occur not only through dysfunction in the primarily damaged site, but also in connected areas, both in the damaged and in the contralateral hemisphere (Feeney & Baron, 1986; Witte & Stoll, 1997). Accordingly, the less focal stimulation provided by tDCS might prove to be more effective. Conversely, the superior temporal and spatial resolution of TMS is more advantageous in order to probe neurophysiological effects on specific brain circuits. In contrast, the simplicity and low cost of tDCS may be better suited for investigations that rely on modulatory effects on less selective populations of neurons, as required in some clinical studies. Moreover, the data on tDCS-induced facilitation of cognitive functions in healthy participants are promising, with effects that might last longer than those produced by rTMS (see Dockery et al., 2009).

As for the phase of learning of a cognitive task, the study by Dockery et al. (2009) provides an illustrative example. Anodal tDCS improves performance in the Tower of Hanoi task only in a later phase of learning, while in the early stages, it is cathodal tDCS that exhibits enhancing effects. These findings have been accounted for by suggesting that cathodal tDCS may reduce neuronal noise, so facilitating the early stages of learning (when more noise is present), while anodal tDCS may enhance behavioural performance, when participants have already become proficient, and less noise is present (see Dockery et al., 2009, for a further detailed discussion, also in relationship to dopamine levels, and homeostatic cortical mechanisms). A similar interpretation in terms of reduction of "neuronal noise" applies to the effects of anodal vs. cathodal tDCS over MT/V5 on the perception of coherent visual motion in the presence vs. absence of visual distracters (Antal, Nitsche, Kruse, et al., 2004).

Additionally, the demographic parameters of the investigated population are a relevant factor, with, for instance, age-related effects (Boggio et al., 2010; Fecteau, Knoch, et al., 2007).

In conclusion, the evidence from NIBS studies in healthy participants indicates that behavioural performance may be facilitated in a variety of conditions, ranging from elementary sensory to higher-order processing. These findings pave the way for studies applying these methods in brain-damaged/dysfunctional populations, with the aim of enhancing the effects of behavioural rehabilitation procedures.

REFERENCES

Accornero, N., Li Voti, P., La Riccia, M., & Gregori, B. (2007). Visual evoked potentials modulation during direct current cortical polarization. *Experimental Brain Research, 178,* 261–266.

Allison, T., McCarthy, G., Wood, C. C., Darcey, T. M., Spencer, D. D., & Williamson, P. D. (1989). Human cortical potentials evoked by stimulation of the median nerve. I. Cytoarchitectonic areas generating short-latency activity. *62,* 694–710.

Allison, T., McCarthy, G., Wood, C. C., & Jones, S. J. (1991). Potentials evoked in human and monkey cerebral cortex by stimulation of the median nerve. A review of scalp and intracranial recordings. *Brain, 114,* 2465–2503.

Allison, T., Wood, C. C., McCarthy, G., & Spencer, D. D. (1991). Cortical somatosensory evoked potentials. II. Effects of excision of somatosensory or motor cortex in humans and monkeys. *Journal of Neurophysiology, 66,* 64–82.

Ansburg, P. I., & Hill, K. (2003). Creative and analytic thinkers differ in their use of attentional resources. *Personality and Individual Differences, 34,* 1141–1152.

Antal, A., Brepohl, N., Poreisz, C., Boros, K., Csifcsak, G., & Paulus, W. (2008). Transcranial direct current stimulation over somatosensory cortex decreases experimentally induced acute pain perception. *Clinical Journal of Pain, 24,* 56–63.

Antal, A., Kincses, T. Z., Nitsche, M. A., Bartfai, O., & Paulus, W. (2004). Excitability changes induced in the human primary visual cortex by transcranial direct current stimulation: Direct electrophysiological evidence. *Investigative Ophthalmology and Visual Science, 45,* 702–707.

Antal, A., Kincses, T. Z., Nitsche, M. A., & Paulus, W. (2003a). Manipulation of phosphene thresholds by transcranial direct current stimulation in man. *Experimental Brain Research, 150,* 375–378.

Antal, A., Kincses, T. Z., Nitsche, M. A., & Paulus, W. (2003b). Modulation of moving phosphene thresholds by transcranial direct current stimulation of V1 in human. *Neuropsychologia, 41,* 1802–1807.

Antal, A., Nitsche, M. A., Kincses, T. Z., Kruse, W., Hoffmann, K. P., & Paulus, W. (2004). Facilitation of visuo-motor learning by transcranial direct current stimulation of the motor and extrastriate visual areas in humans. *European Journal of Neuroscience, 19,* 2888–2892.

Antal, A., Nitsche, M. A., Kruse, W., Kincses, T. Z., Hoffmann, K. P., & Paulus, W. (2004). Direct current stimulation over V5 enhances visuomotor coordination by improving motion perception in humans. *Journal of Cognitive Neuroscience, 16,* 521–527.

Antal, A., Nitsche, M. A., & Paulus, W. (2001). External modulation of visual perception in humans. *NeuroReport, 12,* 3553–3555.

Antal, A., Nitsche, M. A., & Paulus, W. (2006). Transcranial direct current stimulation and the visual cortex. *Brain Research Bulletin, 68,* 459–463.

Antal, A., & Paulus, W. (2008). Transcranial direct current stimulation and visual perception. *Perception, 37,* 367–374.

Antal, A., Varga, E. T., Kincses, T. Z., Nitsche, M. A., & Paulus, W. (2004). Oscillatory brain activity and transcranial direct current stimulation in humans. *NeuroReport, 15,* 1307–1310.

Antal, A., Varga, E. T., Nitsche, M. A., Chadaide, Z., Paulus, W., Kovács, G., & Vidnyánszky, Z. (2004). Direct current stimulation over MT+/V5 modulates motion aftereffect in humans. *Neuroreport, 15,* 2491–2494.

Bachmann, C. G., Muschinsky, S., Nitsche, M. A., Rolke, R., Magerl, W., Treede, R. D., Paulus, W., & Happe, S. (2010). Transcranial direct current stimulation of the motor cortex induces distinct changes in thermal and mechanical sensory percepts. *Clinical Neurophysiology, 121,* 2083–2089.

Been, G., Ngo, T. T., Miller, S. M., & Fitzgerald, P. B. (2007). The use of tDCS and CVS as methods of non-invasive brain stimulation. *Brain Research Reviews, 56,* 346–361.

Bisiach, E., & Vallar, G. (2000). Unilateral neglect in humans. In F. Boller, J. Grafman, & G. Rizzolatti (Eds.), *Handbook of Neuropsychology* (2nd ed., Vol. 1, pp. 459–502). Amsterdam: Elsevier Science.

Bodis-Wollner, I., Davis, J., Tzelepi, A., & Bezerianos, T. (2001). Wavelet transform of the EEG reveals differences in low and high gamma responses to elementary visual stimuli. *Clinical Electroencephalography, 32,* 139–144.

Boggio, P. S., Campanhã, C., Valasek, C. A., Fecteau, S., Pascual-Leone, A., & Fregni, F. (2010). Modulation of decision-making in a gambling task in older adults with transcranial direct current stimulation. *European Journal of Neuroscience, 31,* 593–597.

Boggio, P. S., Rocha, R. R., da Silva, M. T., & Fregni, F. (2008). Differential modulatory effects of transcranial direct current stimulation on a facial expression go-no-go task in males and females. *Neuroscience Letters, 447,* 101–105.

Boggio, P. S., Zaghi, S., & Fregni, F. (2009). Modulation of emotions associated with images of human pain using anodal transcranial direct current stimulation (tDCS). *Neuropsychologia, 47,* 212–217.

Boggio, P. S., Zaghi, S., Lopes, M., & Fregni, F. (2008). Modulatory effects of anodal transcranial direct current stimulation on perception and pain thresholds in healthy volunteers. *European Journal of Neurology, 15,* 1124–1130.

Bolognini, N., Fregni, F., Casati, C., Olgiati, E., & Vallar, G. (2010). Brain polarization of parietal cortex augments training-induced improvement of visual exploratory and attentional skills. *Brain Research, 1349,* 76–89.

Bolognini, N., Olgiati, E., Rossetti, A., & Maravita, A. (2010). Enhancing crossmodal audiovisual processing by brain polarization of the parietal cortex. *European Journal of Neuroscience, 31,* 1800–1806.

Bolognini, N., & Ro, T. (2010). Transcranial magnetic stimulation: Disrupting neural activity to alter and assess brain function. *Journal of Neuroscience, 30,* 9647–9650.

Bolognini, N., Rossetti, A., Casati, C., Mancini, F., & Vallar, G. (2011). Neuromodulation of multisensory perception: A tDCS study of the sound-induced flash illusion. *Neuropsychologia, 49,* 231–237.

Bolognini, N., & Vallar, G. (2010). The Oxford Handbook of Transcranial Stimulation (Book review). *Archives of Neurology, 67,* 775–776.

Born, R. T., & Bradley, D. C. (2005). Structure and function of visual area MT. *Annual Review of Neuroscience, 28,* 157–189.

Boroojerdi, B., Phipps, M., Kopylev, L., Wharton, C. M., Cohen, L. G., & Grafman, J. (2001). Enhancing analogic reasoning with rTMS over the left prefrontal cortex. *Neurology, 56,* 526–528.

Boroojerdi, B., Prager, A., Muellbacher, W., & Cohen, L. G. (2000). Reduction of human visual cortex excitability using 1-Hz transcranial magnetic stimulation. *Neurology, 54,* 1529–1531.

Brighina, F., Palermo, A., & Fierro, B. (2009). Cortical inhibition and habituation to evoked potentials: Relevance for pathophysiology of migraine. *Journal of Headache Pain, 10,* 77–84.

Cappa, S. F., Sandrini, M., Rossini, P. M., Sosta, K., & Miniussi, C. (2002). The role of the left frontal lobe in action naming: rTMS evidence. *Neurology, 59,* 720–703.

Cattaneo, Z., Rota, F., Vecchi, T., & Silvanto, J. (2008). Using state-dependency of transcranial magnetic stimulation (TMS) to investigate letter selectivity in the left posterior parietal cortex: A comparison of TMS-priming and TMS-adaptation paradigms. *European Journal of Neuroscience, 28,* 1924–1929.

Cattaneo, Z., Rota, F., Walsh, V., Vecchi, T., & Silvanto, J. (2009). TMS-adaptation reveals abstract letter selectivity in the left posterior parietal cortex. *Cerebral Cortex, 19,* 2321–2325.

Cerruti, C., & Schlaug, G. (2009). Anodal transcranial direct current stimulation of the prefrontal cortex enhances complex verbal associative thought. *Journal of Cognitive Neuroscience, 21,* 1980–1987.

Chatterjee, A. (2004). Cosmetic neurology: The controversy over enhancing movement, mentation, and mood. *Neurology, 63,* 968–974.

Chi, R. P., & Snyder, A. W. (2011). Facilitate insight by non-invasive brain stimulation. *PLoS One, 6,* e16655.

Csifcsak, G., Antal, A., Hillers, F., Levold, M., Bachmann, C. G., Happe, S., Nitsche, M. A., Ellrich, J., & Paulus, W. (2009). Modulatory effects of transcranial direct current stimulation on laser-evoked potentials. *Pain Medicine, 10,* 122–132.

Csifcsak, G., Nitsche, M. A., Baumgärtner, U., Paulus, W., Treede, R.-D., & Antal, A. (2009). Electrophysiological correlates of reduced pain perception after theta-burst stimulation. *NeuroReport, 20,* 1051–1055.

Devlin, J. T., & Watkins, K. E. (2007). Stimulating language: Insights from TMS. *Brain, 130,* 610–622.

Dieckhöfer, A., Waberski, T. D., Nitsche, M., Paulus, W., Buchner, H., & Gobbelé, R. (2006). Transcranial direct current stimulation applied over the somatosensory cortex – differential effect on low and high frequency SEPs. *Clinical Neurophysiology, 117,* 2221–2227.

Dockery, C. A., Hueckel-Weng, R., Birbaumer, N., & Plewnia, C. (2009). Enhancement of planning ability by transcranial direct current stimulation. *Journal of Neuroscience, 29,* 7271–7277.

Dräger, B., Breitenstein, C., Helmke, U., Kamping, S., & Knecht, S. (2004). Specific and non-specific effects of transcranial magnetic stimulation on picture–word verification. *European Journal of Neuroscience, 20,* 1681–1687.

Evers, S., Böckermann, I., & Nyhuis, P. W. (2001). The impact of transcranial magnetic stimulation on cognitive processing: An event-related potential study. *Neuroreport, 12,* 2915–2918.

Fecteau, S., Knoch, D., Fregni, F., Sultani, N., Boggio, P., & Pascual-Leone, A. (2007). Diminishing risk-taking behavior by modulating activity in the prefrontal cortex: A direct current stimulation study. *Journal of Neuroscience, 27,* 12500–12505.

Fecteau, S., Pascual-Leone, A., Zald, D. H., Liguori, P., Théoret, H., Boggio, P. S., & Fregni, F. (2007). Activation of prefrontal cortex by transcranial direct current stimulation reduces appetite for risk during ambiguous decision making. *Journal of Neuroscience, 27,* 6212–6228.

Feeney, D. M., & Baron, J.-C. (1986). Diaschisis. *Stroke, 17,* 817–830.

Fertonani, A., Rosini, S., Cotelli, M., Rossini, P. M., & Miniussi, C. (2010). Naming facilitation induced by transcranial direct current stimulation. *Behavioral Brain Research, 208,* 311–318.

Fierro, B., Brighina, F., Vitello, G., Piazza, A., Scalia, S., Giglia, G., Daniele, O., & Pascual-Leone, A. (2005). Modulatory effects of low- and high-frequency repetitive transcranial magnetic stimulation on visual cortex of healthy subjects undergoing light deprivation. *Journal of Physiology, 565,* 659–665.

Fink, G. R., Halligan, P. W., Marshall, J. C., Frith, C. D., Frackowiak, R. S., & Dolan, R. J. (1996). Where in the brain does visual attention select the forest and the trees? *Nature, 382,* 626–628.

Fink, G. R., Halligan, P. W., Marshall, J. C., Frith, C. D., Frackowiak, R. S., & Dolan, R. J. (1997). Neural mechanisms involved in the processing of global and local aspects of hierarchically organized visual stimuli. *Brain, 120,* 1779–1791.

Fiori, V., Coccia, M., Marinelli, C. V., Vecchi, V., Bonifazi, S., Ceravolo, M. G., Provinciali, L., Tomaiuolo, F., & Marangolo, P. (2011). Transcranial direct current stimulation improves word retrieval in healthy and nonfluent aphasic subjects. *Journal of Cognitive Neuroscience, 23*(9), 2309–2323.

Fitzgerald, P. B., Fountain, S., & Daskalakis, Z. J. (2006). A comprehensive review of the effects of rTMS on motor cortical excitability and inhibition. *Clinical Neurophysiology, 117,* 2584–2596.

Flöel, A., Rösser, N., Michka, O., Knecht, S., & Breitenstein, C. (2008). Noninvasive brain stimulation improves language learning. *Journal of Cognitive Neuroscience,* 1415–1422.

Fortis, P., Maravita, A., Gallucci, M., Ronchi, R., Grassi, E., Senna, I., Olgiati, E., Perucca, L., Banco, E., Posteraro, L., Tesio, L., & Vallar, G. (2010). Rehabilitating patients with left spatial neglect by prism exposure during a visuomotor activity. *Neuropsychology, 24,* 681–697.

Fregni, F., Marcondes, R., Boggio, P. S., Marcolin, M. A., Rigonatti, S. P., Sanchez, T. G., Nitsche, M. A., & Pascual-Leone, A. (2006). Transient tinnitus suppression induced by repetitive transcranial magnetic stimulation and transcranial direct current stimulation. *European Journal of Neurology, 13,* 996–1001.

Gandiga, P. C., Hummel, F. C., & Cohen, L. G. (2006). Transcranial DC stimulation (tDCS): A tool for double-blind sham-controlled clinical studies in brain stimulation. *Clinical Neurophysiology, 117,* 845–850.

Gangopadhyay, N., Madary, M., & Spicer, F. (2010). *Perception, Action and Consciousness. Sensorimotor Dynamics and the Two Visual Systems*. Oxford: Oxford University Press.

Garcia-Larrea, L., Frot, M., & Valeriani, M. (2003). Brain generators of laser-evoked potentials: From dipoles to functional significance. *Neurophysiologie Clinique, 33,* 279–292.

Godde, B., Spengler, F., & Dinse, H. R. (1996). Associative pairing of tactile stimulation induces somatosensory cortical reorganization in rats and humans. *NeuroReport, 8,* 281–285.

Harris, I. M., Benito, C. T., Ruzzoli, M., & Miniussi, C. (2008). Effects of right parietal transcranial magnetic stimulation on object identification and orientation judgments. *Journal of Cognitive Neuroscience, 20,* 916–926.

Hecht, D., Walsh, V., & Lavidor, M. (2010). Transcranial direct current stimulation facilitates decision making in a probabilistic guessing task. *Journal of Neuroscience, 30,* 4241–4245.

Herrmann, C. S., Munk, M. H., & Engel, A. K. (2004). Cognitive functions of gamma-band activity: Memory match and utilization. *Trends in Cognitive Sciences, 8,* 347–355.

Ishikawa, S., Matsunaga, K., Nakanishi, R., Kawahira, K., Murayama, N., Tsuji, S., Huang, Y. Z., & Rothwell, J. C. (2007). Effect of theta burst stimulation over the human sensorimotor cortex on motor and somatosensory evoked potentials. *Clinical Neurophysiology, 118,* 1033–1043.

Iyer, M. B., Mattu, U., Grafman, J., Lomarev, M., Sato, S., & Wassermann, E. M. (2005). Safety and cognitive effect of frontal DC brain polarization in healthy individuals. *Neurology, 64,* 872–875.

Kammer, T., Puls, K., Erb, M., & Grodd, W. (2005). Transcranial magnetic stimulation in the visual system. II. Characterization of induced phosphenes and scotomas. *Experimental Brain Research, 160,* 129–140.

Katayama, T., & Rothwell, J. C. (2007). Modulation of somatosensory evoked potentials using transcranial magnetic intermittent theta burst stimulation. *Clinical Neurophysiology, 118,* 2506–2511.

Kleinjung, T., Steffens, T., Londero, A., & Langguth, B. (2007). Transcranial magnetic stimulation (TMS) for treatment of chronic tinnitus: Clinical effects. *Progress in Brain Research, 166,* 359–367.

Klimesch, W., Sauseng, P., & Gerloff, C. (2003). Enhancing cognitive performance with repetitive transcranial magnetic stimulation at human individual alpha frequency. *European Journal of Neuroscience, 17,* 1129–1133.

Kolb, B., Teskey, G. C., & Gibb, R. (2010). Factors influencing cerebral plasticity in the normal and injured brain. *Frontiers in Human Neuroscience, 4,* 204.

Koski, L., Molnar-Szakacs, I., & Iacoboni, M. (2005). Exploring the contributions of premotor and parietal cortex to spatial compatibility using image-guided TMS. *Neuroimage, 24,* 296–305.

Kraft, A., Roehmel, J., Olma, M. C., Schmidt, S., Irlbacher, K., & Brandt, S. A. (2010). Transcranial direct current stimulation affects visual perception measured by threshold perimetry. *Experimental Brain Research, 207,* 283–290.

Lang, N., Siebner, H. R., Ernst, D., Nitsche, M. A., Paulus, W., & Lemon, R. N. (2004). Preconditioning with transcranial direct current stimulation sensitizes the motor cortex to rapid-rate transcranial magnetic stimulation and controls the direction of after-effects. *Biological Psychiatry, 56,* 634–639.

Langguth, B., Eichhammer, P., Wiegand, R., Marienhegen, J., Maenner, P., Jacob, P., & Hajak, G. (2003). Neuronavigated rTMS in a patient with chronic tinnitus. Effects of 4 weeks treatment. *Neuroreport, 14,* 977–980.

Leh, S. E., Ptito, A., Schönwiesner, M., Chakravarty, M. M., & Mullen, K. T. (2010). Blindsight mediated by an S-cone-independent collicular pathway: An fMRI study in hemispherectomized subjects. *Journal of Cognitive Neuroscience, 22,* 670–682.

Lejuez, C. W., Read, J. P., Kahler, C. W., Richards, J. B., Ramsey, S. E., Stuart, G. L., Strong, D. R., & Brown, R. A. (2002). Evaluation of a behavioral measure of risk taking: The Balloon Analogue Risk Task (BART). *Journal of Experimental Psychology Applied, 8,* 75–84.

López-Ibor, J. J., López-Ibor, M. I., & Pastrana, J. I. (2008). Transcranial magnetic stimulation. *Current Opinion in Psichiatry, 21,* 640–644.

Loui, P., Hohmann, A., & Schlaug, G. (2010). Inducing disorders in pitch perception and production: A reverse-engineering approach. *Proceedings of Meetings on Acoustics, 9,* doi: 10.1121/1.3431713.

Mather, G., & Harris, J. (1998). Theoretical models of the motion aftereffect. In G. Mather, F. Verstraten, & S. Anstis (Eds.), *The Motion After-Effect: A Modern Perspective* (pp. 157–185). Boston: Mass.: MIT Press.

Matsunaga, K., Nitsche, M. A., Tsuji, S., & Rothwell, J. C. (2004). Effect of transcranial DC sensorimotor cortex stimulation on somatosensory evoked potentials in humans. *Clinical Neurophysiology, 115,* 456–460.

Mesulam, M.-M. (2002). Functional anatomy of attention and neglect: From neurons to networks. In H.-O. Karnath, A. D. Milner, & G. Vallar (Eds.), *The Cognitive and Neural Bases of Spatial Neglect* (pp. 33–45). Oxford: Oxford University Press.

Milner, A. D., & Goodale, M. (2006). *The Visual Brain in Action* (2nd ed.). Oxford: Oxford University Press.

Miniussi, C., Ruzzoli, M., & Walsh, V. (2010). The mechanism of transcranial magnetic stimulation in cognition. *Cortex, 46,* 128–130.

Mottaghy, F. M., Hungs, M., Brügmann, M., Sparing, R., Boroojerdi, B., Foltys, H., Huber, W., & Töpper, R. (1999). Facilitation of picture naming after repetitive transcranial magnetic stimulation. *Neurology, 53,* 1806–1812.

Mottaghy, F. M., Sparing, R., & Töpper, R. (2006). Enhancing picture naming with transcranial magnetic stimulation. *Behavioral Neurology, 17,* 177–186.

Müri, R. M., Rivaud, S., Gaymard, B., Ploner, C. J., Vermersch, A. I., Hess, C. W., & Pierrot-Deseilligny, C. (1999). Role of the prefrontal cortex in the control of express saccades. A transcranial magnetic stimulation study. *Neuropsychologia, 37,* 199–206.

Navon, D. (1977). Forest before trees: The precedence of global features in visual perception. *Cognitive Psychology, 9,* 353–383.

Nitsche, M. A., Lampe, C., Antal, A., Liebetanz, D., Lang, N., Tergau, F., & Paulus, W. (2006). Dopaminergic modulation of long-lasting direct current-induced cortical excitability changes in the human motor cortex. *European Journal of Neuroscience, 23,* 1651–1657.

Nitsche, M. A., & Paulus, W. (2000). Excitability changes induced in the human motor cortex by weak transcranial direct current stimulation. *Journal of Physiology, 527,* 633–639.

Nitsche, M. A., & Paulus, W. (2001). Sustained excitability elevations induced by transcranial DC motor cortex stimulation in humans. *Neurology, 57,* 1899–1901.

Nitsche, M. A., & Paulus, W. (2009). Noninvasive brain stimulation protocols in the treatment of epilepsy: Current state and perspectives. *Neurotherapeutics, 6,* 244–250.

O'Connell, N. E., Wand, B. M., Marston, L., Spencer, S., & Desouza, L. H. (2010). Non-invasive brain stimulation techniques for chronic pain. *Cochrane Database of Systematic Reviews,* CD008208.

Pascual-Leone, A., Walsh, V., & Rothwell, J. (2000). Transcranial magnetic stimulation in cognitive neuroscience – virtual lesion, chronometry, and functional connectivity. *Current Opinion in Neurobiology, 10,* 232–237.

Penolazzi, B., Di Domenico, A., Marzoli, D., Mammarella, N., Fairfield, B., Franciotti, R., Brancucci, A., & Tommasi, L. (2010). Effects of Transcranial Direct Current Stimulation on episodic memory related to emotional visual stimuli. *PLoS One, 13,* e10623.

Pizzamiglio, L., Guariglia, C., Antonucci, G., & Zoccolotti, P. (2006). Development of a rehabilitative program for unilateral neglect. *Restorative Neurology and Neuroscience, 24,* 337–345.

Plewnia, C., Bartels, M., & Gerloff, C. (2003). Transient suppression of tinnitus by transcranial magnetic stimulation. *Annals of Neurology, 53,* 263–266.

Poreisz, C., Antal, A., Boros, K., Brepohl, N., Csifcsák, G., & Paulus, W. (2008). Attenuation of N2 amplitude of laser-evoked potentials by theta burst stimulation of primary somatosensory cortex. *Experimental Brain Research, 185,* 611–621.

Poreisz, C., Csifcsák, G., Antal, A., Levold, M., Hillers, F., & Paulus, W. (2008). Theta burst stimulation of the motor cortex reduces laser-evoked pain perception. *NeuroReport, 19,* 193–196.

Ragert, P., Dinse, H. R., Pleger, B., Wilimzig, C., Frombach, E., Schwenkreis, P., & Tegenthoff, M. (2003). Combination of 5 Hz repetitive transcranial magnetic stimulation (rTMS) and tactile coactivation boosts tactile discrimination in humans. *Neuroscience Letters, 348,* 105–108.

Ragert, P., Vandermeeren, Y., Camus, M., & Cohen, L. G. (2008). Improvement of spatial tactile acuity by transcranial direct current stimulation. *Clinical Neurophysiology, 119,* 805–811.

Rogalewski, A., Breitenstein, C., Nitsche, M. A., Paulus, W., & Knecht, S. (2004). Transcranial direct current stimulation disrupts tactile perception. *European Journal of Neuroscience, 20,* 313–316.

Rosenkranz, K., Nitsche, M. A., Tergau, F., & Paulus, W. (2000). Diminution of training-induced transient motor cortex plasticity by weak transcranial direct current stimulation in the human. *Neuroscience Letters, 296,* 61–63.

Ruzzoli, M., Marzi, C. A., & Miniussi, C. (2010). The neural mechanisms of the effects of transcranial magnetic stimulation on perception. *Journal of Neurophysiology, 103,* 2982–2989.

Seyal, M., Ro, T., & Rafal, R. (1995). Increased sensitivity to ipsilateral cutaneous stimuli following transcranial magnetic stimulation of the parietal lobe. *Annals of Neurology, 38,* 264–267.

Shallice, T. (1982). Specific impairments of planning. *Philosophical Transactions of the Royal Society (London), B298,* 199–209.

Shams, L., Kamitani, Y., & Shimojo, S. (2000). Illusions. What you see is what you hear. *Nature, 408,* 788.

Shibasaki, H. (2004). Central mechanisms of pain perception. *Supplements to Clinical Neurophysiology, 57,* 39–49.

Siebner, H. R., Hartwigsen, G., Kassuba, T., & Rothwell, J. C. (2009). How does transcranial magnetic stimulation modify neuronal activity in the brain? Implications for studies of cognition. *Cortex, 45,* 1035–1042.

Siebner, H. R., Lang, N., Rizzo, V., Nitsche, M. A., Paulus, W., & Lemon, R. N. (2004). Preconditioning of low-frequency repetitive transcranial magnetic stimulation with transcranial direct current stimulation: Evidence for homeostatic plasticity in the human motor cortex. *Journal of Neuroscience, 24,* 3379–3385.

Silvanto, J., Muggleton, N., & Walsh, V. (2008). State-dependency in brain stimulation studies of perception and cognition. *Trends in Cognitive Sciences, 12,* 447–454.

Silvanto, J., & Pascual-Leone, A. (2008). State-dependency of transcranial magnetic stimulation. *Brain Topography, 21,* 1–10.

Snyder, A. (2009). Explaining and inducing savant skills: Privileged access to lower level, less-processed information. *Philosophical Transactions of the Royal Society of London, B364,* 1399–1405.

Snyder, A., Bahramali, H., Hawker, T., & Mitchell, D. J. (2006). Savant-like numerosity skills revealed in normal people by magnetic pulses. *Perception, 35,* 837–845.

Sparing, R., Dafotakis, M., Meister, I. G., Thirugnanasambandam, N., & Fink, G. R. (2008). Enhancing language performance with non-invasive brain stimulation – a transcranial direct current stimulation study in healthy humans. *Neuropsychologia, 46,* 261–268.

Sparing, R., Mottaghy, F. M., Hungs, M., Brügmann, M., Foltys, H., & Huber, W. (2001). Repetitive transcranial magnetic stimulation effects on language function depend on the stimulation parameters. *Journal of Clinical Neurophysiology, 18,* 326–330.

Stewart, L., Ellison, A., Walsh, V., & Cowey, A. (2001). The role of transcranial magnetic stimulation (TMS) in studies of vision, attention and cognition. *Acta Psychologica, 107,* 275–291.

Stoeckel, C., Gough, P. M., Watkins, K. E., & Devlin, J. T. (2009). Supramarginal gyrus involvement in visual word recognition. *Cortex, 45,* 1091–1096.

Stone, D. B., & Tesche, C. D. (2009). Transcranial direct current stimulation modulates shifts in global/local attention. *NeuroReport, 20,* 1115–1119.

Tadin, D., Silvanto, J., Pascual-Leone, A., & Battelli, L. (2011). Improved motion perception and impaired spatial suppression following disruption of cortical area MT/V5. *Journal of Neuroscience, 31,* 1279–1283.

Tegenthoff, M., Ragert, P., Pleger, B., Schwenkreis, P., Förster, A. F., Nicolas, V., & Dinse, H. R. (2005). Improvement of tactile discrimination performance and enlargement of cortical somatosensory maps after 5 Hz rTMS. *PLoS Biol, 3,* e362.

Töpper, R., Mottaghy, F. M., Brügmann, M., Noth, J., & Huber, W. (1998). Facilitation of picture naming by focal transcranial magnetic stimulation of Wernicke's area. *Experimental Brain Research, 121,* 371–378.

Utz, K. S., Dimova, V., Oppenländer, K., & Kerkhoff, G. (2010). Electrified minds: Transcranial direct current stimulation (tDCS) and galvanic vestibular stimulation (GVS) as methods of non-invasive brain stimulation in neuropsychology – a review of current data and future implications. *Neuropsychologia, 48,* 2789–2810.

Varga, E. T., Elif, K., Antal, A., Zimmer, M., Harza, I., Paulus, W., & Kovács, G. (2007). Cathodal transcranial direct current stimulation over the parietal cortex modifies facial gender adaptation. *Ideggyogy Szemle, 60,* 474–479.

Wagner, T., Fregni, F., Fecteau, S., Grodzinsky, A., Zahn, M., & Pascual-Leone, A. (2007). Transcranial direct current stimulation: A computer-based human model study. *Neuroimage, 35,* 1113–1124.

Walsh, V., & Cowey, A. (1998). Magnetic stimulation studies of visual cognition. *Trends in Cognitive Sciences, 2,* 103–110.

Walsh, V., & Cowey, A. (2000). Transcranial magnetic stimulation and cognitive neuroscience. *Nature Reviews Neuroscience, 1,* 73–79.

Walsh, V., & Pascual-Leone, A. (2003). *Transcranial Magnetic Stimulation: A Neurochronometrics of Mind.* Cambridge, MA: MIT Press.

Wassermann, E. M., Epstein, C. M., Ziemann, U., Walsh, V., Paus, T., & Lisanby, S.H. (Eds.) (2008). *The Oxford Handbook of Transcranial Stimulation.* New York: Oxford University Press.

Waterston, M. L., & Pack, C. C. (2010). Improved discrimination of visual stimuli following repetitive transcranial magnetic stimulation. *PLoS One, 5,* e10354.

Wipfli, M., Felblinger, J., Mosimann, U. P., Hess, C. W., Schlaepfer, T. E., & Müri, R. M. (2001). Double pulse transcranial magnetic stimulation over the frontal eye field facilitates triggering of memory-guided saccades. *European Journal of Neuroscience, 14,* 571–575.

Witte, O. W., & Stoll, G. (1997). Delayed and remote effects of focal cortical infarctions: Secondary damage and reactive plasticity. *Advances in Neurology, 73,* 207–227.

Yamaguchi, S., Yamagata, S., & Kobayashi, S. (2000). Cerebral asymmetry of the "top-down" allocation of attention to global and local features. *Journal of Neuroscience, 20,* RC72.

Yamanaka, K., Yamagata, B., Tomioka, H., Kawasaki, S., & Mimura, M. (2010). Transcranial magnetic stimulation of the parietal cortex facilitates spatial working memory: Near-infrared spectroscopy study. *Cerebral Cortex, 20,* 1037–1045.

Ziemann, U. (2010). TMS in cognitive neuroscience: Virtual lesion and beyond. *Cortex, 46,* 124–127.

Zimerman, M., & Hummel, F. C. (2010). Non-invasive brain stimulation: Enhancing motor and cognitive functions in healthy old subjects. *Frontiers in Aging Neuroscience, 2,* 149.

NEUROPSYCHOLOGICAL REHABILITATION
2011, 21 (5), 650–675

Modulation of motor learning and memory formation by non-invasive cortical stimulation of the primary motor cortex

Satoshi Tanaka[1], Marco Sandrini[2,3], and Leonardo G. Cohen[2]

[1]Division of Cerebral Integration, National Institute for Physiological Sciences, Okazaki, Japan
[2]Human Cortical Physiology and Stroke Neurorehabilitation Section, National Institute of Neurological Disorder and Stroke, National Institute of Health, Bethesda, MD, USA
[3]Center for Neuroscience and Regenerative Medicine at the Uniformed Services University of Health Sciences, Bethesda, MD, USA

Transcranial magnetic (TMS) and direct current (tDCS) stimulation are non-invasive brain stimulation techniques that allow researchers to purposefully modulate cortical excitability in focal areas of the brain. Recent work has provided preclinical evidence indicating that TMS and tDCS can facilitate motor performance, motor memory formation, and motor skill learning in healthy subjects and possibly in patients with brain lesions. Although the optimal stimulation parameters to accomplish these goals remain to be determined, and controlled multicentre clinical studies are lacking, these findings suggest that cortical stimulation techniques could become in the future adjuvant strategies in the rehabilitation of motor deficits. The aim of this article is to critically review these findings and to discuss future directions regarding the

Correspondence should be addressed to Leonardo G. Cohen, Human Cortical Physiology and Stroke Neurorehabilitation Section, National Institute of Neurological Disorders and Stroke, National Institutes of Health, 10 Center Drive Bethesda, Maryland 20892-1430, USA. E-mail: cohenl@ninds.nih.gov

This work was supported by the Intramural Research Program of the NINDS, NIH and grants from the Grants-in-Aid for Scientific Research (KAKENHI) to ST (22700442) and by funding from Department of Defense in the Center for Neuroscience and Regenerative Medicine to MS. Satoshi Tanaka and Marco Sandrini contributed equally to this work.

possibility of combining these techniques with other interventions in neurorehabilitation.

Keywords: Motor learning; Memory; Adaptation; TMS; tDCS; Rehabilitation; Stroke.

INTRODUCTION

Motor learning has been defined as "a set of processes associated with practice or experience leading to relatively permanent changes in the capability for movement" (Schmidt, 1988). Our capacity to plan, learn and retain new motor skills is essential for carrying out daily activities such as writing, typing, driving or playing sports. Patients with motor deficits resulting from brain lesions must confront the need to either develop alternative strategies to accomplish the same goals or relearn the motor programs utilised before the lesion. There are different ways by which these processes could take place. One possibility is to reach such goals through the implementation of different motor strategies (i.e., compensation, Levin, Kleim, & Wolf, 2009). An alternative way is to relearn to perform the task in the same way it was done before the lesion. Clearly, both processes involve fundamentally different pathophysiological mechanisms, even when the goal (i.e., grasp a glass of water) remains the same.

In the past few years, there has been an effort to optimise training strategies after brain lesions such as constraint-induced movement therapy, bilateral arm training, mirror and randomised training schedules or robotic-based approaches. (Cauraugh & Kim, 2003; Cheeran, Cohen et al., 2009; Cramer, 2008; Kantak, Sullivan, Fisher, Knowlton, & Winstein, 2010; Krakauer, 2006; Lo et al, 2009; Luft et al., 2004; Tanaka, Honda, Hanakawa, & Cohen, 2010; Wittenberg et al., 2003). Additionally, new technical approaches have been proposed to facilitate the beneficial effects of training on motor skill learning in the setting of rehabilitation interventions like somatosensory stimulation (Conforto, Cohen, dos Santos, Scaff, & Marie, 2007) and non-invasive brain stimulation techniques, such as transcranial magnetic (TMS) and transcranial direct current (tDCS) stimulation. Within the past two decades these techniques have been used to explore possible causal relations between activity in specific brain areas and particular behaviours (Cohen et al., 1997; Hallett, 2000; Nitsche et al., 2008; Pascual-Leone, Walsh, & Rothwell, 2000; Robertson, Theoret, & Pascual-Leone, 2003; Sandrini, Umiltà, & Rusconi, 2011). Improved understanding of the involvement of a brain region in a type of behaviour was followed by attempts to modulate activity in specific cortical areas with the goal to enhance motor and cognitive performance (Fregni & Pascual-Leone, 2007; Hummel et al., 2005; Hummel & Cohen, 2006; Miniussi et al., 2008; Miniussi & Rossini, 2011; Reis et al., 2008; Tanaka et al., 2011; Tanaka, Hanakawa, Honda, & Watanabe, 2009; Tanaka & Watanabe, 2009; Wasserman & Grafman, 2005; Webster, Celnik, & Cohen, 2006).

Although the neural substrates of motor skill learning (Bo, Langan, & Seidler, 2008; Doyon et al., 2009; Shadmehr & Krakauer, 2008; Seidler, 2010) involve functional changes in a distributed network that includes the primary motor cortex (M1), premotor cortex (PMC), supplementary motor area (SMA), somotosensory cortex (S1), dorsolateral prefrontal cortex (DLPFC), posterior parietal cortex (PPC), cerebellum, thalamic nuclei, and the striatum, most TMS and tDCS studies carried out so far have focused on efforts to modulate activity within M1. Thus, the aim of this article is to critically review the results from studies that showed, by means of cortical stimulation over M1, modulation of motor memory formation and motor skill learning in both healthy humans and stroke patients. Finally, studies using a combination of non-invasive cortical stimulation and other intervention techniques will be briefly reviewed to discuss new potential options for further enhancement of training effects.

MOTOR LEARNING

Studies on motor learning have been carried out with a variety of paradigms, two of which have been more commonly used: skill acquisition and adaptation (Shadmehr & Wise, 2005). Acquisition of a new motor skill involves the ability to perform new movement qualities and/or muscle synergies that enhance performance beyond pre-existing levels. On the other hand, adaptation has been defined as the reduction in errors introduced by altered conditions in order to return to a pre-existent level of performance. Adaptation, unlike skill acquisition, does not require new patterns of muscle activations, i.e., a new capability, but rather a new mapping between well-learned movements and spatial goals (Krakauer, 2009). For example, when learning to perfect a sequence of movements, individuals combine isolated movements into one smooth, concatenated and coherent action, such as when practising a tennis serve. In sensorimotor adaptation, participants modify movements in response to changes in sensory inputs or motor outputs, for example, when adapting the motor commands for arm movements in response to the altered limb dynamics associated with holding a tennis racket (Bo et al., 2008). Operationally, the acquisition of such motor abilities is generally measured by a reduction in reaction time and number of errors, and/or by a change in movement synergy and kinematics (Doyon et al., 2009).

Behavioural and physiological studies have shown that motor skill learning can continue over prolonged time periods as in musicians (Brashers-Krug, Shadmehr, & Bizzi, 1996; Dudai, 2004; Luft & Buitrago, 2005; McGaugh, 2000). Within-session performance improvements (on-line effects) occur during initial stages of a learning session. However, the effects of motor learning can also continue after the end of practice (off-line effects) (Krakauer & Shadmehr, 2006; Muellbacher et al., 2002; Reis et al., 2008; Robertson, Pascual-Leone, & Miall, 2004; Walker, Brakefield, Morgan, Hobson, & Stickgold, 2002). Consolidation is an off-line effect in which the learned skill becomes stable and resistant to disruption by subsequent interference (Brashers-Krug et al., 1996; Krakauer & Shadmehr, 2006; Shadmehr & Brashers-Krug, 1997; Shadmehr & Holcomb, 1997). Another form of conso- lidation is "off-line learning" in which performance improvement occurs between sessions without actual training (Censor & Cohen, 2010; Robertson & Cohen, 2006; Robertson, Pascual-Leone, & Miall, 2004; Robertson, Press, & Pascual-Leone, 2005). In adaptation studies, the successful return to base- line performance after the perturbation occurs often within the sole training session, and therefore the possibility of off-line improvements across days has not been thoroughly tested, although savings, an increase in the rate of re-adaptation, has been documented (Krakauer, Ghez, & Ghilardi, 2005).

Reactivation of previously consolidated memories turns them transiently labile to subsequent degradation, stabilisation or further strengthening, a process referred to as reconsolidation (Censor, Dimyan, & Cohen, 2010; Walker, Brakefield, Hobson, & Stickgold, 2003). Over time, motor skills can be retained after completion of training (long-term retention, Savion-Lemieux & Penhune, 2005) or degraded (Adams, 1952). In the next section, we summarise the results of studies showing modulation of motor skill acquisition and adaptation by non-invasive cortical stimulations accord- ing to these temporally distinct stages of learning.

Encoding of an elementary motor memory

Classen and colleagues (Classen, Liepert, Wise, Hallett, & Cohen, 1998) developed a paradigm to evaluate encoding of an elementary motor memory within the primary motor cortex. The experiment was designed to determine whether training to perform a finger movement in a specific direc- tion opposite that of TMS-evoked movements would result in a change in the direction of subsequent TMS- evoked movements. After the repetitive per- formance of isolated and unidirectional stereotyped thumb movements (30 min), the direction of these movements evoked subsequently by TMS over the M1 was changed into the direction of the training, and the excitability of muscle representations in M1 was changed in favour of the training agonist muscle. Therefore, motor training leads to encoding of kinematic details of the practised movements in the human motor cortex, a form of use-dependent plasticity (UDP). It has been proposed that the mechanisms underlying this form of UDP share similarities with those involved in long-term potentiation (LTP) (Bliss & Lomo 1973; Bütefisch et al., 2000; Rioult-Pedotti, Friedman, Hess, & Donoghue, 1998). UDP plays an important role in motor learning and recovery of motor function after brain lesions (Nudo, Wise, SiFuentes, & Milliken, 1996), such as in patients with stroke (Liepert et al., 1998; Liepert, Bauder, Miltner, Taub, & Weiller, 2000). Therefore, enhancing UDP may result in improvements in the ability of the central nervous system to compensate for the loss of function (Bütefisch et al., 2002; Feeney, Gonzalez, & Law, 1982). One possible strategy was introduced by Bütefisch and co-workers (Bütefisch, Khurana, Kopylev, & Cohen, 2004). They showed that the synchronous application of single-pulse TMS (spTMS) to M1 contralateral to a hand practising thumb movements enhanced the ability of healthy subjects to encode an elementary motor memory in M1. Importantly, this effect was evident when M1 was stimulated in synchrony with the training motions but not when applied in between training movements. A second important finding from this study was that synchronous stimulation applied to M1 ipsilateral to the training hand, cancelled training effects on motor memory formation, consistent with the hypothesis that interhemispheric interactions between M1s contribute to motor memory formation (Duque et al., 2008). A different strategy was adopted by Galea and Celnik (2009). The authors tested the capacity of 30 min of tDCS applied over M1 during motor practice to increase motor memory formation and retention. Anodal tDCS applied over the primary motor cortex enhanced the effect of simple repetitive training in a polarity-specific manner, as reflected by changes in the kinematic characteristics of TMS-evoked movements after anodal, but not cathodal or sham stimulation. This effect was present only when training and stimulation were temporally associated and lasted longer than the effects of training without stimulation.

Although most motor skills are acquired through physical practice, the mere observation of movements has also been shown to lead to subsequent specific performance gains (Brass, Bekkering, & Priz, 2001; Mattar & Gribble, 2005; Petrosini et al., 2003). For example, Stefan and collaborators (Stefan et al., 2005) demonstrated that action observation (AO) of movements congruent with the physically trained (PT) direction (AO congruent) drives reorganisation of motor representations in M1 to form a motor memory of the observed action compared to AO of movements opposite to the physically trained direction (AO incongruent). These findings are consistent with those of previous studies, showing that motor performance may be facilitated even with observation of simple movements (Brass et al., 2001; Porro, Facchin, Fusi, Dri, & Fadiga, 2007). For instance, Porro and colleagues (Porro et al., 2007) demonstrated that observing others' actions can facilitate basic aspects of motor performance, such as force production. Observation of finger movements enhanced the excitability of the corticospinal system targeting the first dorsal interosseous as tested by TMS. Moreover, Stefan and co-workers (Stefan, Classen, Celnik, & Cohen, 2008), using the same paradigm of previous studies (Butefisch et al., 2004; Classen et al., 1998; Galea & Celnik, 2009; Stefan et al., 2005), demonstrated that AO of movements in synchrony with those performed in the PT direction (PT + AO congruent) enhanced training effects relative to movements practised opposite to PT direction (PT + AO incongruent) or to PT alone. On carrying out the same experimental protocol in older people (mean age 65 years compared with mean age 34 years), however, PT or AO alone did not significantly change TMS-evoked thumb movement directions from baseline; only combined PT and AO led to new motor memory formation (Celnik et al., 2006). A similar protocol was tested with participants with chronic stroke resulting in motor memory formation by combined PT and congruent but not incongruent AO (Celnik, Webster, Glasser, & Cohen, 2008). These findings indicate that AO could contribute to neurorehabilitation by enhancing the beneficial effects of training on motor function in a partially paralysed hand. However, the influence of AO in patients with more severe motor impairment has not yet been investigated. While none of the subjects reported experiencing or engaging in motor imagery during training (Pascual-Leone et al., 1995; Ranganathan et al., 2004; Zijdewind, Toering, & Bessem, 2003), a partial contribution could not fully be ruled out.

How are learning mechanisms in M1 accessed by action observation? This is an important question to consider because, as far as we know, the motor cortex does not receive direct input from the visual cortex (Watkins, Strafella, & Paus, 2003). Motor learning by observing can be linked to mirror neurons, discovered in the monkey ventral premotor cortex (Di Pellegrino, Fadiga, Fogassi, Gallese, & Rizzolatti, 1992; Gallese, Fadiga, Fogassi, & Rizzolatti, 1996; Rizzolatti, Fadiga, Gallese, & Fogassi, 1996), and the inferior parietal cortex (Brodmann's area 7b; Fogassi et al., 2005; Gallese, Fogassi, Fadiga, & Rizzolatti, 2002), which increase their activity both when a monkey performs a goal-directed action and observes the same or similar actions performed by others (Gallese et al., 1996). A large set of evidence has been provided that a visuomotor resonant system, sharing some similarities with that described at the single cell level in monkeys, does exist in the human brain (Blakemore & Decety, 2001; Buccino et al., 2001; Fadiga, Fogassi, Pavesi, & Rizzolatti, 1995; Rizzolatti et al., 1996; see also Cattaneo & Rizzolatti, 2009 for a recent review). Moreover, neuroimaging studies in humans suggest a partial overlap between the cortical areas involved in action execution, imagination, and observation (Decety & Grèzes, 1999; Grèzes & Decety, 2001; Lui et al., 2008). Importantly, the PMv is directly connected both to the spinal cord and to M1, and it is these cortico-cortical connections that have been linked to changes in the neural excitability of the motor cortex when human observers watch or listen to another person performing an action, as measured by the amplitude of MEPs elicited by spTMS applied to M1 (see for a review Fadiga, Craighero, & Olivier, 2005).

Regarding the study described above (Celnik et al., 2008), it is possible that changes in cortical excitability identified provide some information on the underlying mechanisms associated with these effects. In this study the effect was associated with an increase in corticomotor excitability of the muscle representations mediating movements in the trained and observed direction, whereas the excitability of the antagonist muscles decreased. According to the authors, the differential modulation of corticomotor excitability of the agonist and antagonist muscles involved in the performed and observed movements suggests a change in the balance of inhibition and excitation within the cortical representation of the thumb. It is likely that Hebbian-like confluence of inputs arriving to the corticospinal neurons within the hand representation of M1 from the PMv and non-primary motor regions (Dum & Strick, 2002; Mima et al., 1999), associated to performance of motor tasks, is the mechanism underlying the corticomotor excitability change. Interestingly, similar brain regions activated by hand movements after stroke may contribute to recovery of motor function (Calautti & Baron, 2003; Ward, 2006; Yozbatiran & Cramer, 2006). Therefore, it is possible that using action observation to activate premotor areas and in turn modulate motor neuronal output may be particularly suited in stroke patients.

In conclusion, it is possible to modulate formation of motor memories within M1, which represents a first step in the complex chain of events leading to stable skill acquisition.

Motor skill acquisition

On-line effects.   The interaction between the two M1s appears to play an important role in motor control in general and in motor sequence learning in particular (Duque et al., 2008; Kobayashi, Hutchinson, Theoret, Schlaug, & Pascual-Leone, 2004; Perez & Cohen, 2008). However, the specific ways in which these interactions operate during motor learning remain to be determined. According to this principle, it would be theoretically possible to facilitate motor learning by enhancing excitability (excitatory TMS or anodal tDCS) in M1 contralateral to the practising hand or by decreasing excitability (inhibitory TMS or cathodal tDCS) in M1 ipsilateral to the training hand (Kapur, 1996; Kinsbourne, 1977; Theoret, Kobayashi, Valero-Cabre, & Pascual-Leone, 2003; Ward & Cohen, 2004).

Several studies have shown that facilitatory tDCS or repetitive TMS (rTMS) over M1 contralateral to the training hand can improve on-line learning of sequential finger movement tasks. Anodal tDCS applied over M1 during practice led to improvement in reaction times in the sequence blocks relative to the random blocks in the serial reaction time task (SRTT), a standard paradigm to test procedural motor learning in which subjects perform sequential finger movements repeatedly without awareness of a sequential order (Nissen & Bullemer, 1997; Robertson, 2007; Willingham, Nissen, & Bullemer, 1989). Remarkably the improvement was restricted to M1 because stimulation of PMC and prefrontal cortex (PFC) had no effect (Nitsche et al., 2003). However, caveats remain in the interpretation of these data as to the specific parameters modified: movement time or reaction times (Ghilardi, Moisello, Silvestri, Ghez, & Krakauer, 2009). Similarly, anodal tDCS improved the number of correct key presses in a polarity-specific manner in healthy subjects while cathodal tDCS failed to induce this effect (Vines, Nair, & Schlaug, 2006). The same stimulation technique resulted in improvements in performance of a visuomotor coordination task (Antal et al., 2004). Improvement of initial performance of SRTT was also observed when 10 Hz alternating current stimulation (tACS) was applied over M1 (Antal, Boris et al., 2008). tACS is a non-invasive means by which alternating currents applied above the skull entrains, in a specific fashion, neural oscillations in the brain (Zaghi, Acar, Hultgren, Boggio, & Fregni, 2010). High-frequency tACS at 80, 140 and 250 Hz seemed to be less effective than low-frequency tACS with 10 Hz concerning SRTT learning (Moliadze, Antal, & Paulus, 2010). Similarly, high-frequency rTMS (10 Hz) delivered over M1 facilitated the accuracy and speed of sequential finger movements during the training period in both healthy subjects (Kim, Park, Ko, Jang, & Lee, 2004) and chronic stroke patients (Kim et al., 2006). In addition, transcranial random noise stimulation (tRNS), in which a random electrical oscillation spectrum was applied over the M1, induced the increase of the cortical excitability and improved the performance of SRTT (Terney, Chaieb, Moliadze, Antal, & Paulus, 2008). These findings are in accordance with human neuroimaging (Honda et al., 1998; Karni et al., 1995; Ungerleider, Doyon, & Karni, 2002) and TMS (Wilkinson et al., 2010) studies that documented an important role of M1 in performance of sequential finger movement tasks. In another motor task, it has been reported that intermittent theta burst stimulation (iTBS, Huang, Edwards, Rounis, Bhatia, & Rothwell, 2005) over M1 improves training effects of a precision grip task in subcortical stroke patients (Ackerley, Stinear, Barber, & Bylow, 2010).

    In contrast to the studies that applied TMS or tDCS to the M1 contralateral to the practising hand, low frequency rTMS (1 Hz) applied to M1 ipsilateral to the training hand, improved performance of a sequential finger movement motor task and was associated with increased intracortical excitability in the contralateral M1 (Kobayashi et al., 2004; Kobayashi, Theoret, &

Pascual-Leone, 2009; Schambra, Sawaki, & Cohen, 2003), possibly by releasing it from transcallosal inhibition from the stimulated M1. However, a recent study in stroke patients reported an opposite effect by demonstrating that continuous TBS (cTBS, Huang et al., 2005) over the contralesional M1 actually impaired upper-limb function and decreased ipsilesional M1 excitability (Ackerley et al., 2010). Therefore, further investigation will be necessary to replicate the effects of inhibitory non-invasive cortical stimulation to the contralesional M1 after stroke and to optimise parameters of stimulation as well. Additionally, we cannot rule out the possibility that individual patients may benefit more from facilitatory stimulation of ipsilesional while others from inhibitory stimulation of contralesional motor regions.

It is important to keep in mind that the effects of stimulating M1 with either TMS or tDCS are likely to be dependent on the complexity of the task as well. For example, Agostino and colleagues (2007) found that performance of relatively simpler repetitive finger abduction movements was not improved by high-frequency rTMS (5 Hz) over M1 contralateral to a training hand, whereas Carey and collaborators (Carey, Fregni, & Pascual-Leone, 2006) showed that 1 Hz rTMS interfered with the motor performance in a task engaging single finger tracking motions when applied ipsilateral to the training hand, but it had no effect when applied contralaterally.

It should be kept in mind that while anodal tDCS over the M1 during rest generally results in an increase in MEP amplitudes (Nitsche & Paulus, 2000), under some circumstances, it may worsen subsequent learning (Antal, Begemeier, Nitsche, & Paulus, 2008; Kuo et al., 2008), an effect that could be explained by homeostatic plasticity rules (Antal, Begemeier et al., 2008; Bienenstock, Cooper, & Munro, 1982;). Thus, this dissociation between effects of tDCS on MEP amplitudes and on learning raise caution when trying to use MEP amplitudes as sole biomarker of cortical plasticity or of likelihood of impact on behaviour.

Off-line effects.   Previous work using TMS provided evidence of the functional relevance of M1 in off-line learning of simple ballistic movements as well as sequential movements (Baraduc, Lang, Rothwell, & Wolpert, 2004; Muellbacher et al., 2002; Robertson et al., 2005). So far, only few studies have investigated whether non-invasive brain stimulation over M1 could facilitate off-line effects of motor skill learning.

In one study (Reis et al., 2009), subjects practised sequential visual isometric pinch task (SVIPT) over five consecutive days while receiving 20 min of anodal tDCS over contralateral M1 during the training period. There was no difference of within-day improvements (on-line effects when considering on average the five training days) between anodal tDCS and sham stimulation, while anodal tDCS largely enhanced between-day improvement (off-line effect) compared to sham. Anodal tDCS did not change the rate of forgetting compared to sham stimulation across the 3-month follow-up period, and consequently the skill measure of subjects who received anodal tDCS remained greater at 3 months. These findings, showing that anodal tDCS enhances offline improvement of the motor skill, but did not overwhelmingly affect online learning or rate of forgetting, support the view that motor skill learning has temporally distinct stages. Furthermore, the documentation of lasting beneficial effects (3 months after training and stimulation) of anodal tDCS may have promising implications for the design of protocols in neurorehabilitation of motor deficits following brain lesions. In a recent study, Fritsch and co-workers (2010) examined the cellular and molecular mechanisms of the anodal tDCS effect on off-line motor improvement. They demonstrated that (1) DCS induced long-lasting LTP in mouse M1 slices when combined with repetitive low frequency synaptic activation (LFS), (2) combined DCS and LFA enhanced brain-derived neurotrophic factor (BDNF)-secretion and TRkB (receptor tyrosine kinase for BDNF) activation, which are known to be involved in various forms of cortical synaptic plasticity, and (3) the presence of the BDNF val66met polymorphism, which is known to affect activity-dependent BDNF secretion, was associated with diminished motor skill acquisition in both humans and mice. From these findings, they proposed that tDCS improve offline learning of motor skill through a form of synaptic plasticity that requires BDNF secretion and TrkB activation within M1, consistent with previous electrophysiological studies in humans (Cheeran, Ritter, Rothwell, & Siebner, 2009; Kleim et al., 2006; McHughen et al., 2010).

Depending on the task, offline improvement of motor skill may or may not require sleep (Robertson, Pascual-Leone, & Press, 2004). Tecchio and co-workers (Tecchio et al., 2010) investigated whether anodal tDCS over M1, applied immediately after the training of sequential finger movements, enhanced early consolidation, assessed by the performance difference between the first block after and the last block before stimulation, compared to sham stimulation. These findings suggest that anodal tDCS applied immediately after training may influence early consolidation in a task-dependent manner.

Sensorimotor adaptation.   Recent studies have used TMS and tDCS to explore the role of M1 in sensorimotor adaptation. In these experiments, subjects adjust their motor behaviour to compensate for a particular external perturbation to return to a stable performance. Following removal of perturbation (de-adaptation) participants typically miss the target but in the opposite direction. These mismatches in, for example, movement extent or direction that occur following the period of exposure have been termed "after-effects". It has been proposed that the presence of after-effects results from a coordinative remapping between sensory representations, suggesting that an internal model has been updated (Shadmehr & Mussa-Ivaldi, 1994).

Richardson and colleagues (2006) showed that 1-Hz rTMS applied to M1 before force field adaptation did not affect the participants' adaptation process per se, but impaired retention relative to control subjects (who did not receive any rTMS) as tested the following day. Baraduc and colleagues (Baraduc et al., 2004) showed that 1 Hz rTMS applied to M1 shortly after a force field motor adaptation paradigm did not disrupt subsequent consolidation of the newly formed internal model. Moreover, spTMS delivered immediately after each reaching trial during adaptation to visual rotations did not impact adaptation but caused faster de-adaptation (forgetting) within the same session relative to spTMS applied 700 milliseconds after the end of each trial or relative to dorsal PMC stimulation (Hadipour-Niktarash, Lee, Desmond, & Shadmehr, 2007). These data suggest that processing in M1 contributes to retention in a time-dependent manner, with a strong contribution early in the inter-trial interval when there is a high probability of coinciding with cortical arrival of error feedback, and weaker contribution at later times. Lastly, Orban de Xivry and colleagues (Orban de Xivry, Criscimagna-Hemminger, & Schadmehr, 2011) controlled the schedule of perturbation (i.e., abrupt, intermediate and gradually developing condition) and attempted to assay the role of M1. To this end, they used spTMS to disrupt the function of M1 during these different types of adaptation. This disruption produced deficits that were specific to the schedule of perturbations because TMS to M1 affected adaptation in the abrupt and intermediate conditions but not in the gradual condition.

Although these TMS studies suggest a possible role of M1 in sensorimotor adaptation, they did not directly test the hypothesis that formation of a new internal model, during adaptation, is modified by cortical stimulation. This hypothesis has been tested recently by Hunter and collaborators (Hunter, Sacco, Nitsche, & Turner, 2009). The authors applied anodal or sham tDCS over M1 during the adaptation phase of a force-field motor adaptation task. The results showed that anodal tDCS, during one session of motor adaptation, strengthens an internal model evidenced as short-lived after-effects in trajectory errors during de-adaptation. Moreover, Brown and colleagues (Brown, Wilson, & Gribble, 2009) provided the first direct evidence that neural representations of motor skills in M1 underlie motor learning by observing. As in Mattar and Gribble (2005), subjects who observed another person learning to reach in a novel force environment imposed by a robot arm performed better when later tested in the same environment than subjects who observed movements in a different environment. Moreover, 1 Hz rTMS to M1 after observation reduced the beneficial effect of observing congruent forces, and even more dramatically, removed the detrimental effect of observing incongruent forces. In a related study described before (Stefan et al., 2005), observation of directionally specific thumb movement increased the likelihood that TMS applied to M1 would elicit thumb movements in the same direction. Whereas this study demonstrates that observation can prime the choice of movement direction, the force learning study (Brown et al., 2009) showed that information about a perturbing force field is encoded by M1 during observation as well.

FACILITATING MOTOR LEARNING WITH COMBINATION OF NON-INVASIVE BRAIN STIMULATION AND OTHER INTERVENTIONS

In the previous section, we reviewed several studies suggesting that non-invasive brain stimulation could facilitate motor memory formation and motor learning. For example, anodal tDCS may modulate formation of an internal model during one session of motor adaptation and this is manifest as a short-lived after-effect on trajectory errors during de-adaptation (Hunter et al., 2009). Another recent study has considered repeated sessions (daily) of anodal tDCS application during motor skill learning and demonstrated an improvement in motor skills via a longer-term consolidation process (Reis et al., 2009). The time span and number of sessions as well as the motor skills (upper arm reaching vs. finger/thumb pinch) of these two studies are different. Nevertheless when considered together, the two studies demonstrated a consistent improvement in motor skill development invoked by anodal tDCS and suggest a possible adjuvant role to other neurorehabilitative techniques (i.e., robot-assisted rehabilitation) in brain-injured individuals.

Combination with rehabilitative behavioural therapy

In pilot studies, constrained-induced movement therapy (CIT), robot-assisted training or physical/occupation therapy were combined with noninvasive brain stimulation in order to test additive or multiplicative effects. CIT is one form of physical therapy in which patients perform massed training of functional tasks with the affected arm and hand while constraining the use of the non-affected upper limb. Several studies have reported that CIT has beneficial effects in stroke patients with hemiparesis (Taub et al., 2006; Winstein et al., 2003; Wolf et al., 2006). One possible mechanism underlying the beneficial effect is decreased inter-hemispheric inhibition due to the diminished use of the undamaged hemisphere and the increased excitability of M1 in the damaged hemisphere (Cicinelli et al., 2003; Liepert et al., 2000). Malcolm and colleagues (2007) tested the beneficial effect of combining high-frequency rTMS with CIT. The authors hypothesised that additional increase of the excitability in the damaged hemisphere using non-invasive brain stimulation might have a greater beneficial effect than application of each intervention alone in neurorehabilitation. However, 2 weeks intervention using 20 Hz rTMS over M1 in the damaged hemisphere immediately after CIT did not improve significantly either the Wolf Motor Function Test (WMFT) or the Motor Activity Log (MAL), which are commonly used to assess changes in upper extremity function after treatment.

In robot-assisted training, the robot helps patients perform physical training. The advantages of robot-assisted training are the controllability of movement and the reliability of measurement (Huang & Krakauer, 2009). Recent review articles have reported the usefulness and improvement of motor impairments by robot-assisted training but the magnitude of these changes is not superior to those provided by trained therapists (Kwakkel, Kollen, & Krebs, 2008; Lo et al., 2010; Prange, Jannink, Groothuis-Oudshoorn, Hermens, & Ijzerman, 2006). In a pilot study, Hesse and collaborators (Hesse et al., 2007) observed that the combination of anodal tDCS with robot-assisted training may improve motor impairment in sub-acute stroke patients. In this study, 10 patients received anodal tDCS over M1 in the affected hemisphere and trained bilateral mirror movements with robotic assistance over six weeks. In three patients, upper arm function assessed by the Fugl-Meyer motor score improved significantly. However, it is not clear whether the behavioural improvement was due to the effect of combined tDCS and robot-aided training or spontaneous recovery.

Finally, a recent study (Lindenberg, Renga, Zhu, Nair, & Schlaug, 2010) tested the efficacy of five consecutive sessions of bilateral stimulation (anodal tDCS to upregulate excitability of ipsilesional motor cortex and simultaneous cathodal tDCS to downregulate excitability of contralesional motor cortex), in combination with physical/occupational therapy (i.e., functional motor tasks to promote sensory-motor integration, coordination of movement and goal-directed activities of practical relevance) in chronic stroke patients. The improvement of motor function, assessed by Fugl-Meyer motor score and WMFT, was greater in the real stimulation group compared to the sham group. The effects outlasted the stimulation by at least 1 week.

Combination with peripheral nerve stimulation

Peripheral nerve stimulation (PNS) has been proposed as a possible intervention method which could facilitate motor function and training effects in stroke patients (Celnik, Hummel, Harris-Love, Wolk, & Cohen, 2007; Sawaki, Wu, Kaelin-Lang, & Cohen, 2006). The mechanisms underlying the effects of PNS on motor function still remain unclear but may include modulation of cortical excitability that outlasts the period of stimulation (Kaelin-Lang et al., 2002). A recent study demonstrated that combining PNS and tDCS can facilitate a beneficial effect of motor training in stroke patients (Celnik, Paik, Vandermeeren, Dimyan, & Cohen, 2009). The authors demonstrated that the combination of

PNS of the paretic hand with anodal tDCS over the ipsilesional M1 before a sequential finger movement training induced greater improvement compared to the use of each intervention alone. This effect outlasted the stimulation and training periods by days. In another study, Koganemaru and colleagues (Koganemaru et al., 2010) examined, in chronic stroke patients, the single intervention effect of repetitive wrist and finger extension exercises aided by neuromuscular stimulation, the single intervention of 5 Hz rTMS over the affected M1 and the combined effect of the two interventions. The findings indicate that combining motor training, neuromuscular stimulation and rTMS can facilitate UDP and achieve functional recovery of motor impairments that cannot be attained by either intervention alone. Moreover, performing this combination of interventions over 6 weeks induced a beneficial effect that remained present to some extent 2 weeks later.

Combination with pharmacological treatment

Recently, pharmacological approaches have been used to modulate specific neurotransmitter systems and facilitate neuro-plasticity and learning (Floel & Cohen, 2010; Floel, Breitenstein et al., 2005; Floel et al., 2008; Floel, Hummel, Breitenstein, Knecht, & Cohen, 2005). For example, medication with levodopa as dopamine agonist significantly improved the formation of motor memory (Floel, Hummel, et al., 2005), procedural motor learning (Rosser et al., 2008) and increased offline gains and decreased forgetting of a motor skill acquisition in chronic stroke (Swayne et al., 2010). Initial studies reported that amphetamine with physical therapy promotes recovery of motor function in stroke patients (Crisostomo, Duncan, Propst, Dawson, & Davis, 1988; Walker-Batson, Smith, Curtis, Unwin, & Greenlee, 1995). However, subsequent studies raised questions about these initial conclusions (Gladstone et al., 2006; Martinsson, Eksborg, & Wahlgren, 2003; Reding, Solomon, & Borucki, 1995; Sonde, Nordstron, Nilsson, Lokk, & Viitanen, 2001). So far, combined use of non-invasive stimulation and pharmacological treatment has been reported in healthy subjects (Kuo et al., 2008). Combined use of anodal tDCS over the M1 and D-cycloserine (CYC) before the SRTT training resulted in an excitability enhancement but worsened the results of subsequent SRTT training, possibly due to homeostatic plasticity rules (Antal, Begemeier et al., 2008; Bienenstock et al., 1982). Please refer to Floel and Cohen (2010) for more in detail discussion of the effects of pharmacological agents on cortical plasticity.

CONCLUSIONS AND PERSPECTIVE

In summary, non-invasive brain stimulation data point to a clear role of M1 in the retention of new motor memories (Galea & Celnik, 2009; Galea, Vazquez,

Pasricha, Orban de Xivry, & Celnik, 2011; Hadipour-Niktarash et al., 2007; Hunter et al., 2009; Muellbacher et al., 2002; Reis et al., 2009; Richardson et al., 2006) and in the consolidation of motor memories as they involve repetitive-based learning (Classen et al., 1998; Butefisch et al., 2000; Kantak et al., 2010; Orban de Xivry et al., 2010), particularly during the late phases of training (Paz, Boraud, Natan, Bergman, & Vaadia, 2003; Paz & Vaadia, 2004).

Another area that will require much more work is the optimisation of stimulation parameters best fit to activate different cortical regions in the desired way. It should be kept in mind that while cortical stimulation is delivered to target one specific brain region in most cases, the behavioural effects of such stimulation may represent the consequence of focal activity in the stimulated region and/or effect on its anatomically interconnected brain regions. Dual site paired-pulse TMS (Koch & Rothwell, 2009; Torriero et al., 2011) and concurrent brain stimulation and neuroimaging (fMRI, PET, EEG) could be powerful tools to address this issue (Antal, Polania, Schmidt-Samoa, Dechent, & Paulus, 2011; Bestmann et al., 2008; Driver, Blankenburg, Bestmann, Vanduffel, & Ruff, 2009; Hanakawa et al., 2009; Lang et al., 2005; Paus, 2005; Polania, Nitsche, & Paulus, 2011; Siebner et al., 2009; Thut & Miniussi, 2009).

In the clinical domain, it would be interesting to determine which patients benefit from different stimulation strategies: up-regulating activity in the ipsilesional M1 or down-regulating activity in the contralesional M1, an important question in neurorehabilitation. Moreover, it will be crucial to optimise stimulation protocols in order to enhance long-term retention of newly acquired skills, to transfer what has been learned to new conditions and task variants, and to document functional recovery in adequately controlled multicentre clinical studies.

While M1 contribution to motor learning and neurorehabilitation is supported by the literature, M1 is not the only region within a distributed network that contributes to different aspects of motor learning. For example, some studies unveiled the involvement of the SMA in intermanual transfer of procedural motor learning (Perez et al., 2007, Perez, Tanaka, Wise, Willingham, & Cohen, 2008) and in processes leading to successful motor memory recall dependent on practice structure (Tanaka et al., 2010), which may also rely to some extent on DLPFC function (Kantak et al., 2010). DLPFC may contribute to learning of a visuomotor task containing a sequence to which subjects were previously exposed by observational learning, whereas the cerebellum interfered with the performance of a newly presented sequence (Torriero, Oliveri, Koch, Caltagirone, Petrosini, 2007) in which error-based learning is prominent (Tseng, Diedrichsen, Krakauer, Shadmehr, & Bastian, 2007). In addition, DLPFC seems to contribute to learning in the early phase of learning, when cognitive demands are higher (e.g., Anguera,

Reuter-Lorenz, Willingham, & Seidler, 2010, 2011; Della-Maggiore & McIntosh, 2005; Fitts & Posner, 1967; Gentili, Bradberry, Oh, Hatfield, & Contreras Vidal, 2011; Redding & Wallace, 1996) and may share neural resources with the declarative memory system (Galea, Albert, Ditye, & Miall, 2010; Keisler & Shadmehr, 2010). All together, advances in our understanding of the role of M1 in motor learning started to shed light on the contribution of nonprimary motor areas as well, probably operating in a functionally integrated manner.

REFERENCES

Ackerley, S. J., Stinear, C. M., Barber, P. A., & Byblow, W. D. (2010). Combing theta burst stimulation with training after subcortical stroke. *Stroke, 41,* 1568–1572.

Adams, J. A. (1952). Warm-up decrement in performance on the pursuit-rotor. *American Journal of Psychology, 65,* 404–414.

Agostino, R., Iezzi, E., Dinapoli, L., Gilio, F., Conte, A., Mari, F., & Berardelli, A. (2007). Effects of 5 Hz subthreshold magnetic stimulation of primary motor cortex on fast finger movements in normal subjects. *Experimental Brain Research, 180*(1), 105–111.

Anguera, J. A., Reuter-Lorenz, P. A., Willingham, D. T., & Seidler, R. D. (2010). Contributions of spatial working memory to visuomotor learning. *Journal of Cognitive Neuroscience, 22*(9), 1917–1930.

Anguera, J. A., Reuter-Lorenz, P. A., Willingham, D. T., & Seidler, R. D. (2011). Failure to engage spatial working memory contributes to age-related declines in visuomotor learning. *Journal of Cognitive Neuroscience, 23*(1), 11–25.

Antal, A., Begemeier, S., Nitsche, M. A., & Paulus, W. (2008). Prior state of cortical activity influences subsequent practicing of a visuomotor coordination task. *Neuropsychologia, 46*(13), 3157–3161.

Antal, A., Boros, K., Poreisz, C., Chaieb, L., Terney, D., & Paulus, W. (2008). Comparatively weak after-effects of transcranial alternating current stimulation (tACS) on cortical excitability in humans. *Brain Stimulation, 1*(2), 97–105.

Antal, A., Nitsche, M. A., Kincses, T. Z., Kruse, W., Hoffmann, K. P., & Paulus, W. (2004). Facilitation of visuo-motor learning by transcranial direct current stimulation of the motor and extrastriate visual areas in humans. *European Journal of Neuroscience, 19*(10), 2888–2892.

Antal, A., Polania, R., Schmidt-Samoa, C., Dechent, P., & Paulus, W. (2011). Transcranial direct current stimulation over the primary motor cortex during fMRI. *NeuroImage, 55*(2), 590–596.

Baraduc, P., Lang, N., Rothwell, J. C., & Wolpert, D. M. (2004). Consolidation of dynamic motor learning is not disrupted by rTMS of primary motor cortex. *Current Biology, 14*(3), 252–256.

Bestmann, S., Ruff, C. C., Blankenburg, F., Weiskopf, N., Driver, J., & Rothwell, J. C. (2008). Mapping causal interregional influences with concurrent TMS-fMRI. *Experimental Brain Research, 191*(4), 383–402.

Bienenstock, E. L., Cooper, L. N., & Munro, P. W. (1982). Theory for the development of neuron selectivity: Orientation specificity and binocular interaction in visual cortex. *Journal of Neuroscience, 2*(1), 32–48.

Blakemore, S. J., & Decety, J. (2001). From the perception of action to the understanding of intention. *Nature Reviews Neuroscience, 2,* 561–567.

Bliss, T. V., & Lomo, T. (1973). Long-lasting potentiation of synaptic transmission in the dentate area of the anaesthetized rabbit following stimulation of the perforant path. *Journal of Physiology, 232,* 331–356.

Bo, J., Langan, J., & Seidler, R. D. (2008). Cognitive neuroscience of skill acquisition. *Advances in Psychology, 139,* 101–112.

Brashers-Krug, T., Shadmehr, R., & Bizzi, E. (1996). Consolidation in human motor memory. *Nature, 382*(6588), 252–255.

Brass, M., Bekkering, H., & Prinz, W. (2001). Movement observation affects movement execution in a simple response task. *Acta Psychologica, 106,* 3–22.

Brown, L. E., Wilson, E. T., & Gribble, P. L. (2009). Repetitive transcranial magnetic stimulation to the primary motor cortex interferes with motor learning by observing. *Journal of Cognitive Neuroscience, 21*(5), 1013–1022.

Buccino, G., Binkofski, F., Fink, G. R., Fadiga, L., Fogassi, L., Gallese, V., et al. (2001). Action observation activates premotor and parietal areas in a somatotopic manner: An fMRI study. *European Journal of Neuroscience, 13,* 400–404.

Butefisch, C. M., Davis, B. C., Sawaki, L., Waldvogel, D., Classen, J., Kopylev, L., et al. (2002). Modulation of use-dependent plasticity by d-amphetamine. *Annals of Neurology, 51,* 59–68.

Bütefisch, C. M., Davis, B. C., Wise, S. P., Sawaki, L., Kopylev, L., Classen, J., et al. (2000). Mechanisms of use-dependent plasticity in the human motor cortex. *Proceedings of the National Academy of Sciences of the United States of America, 97*(7), 3661–3665.

Bütefisch, C. M., Khurana, V., Kopylev, L., & Cohen, L. G. (2004). Enhancing encoding of a motor memory in the primary motor cortex by cortical stimulation. *Journal of Neurophysiology, 91*(5), 2110–2116.

Calautti, C., & Baron, J-C. (2003). Functional neuroimaging studies of motor recovery after stroke in adults: A review. *Stroke, 34,* 1553–1566.

Carey, J. R., Fregni, F., & Pascual-Leone, A. (2006). rTMS combined with motor learning training in healthy subjects. *Restorative Neurology and Neuroscience, 24*(3), 191–199.

Cattaneo, L., & Rizzolatti, G. (2009). The mirror neuron system. *Archives of Neurology, 66*(5), 557–560.

Cauraugh, J. H., & Kim, S. B. (2003). Stroke motor recovery: Active neuromuscular stimulation and repetitive practice schedules. *Journal of Neurology, Neurosurgery and Psychiatry, 74*(11), 1562–1566.

Celnik, P., Hummel, F., Harris-Love, M., Wolk, R., & Cohen, L. G. (2007). Somatosensory stimulation enhances the effects of training functional hand tasks in patients with chronic stroke. *Archives of Physical Medicine and Rehabilitation, 88*(11), 1369–1376.

Celnik, P., Paik, N. J., Vandermeeren, Y., Dimyan, M., & Cohen, L. G. (2009). Effects of combined peripheral nerve stimulation and brain polarization on performance of a motor sequence task after chronic stroke. *Stroke, 40*(5), 1764–1771.

Celnik, P., Stefan, K., Hummel, F., Duque, J., Classen, J., & Cohen, L. G. (2006). Encoding a motor memory in the older adult by action observation. *NeuroImage, 29*(2), 677–684.

Celnik, P., Webster, B., Glasser, D. M., & Cohen, L. G. (2008). Effects of action observation on physical training after stroke. *Stroke, 39*(6), 1814–1820.

Censor, N., & Cohen, L. G. (2011). Using repetitive transcranial magnetic stimulation to study the underlying neural mechanisms of human motor learning and memory. *Journal of Physiology, 589*(Pt 1), 21–28.

Censor, N., Dimyan, M. A., & Cohen, L. G. (2010). Modification of existing human motor memories is enabled by primary cortical processing during memory reactivation. *Current Biology, 20*(17), 1545–1549.

Cheeran, B., Cohen, L., Dobkin, B., Ford, G., Greenwood, R., Howard, D., et al. (2009). The future of restorative neurosciences in stroke: Driving the translational research pipeline from basic science to rehabilitation of people after stroke. *Neurorehabilitation and Neural Repair, 23*(2), 97–107.

Cheeran, B. J., Ritter, C., Rothwell, J. C., & Siebner, H. R. (2009). Mapping genetic influences on the corticospinal motor system in humans. *Neuroscience, 164*(1), 156–163.

Cicinelli, P., Pasqualetti, P., Zaccagnini, M., Traversa, R., Oliveri, M., & Rossini, P. M. (2003). Interhemispheric asymmetries of motor cortex excitability in the postacute stroke stage: A paired-pulse transcranial magnetic stimulation study. *Stroke, 34*(11), 2653–2658.

Classen, J., Liepert, J., Wise, S. P., Hallett, M., & Cohen, L. G. (1998). Rapid plasticity of human cortical movement representation induced by practice. *Journal of Neurophysiology, 79*(2), 1117–1123.

Cohen, L. G., Celnik, P., Pascual-Leone, A., Corwell, B., Falz, L., Dambrosia, J., et al. (1997). Functional relevance of cross-modal plasticity in blind humans. *Nature, 389*(6647), 180–183.

Conforto, A. B., Cohen, L. G., dos Santos, R. L., Scaff, M., & Marie, S. K. (2007). Effects of somatosensory stimulation on motor function in chronic cortico-subcortical strokes. *Journal of Neurology, 254*(3), 333–339.

Cramer, S. C. (2008). Repairing the human brain after stroke. II. Restorative therapies. *Annals of Neurology, 63*(5), 549–560.

Crisostomo, E. A., Duncan, P. W., Propst, M. A., Dawson, D. B., & Davis, J. N. (1988). Evidence that amphetamine with physical therapy promotes recovery of motor function in stroke patients. *Annals of Neurology, 23,* 94–97.

Decety, J., & Grèzes, J. (1999). Neural mechanisms subserving the perception of human actions. *Trends in Cognitive Sciences, 3,* 172–177.

Della-Maggiore, V., & McIntosh, A. R. (2005). Time course of changes in brain activity and functional connectivity associated with long-term adaptation to a rotational transformation. *Journal of Neurophysiology, 93,* 2254–2262.

Di Pellegrino, G., Fadiga, L., Fogassi, L., Gallese, V., & Rizzolatti, G. (1992). Understanding motor events: A neurophysiological study. *Experimental Brain Research, 91,* 176–180.

Doyon, J., Bellec, P., Amsel, R., Penhune, V., Monchi, O., Carrier, J., et al. (2009). Contributions of the basal ganglia and functionally related brain structures to motor learning. *Behavioral Brain Research, 199*(1), 61–75.

Driver, J., Blankenburg, F., Bestmann, S., Vanduffel, W., & Ruff, C. C. (2009). Concurrent brain-stimulation and neuroimaging for studies of cognition. *Trends in Cognitive Sciences, 13*(7), 319–327.

Dudai, Y. (2004). The neurobiology of consolidations, or, how stable is the engram? *Annual Review of Psychology, 55,* 51–86.

Dum, R. P., & Strick, P. L. (2002). Motor areas in the frontal lobe of the primate. *Physiology and Behavior, 77,* 677–682.

Duque, J., Mazzocchio, R., Stefan, K., Hummel, F., Olivier, E., & Cohen, L. G. (2008). Memory formation in the motor cortex ipsilateral to a training hand. *Cerebral Cortex, 18*(6), 1395–1406.

Fadiga, L., Craighero, L., & Olivier, E. (2005). Human motor cortex excitability during the perception of others' action. *Current Opinion in Neurobiology, 15*(2), 213–218.

Fadiga, L., Fogassi, L., Pavesi, G., & Rizzolatti, G. (1995). Motor facilitation during action observation: A magnetic stimulation study. *Journal of Neurophysiology, 73*(6), 2608–2611.

Feeney, D. M., Gonzalez, A., & Law, W. A. (1982). Amphetamine, haloperidol, and experience interact to affect rate of recovery after motor cortex injury. *Science, 217*(4562), 855–857.

Fischer, S., Nitschke, M. F., Melchert, U. H., Erdmann, C., & Born, J. (2005). Motor memory consolidation in sleep shapes more effective neuronal representations. *Journal of Neuroscience, 25*(49), 11248–11255.

Fitts, P. M., & Posner, M. I. (1967). *Human performance.* Belmont, CA: Brooks/Cole Publishing.

Floel, A., Breitenstein, C., Hummel, F., Celnik, P., Gingert, C., Sawaki, L., et al. (2005). Dopaminergic influences on formation of a motor memory. *Annals of Neurology, 58*(1), 121–130.

Floel, A., & Cohen, L. G. (2010). Recovery of function in humans: Cortical stimulation and pharmacological treatments after stroke. *Neurobiology of Disease, 37*(2), 243–251.

Floel, A., Garraux, G., Xu, B., Breitenstein, C., Knecht, S., Herscovitch, P., et al. (2008). Levodopa increases memory encoding and dopamine release in the striatum in the elderly. *Neurobiology of Aging, 29*(2), 267–279.

Floel, A., Hummel, F., Breitenstein, C., Knecht, S., & Cohen, L. G. (2005). Dopaminergic effects on encoding of a motor memory in chronic stroke. *Neurology, 65*(3), 472–474.

Fogassi, L., Ferrari, P. F., Gesierich, B., Rozzi, S., Chersi, F., & Rizzolatti, G. (2005). Parietal lobe: From action organization to intention understanding. *Science, 308,* 662–667.

Fregni, F., & Pascual-Leone, A. (2007). Technology insight: Noninvasive brain stimulation in neurology – perspectives on the therapeutic potential of rTMS and tDCS. *Nature Clinical Practice Neurology, 3*(7), 383–393.

Fritsch, B., Reis, J., Martinowich, K., Schambra, H. M., Ji, Y., Cohen, L. G., et al. (2010). Direct current stimulation promotes BDNF-dependent synaptic plasticity: Potential implications for motor learning. *Neuron, 66*(2), 198–204.

Galea, J. M., Albert, N. B., Ditye, T., & Miall, R. C. (2010). Disruption of the dorsolateral prefrontal cortex facilitates the consolidation of procedural skills. *Journal of Cognitive Neuroscience, 22*(6), 1158–1164.

Galea, J. M., & Celnik, P. (2009). Brain polarization enhances the formation and retention of motor memories. *Journal of Neurophysiology, 102*(1), 294–301.

Galea, J. M., Vazquez, A., Pasricha, N., Orban de Xivry, J. J., & Celnik, P. (2011). Dissociating the roles of the cerebellum and motor cortex during adaptive learning: The motor cortex retains what the cerebellum learns. *Cerebral Cortex, 21*(8), 1761–1770.

Gallese, V., Fadiga, L., Fogassi, L., & Rizzolatti, G. (1996). Action recognition in the premotor cortex. *Brain, 119,* 593–609.

Gallese, V., Fogassi, L., Fadiga, L., & Rizzolatti, G. (2002). Action representation and the inferior parietal lobule. In W. Prinz & B. Hommel (Eds.), *Attention and performance: XIX. Common mechanisms in perception and action* (pp. 247–266). Oxford, UK: Oxford University Press.

Gentili, R. J., Bradberry, T. J., Oh, H., Hatfield, B. D., & Contreras Vidal, J. L. (2011). Cerebral cortical dynamics during visuomotor transformation: Adaptation to a cognitive-motor executive challenge. *Psychophysiology, 48*(6), 813–824.

Ghilardi, M. F., Moisello, C., Silvestri, G., Ghez, C., & Krakauer, J. W. (2009). Learning of a sequential motor skill comprises explicit and implicit components that consolidate differently. *Journal of Neurophysiology, 101*(5), 2218–2229.

Gladstone, D. J., Danells, C. J., Armesto, A., McIlroy, W. E., Staines, W. R., Graham, S. J., et al. (2006). Subacute therapy with amphetamine and rehabilitation for stroke study investigators. Physiotherapy coupled with dextroamphetamine for rehabilitation after hemiparetic stroke: A randomized, double-blind, placebo-controlled trial. *Stroke, 37*(1), 179–185.

Grèzes, J., & Decety, J. (2001). Functional anatomy of execution, mental simulation, observation, and verb generation of actions: A meta-analysis. *Human Brain Mapping, 12*(1), 1–19.

Hadipour-Niktarash, A., Lee, C. K., Desmond, J. E., & Shadmehr, R. (2007). Impairment of retention but not acquisition of a visuomotor skill through time-dependent disruption of primary motor cortex. *Journal of Neuroscience, 27*(49), 13413–13419.

Hallett, M. (2000). Transcranial magnetic stimulation and the human brain. *Nature, 406*(6792), 147–150.

Hanakawa, T., Mima, T., Matsumoto, R., Abe, M., Inouchi, M., Urayama, S., et al. (2009). Stimulus-response profile during single-pulse transcranial magnetic stimulation to the primary motor cortex. *Cerebral Cortex, 19*(11), 2605–2615.

Hesse, S., Werner, C., Schonhardt, E. M., Bardeleben, A., Jenrich, W., & Kirker, S. G. (2007). Combined transcranial direct current stimulation and robot-assisted arm training in subacute stroke patients: A pilot study. *Restorative Neurology and Neuroscience, 25*(1), 9–15.

Honda, M., Deiber, M. P., Ibanez, V., Pascual-Leone, A., Zhuang, P., & Hallett, M. (1998). Dynamic cortical involvement in implicit and explicit motor sequence learning. A PET study. *Brain, 121*(11), 2159–2173.

Huang, Y. Z., Edwards, M. J., Rounis, E., Bhatia, K. P., & Rothwell, J. C. (2005). Theta burst stimulation of the human motor cortex. *Neuron, 45*(2), 201–206.

Huang, V. S., & Krakauer, J. W. (2009). Robotic neurorehabilitation: A computational motor learning perspective. *Journal of Neuroengineering and Rehabilitation, 6,* 5.

Hummel, F., Celnik, P., Giraux, P., Floel, A., Wu, W. H., Gerloff, C., et al. (2005). Effects of non-invasive cortical stimulation on skilled motor function in chronic stroke. *Brain, 128*(3), 490–499.

Hummel, F. C., & Cohen, L. G. (2006). Non-invasive brain stimulation: A new strategy to improve neurorehabilitation after stroke? *Lancet Neurology, 5*(8), 708–712.

Hunter, T., Sacco, P., Nitsche, M. A., & Turner, D. L. (2009). Modulation of internal model formation during force field-induced motor learning by anodal transcranial direct current stimulation of primary motor cortex. *Journal of Physiology, 587*(12), 2949–2961.

Kaelin-Lang, A., Luft, A. R., Sawaki, L., Burstein, A. H., Sohn, Y. H., & Cohen, L. G. (2002). Modulation of human corticomotor excitability by somatosensory input. *Journal of Physiology, 540*(2), 623–633.

Kantak, S. S., Sullivan, K. J., Fisher, B. E., Knowlton, B. J., & Winstein, C. J. (2010). Neural substrates of motor memory consolidation depend on practice structure. *Nature Neuroscience, 13*(8), 923–925.

Kapur, N. (1996). Paradoxical functional facilitation in brain-behavior research: A critical review. *Brain, 119,* 1775–1790.

Karni, A., Meyer, G., Jezzard, P., Adams, M. M., Turner, R., & Ungerleider, L. G. (1995). Functional MRI evidence for adult motor cortex plasticity during motor skill learning. *Nature, 377*(6545), 155–158.

Keisler, A., & Shadmehr, R. A. (2010). Shared resource between declarative memory and motor memory. *Journal of Neuroscience, 30*(44), 14817–14823.

Kim, Y. H., Park, J. W., Ko, M. H., Jang, S. H., & Lee, P. K. (2004). Facilitative effect of high frequency subthreshold repetitive transcranial magnetic stimulation on complex sequential motor learning in humans. *Neuroscience Letters, 367*(2), 181–185.

Kim, Y. H., You, S. H., Ko, M. H., Park, J. W., Lee, K. H., Jang, S. H., et al. (2006). Repetitive transcranial magnetic stimulation-induced corticomotor excitability and associated motor skill acquisition in chronic stroke. *Stroke, 37*(6), 1471–1476.

Kinsbourne, M. (1977). Hemi-neglect and hemisphere rivalry. *Advances in Neurology, 18,* 41–49.

Kleim, J. A., Chan, S., Pringle, E., Schallert, K., Procaccio, V., Jimenez, R., & Cramer, S. C. (2006). BDNF val66met polymorphism is associated with modified experience-dependent plasticity in human motor cortex. *Nature Neuroscience, 9*(6), 735–737.

Kobayashi, M., Hutchinson, S., Theoret, H., Schlaug, G., & Pascual-Leone, A. (2004). Repetitive TMS of the motor cortex improves ipsilateral sequential simple finger movements. *Neurology, 62*(1), 91–98.

Kobayashi, M., Theoret, H., & Pascual-Leone, A. (2009). Suppression of ipsilateral motor cortex facilitates motor skill learning. *European Journal of Neuroscience, 29*(4), 833–836.

Koch, G., & Rothwell, J. C. (2009). TMS investigations into the task-dependent functional interplay between human posterior parietal and motor cortex. *Behavioural Brain Research, 202*(2), 147–152.

Koganemaru, S., Mima, T., Thabit, M. N., Ikkaku, T., Shimada, K., Kanematsu, M., et al. (2010). Recovery of upper-limb function due to enhanced use-dependent plasticity in chronic stroke patients. *Brain, 133*(11), 3373–3384.

Krakauer, J. W. (2006). Motor learning: Its relevance to stroke recovery and neurorehabilitation. *Current Opinion in Neurology, 19*(1), 84–90.

Krakauer, J. W. (2009). Motor learning and consolidation: The case of visuomotor rotation. *Advances in Experimental Medicine and Biology, 629,* 405–421.

Krakauer, J. W., Ghez, C., & Ghilardi, M. F. (2005). Adaptation to visuomotor transformations: Consolidation, interference, and forgetting. *Journal of Neuroscience, 25*(2), 473–478.

Krakauer, J. W., & Shadmehr, R. (2006). Consolidation of motor memory. *Trends in Neuroscience, 29*(1), 58–64.

Kuo, M. F., Unger, M., Liebetanz, D., Lang, N., Tergau, F., Paulus, W., et al. (2008). Limited impact of homeostatic plasticity on motor learning in humans. *Neuropsychologia, 46*(8), 2122–2128.

Kwakkel, G., Kollen, B. J., & Krebs, H. I. (2008). Effects of robot-assisted therapy on upper limb recovery after stroke: A systematic review. *Neurorehabilitation and Neural Repair, 22*(2), 111–121.

Lang, N., Siebner, H. R., Ward, N. S., Lee, L., Nitsche, M. A., Paulus, W., et al. (2005). How does transcranial DC stimulation of the primary motor cortex alter regional neuronal activity in the human brain? *European Journal of Neuroscience, 22*(2), 495–504.

Levin, M. F., Kleim, J. A., & Wolf, S. L. (2009). What do motor "recovery" and "compensation" mean in patients following stroke? *Neurorehabilitation and Neural Repair, 23*(4), 313–319.

Liepert, J., Bauder, H., Miltner, W. H. R., Taub, E., & Weiller, C. (2000). Treatment-induced cortical reorganization after stroke in humans. *Stroke, 31*(6), 1210–1216.

Liepert, J., Miltner, W. H. R., Bauder, H., Sommer, M., Dettmers, C., Taub, E., et al. (1998). Motor cortex plasticity during constraint-induced movement therapy in stroke patients. *Neuroscience Letters, 250*(1), 5–8.

Lindenberg, R., Renga, V., Zhu, L. L., Nair, D., & Schlaug, G. (2010). Bihemispheric brain stimulation facilitates motor recovery in chronic stroke patients. *Neurology, 75*(24), 2176–2184.

Lo, A. C., Guarino, P., Krebs, H. I., Volpe, B. T., Bever, C. T., Duncan, P. W., et al. (2009). Multicenter randomized trial of robot-assisted rehabilitation for chronic stroke: Methods and entry characteristics for VA ROBOTICS. *Neurorehabilitation and Neural Repair, 23*(8), 775–783.

Lo, A. C., Guarino, P. D., Richards, L. G., Haselkorn, J. K., Wittenberg, G. F., Federman, D. G., et al. (2010). Robot-assisted therapy for long-term upper-limb impairment after stroke. *New England Journal of Medicine, 362*(19), 1772–1783.

Luft, A. R., & Buitrago, M. M. (2005). Stages of motor skill learning. *Molecular Neurobiology, 32*(3), 205–216.

Luft, A. R., McCombe-Waller, S., Whitall, J., Forrester, L. W., Macko, R., et al. (2004). Repetitive bilateral arm training and motor cortex activation in chronic stroke: A randomized controlled trial. *Journal of American Medical Association, 292*(15), 1853–1861.

Lui, F., Buccino, G., Duzzi, D., Benuzzi, F., Crisi, G., Baraldi, P., et al. (2008). Neural substrates for observing and imagining non object-directed actions. *Social Neuroscience, 3*(3–4), 261–275.

Malcolm, M. P., Triggs, W. J., Light, K. E., Gonzalez Rothi, L. J., Wu, S., Reid, K., et al. (2007). Repetitive transcranial magnetic stimulation as an adjunct to constraint-induced therapy: An exploratory randomized controlled trial. *American Journal of Physical Medicine and Rehabilitation, 86*(9), 707–715.

Martinsson, L., Eksborg, S., & Wahlgren, N. G. (2003). Intensive early physiotherapy combined with dexamphetamine treatment in severe stroke: A randomized, controlled pilot study. *Cerebrovascular Disease*, *16*, 338–345.

Mattar, A. A. G., & Gribble, P. L. (2005). Motor learning by observing. *Neuron*, *46*(1), 153–160.

McGaugh, J. L. (2000). Memory – a century of consolidation. *Science*, *287*(5451), 248–251.

McHughen, S. A., Rodriguez, P. F., Kleim, J. A., Kleim, E. D., Marchal Crespo, L., Procaccio, V., & Cramer, S. C. (2010). BDNF val66met polymorphism influences motor system function in the human brain. *Cerebral Cortex*, *20*(5), 1254–1262.

Mima, T., Sadato, N., Yazawa, S., Hanakawa, T., Fukuyama, H., Yonekura, Y., & Shibasaki, H. (1999). Brain structures related to active and passive finger movements in man. *Brain*, *122*, 1989–1997.

Miniussi, C., Cappa, S. F., Cohen, L. G., Floel, A., Fregni, F., Nitsche, M. A., et al. (2008). Efficacy of repetitive transcranial magnetic stimulation/transcranial direct current stimulation in cognitive neurorehabilitation. *Brain Stimulation*, *1*(4), 326–336.

Miniussi, C., & Rossini, P. M. (2011). Transcranial magnetic stimulation in cognitive rehabilitation. *Neuropsychological Rehabilitation*, *21*(5), 579–601.

Moliadze, V., Antal, A., & Paulus, W. (2010). Boosting brain excitability by transcranial high frequency stimulation in the ripple range. *Journal of Physiology*, *588*(24), 4891–4904.

Muellbacher, W., Ziemann, U., Wissel, J., Dang, N., Kofler, M., Facchini, S., et al. (2002). Early consolidation in human primary motor cortex. *Nature*, *415*(6872), 640–644.

Nissen, M., & Bullemer, P. (1987). Attentional requirements of learning: Evidence from performance measures. *Cognitive Psychology*, *19*, 1–32.

Nitsche, M. A., Cohen, L. G., Wassermann, E. M., Priori, A., Lang, N., Antal, A., et al. (2008). Transcranial direct current stimulation: State of the art. *Brain Stimulation*, *1*(3), 206–223.

Nitsche, M. A., & Paulus, W. (2000). Excitability changes induced in the human motor cortex by weak transcranial direct current stimulation. *Journal of Physiology*, *3*, 633–639.

Nitsche, M. A., Schauenburg, A., Lang, N., Liebetanz, D., Exner, C., Paulus, W., et al. (2003). Facilitation of implicit motor learning by weak transcranial direct current stimulation of the primary motor cortex in the human. *Journal of Cognitive Neuroscience*, *15*(4), 619–626.

Nudo, J. R., Wise, B. M., SiFuentes, F. S., & Milliken, G. W. (1996). Neural substrates for the effects of rehabilitative training on motor recovery after ischemic infarct. *Science*, *272*(5269), 1791–1794.

Orban de Xivry, J. J., Criscimagna-Hemminger, S. E., & Schadmehr, R. (2011). Contributions of the motor cortex to adaptive control of reaching depend on the perturbation schedule. *Cerebral Cortex*, *21*(7), 1475–1484.

Pascual-Leone, A., Dang, N., Cohen, L. G., Brasil-Neto, J. P., Cammarota, A., & Hallett, M. (1995). Modulation of muscle responses evoked by transcranial magnetic stimulation during the acquisition of newfine motor skills. *Journal of Neurophysiology*, *74*, 1037–1045.

Pascual-Leone, A., Walsh, V., & Rothwell, J. (2000). Transcranial magnetic stimulation in cognitive neuroscience – virtual lesion, chronometry, and functional connectivity. *Current Opinion in Neurobiology*, *10*(2), 232–237.

Paus, T. (2005). Inferring causality in brain images: A perturbation approach. *Philosophical Transactions of the Royal Society of London, Series B, Biological Sciences*, *360*(1457), 1109–1114.

Paz, R., Boraud, T., Natan, C., Bergman, H., & Vaadia, E. (2003). Preparatory activity in motor cortex reflects learning of local visuomotor skills. *Nature Neuroscience*, *6*(8), 882–890.

Paz, R., & Vaadia, E. (2004). Specificity of sensorimotor learning and the neural code: Neuronal representations in the primary motor cortex. *Journal of Physiology Paris*, *98*(4–6), 331–348.

Perez, M. A., & Cohen, L. G. (2008). Mechanisms underlying functional changes in the primary motor cortex ipsilateral to an active hand. *Journal of Neuroscience, 28*(22), 5631–5640.

Perez, M. A., Tanaka, S., Wise, S. P., Sadato, N., Tanabe, H. C., Willingham, D. T., et al. (2007). Neural substrates of intermanual transfer of a newly acquired motor skill. *Current Biology, 17*(21), 1896–1902.

Perez, M. A., Tanaka, S., Wise, S. P., Willingham, D. T., & Cohen, L. G. (2008). Time-specific contribution of the supplementary motor area to intermanual transfer of procedural knowledge. *Journal of Neuroscience, 28*(39), 9664–9669.

Petrosini, L., Graziano, A., Mandolesi, L., Neri, P., Molinari, M., & Leggio, M. G. (2003). Watch how to do it! New advances in learning by observation. *Brain Research Reviews, 42*(3), 252–264.

Polanía, R., Nitsche, M. A., & Paulus, W. (2011). Modulating functional connectivity patterns and topological functional organization of the human brain with transcranial direct current stimulation. *Human Brain Mapping, 32*(8), 1236–1249.

Porro, C. A., Facchin, P., Fusi, S., Dri, G., & Fadiga, L. (2007). Enhancement of force after action observation: Behavioural and neurophysiological studies. *Neuropsychologia, 45*(13), 3114–3121.

Prange, G. B., Jannink, M. J., Groothuis-Oudshoorn, C. G., Hermens, H. J., & Ijzerman, M. J. (2006). Systematic review of the effect of robot-aided therapy on recovery of the hemiparetic arm after stroke. *Journal of Rehabilitation Research and Development, 43*(2), 171–184.

Ranganathan, V. K., Siemionow, V., Liu, J. Z., Sahgal, V., & Yue, G. H. (2004). From mental power to muscle power – gaining strength by using the mind. *Neuropsychologia, 42,* 944–956.

Redding, G. M, & Wallace, B. (1996). Adaptive spatial alignment and strategic perceptual-motor control. *Journal of Experimental Psychology: Human Perception and Performance, 22,* 379–394.

Reding, M. J., Solomon, B., & Borucki, S. J. (1995). Effect of dextroamphetamine on motor recovery after stroke. *Neurology, 45,* A222.

Reis, J., Robertson, E., Krakauer, J. W., Rothwell, J., Marshall, L., Gerloff, C., et al. (2008). Consensus: "Can tDCS and TMS enhance motor learning and memory formation?" *Brain Stimulation, 1*(4), 363–369.

Reis, J., Schambra, H. M., Cohen, L. G., Buch, E. R., Fritsch, B., Zarahn, E., et al. (2009). Non-invasive cortical stimulation enhances motor skill acquisition over multiple days through an effect on consolidation. *Proceedings of the National Academy of Sciences of the United States of America, 106*(5), 1590–1595.

Richardson, A. G., Overduin, S. A., Valero-Cabre, A., Padoa-Schioppa, C., Pascual-Leone, A., Bizzi, E., et al. (2006). Disruption of primary motor cortex before learning impairs memory of movement dynamics. *Journal of Neuroscience, 26*(48), 12466–12470.

Rioult-Pedotti, M. S., Friedman, D., Hess, G., & Donoghue, J. P. (1998). Strengthening of horizontal cortical connections following skill learning. *Nature Neuroscience, 1*(3), 230–234.

Rizzolatti, G., Fadiga, L., Gallese, V., & Fogassi, L. (1996). Premotor cortex and the recognition of motor actions. *Cognitive Brain Research, 3,* 131–141.

Rizzolatti, G., Fadiga, L., Matelli, M., Bettinardi, V., Paulesu, E., Perani, D., et al. (1996). Localization of grasp representations in humans by PET: 1. Observation versus execution. *Experimental Brain Research, 111,* 246–252.

Robertson, E. M. (2007). The serial reaction time task: Implicit motor skill learning? *Journal of Neuroscience, 27*(38), 10073–10075.

Robertson, E. M., & Cohen, D. A. (2006). Understanding consolidation through the architecture of memories. *Neuroscientist, 12*(3), 261–271.

Robertson, E. M., Pascual-Leone, A., & Miall, R. C. (2004). Current concepts in procedural consolidation. *Nature Reviews Neuroscience, 5*(7), 576–582.

Robertson, E. M., Pascual-Leone, A., & Press, D. Z. (2004). Awareness modifies the skill-learning benefits of sleep. *Current Biology, 14*(3), 208–212.

Robertson, E. M., Press, D. Z., & Pascual-Leone, A. (2005). Off-line learning and the primary motor cortex. *Journal of Neuroscience, 25*(27), 6372–6378.

Robertson, E. M., Theoret, H., & Pascual-Leone, A. (2003). Studies in cognition: The problems solved and created by transcranial magnetic stimulation. *Journal of Cognitive Neuroscience, 15*(7), 948–960.

Rosser, N., Heuschmann, P., Wersching, H., Breitenstein, C., Knecht, S., & Floel, A. (2008). Levodopa improves procedural motor learning in chronic stroke patients. *Archives of Physical Medicine and Rehabilitation, 89,* 1633–1641.

Sandrini, M., Umiltà, C., & Rusconi, E. (2011). The use of transcranial magnetic stimulation in cognitive neuroscience: A new synthesis of methodological issues. *Neuroscience and Biobehavioral Reviews, 35*(3), 516–536.

Savion-Lemieux, T., & Penhune, V. B. (2005). The effects of practice and delay on motor skill learning and retention. *Experimental Brain Research, 161,* 423–431.

Sawaki, L., Wu, C. W., Kaelin-Lang, A., & Cohen, L. G. (2006). Effects of somatosensory stimulation on use-dependent plasticity in chronic stroke. *Stroke, 37*(1), 246–247.

Schambra, H. M., Sawaki, L., & Cohen, L. G. (2003). Modulation of excitability of human motor cortex (M1) by 1 Hz transcranial magnetic stimulation of the contralateral M1. *Clinical Neurophysiology, 114*(1), 130–133.

Schmidt, R. A. (1988). *Motor control and learning: A behavioral emphasis* (2nd ed.). Champaign, IL: Human Kinetics.

Seidler, R. D. (2010). Neural correlates of motor learning, transfer of learning, and learning to learn. *Exercise and Sport Sciences Reviews, 38*(1), 3–9.

Shadmehr, R., & Brashers-Krug, T. (1997). Functional stages in the formation of human long-term motor memory. *Journal of Neuroscience, 17*(1), 409–419.

Shadmehr, R., & Holcomb, H. H. (1997). Neural correlates of motor memory consolidation. *Science, 277*(5327), 821–825.

Shadmehr, R., & Krakauer, J. W. (2008). A computational neuroanatomy for motor control. *Experimental Brain Research, 185*(3), 359–381.

Shadmehr, R., & Mussa-Ivaldi, F. A. (1994). Adaptive representation of dynamics during learning of a motor task. *Journal of Neuroscience, 14*(5), 3208–3224.

Shadmehr, R., & Wise, S. P. (2005). *The computational neurobiology of reaching and pointing: A foundation for motor learning.* Cambridge, MA: The MIT Press.

Siebner, H. R., Bergmann, T. O., Bestmann, S., Massimini, M., Johansen-Berg, H., Mochizuki, H., et al. (2009). Consensus paper: Combining transcranial stimulation with neuroimaging. *Brain Stimulation, 2*(2), 58–80.

Sonde, L., Nordstrom, M., Nilsson, C. G., Lokk, J., & Viitanen, M. (2001). A double-blind placebo-controlled study of the effects of amphetamine and physiotherapy after stroke. *Cerebrovascular Disease, 17,* 590–599.

Stefan, K., Classen, J., Celnik, P., & Cohen, L. G. (2008). Concurrent action observation modulates practice-induced motor memory formation. *European Journal of Neuroscience, 27*(3), 730–738.

Stefan, K., Cohen, L. G., Duque, J., Mazzocchio, R., Celnik, P., Sawaki, L., et al. (2005). Formation of a motor memory by action observation. *Journal of Neuroscience, 25*(41), 9339–9346.

Swayne, O. B., Dymyan, M., Teo, J. H., Reis, J., Rothwell, J. C., & Cohen, L. G. (2010). Levodopa results in offline gains and decreased forgetting of a newly learned motor skill after chronic stroke. *Society for Neuroscience 40th Annual Meeting, 898.2.*

Tanaka, S., Hanakawa, T., Honda, M., & Watanabe, K. (2009). Enhancement of pinch force in the lower leg by anodal transcranial direct current stimulation. *Experimental Brain Research, 196*(3), 459–465.

Tanaka, S., Honda, M., Hanakawa, T., & Cohen, L. G. (2010). Differential contribution of the supplementary motor area to stabilization of a procedural motor skill acquired through different practice schedules. *Cerebral Cortex, 20*(9), 2114–2121.

Tanaka, S., Takeda, K., Otaka, Y., Kita, K., Osu, R., Honda, M., et al. (2011). Single session of transcranial direct current stimulation transiently increases knee extensor force in patients with hemiparetic stroke. *Neurorehabiltation and Neural Repair, 25*(6), 537–548.

Tanaka, S., & Watanabe, K. (2009). Transcranial direct current stimulation – a new tool for human cognitive neuroscience. *Brain and Nerve, 61*(1), 53–64.

Taub, E., Uswatte, G., King, D. K., Morris, D., Crago, J. E., & Chatterjee, A. (2006). A placebo-controlled trial of constraint-induced movement therapy for upper extremity after stroke. *Stroke, 37*(4), 1045–1049.

Tecchio, F., Zappasodi, F., Assenza, G., Tombini, M., Vollaro, S., Barbati, G., et al. (2010). Anodal transcranial direct current stimulation enhances procedural consolidation. *Journal of Neurophysiology, 104*(2), 1134–1140.

Terney, D., Chaieb, L., Moliadze, V., Antal, A., & Paulus, W. (2008). Increasing human brain excitability by transcranial high-frequency random noise stimulation. *Journal of Neuroscience, 28*(52), 14147–14155.

Theoret, H., Kobayashi, M., Valero-Cabre, A., & Pascual-Leone, A. (2003). Exploring paradoxical functional facilitation with TMS. *Supplements of Clinical Neurophysiology, 56,* 211–219.

Thut, G., & Miniussi, C. (2009). New insights into rhythmic brain activity from TMS-EEG studies. *Trends in Cognitive Sciences, 13*(4), 182–189.

Torriero, S., Oliveri, M., Koch, G., Caltagirone, C., & Petrosini, L. (2007). The what and how of observational learning. *Journal of Cognitive Neuroscience, 19*(10), 1656–1663.

Torriero, S., Oliveri, M., Koch, G., Lo Gerfo, E., Salerno, S., Ferlazzo, F., et al. (2011). Changes in cerebello-motor connectivity during procedural learning by actual execution and observation. *Journal of Cognitive Neuroscience, 23*(2), 338–348.

Tseng, Y. W., Diedrichsen, J., Krakauer, J. W., Shadmehr, R., & Bastian, A. J. (2007). Sensory prediction errors drive cerebellum–dependent adaptation of reaching. *Journal of Neurophysiology, 98*(1), 54–62.

Ungerleider, L. G., Doyon, J., & Karni, A. (2002). Imaging brain plasticity during motor skill learning. *Neurobiology of Learning and Memory, 78*(3), 553–564.

Vines, B. W., Nair, D. G., & Schlaug, G. (2006). Contralateral and ipsilateral motor effects after transcranial direct current stimulation. *Neuroreport, 17*(6), 671–674.

Walker, M. P., Brakefield, T., Hobson, J. A., & Stickgold, R. (2003). Dissociable stages of human memory consolidation and reconsolidation. *Nature, 425,* 616–620.

Walker, M. P., Brakefield, T., Morgan, A., Hobson, J. A., & Stickgold, R. (2002). Practice with sleep makes perfect: Sleep-dependent motor skill learning. *Neuron, 35*(1), 205–211.

Walker-Batson, D., Smith, P., Curtis, S., Unwin, H., & Greenlee, R. (1995). Amphetamine paired with physical therapy accelerates motor recovery after stroke – further evidence. *Stroke, 26,* 2254–2259.

Ward, N. S. (2006). The neural substrates of motor recovery after focal damage to the central nervous system. *Archives of Physical Medicine and Rehabilitation, 87,* 30–35.

Ward, N. S., & Cohen, L. G. (2004). Mechanisms underlying recovery of motor function after stroke. *Archives of Neurology, 61*(12), 1844–1848.

Wassermann, E. M., & Grafman, J. (2005). Recharging cognition with DC brain polarization. *Trends in Cognitive Sciences, 9*(11), 503–505.

Watkins, K. E., Strafella, A. P., & Paus, T. (2003). Seeing and hearing speech excites the motor system involved in speech production. *Neuropsychologia, 41,* 989–994.

Webster, B. R., Celnik, P. A., & Cohen, L. G. (2006). Noninvasive brain stimulation in stroke rehabilitation. *NeuroRx, 3*(4), 474–481.

Wilkinson, L., Teo, J. T., Obeso, I., Rothwell, J. C., & Jahanshahi, M. (2010). The contribution of primary motor cortex is essential for probabilistic implicit sequence learning: Evidence from theta burst magnetic stimulation. *Journal of Cognitive Neuroscience, 22*(3), 427–436.

Willingham, D. B., Nissen, M. J., & Bullemer, P. (1989). On the development of procedural knowledge. *Journal of Experimental Psychology: Learning, Memory and Cognition, 15*(6), 1047–1060.

Winstein, C. J., Miller, J. P., Blanton, S., Taub, E., Uswatte, G., Morris, D., et al. (2003). Methods for a multisite randomized trial to investigate the effect of constraint-induced movement therapy in improving upper extremity function among adults recovering from a cerebrovascular stroke. *Neurorehabilitation and Neural Repair, 17*(3), 137–152.

Wittenberg, G. F., Chen, R., Ishii, K., Bushara, K. O., Eckloff, S., Croarkin, E., et al. (2003). Constraint-induced therapy in stroke: Magnetic-stimulation motor maps and cerebral activation. *Neurorehabilitation and Neural Repair, 17*(1), 48–57.

Wolf, S. L., Winstein, C. J., Miller, J. P., Taub, E., Uswatte, G., Morris, D., et al. (2006). Effect of constraint-induced movement therapy on upper extremity function 3 to 9 months after stroke: The EXCITE randomized clinical trial. *Journal of the American Medical Association, 296*(17), 2095–2104.

Yozbatiran, N., & Cramer, S. C. (2006). Imaging motor recovery after stroke. *NeuroRx, 3*, 482–488.

Zaghi, S., Acar, M., Hultgren, B., Boggio, P. S., & Fregni, F. (2010). Noninvasive brain stimulation with low-intensity electrical currents: Putative mechanisms of action for direct and alternating current stimulation. *Neuroscientist, 16*(3), 285–307.

Zijdewind, I., Toering, S. T., & Bessem, B. (2003). Effects of imagery motor training on torque production of ankle plantar flexor muscles. *Muscle Nerve, 28,* 168–173.

NEUROPSYCHOLOGICAL REHABILITATION
2011, 21 (5), 676–702

Ameliorating spatial neglect with non-invasive brain stimulation: From pathophysiological concepts to novel treatment strategies

M. D. Hesse, R. Sparing, and G. R. Fink

Cognitive Neurology Section, Institute of Neuroscience and Medicine (INM-3), Research Center Juelich, Juelich, Germany, and Department of Neurology, University of Cologne, Germany

Neglect is a multifaceted, complex syndrome, in which patients fail to detect or respond to stimuli or parts thereof located contralesionally. Non-invasive brain stimulation by means of transcranial magnetic stimulation (TMS) or transcranial direct current stimulation (tDCS) may not only be useful as diagnostic research tools to explore the pathophysiology of neglect, but also for ameliorating its symptoms. Current approaches for modulating neglect non-invasively are mainly based on the neurophysiological concept of interhemispheric inhibition, which suggests a pathological overactivation of the contralesional hemisphere due to reduced inhibitory influences from the lesioned one. Within this framework, non-invasive brain stimulation mainly aims to inhibit the contralesional hemisphere to allow for rebalancing the system. However, facilitatory protocols for enhancing the ipsilesional neural circuitry might also prove useful. In this review, we discuss the contribution of non-invasive brain stimulation to current pathological concepts of neglect, the promising results of the proof-of-principle studies currently available as well as the specific aspects to be systematically investigated before broader clinical trials may eventually suggest a routine clinical application.

Correspondence should be addressed to Maike D. Hesse MD, Department of Neurology, University Hospital, University of Cologne, Kerpener Str. 62, 50924 Cologne, Germany. E-mail: m.hesse@fz-juelich.de

M. D. Hesse was supported by a grant of the Medical Faculty of the University of Cologne (Fortune No. 64/2010).

http://www.psypress.com/neurorehab   http://dx.doi.org/10.1080/09602011.2011.573931

Keywords: Non-invasive neuromodulation; Neglect; Stroke; Plasticity; Recovery of function.

INTRODUCTION

Starting off as a valuable diagnostic tool in clinical neurophysiology, non-invasive brain stimulation by means of transcranial magnetic stimulation (TMS) or transcranial direct current stimulation (tDCS) is now – with new stimulation protocols at hand allowing for prolonged effects – at the edge of becoming an adjuvant tool to support recovery of function after stroke (for reviews see Edwards & Fregni, 2008; Harris-Love & Cohen, 2006; Hummel & Cohen, 2006; for methods see Sparing & Mottaghy, 2008). In this review, we focus on the application of these techniques in the context of neglect, a complex, multifaceted multimodal disorder associated with a failure to attend to the contralesional side of space or an object, most commonly observed following right hemisphere damage. Neglect limits the degree of active participation in rehabilitation programmes and is thus associated with poor functional recovery and less successful social reintegration (Arene & Hillis, 2007). In the following we discuss the contribution of non-invasive brain stimulation to the characterisation of the pathophysiology underlying neglect as well as its potential to subserve rehabilitation.

SPATIAL NEGLECT: A MULTIFACETED SYNDROME

Spatial (hemi-)neglect or (hemi-)inattention are clinical terms used to describe a number of different clinical symptoms which have in common the patient's failure to attend, respond adequately, or orient voluntarily to people or objects located at the side of space contralateral to the lesion (Bisiach & Vallar, 2000; Heilman, Watson, & Valenstein, 2003; Husain, 2008; Mesulam, 1981). One particularly interesting feature observed in many cases of neglect is the phenomenon of extinction: Objects or targets may be particularly omitted if stimuli within the ipsilesional space are present that "magnetically" attract attention. Although visuospatial attention is mediated by a widely distributed network of areas in the parietal and frontal cortices of both hemispheres, chronic visuospatial neglect is most reliably observed following lesions in the right hemisphere, and in particular following damage to the posterior parietal cortex (PPC) and the temporoparietal junction (TPJ) (Corbetta, Kincade, Ollinger, McAvoy, & Shulman, 2000; Halligan, Fink, Marshall, & Vallar, 2003; Husain & Nachev, 2007; Mort et al., 2003; Vallar & Perani, 1986). Within the PPC, whether the right supramarginal gyrus (SMG) (Committeri et al., 2007; Doricchi & Tomaiuolo, 2003; Vallar & Perani, 1986) or the right angular gyrus (ANG) (Hillis et al, 2005; Mort et al., 2003) play a predominant role in the manifestation of neglect is still a matter of debate. Patients with neglect symptoms may not only present with cortical, but also with subcortical stroke. Consistent with previous hypotheses, damage to cortical regions may provoke modular deficits, whereas subcortical lesions may disrupt fronto-parietal connections and affect several cortical modules within a disturbed network, aggravating the clinical presentation (Bartolomeo, Thiebaut de Schotten, & Doricchi, 2007; Doricchi & Tomaiuolo, 2003; Verdon et al., 2010).

Different neuropsychological tests have been applied to test for symptoms of neglect. Traditionally neglect is assessed by the line bisection task, in which lines are typically bisected towards the ipsilesional side, or the length judgement task of pre-bisected lines (also known as the Landmark task), and by various cancellation tasks, scene copying, clock drawing or text reading, in which contralesional targets, object parts or words are omitted. Several dissociations of performance have been described for these tasks (e.g., Binder, Marshall, Lazar, Benjamin, & Mohr, 1992; Halligan & Marshall, 1992; Vallar, 1998). For example, Daffner, Ahern, Weintraub, and Mesulam (1990) reported an interesting case with two sequential focal right hemisphere strokes, the first affecting the right frontal lobe causing motor neglect and the second affecting the right parietal lobe eliciting additional perceptual-sensory aspects of neglect. Likewise, spatial attention within the personal or extrapersonal space may be differentially affected (Committeri et al., 2007; Halligan & Marshall, 1995; Weiss et al., 2000).

Individual reports focusing on different aspects of neglect caused difficulties in finding a clear correspondence between behavioural dissociations and different lesion localisations (Coulthard, Parton, & Husain, 2006). In order to overcome these difficulties, Verdon et al. (2010) used a battery of different clinical tests for a data-driven symptom-lesion mapping. Based on the performance in the individual tests, they identified distinct symptom-profile components related to perceptive/visuospatial, exploratory/visuomotor and allocentric/object-centred aspects of spatial neglect, which mapped to distinct lesion locations, namely the right inferior parietal lobule for the perceptive/visuospatial component, the right dorsolateral prefrontal cortex for the exploratory/visuomotor component, and deep temporal lobe regions for the allocentric/object-centred component.

In general, however, patients with neglect have relatively large lesions, which arc likely to disrupt several functional modules. The exact combination of deficits observed in an individual is thus likely to depend upon the extent and distribution of the lesion and its local and distant (i.e., diaschitic) effects (Bartolomeo et al., 2007; He et al., 2007; Verdon et al., 2010). Finally, compensatory strategies in one domain but not another may add to the multi-faceted nature of the syndrome.

NETWORKS OF ATTENTION AND THE CONCEPT OF INTERHEMISPHERIC RIVALRY

Going beyond concepts of localised specialised brain functions and their disturbance due to a focal lesion, neglect is more and more regarded in terms of a dysfunction and disequilibrium of the fronto-parietal networks of attention. Within these networks, spatial attention is controlled by both intra- and inter-hemispheric connections. Focusing on these aspects, the concept of inter-hemispheric rivalry originally proposed by Kinsbourne (1977, 1994) suggests that both parietal cortices exert reciprocal interhemispheric inhibition. Damage to the right parietal cortex causes disinhibition and thus pathological over-activation of the left hemisphere, aggravating the bias to attend to the right and hence to neglect the left side (Figure 1).

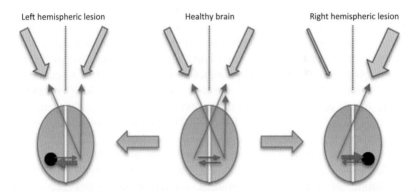

Figure 1. Model of interhemispheric rivalry within a simplified network of spatial attention. A right hemispheric dominance of attention is suggested to explain the predominant occurrence of neglect following right hemispheric lesions. The arrows in front of the head represent visual input, weighted by spatial attention according to their width. *Middle*: In the healthy brain, the left hemisphere directs attention to the right side of visual space (Bisiach & Vallar, 2000; Mesulam, 2002), while the right hemisphere accounts for both sides of space. Interhemispheric connections exert interhemispheric inhibition subserving spatial orientation depending on attentional selection (Rossi & Rossini, 2004). *Left*: Following left hemispheric lesions, the preserved right hemispheric (stimulus-driven) orienting compensates for a diminished voluntary exploration of the right hemispace. *Right*: A right hemispheric lesion results in diminished voluntary orienting towards the contralesional left hemispace in addition to a general lack of stimulus-driven attentional orientation. Interhemispheric inhibition adds to this attentional bias towards the right side of space by disinhibition of the left hemisphere, which in turn causes excessive inhibition from the left to the right hemisphere. [To view this figure in colour, please visit the online version of this journal.]

Recent findings indicate an even greater complexity than originally assigned to this network model, with two complementary networks mediating top-down and bottom-up mechanisms of attention: A bihemispheric dorsal frontoparietal network, including the intraparietal sulcus (IPS), the superior parietal lobule (SPL) and the frontal eye field, which mediates top-down control with voluntary attentional orientation to the contralateral hemispace, and a right-biased ventral frontoparietal network, including the right TPJ, midfrontal gyrus and the inferior frontal gyrus, which responds when behaviourally relevant objects or targets are detected (Corbetta et al., 2000; Corbetta and Shulman, 2002; Hopfinger, Buonocore, & Mangun, 2000). Neglect and its predominant occurrence following right hemispheric lesions may thus be explained by two complementary pathomechanisms: A right hemispheric lesion may result in diminished voluntary orienting towards the contralesional left hemispace in addition to a general lack of stimulus-driven attentional orientation. In contrast, following left hemispheric lesions, the preserved stimulus-driven orienting of attention might compensate for a diminished voluntary exploration of right hemispace. Furthermore, differential effects of lesions affecting the right PPC versus the right TPJ may be envisioned by this model.

Supporting evidence for the basic concept of interhemispheric rivalry stems from clinical observation of a patient who suffered from sequential strokes in both hemispheres with a severe unilateral spatial neglect after a first right-sided parietal infarct (involving the most caudal part of the right angular gyrus) and abrupt disappearance of the neglect after a second left-sided frontal infarct involving the left frontal eye field (Vuilleumier, Hester, Assal, & Regli, 1996). Further evidence supporting the concept of interhemispheric rivalry stems from fMRI showing hyperactivity of the left undamaged hemisphere in neglect patients (Corbetta, Kincade, Lewis, Snyder, & Spair, 2005). The concept of interhemispheric rivalry particularly provides an explanation for the phenomenon of extinction, with simultaneous presentation of a competing stimulus activating the intact hemisphere, thereby leading to a further suppression of the lesioned hemisphere, which reduces the "perceptual weight" of the contralesional stimulus. It also provides the basis for the main strategy of therapeutic non-invasive brain stimulation attempting to countervail this interhemispheric imbalance by inhibiting the over-active contralesional hemisphere, as we will discuss later.

ANIMAL RESEARCH ON NEGLECT

Few studies have used electrical brain stimulation in animal models to identify direct neuronal effects of these techniques on visual attention. Methodological constraints may account for this, since spatial accuracy of TMS in small animals with standard coils is poor and excessive coil heating may be associated with intensive stimulation. Thus, most important contributions from animal models result from other permanent and/or transient lesion techniques: In 1966 James Sprague published a seminal paper that described a visual recovery phenomenon in the cat that has since been called the "Sprague effect". In cats a large unilateral visual cortical lesion produces an enduring hemianopia (i.e., blindness in half of the visual field). Sprague observed a dramatic recovery of the cat's visual orienting ability to stimuli presented in the previously blind hemifield, when the superior colliculus contralateral to the cortical lesion was ablated. This remarkable observation demonstrated that a second lesion may at least in part counteract the effects of a first lesion and ameliorate symptoms induced by the first lesion. Later studies, using a method of reversible cooling deactivation in cats, could likewise demonstrate that visual neglect, induced by unilateral deactivation of the posterior parietal cortex, could be reversed by additional deactivation of the homologue area of the opposite hemisphere (Lomber and Payne, 1996; Lomber, Payne, Bilgetag, & Rushmore, 2002; Lynch & McLaren, 1989; Payne, Lomber, Rushmore, & Pascual-Leone, 2003; Payne & Rushmore, 2003). Valero-Cabré and co-workers finally succeeded in the development of rTMS and tDCS animal models. Stimulation of the cat parietal cortex modulated visual-spatial processing and induced visuotopically specific neglect-like syndromes using rTMS (Valero-Cabré, Pascual-Leone, & Rushmore, 2008, Valero-Cabré, Payne, & Pascual-Leone, 2007; Valero-Cabré Payne, Rushmore, Lomber, & Pascual-Leone, 2005; Valero-Cabré, Rushmore, & Payne, 2006) as well as using cathodal tDCS (Schweid, Rushmore, & Valero-Cabré, 2008).

INVESTIGATING VISUOSPATIAL FUNCTIONS IN HEALTHY SUBJECTS BY TMS AND tDCS

During the past two decades, the modulation of visuospatial functions by TMS contributed significantly to the refinement of our understanding of the pathophysiology underlying neglect. Researchers made use of the perturbation approach of TMS in order to create "virtual patients", by transiently inducing a neglect-like behaviour in normal subjects (for reviews see Bartolomeo, 2007; Fierro, Brighina, & Bisiach, 2006; Hillis, 2006; Minussi et al., 2008; Pascual-Leone, Walsh, & Rothwell, 2000; Utz, Dimova, Oppenlander, & Kerkhoff, 2010).

Similarly to the diagnostic testing of patients, different tasks were used to define "neglect-like symptoms" in healthy subjects, targeting different cortical areas for stimulation in order to determine those structures actually involved in the respective processing.

Behavioural tasks used to detect neglect-like symptoms

Visual extinction was investigated using a visuospatial detection task with single or bilateral targets presented to the right or left visual hemifield, generally at detection threshold. Decreased detection rates of left targets at bilateral simultaneous presentation were shown following right parietal TMS. This extinction-like phenomenon could be induced using rTMS (Hilgetag, Theoret, & Pascual-Leone, 2001; Jin & Hilgetag, 2008; Pascual-Leone et al., 1994), as well as single pulse TMS (Dambeck et al., 2006; Meister et al., 2006; Müri et al., 2002), but also by tDCS, as demonstrated lately by Sparing and coauthors (2009). Similarly, rTMS of the parietal cortex reduced detection of contralateral somatosensory stimuli at bilateral presentation (Nager, Wolters, Munte, & Johannes, 2004; Seyal, Ro, & Rafal, 1995).

Cued-reaction tasks using valid and invalid spatial cues suggest enhanced engagement as well as a reduced ability to disengage when stimuli are presented in the right hemispace following rTMS over the right parietal cortex, as reaction times to left targets following invalid right cues increased (Chambers, Stokes, Janko, & Mattingly, 2006; Rounis, Yarrow, & Rothwell, 2007; Rushworth, Ellison, & Walsh, 2001; Thut, Nietzel, & Pascual-Leone, 2005). This effect was not accomplished by rTMS over the left parietal cortex (Rushworth et al., 2001) or bilateral dorsolateral prefrontal cortex (DLPFC) (Rounis et al., 2007). Despite the fact that right parietal TMS modulates both visuospatial attention as well as visuospatial detection, these high-level cognitive functions do not seem to share linear or simple relationships, as the decrease in detection rates of masked stimuli and the increase in reaction times to invalidly cued targets did not correlate at the individual level (Babiloni et al., 2007).

Using the line bisection task or the Landmark task (i.e., judgements of pre-bisected lines), a clear rightward bias could be demonstrated following right parietal rTMS (Bjoertomt et al. 2002; Brighina et al., 2002; Fierro et al., 2000), as well as single-pulse TMS (Fierro, Brighina, Piazza, Oliveri, & Bisiach, 2001; Pourtois, Vandermeeren, Olivier, & de Gelder, 2001). Interestingly, using off-line high-frequency, i.e., excitatory, rTMS over 10 minutes before the judgements of pre-bisected lines, Kim et al. (2005) showed facilitative effects on visuospatial attention to the contralateral hemispace bilaterally, but found an inhibitory effect to the ipsilateral hemispace only in the left PPC. Ghacibeh et al. (2007) were able to dissect neglect into visuospatial and motor-intentional components by comparison of parietal and frontal rTMS. Subjects performed a line bisection task with the direct view on the hands precluded while the hand movements were presented on a video screen either in a direct or mirrored fashion. In contrast to right parietal rTMS, rTMS over the right frontal cortex caused a rightward deviation independent of the visual feedback.

To simulate better everyday behaviour, Nyffeler et al. (2008) used a visual exploration task with colour photographs of real-life scenes and monitored eye movements to evaluate attentional deficits as shown in neglect patients. Theta-burst stimulation (TBS), a recent protocol, originally used to induce long-term potentiation or long-term depression in brain slices (Larson, Wong, & Lynch, 1986), applied to the right PPC induced neglect-like behaviour with reduced eye movements and fixations to the left hemispace.

Targeted sites in brain stimulation studies on neglect

Compared to vascular lesions, which are variable in size and location within the vascular territories, TMS is capable of inducing much more focal and consistent lesions, allowing for a more precise mapping of brain function. The interindividual anatomical differences, however, need to be respected and addressed by appropriate targeting strategies (Sparing, Buelte, Meister, Paus, & Fink, 2008; Sparing, Hesse, & Fink, 2010; Sparing & Mottaghy, 2008).

Most studies demonstrated neglect-like symptoms induced by stimulation of the right PPC. In some of those studies, the left PPC, the occipital cortex, the prefrontal cortex and the superior temporal gyrus (STG) served for control. rTMS over the right dorsal PPC was shown to (1) cause visual extinction (Dambeck et al., 2006; Hilgetag et al., 2001), as well as a rightward bias in a line bisection task (Bjoertomt, Cowey, & Walsh, 2002; Ellison, Schindler, Pattison, & Milner, 2004; Ghacibeh et al., 2007; Oliveri & Vallar, 2009); (2) impair spatial reorientation to invalidly cued left targets (Rounis et al., 2007; Rushworth et al., 2001; Thut et al., 2005); and (3) enhance target detection in the ipsilesional hemispace (Chambers et al., 2006; Hilgetag et al., 2001). The differential roles particularly of the SMG and ANG within the PPC, however, are still a matter of debate: Rushworth et al. (2001) for instance demonstrated that rTMS over the right ANG increases reaction times to invalidly cued left targets with no effect of rTMS over the right supramarginal gyrus SMG, while Oliveri and Vallar (2009) induced a rightward bias in the line bisection task by rTMS over the right SMG, with stimulation over the right ANG as well as STG being ineffective. Most likely these differential results relate to the tasks and functional differences of ANG and SMG, respectively.

Evidence for the concept of interhemispheric rivalry

Apart from the animal and fMRI studies mentioned above, brain stimulation studies also provide evidence supporting the model of interhemispheric rivalry. Enhanced sensitivity and lowered detection thresholds within the hemispace ipsilateral to the stimulation have also been interpreted as being indicative of disinhibition of the contralateral hemisphere (Babiloni et al., 2007; Hilgetag et al., 2001; Seyal et al., 1995). Pathological hyperexcitability of the left hemisphere has recently been shown by a twin coil approach, with a conditioning pulse over the left PPC prior to the stimulation of the left motor cortex showing an increased left PPC-motor-cortex circuit excitability in neglect patients compared with right hemispheric stroke patients without neglect (Koch et al., 2008).

Most importantly, however, restorative features could be demonstrated in healthy subjects using double stimulation protocols: While confirming extinction-like phenomena following unilateral stimulation applied to the right parietal cortex, Dambeck et al. (2006) as well as Fierro et al. (2006) showed that paired bilateral TMS did not elicit neglect-like deficits in healthy subjects in a cued target-detection or line-bisection task, respectively. Thus, the contralateral pulse restored the neglect-like symptoms induced by the first pulse, most likely by rebalancing the system. Similarly, the initial rightward shift of mean cumulative fixation following TBS over right PPC (Cazzoli, Wurtz, Muri, Hess, & Nyffeler, 2009) could be reversed by TBS of left PPC. Importantly, left PPC stimulation alone had no significant effect on visual exploration. These findings indicate that bilateral inhibition restoring an interhemispheric imbalance ameliorates neglect symptoms.

Protocols used in brain stimulation studies on neglect

Different stimulation protocols have been used to induce neglect-like behaviour. Primarily, in an "on-line" approach, short trains of rTMS over seconds interfered with the neuronal processes underlying spatial processing as long as the targeted cortical area was stimulated (Bjoertomt et al., 2002; Ellison et al., 2004; Fierro et al., 2000; Muggleton et al., 2006; Pascual-Leone et al., 1994; Rushworth et al., 2001). Exploring these issues further, application of single TMS pulses investigated the timing of the underlying attentional processes within individual trials (Fierro et al., 2001; Pourtois et al., 2001). Other studies probed long trains of rTMS over minutes to demonstrate effects on attentional tasks administered immediately after the stimulation had ceased in an "off-line" approach (Hilgetag et al., 2001; Rounis et al., 2007; Thut et al., 2005). Duration of these post-stimulation effects (between 10 and 20 minutes), however, hardly lasted longer than the stimulation itself (between 10 and 25 minutes). The recent protocol of TBS proved capable of inducing longer lasting after-effects (Huang, Edwards, Rounis, Bhatia, & Rothwell, 2005). With respect to neglect, a TBS protocol consisting of repeated bursts of three pulses at 30Hz repeated over 44 seconds was shown to induce behavioural effects lasting 30 minutes (Nyffeler et al., 2006a). In addition, repeated TBS applications disproportionately prolonged the post-stimulation effects up to 32 hours (Nyffeler et al., 2006b), rendering these protocols more appropriate for putative treatment purposes. Similarly, the after-effects induced by tDCS, which delivers weak direct currents via two electrodes placed on the scalp to polarise neural tissue, are thought to potentially last up to a few hours (Fregni & Pascual-Leone, 2007; Nitsche & Paulus, 2000; Paulus, 2003; Sparing & Mottaghy, 2008; Wassermann & Grafman, 2005).

Facilitatory vs. inhibitory effects of non-invasive brain stimulation

Depending on the protocol used, brain stimulation may have opposite effects on the underlying brain tissue: low-frequency rTMS (1Hz), continuous TBS as well as cathodal tDCS are assumed to decrease cortical excitability, while high-frequency rTMS (5Hz), intermittent TBS as well as anodal tDCS primarily seem to enhance cortical excitability and thus seem to have facilitatory effects (Hallett, 2007; Nitsche and Paulus, 2000, 2001; Nitsche et al., 2005, 2008; Priori, Berardelli, Rona, Accornero, & Manfredi, 1998; Wagner, Valero-Cabre, & Pascual-Leone, 2007; Vallar & Bolognini, this issue). However, inter-individual variability, as well as state-dependent effects of brain stimulation, challenge this widely held assumption of a clear-cut dichotomy: Cortical preconditioning by rTMS or tDCS showed an enhancement, or even reversal, of inhibitory or facilitatory effects of the succeeding rTMS (Iyer, Schleper, & Wassermann, 2003; Siebner et al., 2004; Silvanto & Pascual-Leone, 2008). These findings point to the importance of taking the status of the targeted tissue into closer consideration, which should particularly apply for lesioned tissue following stroke.

NEUROREHABILITATIVE APPROACHES IN NEGLECT PATIENTS BY MEANS OF TMS AND tDCS

Based on the model of interhemisheric rivalry and the availability of facilitatory and inhibitory protocols, basically two approaches to use non-invasive brain stimulation in neglect patients are conceivable: Inhibiting the contralesional hemisphere and enhancing the lesioned hemisphere (Figure 2A). Most studies thus far have aimed to inhibit the contralateral hemisphere, more specifically, based on evidence for a central role of right parietal cortex in neglect, the left parietal cortex. These studies indeed affirmed that inhibitory rTMS of the unaffected left parietal cortex transiently improves contralesional visuospatial neglect and extinction (for an overview, see Table 1). However, previous TMS/rTMS studies on patients did not directly compare "inhibitory" and "facilitatory" stimulation protocols. In contrast, using tDCS, Sparing and co-authors (2009) observed a clear interaction between stimulation side and type of stimulation with both contralesional inhibition as well as ipsilesional facilitation ameliorating neglect symptoms (see Figure 2B). Ko and co-workers (2008) also demonstrated an enhancement of performance resulting from a "facilitatory" stimulation of the lesioned cortex in neglect patients. While for obvious reasons fully restoring functions of the lesioned site seems out of reach, facilitating protocols

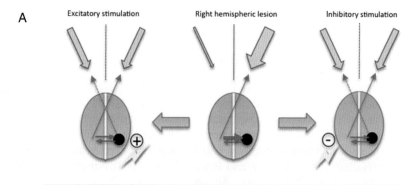

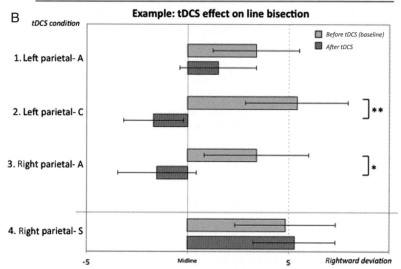

Figure 2A. Model of effect of non-invasive brain stimulation on brains with right hemispheric lesions. The arrows in front of the head represent visual input, weighted by spatial attention according to their width. *Middle*: A right hemispheric lesion causing diminished voluntary and stimulus-driven orienting towards the contralesional left hemispace, with interhemispheric inhibition enhancing this attentional bias. *Left*: Facilitating right parietal stimulation augments activity of the right hemisphere, increasing interhemispheric inhibition from the right to the left hemisphere and thereby rebalancing the interhemispheric interactions. *Right*: Inhibitory left parietal stimulation releases the right hemisphere from excessive inhibition by the left hemisphere, thus reconstituting interhemisphere balance of attentional networks. **2B.** Results adapted with permission from Sparing et al. (2009). Neglect patients were tested with a computerised line bisection task. In all four baseline conditions (bars in light grey), patients showed a rightward deviation reflecting left hemispatial neglect. Both, $tDCS_{anodal}$ of the lesioned (right) hemisphere (3), and $tDCS_{cathodal}$ of the unlesioned (left) hemisphere (2), caused a significant reduction in the rightward bias (mm). No significant modulatory effect on deviation was observed following $tDCS_{anodal}$ of the unlesioned hemisphere (1), or $tDCS_{sham}$ (4). A = $tDCS_{anodal}$; S = $tDCS_{sham}$; C = $tDCS_{cathodal}$. $^{**}p < .01$, $^{*} p < .05$. [To view this figure in colour, please visit the online version of this Journal.]

TABLE 1

Studies currently available evaluating the effects of TMS/tDCS in neglect patients

		Protocol /technique	Subjects	Time post stroke	Targeted region[1]	Main experimental task (test dates)	Main results
TMS	On-line	Oliveri et al., 1999	Single-pulse TMS 4 sessions (4 target regions) fig-of-eight coil, 110% MT	14 patients right BD (8 visuospatial hemineglect; 6 contralat. somatosensory deficits)	1–4 months	Frontal cortex (F3, F4), parietal cortex (P3, P4)	Discrimination of electrical tactile stimuli (on-line)	Left frontal TMS reduces contralesional extinction in patients with unilateral right brain damage
		Oliveri et al., 2001	25 Hz rTMS; trains of 10 pulses, fig-of-eight coil, 115% MT	5 patients right BD (1 P, 1 F, 1 F-T, 2 P-T lesion); 2 patients left BD (1 P-T, 1 F-P-T lesion)	1 to 48 weeks	Right / left parietal cortex (P5, P6)	Length judgement of prebisected lines (on-line)	rTMS of the unaffected hemisphere transiently decreased the magnitude of neglect
	Off-line, single session	Koch et al., 2008	1 Hz rTMS; 600 pulses, fig-of-eight coil, 90%/110% MT (Exp.1: twin-coil TMS; Exp.2: rTMS+twin-coil)	12 patients right BD (for lesion maps see original paper)	4 to 24 weeks	Left parietal cortex (P3), left motor cortex (M1) defined by TMS mapping	Measurement of MEP amplitude, naming of visual chimeric objects pre, post)	Neglect symptoms as well as pathological hyperexcitability of left PPC-M1 circuits (correlating with degree of neglect on clinical cancellation tests) are reduced following 1 Hz rTMS
		Nyffeler et al., 2009	Continuous TBS (801 pulses in 267 bursts of 3 pulses at 30 Hz, interburst interval 100 ms; 2 (or 4) trains of 44s in one session at 0, 15 (& 60, 75) min. round coil, 100% MT	11 patients right BD for lesion maps see original paper	2 weeks to 36 months	Left parietal cortex (P3), control: no stim., sham stimulation over vertex	Subtest of the Vienna Test System (2xTBS: pre, +1, 8h; 4xTBS: pre, +1, 3, 8, 24, 32, 96h)	Two TBS trains increased detection rate of and reduced reaction times to left targets for up to 8 hours. 4 TBS trains showed same effect for up to 32 hours, effect declines after 96h.
	Off-line, multiple session	Brighina et al., 2003	1 Hz rTMS; 900 pulses, 7 sessions (every other day) over 14 days, fig-of-eight coil, 90% MT	3 patients right BD (2 T-P, 1 F-P lesion)	3 to 5 months	Left parietal cortex (P5)	Length judgement of prebisected lines, line bisection, clock drawing (-2wks, pre, post, +2wks)	rTMS induced a significant improvement of visuo-spatial performance that remained quite unchanged after 15 days

(Continued)

Table 1. Continued.

	Protocol /technique	Subjects	Time post stroke	Targeted region[1]	Main experimental task (test dates)	Main results
Shindo et al., 2006	0.9 Hz rTMS; 900 pulses, 6 sessions within 14 days, fig-of-eight coil, 95% MT	2 patients right BD (1 F-P, 1 P-T)	6 months	Left parietal cortex (P5)	Subtests of the Behavioural Inattention Test (BIT) (−2wks, −1d, +1d, +2wks, +4wks, +6wks)	rTMS decreased unilateral spatial neglect for at least 6 weeks
Song et al., 2009	0.5 Hz rTMS; 450 pulses, 2 sessions each day over 14 days,	7 patients right BD (very heterogenous group)	3 to 8 weeks	Left parietal cortex (P3)	Line bisection and line cancellation tests (−2wks, pre, post, +2wks)	rTMS improved visual spatial neglect in both tests up to 14 days after treatment
Lim et al., 2010	Fig-of-eight coil, 90% MT 1 Hz rTMS; 900 pulses, 5 days/week for 2 weeks,fig-of-eight coil, 90% MT	7 patients right BD for lesion maps see original paper)	1 to 44 weeks	Left parietal cortex (P5)	Line bisection, Albert test (line cancellation) (−1d, +1d)	rTMS improved performance in line bisection test, but not line cancellation at end of treatment

targeting the lesioned hemisphere may still contribute to the amelioration of neglect. Whether this effect may be best achieved by direct enhancement of attention-mediating right hemispheric structures or interhemispheric inhibition on the contralesional cortex remains to be investigated.

Table 1 provides an overview of the studies currently available on non-invasive stimulation in the treatment of neglect. Studies vary with respect to many issues: Oliveri et al. studied on-line effects of single pulse (1999) as well as repetitive TMS (2001), on bilateral parietal cortex, while all other studies assessed off-line after-effects. Koch et al. (2008) demonstrated a reduction of neglect symptoms directly after a single session of rTMS along with the normalisation of a pathologically increased left PPC-M1 circuit excitability as assessed in a double stimulation approach. Using a new TBS stimulation protocol, Nyffeler, Cazzoli, Hess, and Muri (2009) pursued after-effects of two or four TBS trains vs. sham stimulation and control for up to 8 (2 x TBS) or 96 hours (4 x TBS). They showed an increased detection rate for stimuli presented in the left hemispace along with reduced reaction times for up to 32 hours following four TBS trains. Four further studies showed positive effects of multiple sessions of inhibitory low frequency rTMS over a period of two weeks with frequency of treatment ranging from three sessions per week to twice a day (Brighina et al., 2003; Lim, Kang, & Paik, 2010; Shindo et al., 2006; Song et al., 2009). Neglect symptoms were assessed prior to as well as after the period of intervention, without intermediate testing following individual sessions. Finally, two studies investigated the effects of single tDCS sessions showing improved figure cancellation and/or line bisection immediately after ipsilesional anodal and/or contralesional cathodal tDCS (Ko et al., 2008; Sparing et al., 2009).

Reviewing the findings of these heterogeneous studies currently available, some important methodological issues of therapeutic TMS/tDCS studies in visuospatial neglect become obvious, which we discuss below.

METHODOLOGICAL KEY POINTS

How to determine efficacy and clinical relevance of the treatment

As discussed above, neglect is a heterogeneous disorder with varying clinical presentations, lesion location and size of lesion. With inconsistent correlations of performance in different tests, it seems a challenging task to reliably measure the effects of neurorehabilitation and its impact on daily living. The studies listed in Table 1 showed improvements in different tasks used to survey the course of the treatment or individual treatment sessions. Interestingly, Sparing et al. (2009) as well as Lim et al. (2010) were able to detect significant behavioural changes in one test, the line bisection task, following tDCS or rTMS, but not in the other (TAP task or line cancellation, respectively). How should we deal with dissociations of treatment effects, which may reflect the interindividual diversity of the neglect syndrome due, for instance, to different lesion sites affecting different cognitive domains (Marshall & Halligan, 1995; Vallar, 1998)?

Even less clear is the question of how individual performance in neuropsychological tests relates to the patients' deficits in their activities of daily living – and thus how to extrapolate the effect of brain stimulation on daily living from those test results. Although the presence of neglect is well known to affect the outcome of rehabilitation, the exact impact of neglect as such on the patients' daily life is hardly examined – partially due to a lack of adequate tests (Eschenbeck et al., 2010).

In addition to its diversity, neglect generally does not present on its own, but is often associated with somatosensory deficits, hemiparesis, hemianopia or anosognosia. Depending on lesion size and location, the combination with other neurological deficits may not simply add up but disproportionately potentiate thereby affecting or even limiting the rehabilitative potential of non-invasive stimulation. A special problem in this vein may be imposed by the additional presence of hemianopia. Dissociating true hemianopia, i.e., primary visual field defects, from pseudo-hemianopia induced by neglect is not an easy task and hardly feasible during a standard neurological examination. Electrophysiological examination may show normal visual evoked potentials in such patients (Vallar, Sandroni, Rusconi, & Barbieri, 1991), indicating intact primary visual processing. Specific neuropsychological testing may reveal that the visual field defect vanishes when the gaze is directed towards the right side (Kooistra & Heilman, 1989), indicating a pseudo-hemianopia related to neglect only. However, if both deficits are present, the coincidence of left unilateral spatial hemineglect and homonymous hemianopia evokes an even more severe inattention to the left side (Cassidy, Bruce, Lewis, & Gray, 1999). Zihl (1995) reported that 60% of their patients with homonymous hemianopia, but without signs of neglect, had impaired visual scanning behaviour. The presence of additional deficits thus needs to be taken into account when determining an accomplishable goal as well as when judging the effectiveness of the treatment.

Where to stimulate? Anatomy, pathophysiological concepts and neuronavigation

Consistent with the classic concept of hemispheric rivalry originally proposed by Kinsbourne (1977, 1994), the available results of TMS and tDCS studies performed in the context of neglect and spatial processing suggest that both targeting the intact left hemisphere with inhibitory as well as the lesioned right hemisphere with facilitatory stimulation protocols are promising. Both approaches aim at "strengthening" the right hemisphere. Supposing that inter-hemispheric rivalry indeed exists, and that it exerts its effect upon corre-sponding bi-hemispheric locations, left hemispheric stimulation should target structures corresponding to neglect-defining structures in the right hemisphere. Hence, thus far, PPC was the primary target of stimulation in all studies.

Future protocols might aim at individually adapting the site of stimulation to the structures affected, rather than using a single target location for all neglect patients. Anatomical landmarks of the lesion or functional character-istics of the deficit may be used to define the individual target area. For example, line bisection, repeatedly shown to draw upon PPC along the IPS (Fink et al., 2000, 2003; Fink, Marshall, Weiss, & Zilles, 2001), improved with PPC stimulation (Lim et al., 2010; Sparing et al., 2009). Thus the site of stimulation may determine which component of neglect is modulated. Patients with intentional neglect, inducible by frontal rTMS, might benefit from frontal stimulation (Ghacibeh et al., 2007). Whether targeting other structures within the frontoparietal networks is similarly effective has not yet been studied.

From a theoretical point of view, more sophisticated network models of attention accounting for neglect symptoms need to be incorporated into the classic concept of hemispheric rivalry. One might hypothesise that the concept of interhemispheric rivalry applies well to the bilaterally distributed dorsal frontoparietal network of voluntary top-down attention. Whether it similarly suits the right biased ventral frontoparietal network of bottom-up orientation has not yet been investigated.

The precise and reliable localisation of the target area is not a simple task either. Regarding a functional approach, TMS outside the motor and visual cortex does not result in an overt response such as muscle twitches or visual sensations (i.e., phosphenes). Nevertheless, feasible "hunting" methods for the IPS or ANG have been proposed by Oliver, Bjoertomt, Driver, Greenwood, and Rothwell (2009) and Göbel, Walsh, and Rothworth (2001), showing specific localised disruptive effects of rTMS on a visuospa-tial or number comparison task, respectively. For the lesioned, and, therefore, malfunctioning hemisphere, however, hunting procedures may be less reliable. Spatial tracking of the target area by the International 10–20 EEG system relies on cranial landmarks (e.g., nasion, inion, and preauricular points), but does not allow to account for interindividual neuroanatomical differences (Binnie, Dekker, Smit, & Van der Linden, 1982; Myslobodsky, Coppola, Bar-Ziv, & Weinberger, 1990) resulting in interindividual vari-ations in electrode position up to the range of 20 mm (Herwig, Satrap, & Schönfeldt-Lecuona, 2003). Optically tracked frameless stereotaxic neurona-vigation systems, which incorporate individual MRI data, provide an alterna-tive means to tackle this problem, allowing for an accuracy within the millimetre range (Sack et al., 2009; Schönfeldt-Lecuona et al., 2005; Sparing & Mottaghy, 2008; Sparing et al., 2010).

On the other hand, high focal precision may not be a desirable goal for therapeutic stimulation. Circumscribed application may have focused effects, which may prove less suitable for covering the aspect of disturbed neural networks underlying the neglect syndrome. This might generally speak in favour of a more extended area upon which stimulation exerts its effects, possibly favouring the use of tDCS as a less focal method (see also Vallar and Bolognini, this issue). In Sparing et al.'s study (2009), the stimulation area may not have been sufficiently large to cover the full range of neglect symptoms, as suggested by the fact that TAP test performance was not improved by tDCS. Size of lesion correlated negatively with the effect of treatment. While larger lesions generally go along with more severe deficits and less rehabilitative potential, a disadvantageous ratio between lesion size and the area which may be targeted by the stimulation may additionally influence effectiveness of stimulation.

How to stimulate? Intensity, duration or frequency of stimulation sessions

Stimulation protocols and individual parameters such as stimulation intensities are usually derived from neurophysiological studies of motor cortex excitability. Optimal stimulation parameters for non-motor areas are presently unknown. With respect to treatment effects, dose-finding studies varying systematically intensity and duration of stimulation or frequency of sessions have not been conducted thus far. Likewise, cumulative effects of multisession TMS have scarcely been investigated systematically. The four multisession rTMS treatment studies on neglect neither assessed neglect symptoms after individual sessions nor varied treatment duration. Therefore, at present no conclusions on the cumulative nature of the effects can be drawn. Nyffeler et al. (2009) showed that four vs. two TBS trains applied within 75 and 15 minutes, respectively, significantly increased the number of perceived left visual targets along with decreased reaction times for up to 32 vs. 8 hours. However, while the effect of four TBS trains was observed to decline 96 hours after stimulation, the persisting effect of two consecutive TBS trains had not been followed-up beyond 8 hours. In an rTMS study on cats, Valero-Cabré and co-authors (2008) demonstrated that a series of rTMS sessions on consecutive days over the right parietal cortex progressively induced visuospatial neglect-like after-effects of greater magnitude and spatial extent, without prolonging the duration of the effect, suggesting an increased facilitation to subsequent TMS-induced disruptions, but no accumulation. Comparison between effects of multi-session rTMS and TBS, as well as between humans and cats, may not be permitted, and benefits on injured brains may vary from short to long-term effects of disturbance on intact neuronal systems. It is conceivable that the healthy brain may resist or overcome the induced disturbance of balance with the effects lacking or wearing off over time, while dysbalanced networks in a lesioned brain may be rebalanced. In addition, we envision that an unbalanced network in the lesioned brain (temporarily) overcoming its unbalance by neurostimulation may try to stabilise the induced balanced status.

Indeed, normalisation of over-excitability of the left PPC-M1-circuitry was specific for neglect patients; no change in excitability was observed in the control group of right hemispheric patients without neglect (Koch et al., 2008). In the four multisession studies presented, treatment continued over two weeks. Whether patients would benefit from a longer treatment cycle or a second cycle after a pause remains to be elucidated. Finally, preconditioning of brain tissue by preceding TMS (Iyer et al., 2003) or tDCS (Lang et al., 2004; Siebner et al., 2004) may open up further avenues for future stimulation protocols worth investigating.

Along with the development of treatment protocols, putative adverse effects and risks of the use of rTMS and tDCS should also be assessed carefully. The dosage should generally be limited according to published safety guidelines (e.g., Nitsche et al., 2003; Poreisz, Boros, Antal, & Paulus, 2007; Wassermann et al., 1996). Although current data do not hint at adverse side effects, the particular risks of repetitive stimulation sessions as well as novel protocols such as TBS (Huang et al., 2005) or combinations with pre-conditioning TMS (Iyer et al., 2003) or tDCS (Lang et al., 2004; Siebner et al., 2004) should be concurrently addressed in future investigations.

When to intervene? Acute vs. chronic stage

Another concern is whether stimulation protocols should start in the acute phase, i.e. within the first few days following the onset of stroke, or later. Groups of patients are heterogeneous (see Table 1), also with respect to the time point of stimulation following stroke onset, showing positive effects of stimulation both in the subacute and chronic phase of stroke. Whether the extent of short-term effects differ when applied in the acute compared with the chronic phase has not been investigated systematically. Moreover, long-term treatment and long-term effects studied so far were limited to a period of 6 weeks (Shindo et al., 2006), with most studies only testing for short-term effects.

Current studies do not suggest any negative effects of stimulation depending on the stage of the disease. However, systematic studies are lacking that investigate whether acutely damaged and vulnerable tissue, in particular any tissue at risk at the borders of the lesion, reacts differently to stimulation. Furthermore stimulation protocols should not inhibit adaptive processes prone to restore the affected neural networks. Finally, patients should not only benefit from early stimulation protocols, but any benefit achieved should be long-lasting and not reachable to the same degree by the same therapy starting at a later time point in order to justify a very early onset of the treatment. If any maladaptive processes resulting from interhemispheric disinhibition should prove irreversible, one might postulate a preventive effect of early-onset stimulation therapy, which could not be regained at later time-points. To the best of our knowledge, these aspects have not been investigated.

Whom to treat? Considering lesion location, size and clinical presentation

Likewise, whether lesion location or size may predict who will or will not benefit from brain stimulation in order to allow for categorising patients and adapting treatment to the individual needs has not been investigated systematically. Patient groups reported are usually very heterogeneous as far as lesion size and location is concerned (see Table 1). Sparing et al. (2009) demonstrated a negative correlation of stimulation effect with lesion size indicating that those patients with larger lesions improve less. Apart from this finding, only four out of the 10 stimulation treatment studies with neglect patients report lesion maps and lesion size or volume – without striving for any correlation with treatment effects. In order to demonstrate a robust effect, however, selection of patient groups seems important: In comparison to more homogeneous groups of healthy individuals, stimulation induced much more variable behavioural effects in patients.

What to add to stimulation? Combination with rest, physical and/or occupational therapy

This aspect addresses the setting in which a neuromodulatory approach may be embedded. Again, this issue has not been explored. Should stimulation be applied separately or can its effects be enhanced when combined with physical or occupational therapy? If a combination is favourable, should stimulation be simultaneous to other treatment, or rather following or preceding it? In other words, should stimulation take place during rest or in combination with certain tasks? If the latter was the case, which tasks would be best suited to enhance the stimulation effect? The demonstration of state-dependent effects of stimulation (Silvanto, Muggleton, & Walsh, 2008, Silvanto & Pascual-Leone, 2008) suggests that these aspects may indeed be relevant.

In a study by Song et al. (2009) all patients were given conventional rehabilitation treatment, while the treatment group also received inhibitory rTMS applied to the left parietal cortex, unrelated to treatment, for 14 consecutive days twice a day for 15 minutes. Only the rTMS treatment group improved in both the line bisection as well as the line cancellation task. In a different study by Lim et al. (2010), patients received a session of 1 Hz rTMS applied to the left parietal cortex, immediately prior to the 30-minute session of occupational therapy for a total of 10 days within a 14-day period. Six out of 7 patients of the combined treatment group improved with respect to the line bisection task (compared to 2 out of 7 in the control group), however, there is no comment on whether improvements correlated with any parameter reflecting activities of daily living.

CONCLUSION

The currently available proof-of-principle studies of non-invasive brain stimulation in the treatment of neglect give rise to optimism for applying neuromodulatory approaches in the rehabilitation of a so far quite daunting condition. Other therapeutic approaches, such as spatial training, prism adaptation (Fortis et al., 2010), pharmacological treatment (for review see Sivan, Neumann, Kent, Stroud, & Bhakta, 2010) or neck vibration (for reviews for the main approaches see Kerkhoff, 2003; Pizzamiglio, Guariglia, Antonucci, & Zoccolotti, 2006; Rode et al., 2006), also show encouraging effects. Particularly appealing for the brain stimulation approach is, however, the hypothesised pathophysiological concept of hemispheric rivalry, for which current findings provide compelling evidence. Along with functional topography of subcomponents of neglect to be refined by future investigations, more sophisticated network models of attention should be incorporated into the concept of hemispheric rivalry. Finally, larger double-blind, placebo-controlled trials are needed, that systematically study optimal stimulation protocols, possibly individualised for site, intensity, frequency, and duration of stimulation, onset of treatment, co-therapy, and prognostic criteria, before any systematic application in the clinical routine may be pursued. Tackling those aspects, non-invasive brain stimulation may not only excite the so-far very limited treatment options of neglect, but conversely, neglect may also provide a stimulating example of where therapeutic application of non-invasive brain stimulation may be heading in the future.

REFERENCES

Arene, N. U., & Hillis, A. E. (2007). Rehabilitation of unilateral spatial neglect and neuroimaging. *Europa Medicophysica, 43,* 255–269.

Babiloni, C., Vecchio, F., Rossi, S., De Capua, A., Bartalini, S., Ulivelli, M., & Rossini, P. M. (2007). Human ventral parietal cortex plays a functional role on visuospatial attention and primary consciousness: A repetitive transcranial magnetic stimulation study. *Cerebral Cortex, 17,* 1486–1492.

Bartolomeo, P. (2007). Visual neglect. *Current Opinion in Neurology, 20,* 381–6.

Bartolomeo, P., Thiebaut de Schotten, M., & Doricchi, F. (2007). Left unilateral neglect as a disconnection syndrome. *Cerebral Cortex, 17,* 2479–2490.

Binder, J., Marshall, R., Lazar, R., Benjamin, J., & Mohr, J. P. (1992). Distinct syndromes of hemineglect. *Archives in Neurology, 49,* 1187–1194.

Binnie, C. D., Dekker, E., Smit, A., & Van der Linden, G. (1982). Practical considerations in the positioning of EEG electrodes. *Electroencephalography and Clinical Neurophysiology, 53,* 453–458.

Bisiach, E., & Vallar, G. (2000). Unilateral neglect in humans. In F. Boller, J. Grafman, & G. Rizzolatti (Eds.), *Handbook of neuropsychology,* (2nd ed., Vol. 1, pp. 459–502). Amsterdam: Elsevier Science.

Bjoertomt, O., Cowey, A., & Walsh, V. (2002). Spatial neglect in near and far space investigated by repetitive transcranial magnetic stimulation. *Brain, 125,* 2012–2022.

Brighina, F., Bisiach, E., Oliveri, M., Piazza, A., La Bua, V., Daniele, O., & Fierro, B. (2003). 1 Hz repetitive transcranial magnetic stimulation of the unaffected hemisphere ameliorates contralesional visuospatial neglect in humans. *Neuroscience Letters, 336,* 131–133.

Brighina, F., Bisiach, E., Piazza, A., Oliveri, M., La Bua, V., Daniele, O., & Fierro, B. (2002). Perceptual and response bias in visuospatial neglect due to frontal and parietal repetitive transcranial magnetic stimulation in normal subjects. *Neuroreport, 13,* 2571–2575.

Cassidy, T. P., Bruce, D. W., Lewis, S., & Gray, C. S. (1999). The association of visual field deficits and visuo-spatial neglect in acute right-hemisphere stroke patients. *Age and Ageing, 28,* 257–260.

Cazzoli, D., Wurtz, P., Müri, R. M., Hess, C. W., & Nyffeler, T. (2009). Interhemispheric balance of overt attention: A theta burst stimulation study. *European Journal of Neuroscience, 29,* 1271–1276.

Chambers, C. D., Stokes, M. G., Janko, N. E., & Mattingley, J. B. (2006). Enhancement of visual selection during transient disruption of parietal cortex. *Brain Research, 1097,* 149–155.

Committeri, G., Pitzalis, S., Galati, G., Patria, F., Pelle, G., Sabatini, U., et al. (2007). Neural bases of personal and extrapersonal neglect in humans. *Brain, 130,* 431–441.

Corbetta, M., Kincade, M. J., Lewis, C., Snyder, A. Z., & Sapir, A. (2005). Neural basis and recovery of spatial attention deficits in spatial neglect. *Nature Neuroscience, 8,* 1603–1610.

Corbetta, M., Kincade, J. M., Ollinger, J. M., McAvoy, M. P., & Shulman, G. L. (2000). Voluntary orienting is dissociated from target detection in human posterior parietal cortex. *Nature Neuroscience, 3,* 292–297.

Corbetta, M., & Shulman, G. L. (2002). Control of goal-directed and stimulus-driven attention in the brain. *Nature Reviews in Neuroscience, 3,* 201–215.

Coulthard, E., Parton, A., & Husain, M. (2006). Action control in visual neglect. *Neuropsychologia, 44,* 2717–2733.

Daffner, K. R., Ahern, G. L., Weintraub, S., & Mesulam, M. M. (1990). Dissociated neglect behavior following sequential strokes in the right hemisphere. *Annals of Neurology, 28,* 97–101.

Dambeck, N., Sparing, R., Meister, I. G., Wienemann, M., Weidemann, J., Topper, R., & Boroojerdi, B. (2006). Interhemispheric imbalance during visuospatial attention investigated by unilateral and bilateral TMS over human parietal cortices. *Brain Research, 1072,* 194–199.

Doricchi, F., & Tomaiuolo, F. (2003). The anatomy of neglect without hemianopia: A key role for parietal-frontal disconnection? *NeuroReport, 14,* 2239–2243.

Edwards, D., & Fregni, F. (2008). Modulating the healthy and affected motor cortex with repetitive transcranial magnetic stimulation in stroke: Development of new strategies for neurorehabilitation. *NeuroRehabilitation, 23,* 3–14.

Ellison, A., Schindler, I., Pattison, L. L., & Milner, A. D. (2004). An exploration of the role of the superior temporal gyrus in visual search and spatial perception using TMS. *Brain, 127,* 2307–2315.

Eschenbeck, P., Vossel, S., Weiss, P. H., Saliger, J., Karbe, H., & Fink, G. R. (2010). Testing for neglect in right-hemispheric stroke patients using a new assessment battery based upon standardized activities of daily living (ADL). *Neuropsychologia, 48,* 3488–3496.

Fierro, B., Brighina, F., & Bisiach, E. (2006). Improving neglect by TMS. *Behavioural Neurology, 17,* 169–176.

Fierro, B., Brighina, F., Oliveri, M., Piazza, A., La, Bua, V., Buffa, D., & Bisiach, E. (2000). Contralateral neglect induced by right posterior parietal rTMS in healthy subjects. *Neuroreport, 11,* 1519–1521.

Fierro, B., Brighina, F., Piazza, A., Oliveri, M., & Bisiach, E. (2001). Timing of right parietal and frontal cortex activity in visuo-spatial perception: A TMS study in normal individuals. *Neuroreport, 12,* 2605–2607.

Fink, G. R., Marshall, J. C., Shah, N. J., Weiss, P. H., Halligan, P. W., Grosse-Ruyken, M., et al. (2000). Line bisection judgments implicate right parietal cortex and cerebellum as assessed by fMRI. *Neurology, 54,* 1324–1331.

Fink, G. R., Marshall, J. C., Weiss, P. H., Stephan, T., Grefkes, C., Shah, N. J., et al (2003). Performing allocentric visuospatial judgments with induced distortion of the egocentric reference frame: An fMRI study with clinical implications. *Neuroimage, 20,* 1505–1517.

Fink, G. R., Marshall, J. C., Weiss, P. H., & Zilles, K. (2001). The neural basis of vertical and horizontal line bisection judgments: An fMRI study of normal volunteers. *Neuroimage, 14,* 59–67.

Fortis, P., Maravita, A., Gallucci, M., Ronchi, R., Grassi, E., Senna, I., et al. (2010). Rehabilitating patients with left spatial neglect by prism exposure during a visuomotor activity. *Neuropsychology, 24,* 681–697.

Fregni, F., & Pascual-Leone, A. (2007). Technology insight: Noninvasive brain stimulation in neurology perspectives on the therapeutic potential of rTMS and tDCS. *Nature Clinical Practice Neurology, 3,* 383–393.

Ghacibeh, G. A., Shenker, J. I., Winter, K. H., Triggs, W. J., & Heilman, K. M. (2007). Dissociation of neglect subtypes with transcranial magnetic stimulation. *Neurology, 69,* 1122–1127.

Göbel, S., Walsh, V., & Rushworth, M. F. (2001). The mental number line and the human angular gyrus. *Neuroimage, 14,* 1278–1289.

Hallett, M. (2007). Transcranial magnetic stimulation: A primer. *Neuron, 55,* 187–199.

Halligan, P. W., Fink, GR., Marshall, J. C., & Vallar, G. (2003). Spatial cognition: Evidence from visual neglect. *Trends in Cognitive Science, 7,* 125–133.

Halligan, P. W., & Marshall, J. C. (1992). Left visuo-spatial neglect: A meaningless entity? *Cortex, 28,* 525–535.

Halligan, P. W., & Marshall, J. C. (1995). Lateral and radial neglect as a function of spatial position: A case study. *Neuropsychologia, 33,* 1697–1702.

Harris-Love, M. L., & Cohen, L. G. (2006). Noninvasive cortical stimulation in neurorehabilitation: A review. *Archives of Physical Medicine and Rehabilitation, 87,* 84–93.

He, B. J., Snyder, A. Z., Vincent, J. L., Epstein, A., Shulman, G. L., & Corbetta, M. (2007). Breakdown of functional connectivity in frontoparietal networks underlies behavioral deficits in spatial neglect. *Neuron, 53,* 905–918.

Heilman, K. M., Watson, R. T., & Valenstein, E. (2003). Neglect and related disorders. In K. M. Heilman & E. Valenstein (Eds.), *Clinical Neuropsychology,* (4th ed., pp. 296–346). New York: Oxford University Press.

Herwig, U., Satrapi, P., & Schönfeldt-Lecuona, C. (2003). Using the international 10-20 EEG system for positioning of transcranial magnetic stimulation. *Brain Topography, 16,* 95–99.

Hilgetag, C. C., Théoret, H., & Pascual-Leone, A. (2001). Enhanced visual spatial attention ipsi-lateral to rTMS-induced 'virtual lesions' of human parietal cortex. *Natue Neuroscience, 4,* 953–957.

Hillis, A. E. (2006). Neurobiology of unilateral spatial neglect. *Neuroscientist, 12,* 153–163.

Hillis, A. E., Newhart, M., Heidler, J., Barker, P. B., Herskovits, E. H., & Degaonkar, M. (2005). Anatomy of spatial attention: Insights from perfusion imaging and hemispatial neglect in acute stroke. *Journal of Neuroscience, 25,* 3161–3167.

Hopfinger, J. B., Buonocore, M. H., & Mangun, G. R. (2000). The neural mechanisms of top-down attentional control. *Nature Neuroscience, 3,* 284–291.

Huang, Y. Z., Edwards, M. J., Rounis, E., Bhatia, K. P., & Rothwell, J. C. (2005). Theta burst stimulation of the human motor cortex. *Neuron, 45,* 201–206.

Hummel, F. C., & Cohen, L. G. (2006). Non-invasive brain stimulation: A new strategy to improve neurorehabilitation after stroke? *Lancet Neurology, 5,* 708–712.

Husain, M. (2008). Hemispatial neglect. In G. Goldenberg & B. L. Miller (Eds.), *Handbook of Clinical Neurology* (Vol. 88, pp. 359–372). Amsterdam: Elsevier.

Husain, M., & Nachev, P. (2007). Space and the parietal cortex. *Trends in Cognitive Science, 11,* 30–36.

Iyer, M. B., Schleper, N., & Wassermann, E. M. (2003). Priming stimulation enhances the depressant effect of low-frequency repetitive transcranial magnetic stimulation. *Journal of Neuroscience, 23,* 10867–10872.

Jin, Y., & Hilgetag, C. C. (2008). Perturbation of visuospatial attention by high-frequency offline rTMS. *Expimental Brain Research, 189,* 121–128.

Kerkhoff, G. (2003). Modulation and rehabilitation of spatial neglect by sensory stimulation. *Progress in Brain Research, 142,* 257–271.

Kim, Y. H., Min, S. J., Ko, M. H., Park, J. W., Jang, S. H., & Lee, P. K. (2005). Facilitating visuospatial attention for the contralateral hemifield by repetitive TMS on the posterior parietal cortex. *Neuroscience Letters, 382,* 280–285.

Kinsbourne, M. (1977). Hemi-neglect and hemisphere rivalry. *Advance in Neurology, 18,* 41–49.

Kinsbourne, M. (1994). Mechanisms of neglect: Implications for rehabilitation. *Neuropsychological Rehabilitation, 4,* 151–153.

Ko, M. H., Han, S. H., Park, S. H., Seo, J. H., & Kim, Y. H. (2008). Improvement of visual scanning after DC brain polarization of parietal cortex in stroke patients with spatial neglect. *Neuroscience Letters, 448,* 171–174.

Koch, G., Oliveri, M., Cheeran, B., Ruge, D., Lo Gerfo, E., Salerno, S., Torriero, S., Marconi, B., Mori, F., Driver, J., Rothwell, J. C., & Caltagirone, C. (2008). Hyperexcitability of parietal-motor functional connections in the intact left-hemisphere of patients with neglect. *Brain, 131,* 3147–3155.

Kooistra, C. A., & Heilman, K. M. (1989). Hemispatial visual inattention masquerading as hemianopia. *Neurology, 39,* 1125–1127.

Lang, N., Siebner, H. R., Ernst, D., Nitsche, M. A., Paulus, W., Lemon, R. N., & Rothwell, J. C. (2004). Preconditioning with transcranial direct current stimulation sensitizes the motor cortex to rapid-rate transcranial magnetic stimulation and controls the direction of after-effects. *Biological Psychiatry, 56,* 634–639.

Larson, J., Wong, D., & Lynch, G. (1986). Patterned stimulation at the theta frequency is optimal for the induction of hippocampal long-term potentiation. *Brain Research, 368,* 347–350.

Lim, J. Y., Kang, E. K., & Paik, N. J. (2010). Repetitive transcranial magnetic stimulation to hemispatial neglect in patients after stroke: An open-label pilot study. *Journal of Rehabilitation Medicine, 42,* 447–452.

Lomber, S. G., & Payne, B. R. (1996). Removal of two halves restores the whole: Reversal of visual hemineglect during bilateral cortical or collicular inactivation in the cat. *Visual Neuroscience, 13,* 1143–1156.

Lomber, S. G., Payne, B. R., Hilgetag, C. C., & Rushmore, J. (2002). Restoration of visual orienting into a cortically blind hemifield by reversible deactivation of posterior parietal cortex or the superior colliculus. *Expimentalk Brain Research, 142,* 463–474.

Lynch, J. C., & McLaren, J. W. (1989). Deficits of visual attention and saccadic eye movements after lesions of parietooccipital cortex in monkeys. *Journal of Neurophysioogy, 61,* 74–90.

Marshall, J. C., & Halligan, P. W. (1995). Within- and between-task dissociations in visuospatial neglect: A case study. *Cortex, 31,* 367–376.

Meister, I. G., Wienemann, M., Buelte, D., Grünewald, C., Sparing, R., Dambeck, N., & Boroojerdi, B. (2006). Hemiextinction induced by transcranial magnetic stimulation over the right temporo-parietal junction. *Neuroscience, 142,* 119–123.

Mesulam, M. M. (1981). A cortical network for directed attention and unilateral neglect. *Annals of Neurology, 10,* 309–325.

Mesulam, M. M. (2002). Functional anatomy of attention and neglect: From neurons to networks. In H.-O. Karnath, A. D. Milner, & G. Vallar (Eds.), *The Cognitive and Neural Bases of Spatial Neglect* (pp. 33–45). Oxford: Oxford University Press.

Miniussi, C., Cappa, S. F., Cohen, L. G., Floel, A., Fregni, F., Nitsche, M. A., et al. (2008). Efficacy of repetitive transcranial magnetic stimulation/transcranial direct current stimulation in cognitive neurorehabilitaion. *Brain Stimulation, 1,* 326–336.

Mort, D. J., Malhotra, P., Mannan, S. K., Rorden, C., Pambakian, A., Kennard, C., & Husain, M. (2003). The anatomy of visual neglect. *Brain, 126,* 1986–1997.

Muggleton, N. G., Postma, P., Moutsopoulou, K., Nimmo-Smith, I., Marcel, A., & Walsh, V. (2006). TMS over right posterior parietal cortex induces neglect in a scene-based frame of reference. *Neuropsychologia, 44,* 1222–12229.

Müri, R. M., Bühler, R., Heinemann, D., Mosimann, U. P., Felblinger, J., Schlaepfer, T. E., & Hess, C. W. (2002). Hemispheric asymmetry in visuospatial attention assessed with transcranial magnetic stimulation. *Expimental Brain Research, 143,* 426–430.

Myslobodsky, M. S., Coppola, R., Bar-Ziv, J., & Weinberger, D. R. (1990). Adequacy of the International 10-20 electrode system for computed neurophysiologic topography. *Journal of Clinical Neurophysiology, 7,* 507–518.

Nager, W., Wolters, C., Münte, T. F., & Johannes, S. (2004). Transcranial magnetic stimulation to the parietal lobes reduces detection of contralateral somatosensory stimuli. *Acta Neurologica Scandinavica, 109,* 146–150.

Nitsche, M. A., Cohen, L. G., Wassermann, E. M., Priori, A., Lang, N., Antal, A., et al. (2008). Transcranial direct current stimulation: State of the art 2008. *Brain Stimulation, 1,* 206–223.

Nitsche, M. A., Liebetanz, D., Antal, A., Lang, N., Tergau, F., & Paulus, W. (2003). Modulation of cortical excitability by weak direct current stimulation – technical, safety and functional aspects. *Supplements in Clinical Neurophysiology, 56,* 255–276.

Nitsche, M. A., & Paulus, W. (2000). Excitability changes induced in the human motor cortex by weak transcranial direct current stimulation. *Journal of Physiology, 527,* 633–639.

Nitsche, M. A., & Paulus, W. (2001). Sustained excitability elevations induced by transcranial DC motor cortex stimulation in humans. *Neurology, 57,* 1899–1901.

Nitsche, M. A., Seeber, A., Frommann, K., Klein, C. C., Rochford, C., Nitsche, M. S., et al. (2005). Modulating parameters of excitability during and after transcranial direct current stimulation of the human motor cortex. *Journal of Physiology, 568,* 291–303.

Nyffeler, T., Cazzoli, D., Hess, C. W., & Müri, R. M. (2009). One session of repeated parietal theta burst stimulation trains induces long-lasting improvement of visual neglect. *Stroke, 40,* 2791–2796.

Nyffeler, T., Cazzoli, D., Wurtz, P., Lüthi, M., von Wartburg, R., Chaves, S., Déruaz, A., Hess, C. W., & Müri, R. M. (2008). Neglect-like visual exploration behaviour after theta burst transcranial magnetic stimulation of the right posterior parietal cortex. *European Journal of Neuroscience, 27,* 1809–1813.

Nyffeler, T., Wurtz, P., Lüscher, H. R., Hess, C. W., Senn, W., Pflugshaupt, T., von Wartburg, R., Lüthi, M., & Müri, R. M. (2006a). Repetitive TMS over the human oculomotor cortex: Comparison of 1-Hz and theta burst stimulation. *Neuroscience Letters, 409,* 57–60.

Nyffeler, T., Wurtz, P., Lüscher, H. R., Hess, C. W., Senn, W., Pflugshaupt, T., von Wartburg, R., Lüthi, M., & Müri, R. M. (2006b). Extending lifetime of plastic changes in the human brain. *European Journal of Neuroscience, 24,* 2961–2966.

Oliver, R., Bjoertomt, O., Driver, J., Greenwood, R., & Rothwell, J. (2009). Novel 'hunting' method using transcranial magnetic stimulation over parietal cortex disrupts visuospatial sensitivity in relation to motor thresholds. *Neuropsychologia, 47,* 3152–3161.

Oliveri, M., Bisiach, E., Brighina, F., Piazza, A., La Bua, V., Buffa, D., & Fierro, B. (2001). rTMS of the unaffected hemisphere transiently reduces contralesional visuospatial hemi-neglect. *Neurology, 57,* 1338–1340.

Oliveri, M., Rossini, P. M., Traversa, R., Cicinelli, P., Filippi, M. M., Pasqualetti, P., Tomaiuolo, F., & Caltagirone, C. (1999). Left frontal transcranial magnetic stimulation reduces contralesional extinction in patients with unilateral right brain damage. *Brain, 122,* 1731–1739.

Oliveri, M., & Vallar, G. (2009). Parietal versus temporal lobe components in spatial cognition: Setting the mid-point of a horizontal line. *Journal of Neuropsychology, 3,* 201–211.

Pascual-Leone, A., Gomez-Tortosa, E., Grafman, J., Alway, D., Nichelli, P., & Hallett, M. (1994). Induction of visual extinction by rapid-rate transcranial magnetic stimulation of parietal lobe. *Neurology, 44,* 494–498.

Pascual-Leone, A., Walsh, V., & Rothwell, J. (2000). Transcranial magnetic stimulation in cognitive neuroscience: Virtual lesion, chronometry, and functional connectivity. *Current Opinion in Neurobioogy, 10,* 232–237.

Paulus, W. (2003). Transcranial direct current stimulation (tDCS). *Supplements in Clinical Neurophysiology, 56,* 249–254.

Payne, B. R., Lomber, S. G., Rushmore, R. J., & Pascual-Leone, A. (2003b). Cancellation of visuospatial lesion-induced spatial neglect. *Experimental Brain Research, 150,* 395–398.

Payne, B. R., & Rushmore, R. J. (2003a). Animal models of cerebral neglect and its cancellation. *Neuroscientist, 9,* 446–454.

Pizzamiglio, L., Guariglia, C., Antonucci, G., & Zoccolotti, P. (2006). Development of a rehabilitative program for unilateral neglect. *Restorative Neurology and Neuroscience, 24,* 337–345.

Poreisz, C., Boros, K., Antal, A., & Paulus, W. (2007). Safety aspects of transcranial direct current stimulation concerning healthy subjects and patients. *Brain Research Bulletin, 72,* 208–214.

Pourtois, G., Vandermeeren, Y., Olivier, E., & de Gelder, B. (2001). Event-related TMS over the right posterior parietal cortex induces ipsilateral visuo-spatial interference. *Neuroreport, 12,* 2369–2374.

Priori, A., Berardelli, A., Rona, S., Accornero, N., & Manfredi, M. (1998). Polarization of the human motor cortex through the scalp. *Neuroreport, 9,* 2257–2260.

Rode, G., Klos, T., Courtois-Jacquin, S., Rossetti, Y., & Pisella, L. (2006). Neglect and prism adaptation: A new therapeutic tool for spatial cognition disorders. *Restorative Neurology and Neuroscience, 24,* 347–356.

Rossi, S., & Rossini, P. M. (2004). TMS in cognitive plasticity and the potential for rehabilitation. *Trends in Cognitive Sciences, 8,* 273–279.

Rounis, E., Yarrow, K., & Rothwell, J. C. (2007). Effects of rTMS conditioning over the fronto-parietal network on motor versus visual attention. *Journal of Cognitive Neuroscience, 19,* 513–524.

Rushworth, M. F., Ellison, A., & Walsh, V. (2001). Complementary localization and lateralization of orienting and motor attention. *Nature Neuroscience, 4,* 656–661.

Sack, A. T., Cohen Kadosh, R., Schuhmann, T., Moerel, M., Walsh, V., & Goebel, R. (2009). Optimizing functional accuracy of TMS in cognitive studies: A comparison of methods. *Journal of Cognitive Neuroscience, 21,* 207–221.

Schönfeldt-Lecuona, C., Thielscher, A., Freudenmann, R. W., Kron, M., Spitzer, M., & Herwig, U. (2005). Accuracy of stereotaxic positioning of transcranial magnetic stimulation. *Brain Topography, 17,* 253–259.

Schweid, L., Rushmore, R. J., & Valero-Cabré, A. (2008). Cathodal transcranial direct current stimulation on posterior parietal cortex disrupts visuo-spatial processing in the contralateral visual field. *Experimental Brain Research, 186,* 409–417.

Seyal, M., Ro, T., & Rafal, R. (1995). Increased sensitivity to ipsilateral cutaneous stimuli following transcranial magnetic stimulation of the parietal lobe. *Annals of Neurology, 38,* 264–267.

Shindo, K., Sugiyama, K., Huabao, L., Nishijima, K., Kondo, T., & Izumi, S. (2006). Long-term effect of low-frequency repetitive transcranial magnetic stimulation over the unaffected posterior parietal cortex in patients with unilateral spatial neglect. *Journal of Rehabilitation Medicine, 38,* 65–67.

Siebner, H. R., Lang, N., Rizzo, V., Nitsche, M. A., Paulus, W., Lemon, R. N., & Rothwell, J. C. (2004). Preconditioning of low-frequency repetitive transcranial magnetic stimulation with transcranial direct current stimulation: Evidence for homeostatic plasticity in the human motor cortex. *Journal of Neuroscience, 24,* 3379–3385.

Silvanto, J., Muggleton, N., & Walsh, V. (2008b). State-dependency in brain stimulation studies of perception and cognition. *Trends in Cognitive Science, 12,* 447–454.

Silvanto, J., & Pascual-Leone, A. (2008a). State-dependency of transcranial magnetic stimulation. *Brain Topography, 21,* 1–10.

Sivan, M., Neumann, V., Kent, R., Stroud, A., & Bhakta, B. B. (2010). Pharmacotherapy for treatment of attention deficits after non-progressive acquired brain injury: A systematic review. *Clinical Rehabilitation, 24,* 110–121.

Song, W., Du, B., Xu, Q., Hu, J., Wang, M., & Luo, Y. (2009). Low-frequency transcranial magnetic stimulation for visual spatial neglect: A pilot study. *Journal of Rehabilitation Medicine, 41,* 162–165.

Sparing, R., Buelte, D., Meister, I. G., Paus, T., & Fink, G. R. (2008). Transcranial magnetic stimulation and the challenge of coil placement: A comparison of conventional and stereotaxic neuronavigational strategies. *Human Brain Mapping, 29,* 82–96.

Sparing, R., Hesse, M. D., & Fink, G. R. (2010). Neuronavigation for transcranial magnetic stimulation (TMS): Where we are and where we are going. *Cortex, 46,* 118–120.

Sparing, R., & Mottaghy, F. M. (2008). Noninvasive brain stimulation with transcranial magnetic or direct current stimulation (TMS/tDCS): From insights into human memory to therapy of its dysfunction. *Methods, 44,* 287–348.

Sparing, R., Thimm, M., Hesse, M. D., Küst, J., Karbe, H., & Fink, G. R. (2009). Bidirectional alterations of interhemispheric parietal balance by non-invasive cortical stimulation. *Brain, 132,* 3011–3020.

Sprague, J. M. (1966). Interaction of cortex and superior colliculus in mediation of visually guided behavior in the cat. *Science, 153,* 1544–1547.

Thut, G., Nietzel, A., & Pascual-Leone, A. (2005). Dorsal posterior parietal rTMS affects voluntary orienting of visuospatial attention. *Cerebral Cortex, 15,* 628–638.

Utz, K. S., Dimova, V., Oppenländer, K., & Kerkhoff, G. (2010). Electrified minds: Transcranial direct current stimulation (tDCS) and galvanic vestibular stimulation (GVS) as methods of non-invasive brain stimulation in neuropsychology: A review of current data and future implications. *Neuropsychologia, 48,* 2789–2810.

Valero-Cabré, A., Pascual-Leone, A., & Rushmore, R. J. (2008). Cumulative sessions of repetitive transcranial magnetic stimulation (rTMS) build up facilitation to subsequenct TMS-mediated behavioral disruptions. *European Journal of Neuroscience, 27,* 765–774.

Valero-Cabré, A., Payne, B. R., & Pascual-Leone, A. (2007). Opposite impact on 14C-2-deoxy-glucose brain metabolism following patterns of high and low frequency repetitive transcranial magnetic stimulation in the posterior parietal cortex. *Expimental Brain Research, 176,* 603–615.

Valero-Cabré, A., Payne, B. R., Rushmore, J., Lomber, S. G., & Pascual-Leone, A. (2005). Impact of repetitive transcranial magnetic stimulation of the parietal cortex on metabolic brain activity: A 14C-2DG tracing study in the cat. *Experimental Brain Research, 163,* 1–12.

Valero-Cabré, A., Rushmore, R. J., & Payne, B. R. (2006). Low frequency transcranial magnetic stimulation on the posterior parietal cortex induces visuotopically specific neglect-like syndrome. *Experimental Brain Research, 172,* 14–21.

Vallar, G. (1998). Spatial hemineglect in humans. *Trends in Cognitive Sciences, 2,* 87–97.

Vallar, G., & Perani, D. (1986). The anatomy of unilateral neglect after right-hemisphere stroke lesions. A clinical/CT-scan correlation study in man. *Neuropsychologia, 24,* 609–622.

Vallar, G., Sandroni, P., Rusconi, M. L., & Barbieri, S. (1991). Hemianopia, hemianesthesia and spatial neglect. A study with evoked potentials. *Neurology, 41,* 1918–1922.

Verdon, V., Schwartz, S., Lovblad, K. O., Hauert, C. A., & Vuilleumier, P. (2010). Neuroanatomy of hemispatial neglect and its functional components: A study using voxel-based lesion-symptom mapping. *Brain, 133,* 880–894.

Vuilleumier, P., Hester, D., Assal, G., & Regli, F. (1996). Unilateral spatial neglect recovery after sequential strokes. *Neurology, 46,* 184–189.

Wagner, T., Valero-Cabre, A., & Pascual-Leone, A. (2007). Noninvasive human brain stimulation. *Annual Reviews in Biomedical Engineering, 9,* 527–565.

Wassermann, E. M., & Grafman, J. (2005). Recharging cognition with DC brain polarization. *Trends in Cognitive Science, 9,* 503–505.

Wassermann, E. M., Grafman, J., Berry, C., Hollnagel, C., Wild, K., Clark, K., & Hallett, M. (1996). Use and safety of a new repetitive transcranial magnetic stimulator. *Electroencephalographyy and Clinical Neurophysiology, 101,* 412–417.

Weiss, P. H., Marshall, J. C., Wunderlich, G., Tellmann, L., Halligan, P. W., Freund, H. J., Zilles, K., & Fink, G. R. (2000). Neural consequences of acting in near versus far space: A physiological basis for clinical dissociations. *Brain, 123,* 2531–2541.

Zihl, J. (1995). Visual scanning behavior in patients with homonymous hemianopia. *Neuropsychologia, 33,* 287–303.

NEUROPSYCHOLOGICAL REHABILITATION
2011, 21 (5), 703–716

Non-invasive brain stimulation to assess and modulate neuroplasticity in Alzheimer's disease

Paulo Sérgio Boggio[1], Claudia Aparecida Valasek[1], Camila Campanhã[1], Ana Carolina Alem Giglio[1], Nathalia Ishikawa Baptista[1], Olivia Morgan Lapenta[1], and Felipe Fregni[2]

[1]Social and Cognitive Neuroscience Laboratory and Developmental Disorders Program, Center for Health and Biological Sciences, Mackenzie Presbyterian University, Sao Paulo, Brazil
[2]Laboratory of Neuromodulation, Department of Physical Medicine and Rehabilitation, Spaulding Rehabilitation Hospital and Massachusetts General Hospital, Harvard Medical School, Boston, MA

Alzheimer's disease (AD) is a neurodegenerative and progressive disease related to a gradual decline in cognitive functions such as memory, attention, perceptual-spatial abilities, language, and executive functions. Recent evidence has suggested that interventions promoting neural plasticity can induce significant cognitive gains especially in subjects at risk of or with mild AD. Transcranial magnetic stimulation (TMS) and transcranial direct current stimulation (tDCS) are non-invasive techniques that can induce significant and long-lasting changes in focal and non-focal neuroplasticity. In this review, we present initial preliminary evidence that TMS and tDCS can enhance performance in cognitive functions typically impaired in AD. Also, we reviewed the initial six studies on AD that presented early findings showing cognitive

Correspondence should be addressed to Paulo Sérgio Boggio, Social and Cognitive Neuroscience Laboratory and Developmental Disorders Program, Center for Health and Biological Sciences, Mackenzie Presbyterian University, Rua Piaui, 181, 10°andar, Sao Paulo, SP, 01241-001. E-mails: psboggio@gmail.com; paulo.boggio@mackenzie.br

We would like to thank Kayleen Weaver, BA, for her careful proofreading of this manuscript. PSB is supported by a CNPq researcher grant (305718/2009-6); FF is supported by a grant from RJG foundation; CC is supported by a PhD grant (FAPESP- 2010/20063-9); CAV is supported by a Master grant (FAPESP- 2010/14656-7); OML is supported by a Master grant (CAPES-PROSUP - IES Modality I); and ACAG and NIB are supported by student grants (CNPq).

gains such as in recognition memory and language associated with TMS and tDCS treatment. In addition, we showed that TMS has also been used to assess neuroplasticity changes in AD supporting the notion that cortical excitability is changed in AD due to the neurodegenerative process. Due to the safe profile, cost of these tools, and initial clinical trials results, further studies are warranted in order to replicate and extend the initial findings of rTMS and tDCS as cognitive enhancers in AD. Further trials should explore different targets of stimulation along with different paradigms of stimulation including combination with behavioural interventions.

Keywords: tDCS; TMS; Cognitive rehabilitation.

INTRODUCTION

Alzheimer's disease (AD) is a neurodegenerative and progressive disease. It is the most common type of dementia (60% to 80% of the cases) (Thies & Blailer, 2011). It is related to a progressive decline in cognitive functions such as memory, attention, perceptual-spatial abilities, language, and executive functions. Behavioural and affective disorders, such as agitation and depression are also frequently presented. In fact, approximately 50% of AD patients have depression as a comorbid condition (Modrego, 2010).

Genes and environmental components play a role in AD. Four genes are associated with predisposition to AD: apolipoprotein E (APOE), amyloid precursor protein (APP), presenilin 1 (PS1), and presenilin 2 (PS2) (for a review see Bertram, Lill, & Tanzi, 2010). In general, AD neuropathology is related to an abnormal aggregation and deposition of two proteins in the brain – tau and amyloid-β (Aβ) (for review see Ballatore, Lee, & Trojanowski, 2007; Dubois et al., 2010; Maccioni, Muñoz, & Barbeito, 2001).

The incidence of AD increases with age, but AD is not a normal consequence of ageing (Bishop, Lu, Yanker, 2010; Nelson et al., 2011). It is estimated that AD affects 4% of people under 65 years of age, 6% of people between 65 and 74 years of age, and 45% between 75 and 84 years of age; 45% are above 85 years of age (Thies & Blialier, 2011). In 2010, it was estimated that there were 35.5 million individuals with dementia in the world (Alzheimer's Disease International, 2010) with a prediction that this number will increase to 65.7 million people by 2030, and 115.4 million by 2050.

The World Alzheimer Report 2010 (Alzheimer's Disease International, 2010) estimated that the total costs of dementia in 2010 were $604 billion (USD). Given the importance of AD for public health, development of treatments and studies understanding the pathophysiological mechanisms of this disease are necessary. To date, most of these treatments attempt to slow down the progression of disease by increasing cholinergic activity.

However, current treatments are still associated with small effect sizes. More-over, pharmacological treatments are associated with significant adverse effects and, in addition, cannot be used to induce plasticity changes in specific neural networks. Recent evidence has suggested that subjects at risk of devel-oping AD have a highly plastic brain (Belleville et al., 2011) and thus inter-ventions promoting plasticity in specific neural networks are extremely desirable in AD, and may result in reducing the behavioural consequences of AD.

Given the role of rTMS and tDCS to induce and measure neuroplasticity, these tools may have a significant impact for the treatment of AD. In this review, we present an overview of AD, discussing aspects such as impaired cognitive functions, and then a discussion of the role of rTMS and tDCS as assessment and intervention tools. We present evidence that these non-invasive techniques of brain stimulation are capable of improving cognitive functions typically impaired in patients with AD, such as memory, visuo-spatial functions, attention, language, and executive functions. Finally, we review the rTMS and tDCS studies conducted in patients with AD.

NEUROPSYCHOLOGICAL DEFICITS IN AD PATIENTS

AD is a progressive and degenerative process in the basal forebrain, which contains a large number of cholinergic neurons resulting in a decrease of acetylcholine (for a review see Schliebs & Arendt, 2011). The decrease in acetylcholine activity in AD leads to a widespread change in cortical activity, thus leading to a significant cognitive decline across several domains. The understanding of domains affected by this condition is useful to plan for inter-ventions aiming at focal modulation of cortical activity.

Patients with AD present a progressive decline of functional abilities and some cognitive domains such as memory, attention, perception and language. Behavioural changes are also reported. As the disease progresses, the ability to perform daily activities is impaired. The sequence in which cognitive losses occur varies among patients (Stopford, Snowden, Thompson, & Neary, 2008).

Memory impairment is one of the main features of AD. In early stages of the disease, there are observed difficulties in episodic (see Dickerson & Eichenbaum, 2009), semantic (Peters et al., 2009) and working memory (for review see Huntley & Howard, 2010; Storandt, 2008). The use of recog-nition lists (cues) or repetitive stimuli as a training strategy does not always result in improved performance in AD patients. Also, AD patients do not benefit from establishing conceptual relationships such as semantic categories in a list of words, in contrast to normal subjects (Plancher, Guyard, Nicolas, & Piolino, 2009). However, Clare, Wilson, Carter, Roth, and Hodges (2002) showed improvement in face-naming after training using errorless learning procedures in the early stage of AD. These findings suggest that relatively well-preserved skills may be used as a target for memory rehabilitation interventions at early stages.

Another function typically compromised by AD is visuo-spatial ability. It involves the identification and location of stimuli, and deficits of this function are usually related to changes in the dorsal occipital-temporal pathway (Nguyen, Chubb, & Huff, 2003).

Attention deficits are also observed in AD. Usually, changes are observed in span, focus, and selective and divided attention (Belleville et al., 2008; Festa, Heindel, & Ott, 2010; Thomas et al., 2010). AD also comprises executive functions impairing decision making (Gleichgerrcht, Ibáñez, Roca, Torralva, & Manes, 2010).

Finally, AD alters language abilities. Patients with AD have disorders of oral language comprehension. They have difficulty establishing inferences and comprehending ambiguous sentences. De Lira et al. (2011) found poor performance in microlinguistics at the lexical and syntactic aspects in participants with AD, being most affected at the lexical level.

In a recent study by Báez, Mendoza, Reyes, Matallana, and Montañés (2009), patients showed lower performance interpreting the meaning of proverbs, supporting the hypothesis of difficulty in semantic processing of language. Some aspects of language, such as the repetition of simple phrases, seem to be preserved in early stages of the disease. In addition, naming deficits related to semantic knowledge impairment or failures of object name retrieval are observed in AD patients. Alterations to both temporal and frontal areas underlie these deficits, respectively (Melrose et al., 2009).

Mapping cognitive deficits in AD is important to understand the differences in changes in neural networks. In fact, cognitive decline is not homogeneous across subjects with AD and pathological features might affect networks differently. For instance, a recent study in mild cognitive impairment (that might be the precursor for AD) has shown that specific changes in atrophy were correlated with dysfunctions of different cognitive domains. For instance, left temporal lobe atrophy was associated with naming decline, whereas bilateral temporal, left frontal, and left anterior cingulate atrophy were associated with language changes, specifically semantic fluency. Left entorhinal atrophy, on the other hand, was associated with memory decline and, finally, executive dysfunction was associated with bilateral frontal atrophy (McDonald et al., 2010). These data support the notion that cognitive decline depends on neural networks that are affected during progression of disease and thus give additional support to the use of focal brain stimulation to activate specific neural networks in order to induce behavioural gains in AD.

TMS AND tDCS AS ASSESSMENT TOOLS FOR AD-RELATED NEUROPLASTICITY CHANGES

For detailed information on these techniques please refer to the respective articles in this issue. Single and paired-pulse TMS can assess cortical excitability. Therefore, it can be a co-adjuvant diagnostic tool to assess plastic changes associated with interventions such as to measure drug response, and in addition it might be a useful neurophysiological index of cortical hyperexcitability in AD (Pennisi et al., 2011).

TMS studies have shown several abnormalities of motor cortex excitability (for a systematic review see Freitas, Mondragón-Llorca, & Pascual-Leone, 2011). Perretti et al. (1996) found a higher motor evoked potential (MEP) threshold in abductor pollicis brevis (APB) in 40% of moderate to severe AD patients. MEP was not obtained in the relaxed tibialis anterior muscles in 8 of 15 patients. Although these patients presented no clinical signs of motor system changes, these data suggest an overall change in corticospinal excitability.

With paired pulse TMS, it is possible to investigate localised changes in cortical inhibition and facilitation. Liepert, Bar, Meske, and Weiller (2001) investigated 11 mild to moderate AD patients who did not present clinical signs of motor dysfunction. As compared to a healthy control group, they found a reduction of cortical inhibition as indexed by larger MEP amplitudes. When interstimulus intervals (ISIs) were 2, 3 and 4 ms, the authors did not find significant differences between groups with respect to cortical facilitation (but significant differences were found when ISIs were 8, 10, 15 and 20 ms). In addition, there was a correlation between AD severity (as indexed by Clinical Dementia Rating) and the mean value of cortical inhibition. Also, cortical inhibition increased after treatment with donepezil in a daily regimen. Alagona et al. (2001) investigated changes of cortical excitability in 21 AD patients at different stages of the disease (mild, moderate, and severe). Motor threshold of patients was lower than the healthy control group and was correlated with the severity stage. Also, they found an increase in MEP amplitude and a reduction of the silent period duration. These findings at subclinical motor impairment stages are probably associated with a cholinergic deficit.

Also important, it has been shown that short latency afferent inhibition (SAI), related to central cholinergic transmission, is smaller in AD patients as compared to healthy subjects (Chen et al., 2008; Di Lazzaro et al., 2002) and can discriminate AD patients from mild cognitive impairment (MCI) patients (Sakuma, Murakami, & Nakashima, 2007) and frontotemporal dementia patients (Di Lazzaro et al., 2006). Particularly important, Nardone et al. (2008) showed that SAI is smaller in early AD patients, which could benefit early diagnosis.

TMS can be useful in understanding neuroplasticity changes associated with AD progression. Koch et al. (2011) found that 1 Hz repetitive transcranial magnetic stimulation (rTMS) did not induce inhibitory effects in AD patients as observed in healthy controls. L-Dopa did not modulate the effects of rTMS in AD patients showing that synaptic potential plasticity, such as long-term depression, might be impaired in these patients. Martorana et al. (2008) showed that L-Dopa can reverse the impairment of intra-cortical inhibition in AD patients. Although there are no studies to date, tDCS is also another potential tool to be used to induce non-focal plasticity changes (Brunoni et al., 2011). Because tDCS induces changes in neuronal membrane resting threshold, it can provide different insights on plasticity changes as compared with rTMS that induces a modulatory effect that is activity dependent.

The investigation of motor cortex excitability is also interesting to explicate deficits of functional connectivity between language and motor-related brain areas. Bracco et al. (2009) demonstrated that patients with MCI did not present MEP modulation during performance on a linguistic task differently from healthy subjects. Based on this data, TMS along with tDCS might be used as a tool to index progression from MCI to AD.

rTMS AND tDCS AS COGNITIVE ENHANCERS

Both rTMS and tDCS have been shown to be effective cognitive modulators. Their ability to interfere with cognitive functions has been seen in both healthy volunteers and patients with neurological disease (Boggio et al., 2006; Boggio, Khoury, et al., 2009; Fregni et al., 2005; Gagnon, Schneider Grondin, & Blanchet, 2011; Keeser et al., 2011; Kohler, Paus, Buckner, & Milner, 2004; Luber et al., 2007; Solé-Padullés et al., 2006). Studies on the effects of TMS and tDCS on memory, visuo-spatial abilities, attention, executive functions, and language have important implications for AD rehabilitation as these cognitive domains are typically impaired in AD. To date, there are few reports about the effects of rTMS and tDCS on cognitive functions in AD patients. In fact, there are only four papers on the use of rTMS (Bentwich et al., 2011; Cotelli et al., 2006; 2008; 2011) and two on the use of tDCS (Boggio, Khoury, et al., 2008) as cognitive intervention strategies. Thus, a review on the role of brain stimulation as a rehabilitation tool in AD is necessary, as is an overview of the described effects of these techniques in cognition and their impact on quality of life.

rTMS has been shown to be effective for memory improvement in healthy subjects. For instance, the application of 5 Hz rTMS over the midline parietal cortex resulted in a decreased reaction time of a working memory task (Luber et al., 2007). tDCS can also improve working memory. Fregni et al. (2005)

showed that 1 mA anodal tDCS applied over the left prefrontal cortex enhances the performance of healthy subjects in a 3-back task. Interestingly, this effect was also observed by Boggio et al. (2006) in a sample of Parkinson's disease (PD) patients. However, memory improvement in PD patients was only observed with a current intensity of 2mA.

In addition, Marshall, Mölle, Siebner, and Born (2005) used a different protocol of tDCS (intermittent tDCS – 15 sec on and 15 sec off) in healthy subjects. This was applied as bilateral anodal and cathodal stimulation (as well as sham stimulation) at frontocortical electrode sites over the course of 15 min. During stimulation, subjects were given a modified Sternberg task, and the resulting data showed that reaction time decreased during both anodal and cathodal stimulation as compared to placebo. This opposite finding compared with Fregni et al. (2005) underscores the importance of parameters of stimulation in the final results of controlled clinical trials.

These protocols were also extended to stroke patients. Jo et al. (2009) showed that 2 mA anodal tDCS over the left DLPFC enhanced working memory performance of stroke patients. Keeser et al. (2011) found a significant improvement in working memory after anodal tDCS of the left DLPFC. In addition, they found enhanced activity in the left parahippocampal gyrus and an increase of P2 and P3 components for the 2-back task. Finally, two previous studies have demonstrated that tDCS may be useful to reduce false memories due to excessive semantic processing (Boggio, Fregni, et al., 2009; Chi, Fregni, & Snyder, 2010).

Episodic memory formation can also be enhanced by rTMS. Kohler et al. (2004) showed that 7 Hz rTMS applied over the left inferior prefrontal cortex results in enhancement of accuracy as indexed by a word recognition memory task. Gagnon et al. (2011) showed that paired-pulse TMS during the encoding phase of a recognition task shortened the reaction time when applied over the left prefrontal cortex as compared to the right prefrontal cortex or to sham. The effect was the opposite during retrieval; i.e., shorter reaction times after right prefrontal cortex TMS as compared to left prefrontal cortex. The positive effects of TMS on memory performance have also been described among elders with memory dysfunction. Solé-Padullé et al. (2006) showed that rTMS over the prefrontal cortex results in an improvement of associative memory, opening a new avenue for the investigation of patients with memory problems.

The positive effects of rTMS have been demonstrated on the learning process in mice. Ahmed and Wieraszko (2006) demonstrated that 15Hz rTMS improved performance in an object recognition task. Moreover, there was an enhancement of long-term potentiation (LTP) as investigated on hippocampal slices.

tDCS has also been demonstrated as a tool to enhance or facilitate learning. Tecchio et al. (2010) showed that anodal tDCS over M1 after motor training improves consolidation of implicit learning. Clark et al. (2010) showed that 2 mA anodal tDCS over right inferior frontal and right parietal cortex improved learning to identify concealed objects in naturalistic environments.

The positive effects on memory and learning have been extended to other cognitive functions that may potentially have an impact on dementia deficits not directly related to memory. For instance, these positive effects have been seen in language, visuo-spatial, and attention domains. With regard to language, tDCS is related to an enhancement of learning of novel object names (Floel et al., 2008) and improvement of performance on picture naming tasks (Fertonani et al., 2010; Sparing et al., 2008). Naming improvement is also reported with the use of TMS (Cappa, Sandrini, Rossini, Sosta, & Miniussi, 2002; Mottaghy, Sparing, & Topper, 2006; Mottaghy et al., 1999).

tDCS is also capable of modulating visuo-spatial skills. Antal et al. (2004) showed that anodal tDCS over M1 or V5 improves learning of visuo-motor coordination and Bolognini, Fregni, Casati, Olgiati, and Vallar (2010) showed that right posterior parietal cortex anodal stimulation enhances visual search.

Previous findings have also demonstrated that TMS and tDCS can improve some attentional processes and executive functions as indexed by the Stroop task (Boggio et al., 2005;Vanderhasselt, De Raedt, Baeken, Leyman, & D'Haenen, 2006) go-no-go tasks (Boggio et al., 2007), decision making tasks (Boggio et al., 2010; Fecteau et al., 2007; Knoch et al., 2006), and a complex verbal problem-solving task (Cerruti & Schlaug, 2009).

These positive effects suggest its use on brain pathologies. Specifically, tDCS and TMS can enhance memory, attention, visuo-spatial abilities, executive functions and language and therefore it is necessary to investigate if these effects can be transferred to AD patients. Importantly, TMS and tDCS are safe and non-invasive techniques with low occurrences of side-effects when compared to cholinesterase inhibitor (ChE-I) treatment.

To the best of our knowledge, there are only four articles on rTMS (Bentwich et al., 2011; Cotelli et al., 2006; 2008; 2011) and two on tDCS (Boggio, Khoury, et al., 2009; Ferruci et al., 2008) directly investigating the effects of these tools as cognitive enhancers in AD.

Firstly, Cotelli et al. (2006) investigated the effects of rTMS on 15 mild to moderate AD patients all receiving ChEIs. (20 Hz rTMS as well as sham rTMS was delivered over the left or right DLPFC). Magnetic pulses were delivered for 600 ms from the onset of the stimulus presentation. They used a picture naming task as their cognitive measure, using pictures of actions or objects. They found a significant improvement for action naming after both the left and right DLPFC stimulation as compared with sham.

In a subsequent study and using the same paradigm, Cotelli et al. (2008) investigated the effects of rTMS on 24 AD patients divided into two groups, mild and moderate to severe. As previously reported, rTMS of both left and right DLPFC resulted in an improvement in action naming in the mild AD group. In addition, they found an improvement in both action and object naming after rTMS in the moderate to severe group.

In both studies, rTMS was applied in a single session and therefore, long-lasting effects were not assessed. To investigate the cumulative effects of repeated consecutive sessions and possible long-lasting effects, Cotelli et al. (2011) administered a neuropsychological battery of tests including assessment of memory, language, and executive functions. Ten moderate AD patients were assessed before rTMS treatment, at 2, 4 and 12 weeks after the onset of rTMS intervention. Patients were allocated to one of two groups in which they received eiher four weeks of rTMS of the left DLPFC or two weeks of sham rTMS followed by two weeks of active rTMS over the same area. The authors showed a significant effect of rTMS on auditory sentence comprehension. Also, there was no difference on rTMS effects when comparing two and four weeks of treatment showing that two weeks is sufficient to promote a specific language improvement. Moreover, they found long-lasting improvement in sentence comprehension (eight weeks after the end of rTMS treatment).

In contrast Cotelli et al. (2006, 2008, 2011) used an off-line rTMS para-digm. This difference might explain the absence of effect on the picture naming task. Therefore, further investigations should address which kind of effect might be expected using on-line or off-line rTMS. Interestingly, it is also important to investigate the combination of cognitive rehabilitation with non-invasive brain stimulation.

Accordingly, Bentwich et al. (2011) investigated the effects of a combi-nation of cognitive training with rTMS sessions. Eight patients with probable AD received daily rTMS and cognitive training for six weeks followed by a maintenance phase of two sessions per week for an additional three months. rTMS was delivered over Broca's area, Wernicke's area and right DLPFC at one daily session, and left DLPFC, and right and left parietal somatosensory association cortex on the following day. Parallel to each of the cortical stimu-lation sessions, subjects performed tasks of syntax, grammar, comprehension of lexical meaning and categorisation, action and object naming, spatial memory, and spatial attention. The assessments of cognitive performance were performed three weeks before the beginning of the treatment, and six weeks and four and a half months after treatment started. The authors found a significant improvement on ADAS-Cog after both six weeks and four and a half months of the treatment.

On the other hand, there are only two tDCS studies investigating the effects of this technique on AD patients (Boggio, Khoury, et al., 2009; Ferruci et al., 2008). Ferruci et al. (2008) compared the effects of anodal, cathodal and sham tDCS over the temporo-parietal junction in 10 patients with probable AD. Cognitive assessments were performed before and after each tDCS session.

They showed a significant improvement after anodal tDCS on a verbal recognition memory task. Boggio et al. (2009) also investigated the effects of tDCS on a recognition memory test. Ten AD patients received tDCS in three different sessions – 2 mA anodal over the left DLPFC, 2 mA anodal over the left temporal cortex and sham tDCS. Neuropsychological assessment included three cognitive domains: selective attention, working memory and visual recognition memory. All tasks were administered during tDCS. The authors found an improvement of 18% and 13% on the visual recognition memory task during temporal and prefrontal cortex stimulation, respectively.

CONCLUSION

In summary, there is initial evidence that tDCS and TMS can induce cognitive gains in different cognitive domains such as memory, executive functions, language, visuo-spatial abilities and attention in healthy subjects. In addition, preliminary evidence confirms some of these findings in AD patients. Although the safe profile and low cost (considering tDCS) of these tools are attractive as compared to drugs such as ChEIs, it should be underscored that a properly designed study is necessary before any conjecture comparing drugs vs. brain stimulation is made. Furthermore, other studies are needed in order to replicate and extend the initial findings of rTMS and tDCS as cognitive enhancers in AD. Further trials should explore different targets of stimulation along with different paradigms of stimulation including combination with behavioural interventions.

REFERENCES

Ahmed, Z., & Wieraszko, A. (2006). Modulation of learning and hippocampal, neuronal plasticity by repetitive transcranial magnetic stimulation (rTMS). *Bioelectromagnetics, 27*(4), 288–294.

Alagona, G., Bella, R., Ferri, R., Carnemolla, A., Pappalardo, A., Costanzo, E., & Pennisi, G. (2001). Transcranial magnetic stimulation in Alzheimer disease: Motor cortex excitability and cognitive severity. *Neuroscience Letters, 314*(1–2), 57–60.

Alzheimer's Disease International (2010). *World Alzheimer Report 2010*. Retrieved from http://www.alz.co.uk/research/files/WorldAlzheimerReport2010.pdf.

Antal, A., Nitsche, M., Kincses, T., Kruse, W., Hoffmann, K., & Paulus, W. (2004). Facilitation of visuo-motor learning by transcranial direct current stimulation of the motor and extrastriate visual areas in humans. *European Journal of Neuroscience, 19*(10), 2888–2892.

Báez, S., Mendoza, L., Reyes, P., Matallana, D., & Montañés, P. (2009). Interpretation of proverbs and Alzheimer's disease. *Review Neurology, 49,* 566–672.

Ballatore, C., Lee, V. M. Y., & Trojanowski, J. Q. (2007). Tau-mediated neurodegeneration in Alzheimer's disease and related disorders. *Nature Reviews Neuroscience, 8*(9), 663–672.

Belleville, S., Bherer, L., Lepage, E., Chertkow, H., & Gauthier, S. (2008). Task switching capacities in persons with Alzheimer's disease and mild cognitive impairment. *Neuropsychologia, 46*(8), 2225–2233.

Belleville, S., Clément, F., Mellah, S., Gilbert, B., Fontaine, F., & Gauthier, S. (2011). Training-related brain plasticity in subjects at risk of developing Alzheimer's disease. *Brain*, 1–12.

Bentwich, J., Dobronevsky, E., Aichenbaum, S., Shorer, R., Peretz, R., Khaigrekht, M., Marton, R. G., & Rabey, J. M. (2011). Beneficial effect of repetitive transcranial magnetic stimulation combined with cognitive trining for the treatment of Alzheimer's disease: A proof of concept study. *Journal of Neural Transmission*, *118*, 463–471.

Bertram, L., Lill, C. M., & Tanzi, R. E. (2010). The genetics of Alzheimer disease: Back to the future. *Neuron*, *68*(2), 270–281.

Bishop, N. A., Lu, T., & Yankner, B. A. (2010). Neural mechanisms of ageing and cognitive decline. *Nature*, *464*, 529–535.

Boggio, P. S., Bermpohl, F., Vergara, A. O., Muniz, A. L. C. R., Nahas, F. H., Leme, P. B., Rigonatti, S. P., & Fregni, F. (2007). Go-no-go task performance improvement after anodal transcranial DC stimulation of the left dorsolateral prefrontal cortex in major depression. *Journal of Affective Disorders*, *101*(1–3), 91–98.

Boggio, P., Campanhã, C., Valasek, C., Fecteau, S., Pascual-Leone, A., & Fregni, F. (2010). Modulation of decision-making in a gambling task in older adults with transcranial direct current stimulation. *European Journal of Neuroscience*, *31*(3), 593–597.

Boggio, P. S., Ferrucci, R., Rigonatti, S. P., Covre, P., Nitsche, M., Pascual-Leone, A., & Fregni, F. (2006). Effects of transcranial direct current stimulation on working memory in patients with Parkinson's disease. *Journal of the Neurological Sciences*, *249*(1), 31–38.

Boggio, P. S., Fregni, F., Bermpohl, F., Mansur, C. G., Rosa, M., Rumi, D. O., Barbosa, E. R., Rosa, M. O., Pascual-Leone, A., Rigonatti, S. P., Marcolin, M. A., & Silva, M. T. A. (2005). Effect of repetitive TMS and fluoxetine on cognitive function in patients with Parkinson's disease and concurrent depression. *Movement Disorders*, *20*(9), 1178–1219.

Boggio, P. S., Fregni, F., Valasek, C., Ellwood, S., Chi, R., Gallate, J., Pascual-Leone, A., & Snyder, A. (2009). Temporal lobe cortical electrical stimulation during the encoding and retrieval phase reduces false memories. *PLoS One*, *4*(3), e4959.

Boggio, P. S., Khoury, L. P., Martins, D. C. S., Martins, O. E. M. S., De Macedo, E. C., & Fregni, F. (2009). Temporal cortex direct current stimulation enhances performance on a visual recognition memory task in Alzheimer disease. *Journal of Neurology, Neurosurgery and Psychiatry*, *80*(4), 444–447.

Bolognini, N., Fregni, F., Casati, C., Olgiati, E., & Vallar, G. (2010). Brain polarization of parietal cortex augments training-induced improvement of visual exploratory and attentional skills. *Brain Research*, *1349*, 76–89.

Bracco, L., Giovannelli, F., Bessi, V., Borgheresi, A., Tullio, A. D., Sorbi, S., Zaccara, G., & Cincotta, M. (2009). Mild cognitive impairment: Loss of linguistic task-induced changes in motor cortex excitability. *Neurology*, *10*(72), 928–934.

Brunoni, A. B., Nitsche, M., Bolognini, N., Bikson, M., Wagner, T., Merabet, L., Edwards, D. J., Valero-Cabre, A., Rotenberg, A., Pascual-Leone, A., Ferrucci, R., Priori, A., Boggio, P. S., & Fregni, F. (2011). Clinical research with transcranial direct current stimulation (tDCS): Challenges and future directions. *Brain Stimulation*, Advance online publication. doi: 10.1016/j.brs.2011.03.002.

Cappa, S. F., Sandrini, M., Rossini, P. M., Sosta, K., & Miniussi, C. (2002). The role of the left frontal lobe in action naming: rTMS evidence. *Neurology*, *59*(5), 720–723.

Cerruti, C., & Schlaug, G. (2009). Anodal transcranial direct current stimulation of the prefrontal cortex enhances complex verbal associative thought. *Journal of Cognitive Neuroscience*, *21*(10), 1980–1987.

Chen, R., Cros, D., Curra, A., Di Lazzaro, V., Lefaucheur, J., Magistris, M. R., et al. (2008). The clinical diagnostic utility of transcranial magnetic stimulation: Report of an IFCN committee. *Clinical Neurophysiology*, *119*(3), 504–532.

Chi, R. P., Fregni, F., & Snyder, A. W. (2010). Visual memory improved by non-invasive brain stimulation. *Brain Research, 24*(1353), 168–175.

Clare, L., Wilson, B. A., Carter, G., Roth, I., & Hodges, J. R. (2002). Relearning face–name associations in early Alzheimer's disease. *Neuropsychology, 16*(4), 538–547.

Clark, V. P., Coffman, B. A., Mayer, A. R., Weisend, M. P., Lane, T. D., Calhoun, V. D., Raybourn, E. M., Garcia, C. M., & Wassermann, E. M. (2010). tDCS guided using fMRI significantly accelerates learning to identify concealed objects. *NeuroImage, 74*(8), 643–650.

Cotelli, M., Calabria, M., Manenti, R., Rosini, S., Zanetti, O., Cappa, S. F., & Miniussi, C. (2011). Improved language performance in Alzheimer disease following brain stimulation. *Journal of Neurology, Neurosurgery & Psychiatry, 82*(7), 794–797.

Cotelli, M., Manenti, R., Cappa, S. F., Geroldi, C., Zanetti, O., Rossini, P. M., & Miniussi, C. (2006). Effect of transcranial magnetic stimulation on action naming in patients with Alzheimer disease. *Archives Neurology, 63,* 1602–1604.

Cotelli, M., Manenti, R., Cappa, S. F., Zanetti, O., & Miniussi, C. (2008). Transcranial magnetic stimulation improves naming in Alzheimer disease patients at different stages of cognitive decline. *European Journal of Neurology, 15,* 1286–1292.

De Lira, J. O., Ortiz, K. Z., Campanha, A. C., Bertolucci, P. H., & Minett, T. S. (2011). Microlinguistic aspects of the oral narrative in patients with Alzheimer's disease. *International Psychogeriatrics, 23*(3), 404–412.

Dickerson, B. C., & Eichenbaum, H. (2009). The episodic memory system: Neurocircuitry and disorders. *Neuropsychopharmacology,* 1–19.

Di Lazzaro, V., Oliviero, A., Tonali, P. A., Marra, C., Daniele, A., Profice, P., et al. (2002). Noninvasive *in vivo* assessment of cholinergic cortical circuits in AD using transcranial magnetic stimulation. *Neurology, 59*(3), 392–397.

Di Lazzaro, V., Pilato, F., Dileone, M., Saturno, E., Oliviero, A., Marra, C., Daniele, A., Ranieri, F., Gainotti, G., & Tonali, P. A. (2006). *In vivo* cholinergic circuit evaluation in frontotemporal and Alzheimer dementias. *Neurology, 66*(7), 1111–1113.

Dubois, B., Feldman, H. H., Jacova, C., Cummings, J. L., Dekosky, S. T., Barberger-Gateau, P., Delacourte, A., Frisoni, G., Fox, N. C., Galasko, D., Gauthier, S., Hampel, H., Jicha, G. A., Meguro, K., O'Brien, J., Pasquier, F., Robert, P., Rossor, M., Salloway, S., Sarazin, M., de Souza, L. C., Stern, Y., Visser, P. J., & Scheltens, P. (2010). Revising the definition of Alzheimer's disease: A new lexicon. *The Lancet Neurology, 9*(11), 1118–1127.

Fecteau, S., Knoch, D., Fregni, F., Sultani, N., Boggio, P., & Pascual-Leone, A. (2007). Diminishing risk-taking behavior by modulating activity in the prefrontal cortex: A direct current stimulation study. *Journal of Neuroscience, 27*(46), 12500–12505.

Ferrucci, R., Mameli, F., Guidi, I., Mrakic-Sposta, S., Vergari, M., Marceglia, S., Cogiamanian, F., Barbieri, S., Scarpini, E., & Priori, A. (2008). Transcranial direct current stimulation improves recognition memory in Alzheimer disease. *Neurology, 71*(7), 493–498.

Fertonani, A., Rosini, S., Cotelli, M., Rossini, P. M., & Miniussi, C. (2010). Naming facilitation induced by transcranial direct current stimulation. *Behavioural Brain Research, 208*(2), 311–318.

Festa, E. K., Heindel, W. C., & Ott, B. R. (2010). Dual-task conditions modulate the efficiency of selective attention mechanisms in Alzheimer's disease. *Neuropsychologia, 48*(11), 3252–3261.

Flöel, A., Rösser, N., Michka, O., Knecht, S., & Breitenstein, C. (2008). Noninvasive brain stimulation improves language learning. *Journal of Cognitive Neuroscience, 20*(8), 1415–1422.

Fregni, F., Boggio, P., Nitsche, M., Bermpohl, F., Antal, A., Feredoes, E., Marcolin, M. A., Rigonatti, S. P., Silva, M. T. A., Paulus, W., & Pascual-Leone, A. (2005). Anodal transcranial direct current stimulation of prefrontal cortex enhances working memory. *Experimental Brain Research, 166*(1), 23–30.

Freitas, C., Mondragón-Llorca, H., & Pascual-Leone, A. (2011). Noninvasive brain stimulation in Alzheimer's disease: Systematic review and perspectives for the future. *Experimental Gerontology, 46*(8), 611–627.

Gagnon, G., Schneider, C., Grondin, S., & Blanchet, S. (2011). Enhancement of episodic memory in young and healthy adults: A paired-pulse TMS study on encoding and retrieval performance. *Neuroscience Letters, 488*(2), 138–142.

Gleichgerrcht, W., Ibáñez, A., Roca, M., Torralva, T., & Manes, F. (2010). Decision-making cognition in neurodegenerative diseases. *Nature Reviews Neurology, 6,* 611–623.

Huntley, J. D., & Howard, R. J. (2010). Working memory in early Alzheimer's disease: A neuropsychological review. *International Journal of Geriatric Psychiatry, 25*(2), 121–132.

Jo, J. M., Kim, Y. H., Ko, M. H., Ohn, S. H., Joen, B., & Lee, K. H. (2009). Enhancing the working memory of stroke patients using tDCS. *American Journal of Physical Medicine and Rehabilitation, 88*(5), 404–409.

Keeser, D., Padberg, F., Reisinger, E., Pogarell, O., Kirsch, V., Palm, U., Karch, S., Möller, H. J., Nitsche, M. A., & Mulert, C. (2011). Prefrontal direct current stimulation modulates resting EEG and event-related potentials in healthy subjects: A standardized low resolution tomography (sLORETA) study. *NeuroImage, 55*(2), 644–657.

Knoch, D., Gianotti, L., Pascual-Leone, A., Treyer, V., Regard, M., Hohmann, M., & Brugger, P. (2006). Disruption of right prefrontal cortex by low-frequency repetitive transcranial magnetic stimulation induces risk-taking behavior. *Journal of Neuroscience, 26*(24), 6469–6472.

Koch, G., Esposito, Z., Codecà, C., Mori, F., Kusayanagi, H., Monteleone, F., Di Lorenzo, F., Bernardi, G., & Martorana, A. (2011). Altered dopamine modulation of LTD-like plasticity in Alzheimer's disease patients. *Clinical Neurophysiology, 122*(4), 703–707.

Köhler, S., Paus, T., Buckner, R. L., & Milner, B. (2004). Effects of left inferior prefrontal stimulation on episodic memory formation: A two-stage fMRI–rTMS study. *Journal of Cognitive Neuroscience, 16,* 178–188.

Liepert, J., Bär, K. J., Meske, U., & Weiller, C. (2001). Motor cortex disinhibition in Alzheimer's disease. *Clinical Neurophysiology, 112*(8), 1436–1441.

Luber, B., Kinnunen, L. H., Rakitin, B. C., Ellsasser, R., Stern, Y., & Lisanby, S. H. (2007). Facilitation of performance in a working memory task with rTMS stimulation of the precuneus: Frequency- and time-dependent effects. *Brain Research, 1128,* 120–129.

Maccioni, R. B., Muñoz, J. P., & Barbeito, L. (2001). The molecular bases of Alzheimer's disease and other neurodegenerative disorders. *Archives Medical Research, 32*(5), 367–381.

Marshall, L., Mölle, M., Siebner, H. R., & Born, J. (2005). Bifrontal transcranial direct current stimulation slows reaction time in a working memory task. *BMC Neuroscience, 8*(6), 23.

Martorana, A., Stefani, A., Palmieri, M. G., Esposito, Z., Bernardi, G., Sancesario, G., & Pierantozzi, M. (2008). L-dopa modulates motor cortex excitability in Alzheimer's disease patients. *Journal of Neural Transmission, 115*(9), 1313–1319.

McDonald, C. R., Gharapetian, L., McEvoy, L. K., Fennema-Notestine, C., Hagler, D. J. Jr, Holland, D., & Dale, A. M. (2010). Relationship between regional atrophy rates and cognitive decline in mild cognitive impairment. *Neurobiology of Aging*. Advance online publication. doi: 10.1016/j.neurobiolaging.2010.03.015.

Melrose, R. J., Campa, O. M., Harwood, D. G., Osato, S., Mandelkern, M. A., & Sultzer, D. L. (2009). The neural correlates of naming and fluency deficits in Alzheimer's disease: An FDG-PET study. *International Journal of Geriatric Psychiatry, 24,* 885–893.

Modrego, P. J. (2010). Depression in Alzheimer's disease. Pathophysiology, diagnosis, and treatment. *Journal of Alzheimer's Disease, 21*(4), 1077–1087.

Mottaghy, F. M., Hungs, M., Brügmann, M., Sparing, R., Boroojerdi, B., Foltys, H., Huber, W., & Töpper, R. (1999). Facilitation of picture naming after repetitive transcranial magnetic stimulation. *Neurology, 53*(8), 1806–1812.

Mottaghy, F. M., Sparing, R., & Töpper, R. (2006). Enhancing picture naming with transcranial magnetic stimulation. *Behavioural Neurology, 17*(3–4), 177–186.

Nardone, R., Bergmann, J., Kronbichler, M., Kunz, A., Klein, S., Caleri, F., Tezzon, F., Ladurner, G., & Golaszewski, S. (2008). Abnormal short latency afferent inhibition in early Alzheimer's disease: A transcranial magnetic demonstration. *Journal of Neural Transmission, 115*(11), 1557–1562.

Nelson, P. T., Head, E., Schmitt, F. A., Davis, P. R., Neltner, J. H., Jicha, G. A., et al. (2011). Alzheimer's disease is not "brain aging": Neuropathological, genetic, and epidemiological human studies. *Acta Neuropathologica, 121*(5), 571–587.

Nguyen, A. S., Chubb, C., & Huff, F. J. (2003). Visual identification and spatial location in Alzheimer's disease. *Brain and Cognition, 52*(2), 155–166.

Pennisi, G., Ferri, R., Lanza, G., Cantone, M., Pennisi, M., Puglisi, V., Malaguarnera, G., & Bella, R. (2011). Transcranial magnetic stimulation in Alzheimer's disease: A neurophysiological marker of cortical hyperexcitability. *Journal of Neural Transmission, 115*(11), 1557–1562.

Perretti, A., Grossi, D., Fragassi, N., Lanzillo, B., Nolano, M., Pisacreta, A. I., Caruso, G., & Santoro, L. (1996). Evaluation of the motor cortex by magnetic stimulation in patients with Alzheimer disease. *Journal of the Neurological Sciences, 135*(1), 31–37.

Peters, F., Majerus, S., De Baerdemaeker, J., Salmon, E., & Collette, F. (2009). Impaired semantic knowledge underlies the reduced verbal short-term storage capacity in Alzheimer's disease. *Neuropsychologia, 47*(14), 3067–3073.

Plancher, G., Guyard, A, Nicolas, S., & Piolino, P. (2009). Mechanisms underlying the production of false memories for famous people's names in aging and Alzheimer's disease. *Neuropsychologia, 47*(12), 2527–2536.

Sakuma, K., Murakami, T., & Nakashima, A. K. (2007). Short latency afferent inhibition is not impaired in mild cognitive impairment. *Clinical Neurophysiology, 118*(7), 1460–1463.

Schliebs, R., & Arendt, T. (2011). The cholinergic system in aging and neuronal degeneration. *Behavioural Brain Research, 221*(2), 555–563.

Solé-Padullé, C., Bartré s-Faz, D., Junqué, C., Clemente, I. C., Molinuevo, J. L., Bargalló, N., Sánchez-Aldeguer, J., Bosch, B., Falcó, C., & Valls-Solé, J. (2006). Repetitive transcranial magnetic stimulation effects on brain function and cognition among elders with memory dysfunction. A randomized sham-controlled study. *Cerebral Cortex, 16,* 1487–1493.

Sparing, R., Dafotakis, M., Meister, I. G., Thirugnanasambandam, N., & Fink, G. R. (2008). Enhancing language performance with non-invasive brain stimulation – A transcranial direct current stimulation study in healthy humans. *Neuropsychologia, 46*(1), 261–268.

Stopford, C. L., Snowden, J. S., Thompson, J. C., & Neary, D. (2008). Variability in cognitive presentation of Alzheimer's disease. *Cortex, 44,* 185–195.

Storandt, M. (2008). Cognitive deficits in the early stages of Alzheimer's disease. *Current Directions in Psychological Science, 17*(3), 198–202.

Tecchio, F., Zappasodi, F., Assenza, G., Tombini, M., Vollaro, S., Barbati, G., & Rossini, P. M. (2010). Anodal transcranial direct current stimulation enhances procedural consolidation. *Journal of Neurophysiology, 104*(2), 1134–1140.

Thies, W., & Bleiler, L. (2011). 2011 Alzheimer's disease facts and figures. *Alzheimer's and Dementia, 7*(2), 208–244.

Thomas, C., vom Berg, I., Rupp, A., Seidl, U., Schröder, J., Roesch-Ely, D., Kreisel, S. H., Mundt, C., & Weisbrod, M. (2010). P50 gating deficit in Alzheimer dementia correlates to frontal neuropsychological function. *Neurobiology of Aging, 31*(3), 416–424.

Vanderhasselt, M. A, De Raedt, R., Baeken, C., Leyman, L., & D'Haenen, H. (2006). The influence of rTMS over the right dorsolateral prefrontal cortex on intentional set switching. *Experimental Brain Research, 172*(4), 561–565.

NEUROPSYCHOLOGICAL REHABILITATION
2011, 21 (5), 717–741

Anomia training and brain stimulation in chronic aphasia

Maria Cotelli[1], Anna Fertonani[1], Antonio Miozzo[2], Sandra Rosini[1], Rosa Manenti[1], Alessandro Padovani[2], Ana Ines Ansaldo[3], Stefano F. Cappa[4], and Carlo Miniussi[1,5]

[1]IRCCS Centro San Giovanni di Dio Fatebenefratelli, Brescia, Italy
[2]Centre for Brain Aging and Neurodegenerative Disorders, Neurology Unit, University of Brescia, Italy
[3]Département D'orthophonie et Audiologie, Faculté de Médecine, Université de Montréal; Centre de Recherche de l'Institut Universitaire de Gériatrie de Montréal, Canada
[4]Vita-Salute University and San Raffaele Scientific Institute, Milan, Italy
[5]Department of Biomedical Sciences and Biotechnologies, National Neuroscience Institute, University of Brescia, Brescia, Italy

Recent studies have reported enhanced performance on language tasks induced by non-invasive brain stimulation, i.e., repetitive transcranial magnetic stimulation (rTMS), or transcranial direct current stimulation (tDCS), in patients with aphasia due to stroke or Alzheimer's disease (AD). The first part of this article reviews brain stimulation studies related to language recovery in aphasic patients. The second part reports results from a pilot study with three chronic stroke patients who had non-fluent aphasia, where real or placebo rTMS was immediately followed by 25 minutes of individualised speech therapy. Real rTMS consisted of high-frequency rTMS over the left dorsolateral prefrontal cortex (BA 8/9) for 25 minutes. Each patient underwent a total of four weeks of intervention. P1 underwent four weeks of real rTMS

Correspondence should be addressed to Maria Cotelli, PhD, IRCCS Centro San Giovanni di Dio Fatebenefratelli, Via Pilastroni, 4, 25125 Brescia, Italy. E-mail: mcotelli@fatebenefratelli.it

This work was supported by James S. McDonnell Foundation and Associazione Fatebenefratelli per la Ricerca.

(5 days/week) where individualised speech therapy was provided for 25 minutes immediately following each rTMS session. P2 and P3 each underwent two weeks of placebo rTMS, followed immediately by individualised speech therapy; then two weeks of real rTMS, followed immediately by individualised speech therapy. Assessments took place at 2, 4, 12, 24 and 48 weeks post-entry/baseline testing. Relative to entry/baseline testing, a significant improvement in object naming was observed at all testing times, from two weeks post-intervention in real rTMS plus speech therapy, or placebo rTMS plus speech therapy. Our findings suggest beneficial effects of targeted behavioural training in combination with brain stimulation in chronic aphasic patients. However, further work is required in order to verify whether optimal combination parameters (rTMS alone or speech therapy alone) and length of rTMS treatment may be found.

Keywords: TMS; rTMS; Naming; Speech therapy.

INTRODUCTION

Aphasia is a frequent consequence of stroke (Engelter, 2006; Laska, Hellblom, Murray, Kahan, & Von Arbin, 2001) and is associated with increased mortality, decreased rates of functional recovery, and reduced probability of returning to work (Black-Schaffer & Osberg, 1990; Paolucci et al., 1998; Tilling et al., 2001). While there is a general consensus that aphasia rehabilitation is effective (Berthier & Pulvermuller, 2011; Cappa et al., 2003, 2005; Galletta, Rao, & Barrett, 2011), high-quality clinical trials are lacking and there is insufficient evidence indicating which is the best approach to delivering speech and language therapy (Kelly, Brady, & Enderby, 2010). Moreover, recent studies have shown that a high intensity of treatment is crucial for efficacy (Bhogal, Teasell, & Speechley, 2003); however, from a clinical prospective, highly intensive treatments are often impractical.

Within this context, there is increasing interest in the potential enhancement of performance with non-invasive brain stimulation, i.e., repetitive transcranial magnetic stimulation (rTMS) or transcranial direct current stimulation (tDCS), applied to specific cortical areas (Miniussi et al., 2008). Facilitation effects have been observed in patients with stroke and dementia when performing a variety of cognitive tasks. These effects have been related to TMS-induced changes in cortical excitability resulting in functional reorganisation and improved cognitive performance. Specifically, the potential of rTMS or tDCS to trigger adaptive neuroplasticity in neurological patients has been related to three main mechanisms: (1) the reactivation of canonical networks, partly damaged or made dysfunctional by the cerebral lesion; (2) the recruitment of compensatory networks, mostly contralateral homologue cortical regions; and (3) the additional recruitment of perilesional sub-optimally functioning areas (see Miniussi & Rossini, this issue, for a discussion). However, the mechanisms responsible for rTMS- and tDCS-induced changes in neural activity remain largely unknown. There is, however, evidence that rTMS and tDCS techniques can modify neuronal excitation through different mechanisms: TMS elicits action potentials in neurons, whereas tDCS does not (see Paulus, this issue). However, tDCS effectively modifies both the evoked cortical response to afferent stimulation, and the post-synaptic activity level of cortical neurons, presumably by inducing a shift in intrinsic neuronal excitability (Bindman, Lippold, & Redfearn, 1962). In other words, both techniques can modify cortical plasticity by increasing excitability in cortical neurons within a specific network and, in doing so, improve the cognitive ability sustained by the stimulated network.

Specifically, regarding rTMS, there is evidence that the frequency of stimulation modulates neural activity. High-frequency rTMS (≥ 5 Hz), has been shown to increase cortical excitability, whereas low-frequency rTMS (≤ 1 Hz) can inhibit "maladaptive" plasticity, which prevents recovery from aphasia (Martin, Naeser, Ho, Doron, et al., 2009). The administration of rTMS to the anterior portion of the right homologue of Broca's area (pars triangularis) improves picture naming in patients with non-fluent aphasia (Barwood, Murdoch, Whelan, Lloyd, Riek, O'Sullivan, Coulthard, & Wong, 2011; Barwood, Murdoch, Whelan, Lloyd, Riek, O'Sullivan, Coulthard, Wong, et al., 2011; Hamilton et al., 2010; Naeser, Martin, Lundgren, et al., 2010; Naeser, Martin, Nicholas, Baker, Seekins, Helm-Estabrooks, et al., 2005). In a stroke patient with chronic non-fluent aphasia, the same authors reported improvement of language following treatment with continuous positive airway pressure (CPAP) for sleep apnoea, as well as following CPAP plus slow-rTMS, to suppress pars triangularis (Naeser, Martin, Lundgren, et al., 2010). Naeser et al. (Naeser, Martin, Nicholas, Baker, Seekins, Kobayashi, 2010) argue that low-frequency rTMS over the right pars triangularis suppresses maladaptive right hemisphere frontal activations, and thus allows for the activation of left hemispheric perilesional and perisylvian areas, as well as the left supplementary motor area, which support recovery in non-fluent aphasic patients. However, in the study by Martin and co-authors (Martin, Naeser, Ho, Doron, et al., 2009), only one of two patients with chronic non-fluent aphasia showed language improvement following low-frequency rTMS on the right pars triangularis. Martin et al. (Martin, Naeser, Ho, Doron, et al., 2009) argue that the shift to left hemisphere activation post-rTMS observed in the fMRI scans of the good responders supports the idea that restoration of the left hemisphere language network is linked, at least in part, to a better recovery of naming in non-fluent aphasia. Moreover, Martin, Naeser, Ho, Treglia, et al. (2009) reported improved naming performance following a combined behavioural and rTMS treatment in a pilot single-case study, in which rTMS stimulation was immediately followed by constraint-induced language therapy. These pilot data suggest that a combined behavioural-rTMS treatment could be more efficient than behavioural treatment alone.

In this vein, Kakuda, Abo, Kaito, et al. (2010) demonstrated that the application of low-frequency rTMS to an area that is homologous to the most activated area, as evaluated in a pre-treatment fMRI acquisition, resulted in improvement of language abilities in three chronic stroke patients. In a subsequent study, the authors applied rTMS over the left Wernicke's area combined with language therapy in two post-stroke patients with "sensory-dominant" aphasia (Kakuda, Abo, Uruma, et al., 2010). Ten sessions of treatment were delivered during a 6-day hospitalisation period, followed by a weekly outpatient rTMS treatment for 3 months. The study showed an improvement of comprehension abilities in both patients at the end of the 6th day, maintained at the 3-month post-discharge period.

A recent randomised, controlled, blinded pilot study has investigated the effect of low-frequency rTMS over the right-hemispheric pars triangularis portion of the Broca's area homologue in 10 left-brain-damaged patients with post-stroke aphasia (Weiduschat et al., 2011). Patients received, in addition to conventional speech and language therapy, multiple sessions of rTMS. Using positron emission tomography (PET) this study revealed a shift of activation towards the right hemisphere in the placebo group, but not in the real rTMS group of patients. Furthermore, only patients in the real rTMS group improved their performance in the Aachener Aphasia Test (AAT) global score. The authors suggest that low-frequency rTMS applied on the right-hemispheric pars triangularis portion of the Broca's area homologue prevents right-hemispheric lateralisation resulting in a better clinical improvement.

Furthermore, Szaflarski and co-authors (2011) provide preliminary evidence regarding the safety and efficacy of fMRI-guided high-frequency rTMS (intermittent theta burst stimulation) applied to the residual left hemispheric Broca's area in eight left-brain-damaged patients with post-stroke aphasia. The study showed an improvement in semantic fluency after 2 weeks of stimulation that was associated with a significant shift of the fMRI signal to the affected hemisphere. Finally, Jung and co-workers (2010) report a significant improvement of naming and comprehension performances in a post-stroke patient affected by crossed aphasia, following the application of low-frequency rTMS over the left parietal cortex.

tDCS is another way of promoting neuroplasticity to enhance cognitive performance. In tDCS, a weak electrical current is directly applied to the head to generate an electrical field that modulates neuronal activity (see Paulus, this issue). Anodal tDCS (atDCS) has a general facilitation effect and causes membrane depolarisation, whereas cathodal tDCS (ctDCS) has a general inhibitory effect and causes membrane hyperpolarisation (cathodal stimulation, see Liebetanz, Nitsche, Tergau, & Paulus, 2002). Behavioural facilitatory tDCS effects have been highlighted (see Vallar & Bolognini, this issue) with respect to implicit motor learning (Nitsche et al., 2003; Reis et al., 2009), working memory (Fregni et al., 2005; Ohn et al., 2008), pitch memory (Vines, Schnider, & Schlaug, 2006), perception (Antal et al., 2004), and language (Fertonani, Rosini, Cotelli, Rossini, & Miniussi, 2010; Iyer et al., 2005; Sparing, Dafotakis, Meister, Thirugnanasambandam, & Fink, 2008). Interestingly, and particularly relevant to the neurorehabilitation field, these tDCS-induced modifications of cortical excitability and behaviour can outlast the stimulation period itself. Hence, there is growing interest in applying these methodologies therapeutically, in order to potentiate the effects of cognitive rehabilitation, and to reduce cognitive deficits in patients with chronic and neurodegenerative diseases.

Monti and co-authors (2008) reported naming facilitation following cathodal stimulation over the damaged left frontotemporal areas in eight patients with chronic, non-fluent, post-stroke aphasia. Baker, Rorden, and Fridriksson (2010) performed a combined behavioural tDCS study with left-brain-damaged patients receiving 5 days of computerised anomia therapy concurrently with tDCS over the damaged left hemisphere or sham stimulation. This study revealed significantly improved naming accuracy in patients treated with anodal tDCS compared with the sham tDCS patients. In addition, the treatment effect persisted for at least 1 week after treatment. Fridriksson et al. (2011) applied the same procedure used by Baker et al. (2010) in eight left-brain-damaged patients with chronic fluent aphasia, and showed that anodal tDCS administered during language treatment decreased verbal reaction times during naming, as assessed immediately post-treatment and 3 weeks later. Another recent study (Fiori et al., 2011) highlights the beneficial effects of 5 days of anodal tDCS in three aphasic patients. The stimulation was applied to Wernicke's area while patients were executing a naming task. This procedure produced an improvement in naming accuracy that lasted for 3 weeks.

In a randomised, double-blind, sham controlled crossover trial, Floel and co-workers (2011) explored whether anodal tDCS compared to cathodal tDCS and placebo stimulation applied over the right temporo-parietal cortex would improve the success of anomia training in a group of 12 post-stroke aphasic left-brain-damaged patients. This finding indicates that all treatment conditions led to a significant increase of naming ability, with a greater effect of anodal tDCS as compared to cathodal and placebo tDCS.

Kang and colleagues (2011) evaluated the hypothesis that cathodal tDCS applied on the right Broca's homologue could improve picture naming in patients with post-stroke aphasia. Patients received 5 consecutive days of cathodal tDCS followed or preceded (with a minimum interval of 1 week) by 5 days of placebo tDCS and simultaneous language therapy. Results demonstrated that cathodal tDCS applied over the right Broca's homologue

combined with language therapy can improve picture naming task performance in post-stroke aphasic patients.

Furthermore, You, Kim, Chun, Jung, and Park (2011), in a prospective,
double-blind, sham-controlled study assessed whether anodal tDCS delivered
to the left superior temporal gyrus, or cathodal tDCS to the right superior
temporal gyrus in comparison with sham tDCS could ameliorate aphasic
symptoms. Cathodal tDCS over right superior temporal areas brought about
significantly greater improvements in auditory verbal comprehension as
compared to the other two conditions.

In summary, recent studies report enhanced cognitive performance
following rTMS or tDCS, to specific cortical areas in a variety of patients
with neurological diseases (see Table 1). Specifically, in chronic aphasia
patients, non-invasive brain stimulation has been shown to increase the
number of correct responses and to reduce response times. Moreover, recent
studies suggest that these effects can persist over time (Baker et al., 2010;
Barwood, Murdoch, Whelan, Lloyd, Riek, O'Sullivan, Coulthard, & Wong,
2011; Fiori et al., 2011; Floel et al., 2011; Fridriksson et al., 2011; Hamilton
et al., 2010; Kakuda, Abo, Kaito, et al., 2010; Kakuda, Abo, Uruma, et al.,
2010b; Martin, Naeser, Ho, Doron, et al., 2009; Martin, Naeser, Ho, Treglia,
et al., 2009; Naeser, Martin Lundgren, et al., 2010; Naeser, Martin Nicholas,
Baker, Seekins, Helm-Estabrooks, et al., 2005; Naeser, Martin, Nicholas,
Baker, Seekins, Kobayashi, et al., 2005; Naeser, Martin, Treglia, et al., 2010).

The present study reports the results of a combined rTMS anomia training
approach administered to three patients with post-stroke chronic aphasia
(PWAs).

PARTICIPANTS

Three patients with post-stroke chronic aphasia (PWAs) were recruited for the
present study. Time after onset of aphasia varied from 1 year to 4.5 years.
Two PWAs had suffered a left middle cerebral artery infarction, PWA 1
(P1) and PWA 3 (P3), whereas one PWA had a left capsulo-thalamic haem-
orrhage, PWA 2 (P2). P2 and P3 were right-handed, P1 was left-handed. A
clinical assessment showed full awareness of the deficits in each of the
three patients.

Each patient underwent a neurological assessment, complete neuropsychological assessment (see Table 2) and neuroimaging diagnostic procedures (see
Figure 1). They all presented non-fluent speech but no verbal dyspraxia. The
ability to understand single words was preserved. They could repeat and read
single words but had a naming deficit.

Exclusion criteria included clinical evidence of depression, clinical signs
of hearing or vision impairment, a past history of epilepsy, implanted metal
objects, psychosis or major depression, alcohol abuse and drug addiction.

TABLE 1
Different rTMS and tDCS approaches

Study	Number of patients (time post-stroke onset in months)	Lesion site	Type of aphasia	rTMS/tDCS approach	Placebo	Stimulated area	Language training	Outcome measures	Follow up timings from baseline	Results
(Naeser et al., 2005)[1]	1 (77)	LH SCL	P1: NF/G	1 Hz rTMS, 20 m/d (1200 p), 90% of MT, 5 d/w, 2 w	No	RH PTr	No	BNT, BDAE	10, 34 w	Improvement in naming accuracy on BNT and BDAE at 10 and 34 w.
(Naeser et al., 2005)[2]	4 (60–132)	P1–P3: LH FC; P4: LH SCL	P1: A; P2, P3: NF; P4: NF/G	1 Hz rTMS, 20 m/d (1200 p), 90% of MT, 5 d/w, 2 w	No	RH PTr	No	BNT, BDAE	10, 34 w	Improvement of naming of BDAE. Improvements in BNT, animals and tools/implements of BDAE at 10 w, in naming of BNT, animals and tools/implements of BDAE at 34 w.
(Martin et al., 2009)[3]	2 (24–120)	P1: LH FTPC, SCL; P2: LH FTC, SCL	P1, P2: NF	1 Hz rTMS, 20 m/d (1200 p), 90% of MT, 5 d/w, 2 w	No	RH PTr	No	BNT, BDAE	P1: 10, 26, 34, 66, 174 w; P2: 10, 26 w	P1: improvement of naming and longest phrase length at all timepoints. P2: no improvements.
(Martin et al., 2009)[4]	1 (125)	LH SCL	P1: NF/G	1 Hz rTMS, 20 m/d (1200 p), 90% of MT, 5 d/w, 2 w	No	RH PTr	Post, CILT, 180 m	BNT, BDAE	6, 26 w	Improvement of naming of BDAE.

(Continued)

TABLE 1
Continued

Study	Number of patients (time post-stroke onset in months)	Lesion site	Type of aphasia	rTMS/tDCS approach	Placebo	Stimulated area	Language training	Outcome measures	Follow up timings from baseline	Results
(Naeser et al., 2010)[5]	1 (24)	LH FTC, LH SCL	P1: NF	1 Hz rTMS, 20 m/ d (1200 p), 90% of MT, 5 d/w, 2 w	No	RH PTr	No	BNT, BDAE	14, 26, 114 w	Improvement in picture description, auditory comprehension and naming at 14, 26 and 114 w.
(Naeser et al., 2010)[6]	2 (56–149)	**P1**: LH SCL; **P2**:LH FTC, LH SCL	P1: NF/ G, P2: NF	1 Hz rTMS, 20 m/ d (1200 p), 90% of MT, 5 d/w, 2 w	No	RH PTr	Post, CILT180 m	BNT, BDAE	P1: 6, 26 w; P2: 10 w	Improvement of action naming of BDAE, Tools/ implements, Single Word Repetition in P1; naming of BNT, propositional speech in P2.
(Barwood et al., 2011)[7]	12 (24-72); real (6) and placebo (6)	**P1-P6, P8, P10-P12**: LH FTC; **P7**: LH TC; **P9**: LH FTC, RH OC, SCL	P1, P3, P6-P11: NF; P2, P4-P5, P12: NF/ G	1 Hz rTMS, 20 m/ d (1200 p), 90% of MT, 5 d/w, 2 w	Yes	RH PTr	No	BNT, BDAE, SV	10 w	Improvement of naming accuracy on BNT, BDAE, SV object naming accuracy; reduction of object-naming latency.
(Hamilton et al., 2010)	1 (7)	LH FTPC	P1: NF	1 Hz rTMS, 20 m/ d (1200 p), 90% of MT, 5 d/w, 2 w	No	RH PTr	No	BDAE, WAB	10, 26, 42 w	Improvement in picture description. Improvement of naming at 26 w and of spontaneous speech of WAB and picture description at 42 w.

(Kakuda, Abo, Kaito, et al., 2010)	4 (5–28)	**P1:** LH FTC; **P2, P3:** LH FC; **P4:** LH putamen.	P1-P4: MD	1 Hz rTMS, 20 m/ d (1200 p), 90% of MT for 10 treatments, 6 d	No	P1, P2: **RH** FC; P3, P4: LH FC	Post, LT 60 m	WAB, SLTA, SLTA-ST	5 w	Improvement of WAB, SLTA, SLTA-ST in P1 and P2 and of naming of SLTA in P3 and repetition of WAB in P4. Stable at 5 w.
(Kakuda, Abo, Uruma, et al., 2010)	2 (7–8)	**P1–P2:** LH FTPC	P1–P2: SD	1 Hz rTMS, 20 m/ d (1200 p), 90% of MT for 10 treatments, 6 d plus 1 Hz rTMS, 20 m/ d (1200 p), 90% of MT, 1 d/w, 12 w	No	LH W	Post, LT 60 m	SLTA, TT	12 w	Improvement of TT and comprehension of SLTA at 2 and 12 w.
(Jung et al., 2010)	1 (36)	NA	P1:C	1 Hz rTMS, 20 m/ d (1200 p), 90% of MT, 5 d/w, 2 w	No	LH PC	No	MMSE, MAS, K-WAB	None	Improvement of naming and comprehension at 2 w.
(Barwood et al., 2011)[8]	12 (24–72); real (6) and placebo (6)	**P1–P6, P8, P10–P12:** LH FTC; **P7:** LH TC; **P9:** LH FTC, RH OC, SCL	P1, P3, P6–P11: NF; P2, P4–P5, P12: NF/ G	1 Hz rTMS, 20 m/ d (1200 p), 90% of MT, 5 d/w, 2 w	Yes	RH PTr	No	BNT, BDAE, SV	None	Improvement on BNT, BDAE naming accuracy, picture description and repetition, SV naming accuracy and reduction of SV naming latency.
(Szaflarski et al., 2011)	8 (>12, mean: 63)	NA	P1, P3, P4, P6: A; P2, P5, P7, P8: NF	iTBS, 200 s/d (600 p), 80% of MT, 5 d/w, 2 w	No	LH B	No	SF, CAL, COWAT, BNT, PPVT, BDAE	None	Improved SF performance.
(Weiduschat et al., 2011)	10 (1–3) real (6) and placebo (4)	**P1:** FC; **P3:** TC; **P4, P13:** SCL; **P6:** FTC; **P7, P14:** TPC; **P8:** FTPC; **P10, P12:** FC, SCL	P1, P6: NF; P3– NF; P3– P4, P10, P12–P14: F; P7, P8:G	1 Hz rTMS, 20 m/ d (1200 p), 90% of MT, 5 d/w, 2 w	Yes	RH PTr	Post, individualised LT 45 m	AAT	None	Improvement of AAT total score in the real group.

(Continued)

TABLE 1
Continued

Study	Number of patients (time post-stroke onset in months)	Lesion site	Type of aphasia	rTMS/tDCS approach	Placebo	Stimulated area	Language training	Outcome measures	Follow up timings from baseline	Results
(Monti et al., 2008)	8 (24–96) atDCS–ptDCS, ptDCS–atDCS, ctDCS–ptDCS–ctDCS	**P1, P7:** LH FC, SCL; **P2, P8:** LH FPC, SCL; **P3, P5:** LH FTPC, SCL; **P4:** LH SCL; **P6:** FC, SCL	P1, P3, P6, P8: NF; P2, P4, P5, P7: G	atDCS or ctDCS (2 mA),10 m/d, 1 d	Yes	experiment 1: LH B; experiment 2: OC	No	Pictures naming	None	ctDCS over the LH B as compared to ptDCS and atDCS improved naming accuracy.
(Baker et al., 2010)	10 (10–242) atDCS–ptDCS (5), ptDCS–atDCS (5)	**P1-P3, P5-P6, P8:** LH FTC, SCL; **P4, P7, P9-P10:** LH TC	P1, P3, P6, P8: NF; P2, P4, P5, P7, P9, P10: A	atDCS (1 mA), 20 m/d, 5 d/w, 1 w	Yes	fMRI-selected LH FC	During, CAT	Pictures naming	3 w	atDCS plus CAT as compared to ptDCS plus CAT improved naming accuracy (treated and untreated items) and this effect persisted at 3 w.
(Fiori et al., 2011)	3 (21–71) **atDCS**–ptDCS, ptDCS–atDCS	**P1:** LH SCL; **P2:** LH FC, LH SCL; **P3:** LH FTPC, LH SCL	P1–P3: NF	atDCS (1 mA), 20 m/d, 5 d/w, 1 w	Yes	LH W	During, CAT	Pictures naming	3, 5 w	atDCS plus CAT as compared to ptDCS plus CAT improved naming accuracy and reduced reaction times during a picture-naming task at post-treatment assessment and at 3 and 5 w.

(Fridriksson et al., 2011)	8 (10–150) atDCS– ptDCS (4), ptDCS– atDCS (4)	**P1–P8**: PC, LH SCL	P1–P8: F	atDCS (1 mA), 20 m/d, 5 d/w, 1 w	Yes	fMRI-selected LH posterior C	During, CAT	Pictures naming	5 w	atDCS plus CAT as compared to ptDCS plus CAT reduced reaction times during naming task of trained items both at post-tDCS assessment and at 5 w.
(You et al., 2011)	21 (16–36) atDCS(7), ptSCD (7), ctDCS (7)	**P1, P3**: LH TPC; **P2, P11, P14–P16**: LH FC: **P4, P10**: LH TC; **P5**: LH FTC; **P6, P12**: SCL; **P7–P9, P13, P17–P20**: LH FPC, SCL; **P21**: LH PC	P1-P21: G	atDCS or ctDCS (2 mA), 30 m/d, 5 d/w, 2 w	Yes	RH W for ctDCS or LH W for atDCS	No	K-WAB	None	All groups improved as compared to baseline. ctDCS induced a greater improvement in comprehension as compared to atDCS and ptDCS.
(Floel et al., 2011)	12 (14–260) atDCS– ptDCS– ctDCS, ptDCS– atDCS– ctDCS	**P1-P12**: LH FTC	P2–P7, P12: NF; P9:NC; P8:G; P11:F; P1,P10: AM	aTDCS or cTDCS (1mA), 40 m/d, 3 d/w, 1 w	Yes	RH TPC	During, CAT	Pictures naming	2 w	atDCS, ctDCS and ptDCS plus CAT improved naming accuracy compared to baseline. atDCS induced greater effects. Effects stable at 2 w.

(Continued)

TABLE 1
Continued

Study	Number of patients (time post-stroke onset in months)	Lesion site	Type of aphasia	rTMS/tDCS approach	Placebo	Stimulated area	Language training	Outcome measures	Follow up timings from baseline	Results
(Kang et al., 2011)	10 (6–180) ctDCS–ptDCS (5), ptDCS–ctDCS (5)	**P1, P2:** LH FTPC; **P3, P6, P9:** LH FTC; **P4:** LH FC; **P5, P8:** SCL; **P7:** LH TPC; **P10:** LH OC, SCL	**P1–P3:** G; **P4, P7–P9:** NF; **P5,P6:** A; **P10:**MD	ctDCS (2 mA), 20 m/d, 5 d/w, 1 w	Yes	BH	During, LT	BNT	none	ctDCS plus LT as compared to ptDCS plus LT improved naming accuracy.

Not available (NA); repetitive transcranial magnetic stimulation (rTMS); transcranial direct current stimulation (tDCS); intermittent theta burst stimulation (iTBS); transcranial direct current stimulation (tDCS); anodal transcranial direct current stimulation (atDCS); placebo transcranial direct current stimulation (ptDCS); cathodal transcranial direct current stimulation (ctDCS); centre hemisphere (LH); subcortical lesions (SCL); frontal (F); cortex (C); temporal (T); parietal (P); occipital (O); not classified (NC); amnestic aphasia (AM); nonfluent aphasia (NF); global aphasia (G); motor dominant aphasia (MD); sensory dominant aphasia (SD); anomic aphasia (A); fluent aphasia (F); conduction aphasia (C); minutes a day (m/d); pulses (p); motor threshold (MT); days a week (d/w); weeks (w); day (d); Broca's area homologue in the right hemisphere (BH); pars triangularis (PTr); right hemisphere (RH); Broca's area (B); Wernicke's area (W); functional magnetic resonance imaging (fMRI); Communicative Activities Log (CAL); Controlled Oral Word Association Test (COWAT); Constraint-Induced Language Therapy (CILT); minutes (m); language therapy (LT); computerised anomia treatment (CAT); Aachener Aphasie Test (AAT); Boston Naming Test (BNT); Boston Diagnostic Aphasia Exam (BDAE); Mini Mental State Examination (MMSE); Memory Assessment Scale (MAS); Peabody Picture Vocabulary Test (PPVT); Semantic Fluency (SF); Standard Language Test of Aphasia (SLTA); supplementary test of SLTA (SLTA-ST); Snoodgrass and Vanderwart picture naming (SV); Token Test (TT); Korean-Western Aphasia Battery (K-WAB); Western Aphasia Battery (WAB).

[1]Naeser, Martin, Nicholas, Baker, Seekins, Helm-Estabrooks, et al., 2005
[2]Naeser, Martin, Nicholas, Baker, Seekins, Kobayashi, et al., 2005
[3]Martin, Naeser, Ho, Doron, et al., 2009
[4]Martin, Naeser, Ho, Treglia, et al., 2009
[5]Naeser, Martin, Lundgren, et al., 2010
[6]Naeser, Martin, Treglia, et al., 2010
[7]Barwood, Murdoch, Whelan, Lloyd, Riek, O'Sullivan, Coulthard, & Wong, 2011
[8]Barwood, Murdoch, Whelan, Lloyd, Riek, O'Sullivan, Coulthard, Wong, et al., 2011

TABLE 2
Clinical features and baseline language assessment

	P1	P2	P3
Age at entry into this study (years)	41	45	71
Male/female	F	M	M
Education (years)	13	13	5
Aetiology (ischaemic/haemorrhagic)	I	H	I
Time post onset (years)	4.5	1	3.5
Length of a phrase (words)	5	4	1
Neurological symptoms	Hemiparesis	Hemiplegia	Hemiparesis
Handedness	Left	Right	Right
Aachener Aphasie Test (AAT)			
Token Test (Errors)	**19/50**	**38/50**	**27/50**
Repetition	**132/150**	**106/150**	**83/150**
Writing	86/90	**62/90**	**8/90**
Naming	105/120	**94/120**	**13/120**
Comprehension	109/120	**82/120**	**42/120**
Battery for the Analysis of the Aphasic Deficits (BADA)			
Object comprehension subtest	40/40	40/40	38/40
Action comprehension subtest	18/20	20/20	20/20
Object naming subtest	25/30	18/30	4/30
Action naming subtest	21/28	12/28	1/28
Sentence Comprehension	58/60	40/60	44/60

Bold data indicate scores below normal cut-off.

These parameters are consistent with the safety recommendations for rTMS (Rossi, Hallett, Rossini, Pascual-Leone, & Safety of TMS Consensus Group, 2009). The use of psychopharmacological agents that could interfere with the test performance or diagnosis and MRI evidence of relevant cerebro-vascular changes unrelated to the main diagnosis of the patient were additional exclusion criteria.

METHODS

TMS

Patients were randomly assigned to one of two conditions: (1) Real-Real (RR), in which the patient received four weeks of rTMS stimulation of the left dorsolateral prefrontal cortex (DLPFC) combined with the speech therapy (P1); and (2) Placebo-Real (PR), in which patients received left DLPFC placebo stimulation combined with the speech therapy during the first two weeks followed by two weeks of real stimulation combined with speech therapy (P2 and P3). Each week of rTMS treatment consisted of 5

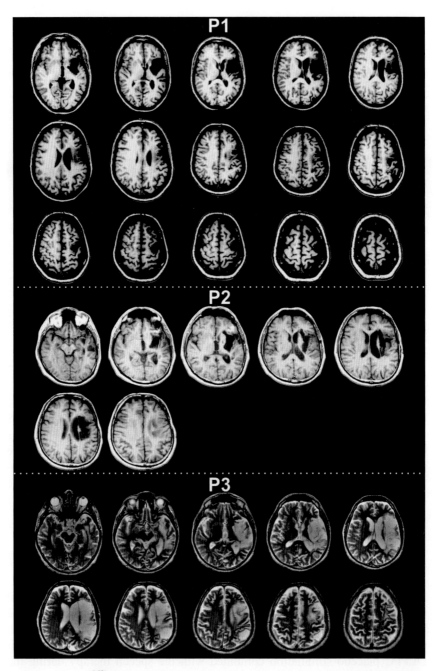

Figure 1. Structural MRIs for each patient. All the axial slices (thickness of 5 mm for P2 and P3 and of 4 mm for P1), where a lesion was present, are shown in a radiological convention (left side of brain is on the right).

sessions that comprised a total of 50 minutes/day (25 minutes of rTMS plus 25 minutes of speech therapy). rTMS was delivered using a Magstim unit featuring a double 70 mm air-cooled coil. Before starting the rTMS treatment, the right motor cortex excitability stimulation threshold was established for each subject (mean $\pm$ *SD*: 54% $\pm$ 10). The stimulation intensity used during the experiment was set to 90% of each subject's motor threshold. Trains of high-frequency (20 Hz) rTMS were delivered in short periods (2 sec duration) separated by longer periods (28 sec) of no stimulation, for each 25-minute daily rTMS session. The total number of pulses for each session was 2000 (40 stimuli/train, 50 trains). These parameters are consistent with safety recommendations for rTMS (Rossi et al., 2009). Furthermore, all participants tolerated rTMS well and did not report any adverse effects. In the placebo condition, a sham coil was used. We localised the target areas using the SofTaxic neuronavigator system (www.emsmedical.net) on an MRI template. Based on these estimated MRIs, the average location of the stimulating points was centred on Talairach coordinates $X = -35$, $Y = 24$, $Z = 48$, corresponding to the left DLPFC (Brodmann Area 8/9). To stimulate the DLPFC, the coil was placed with the junction of the two coil wings above the target point. During the experiment, the coil was fixed with a mechanical support.

Rationale for choosing the DLPFC as the rTMS target area

High-frequency rTMS to the left DLPFC results in reduced action naming latencies in young subjects (Cappa, Sandrini, Rossini, Sosta, & Miniussi, 2002), and in an increased number of correct responses for action naming in patients with mild Alzheimer's disease (AD), for both classes of stimuli (actions and objects) in moderate-to-severe AD patients (Cotelli et al., 2006; Cotelli, Manenti, Cappa, Zanetti, & Miniussi, 2008). Moreover, in an off-line study, a significant effect of left DLPFC stimulation (25 minutes/ day for 5 days/week for 4 weeks) on language functioning, together with a lasting benefit at 6 months, was also found in an AD patient sample (Cotelli et al., 2011). Based on these observations, we hypothesised that high-frequency rTMS stimulation over the left DLPFC would result in improved naming in patients with post-stroke chronic aphasia. An additional hypothesis was that, combining this rTMS treatment with speech therapy, could enhance the improvement of the language deficit.

BEHAVIOURAL ASSESSMENT

Participants were assessed before therapy (baseline), after the first 2 weeks of treatment, and at the end of the 4 weeks of therapy. Tests including the following: a neuropsychological battery for reasoning and verbal fluency

(Lezak, Howieson, & Loring, 2004); the Aachener Aphasie Test (AAT; Luzzatti et al., 1994); the object and action naming subtests, comprehension and sentence comprehension subtests of the Battery for the Analysis of the Aphasic Deficit (BADA; Miceli, Laudanna, Burani, & Capasso, 1994). See Table 2 for details.

Stimuli selection

To select stimuli for the therapy and to test for generalisation effects, all patients completed two oral naming tasks and one oral comprehension task. The oral naming task was repeated twice, on two consecutive days, to ensure a stable baseline before introducing therapy and to select the therapy items. Stimuli for the oral naming task were 340 black-and-white 2-dimensional line drawings representing objects, which were taken from the 795 corpus of objects and nouns of the CRL-IPNP (Center for Research in Language – International Picture Naming Project; http://crl.ucsd.edu) (Bates et al., 2000). These stimuli were normalised with healthy and brain damaged populations across seven international sites and languages; items were coded for a number of variables known to influence naming difficulty (e.g., word frequency, age of acquisition, degree of imageability, etc.). In total, 349 pictures of objects were displayed twice (on two consecutive days) on a computer screen using Presentation software v. 12.0 (neurobehavioural systems: http://www.neurobs.com), with each picture being presented for a maximum of 10 seconds. Each participant was asked to name each picture as accurately as possible, and oral responses were recorded.

In addition, because we aimed to focus the therapy on word production, all misnamed pictures were included in a comprehension task to make sure that the participants understood the word. In the comprehension task, participants were asked whether a picture presented for a maximum of 10 seconds corresponded or not to the spoken word. The participant was questioned about the picture's name during three consecutive trials, including the target's correct name, a semantic distractor and an unrelated distractor (e.g., for the picture of a bottle, the questions were "Is it a bottle?", "Is it a glass?" or "Is it a calendar?", respectively). The presentation of the items and the order of the distractors were randomised. Only items for which no errors were made in any of the three trials were selected for the rehabilitation list.

The rehabilitation list was further split into two sets: the "therapy" list, including the items to be treated; and the "control" list, with items not to be treated (untreated items). The two lists were balanced for a number of variables related to the participant's performance during the assessment of naming abilities; more specifically, these variables included the percent of correct picture naming across assessment sessions (one time or never across two sessions), target word frequency, number of syllables and number of letters, as well as semantic category (i.e., living or non-living). Furthermore, the two sets were split into two balanced sub-sets to be used during the first and the second week of treatment or to be used during the third and the fourth week, respectively (first and second vs. third and fourth).

Given the type of procedure used to select the "therapy" and "control" lists, each participant ended with a personalised set of items, which ensured the within- and across-subject validity of the design.

Therapy protocol

Participants underwent 25 minutes of speech therapy immediately following each rTMS treatment on a daily basis for 4 weeks. In general, the procedure included repetition and reading of the target word to facilitate naming, and an articulatory suppression task (average duration of articulatory suppression: 10 seconds) (Baddeley, Lewis, & Vallar, 1984). For every error, the trial was repeated again (at the end of the list). The patient was seated in front of a computer screen in a quiet room while the therapy protocol was displayed using Presentation software v. 12.0 (neurobehavioural systems: http://www.neurobs.com). The pictures showing the items to be treated and the written words used during the treatment were presented on the computer screen. The treatment involved several steps to elicit the production of a target noun, specifically:

Step 1: Repetition of the target word (the target word was spoken by the therapist and the participant was asked to repeat it three times).

Articulatory suppression task: Interference with articulatory codes caused by the uttering of an irrelevant speech sound (i.e., bla, bla, bla).

In the suppression condition, participants received instructions to start uttering the syllable "bla". The suppression was carried on during the interval between step 1 and step 2 and between step 3 and step 4.

Step 2: Oral picture naming (the target picture was presented on the computer screen and the participant was asked to retrieve its correct name).

Step 3: Reading of the target word (the target written word was presented on the computer screen and the participant was asked to read it).

Articulatory suppression task: Interference with articulatory codes caused by the uttering of an irrelevant speech sound (i.e., bla, bla, bla).

Step 4: Oral picture naming (the target picture was presented on the computer screen and the participant was asked to retrieve its correct name, and say it aloud).

The complete procedure was repeated when at least one of the two requested naming responses was incorrect.

At the end of the therapy, object naming was reassessed, with their respective lists prepared during the pre-therapy assessment. At the end of the first two weeks of treatment, an equal number of treated and untreated items corresponding to the first two weeks were tested, whereas at the end of the

treatment and at follow-up visits, all treated and untreated items corresponding to the four weeks of the experiment were tested.

RESULTS

Significant improvements were found for object naming in the experimental
stimuli set. For each participant, we calculated the baseline for the therapy
and control lists. The percentage correct at baseline for each participant
corresponded to the number of items correctly named in one of the two
naming assessment sessions, divided by two and further divided by the total
number of items in the therapy and control lists (both the therapy and control
lists included the same number of items) multiplied by 100. For each PWA,
a χ^2 comparison, with Yates correction, was applied to compare performance
scores after 2, 4, 12, 24 and 48 weeks, with respect to baseline and for both
the treated and untreated items. In contrast, no changes were recorded in the
standard neuropsychological assessment including formal language assessment
(AAT and BADA) after the therapy.

For treated items, the three PWAs showed improvement after 2 weeks of
combined rTMS-behavioural therapy as compared to baseline, and this
significant improvement persisted at 4, 12, 24 and 48 weeks. Moreover, the
improvement was also significant with untreated items after 2 weeks of combined rTMS and behavioural therapy and at weeks 4, 12, 24 and 48 (see
Figure 2 and Table 3 for details).

Additionally, in order to examine the generalisation of effects to untreated
items, we compared the accuracy scores for trained and untrained items for
each PWA and for each time-point using Yates-corrected χ^2 comparisons.
The results showed a significant effect on treated items (vs. untreated items)
at the 2- and 4-week post-treatment measurement points, in all three cases,
whereas the difference between naming treated and untreated images decreased
over time, and, in most cases, vanished at follow-up assessments beginning at 12
weeks post-entry/baseline in two of the three cases (see Table 3 for details).

DISCUSSION

Our preliminary findings provide additional evidence for the beneficial effects
of brain stimulation in combination with targeted behavioural training in
PWAs suffering from anomia. In particular, a long-lasting effect of combined
rTMS and behavioural therapy was observed; this effect was still present at
48 weeks after the beginning of the combined rTMS-speech therapy intervention on the therapy list, but not on the standardised tests. This result is consistent with previous reports of enhanced cognitive performance following non-
invasive brain stimulation (i.e., rTMS or tDCS) to specific cortical areas in

patients with a variety of neurological diseases (Baker et al., 2010; Berthier, & Pulvermuller, 2011; Cotelli et al., 2006, 2008; Fiori et al., 2011; Martin et al., 2004; Monti et al., 2008; Naeser, Martin, Nicholas, Baker, Seekins,

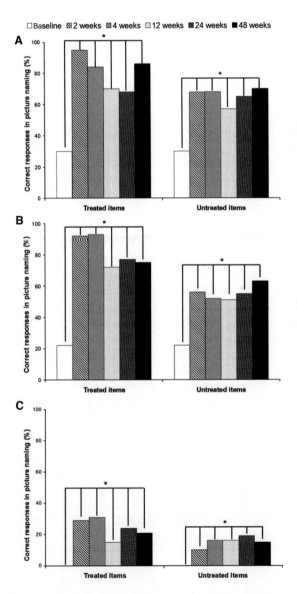

Figure 2. Percentage of correct responses in the picture-naming task for treated and untreated items at baseline and 2, 4, 12, 24 and 48 weeks after the beginning of treatment for patients P1 (A), P2 (B) and P3 (C). * $p < .05$.

TABLE 3
Oral object naming at all time points for treated and untreated items for the three patients (P1, P2, P3)

Timing	Treated items		Untreated items		Treated vs. untreated
	Correctness %	Comparison with baseline	Correctness %	Comparison with baseline	
P1: 4 weeks of real rTMS plus speech therapy					
Baseline	30		30		
2 weeks	95	$\chi^2 = 87.4, p < .001$	68	$\chi^2 = 27.4, p < .001$	$\chi^2 = 22.4, p < .001$
4 weeks	84	$\chi^2 = 57.3, p < .001$	68	$\chi^2 = 27.4, p < .001$	$\chi^2 = 6.2, p = .013$
12 weeks	70	$\chi^2 = 30.4, p < .001$	57	$\chi^2 = 13.8, p < .001$	n.s.
24 weeks	68	$\chi^2 = 27.4, p < .001$	65	$\chi^2 = 23.2, p < .001$	n.s.
48 weeks	86	$\chi^2 = 62.1, p < .001$	70	$\chi^2 = 30.4, p < .001$	$\chi^2 = 6.6, p = .011$
P2: 2 weeks of placebo rTMS plus speech therapy; followed by 2 weeks of real rTMS plus speech therapy					
Baseline	22		22		
2 weeks	92	$\chi^2 = 97.1, p < .001$	56	$\chi^2 = 22.9, p < .001$	$\chi^2 = 31.8, p < .001$
4 weeks	93	$\chi^2 = 100.3, p < .001$	52	$\chi^2 = 18.0, p < .001$	$\chi^2 = 40.1, p < .001$
12 weeks	72	$\chi^2 = 48.2, p < .001$	51	$\chi^2 = 16.9, p < .001$	$\chi^2 = 8.5, p = .004$
24 weeks	77	$\chi^2 = 58.3, p < .001$	55	$\chi^2 = 21.6, p < .001$	$\chi^2 = 9.8, p = .002$
48 weeks	75	$\chi^2 = 54.1, p < .001$	63	$\chi^2 = 32.7, p < .001$	n.s.
P3: 2 weeks of placebo rTMS plus speech therapy; followed by 2 weeks of real rTMS plus speech therapy					
Baseline	0		0		
2 weeks	29	$\chi^2 = 31.6, p < .001$	10	$\chi^2 = 8.5, p < .001$	$\chi^2 = 10.3, p = .001$
4 weeks	31	$\chi^2 = 34.4, p < .001$	16	$\chi^2 = 15.3, p < .001$	$\chi^2 = 5.5, p = .020$
12 weeks	15	$\chi^2 = 14.1, p < .001$	16	$\chi^2 = 15.3, p < .001$	n.s.
24 weeks	24	$\chi^2 = 25.1, p < .001$	19	$\chi^2 = 18.8, p < .001$	n.s.
48 weeks	21	$\chi^2 = 21.3, p < .001$	15	$\chi^2 = 14.1, p < .001$	n.s.

Statistical data (χ^2, Yates correction) are also reported. n.s. = not statistically significant.

Helm-Estabrooks, et al., 2005; Naeser, Martin, Nicholas, Baker, Seekins, Kobayashi, et al., 2005). Moreover, the results of our study are also consistent with previous evidence regarding the increased efficacy of daily combined rTMS or tDCS plus cognitive rehabilitation (Baker et al., 2010; Fiori et al., 2011; Floel et al., 2011; Fridriksson et al., 2011; Kakuda, Abo, Uruma, et al., 2010; Kang et al., 2011; Martin, Naeser, Ho, Treglia, et al., 2009; Naeser, Martin, Treglia, et al., 2010; Weiduschat et al., 2011).

The present study provides additional evidence supporting the use of combined behavioural and brain stimulation approaches to achieve successful outcomes in aphasia therapy. The heterogeneity of the approaches used to date makes comparison of rTMS studies complex, i.e., (1) low-frequency rTMS over the unaffected hemisphere to suppress the presence of over-activation in the right frontal area due, in part, to lack of transcallosal inhibition from the damaged left frontal area; and (2) high-frequency rTMS over the damaged hemisphere aiming at facilitating spared regions surrounding the damaged areas.

Regarding tDCS, both anodal and cathodal stimulation applied over the lesional hemisphere improved language in post-stroke aphasia patients. What are the possible mechanisms responsible for these effects? It has been hypothesised that both tDCS and rTMS can affect the cortical plastic changes following stroke in a positive way and that these effects may outlast the stimulation period (Ridding & Rothwell, 2007).

Several studies support the idea that a favourable recovery from post-stroke aphasia is associated with a predominant reactivation of ipsilesional areas (Heiss, Emunds, & Herholz, 1993; Thiel et al., 1998, 2001; Winhuisen et al., 2005, 2007). Recent reviews highlight that several recruitment mechanisms may occur, including persistent function in spared areas, compensatory recruitment of alternate nodes, and involvement of areas that may hinder recovery (Turkeltaub, Messing, Norise, & Hamilton, 2011). Based on these ideas, we applied high-frequency rTMS over the left DLPFC to increase cortical excitability and our results are consistent with this perspective. No adverse effects have been reported, supporting the safety of this approach (Rossi et al., 2009).

These facilitation effects may be related to changes in cortical excitability and plasticity (Ridding & Rothwell, 2007). One possible explanation for these stimulation effects is that they may be mediated by the enhancement of compensatory modifications in functional networks associated with a specific function (Fridriksson, 2010). These modifications of cortical activity through the use of stimulation may readjust the pathological patterns of brain activity, thus providing an opportunity to normalise activity patterns within the affected functional networks (Thut & Miniussi, 2009).

The present findings suggest that rTMS-induced modulation of short- and/ or long-range cortical synaptic efficacy and connectivity, which potentiates the system within the language network, leads to increased effects of speech therapy (see Miniussi & Rossini, this issue).

The major limitations of this preliminary study were the small number of patients and the lack of a placebo stimulation group, for 2 and 4 weeks, with and without speech therapy. Thus, the main findings of this study, i.e., that combined behavioural-rTMS treatment induced a long-lasting effect on treated items (up to 48 weeks), and contributed to a generalisation of therapy effects to untreated items (observed earlier post-treatment in all three cases, but not always observed later) (Miceli, Amitrano, Capasso, & Caramazza, 1996), need to be confirmed using a larger sample. The inclusion of a control group receiving only language therapy is required to separate the respective contribution of language therapy alone, and in combination with real or placebo rTMS treatments.

REFERENCES

Antal, A., Nitsche, M. A., Kruse, W., Kincses, T. Z., Hoffmann, K. P., & Paulus, W. (2004). Direct current stimulation over V5 enhances visuomotor coordination by improving motion perception in humans. *Journal of Cognitive Neuroscience, 16,* 521–527.

Baddeley, A. D., Lewis, V., & Vallar, G. (1984). Exploring the articulatory loop. *Quarterly Journal of Experimental Psychology, 36,* 233–252.

Baker, J. M., Rorden, C., & Fridriksson, J. (2010). Using transcranial direct-current stimulation to treat stroke patients with aphasia. *Stroke, 41,* 1229–1236.

Barwood, C. H., Murdoch, B. E., Whelan, B. M., Lloyd, D., Riek, S., O'Sullivan, J., Coulthard, A., & Wong, A. (2011). Improved language performance subsequent to low-frequency rTMS in patients with chronic non-fluent aphasia post-stroke. *European Journal of Neurology, 18,* 935–943.

Barwood, C. H., Murdoch, B. E., Whelan, B. M., Lloyd, D., Riek, S., O'Sullivan, J., Coulthard, A., Wong, A., Aitken, P., & Hall, G. (2011). The effects of low frequency Repetitive Transcranial Magnetic Stimulation (rTMS) and sham condition rTMS on behavioural language in chronic non-fluent aphasia: Short term outcomes. *NeuroRehabilitation, 28,* 113–128.

Bates, E., Andonova, E., D'Amico, S., Jacobsen, T., Kohnert, K., Lu, C. C., et al. (2000). Introducing the CRL International Picture-Naming Project (CRL-IPNP). *Center for Research in Language Newsletter La Jolla: University of California San Diego, 12.*

Berthier, M. L., & Pulvermuller, F. (2011). Neuroscience insights improve neurorehabilitation of poststroke aphasia. *Nature Reviews Neurology, 7,* 86–97.

Bhogal, S. K., Teasell, R., & Speechley, M. (2003). Intensity of aphasia therapy, impact on recovery. *Stroke, 34,* 987–993.

Bindman, L. J., Lippold, O. C., & Redfearn, J. W. (1962). Long-lasting changes in the level of the electrical activity of the cerebral cortex produced bypolarizing currents. *Nature, 196,* 584–585.

Black-Schaffer, R. M., & Osberg, J. S. (1990). Return to work after stroke: Development of a predictive model. *Archives of Physical Medicine and Rehabilitation, 71,* 285–290.

Cappa, S. F., Benke, T., Clarke, S., Rossi, B., Stemmer, B., & van Heugten, C. M. (2005). EFNS guidelines on cognitive rehabilitation: Report of an EFNS task force. *European Journal of Neurology, 12,* 665–680.

Cappa, S. F., Benke, T., Clarke, S., Rossi, B., Stemmer, B., van Heugten, C. M., & European Federation of Neurological Societies (2003). EFNS guidelines on cognitive rehabilitation: Report of an EFNS task force. *European Journal of Neurology*, *10*, 11–23.

Cappa, S. F., Sandrini, M., Rossini, P. M., Sosta, K., & Miniussi, C. (2002). The role of the left frontal lobe in action naming: rTMS evidence. *Neurology*, *59*, 720–723.

Cotelli, M., Calabria, M., Manenti, R., Rosini, S., Zanetti, O., Cappa, S. F., et al. (2011). Improved language performance in Alzheimer disease following brain stimulation. *Journal of Neurology, Neurosurgery, & Psychiatry*, *82*, 794–797.

Cotelli, M., Manenti, R., Cappa, S. F., Geroldi, C., Zanetti, O., Rossini, P. M., et al. (2006). Effect of transcranial magnetic stimulation on action naming in patients with Alzheimer disease. *Archives of Neurology*, *63*, 1602–1604.

Cotelli, M., Manenti, R., Cappa, S. F., Zanetti, O., & Miniussi, C. (2008). Transcranial magnetic stimulation improves naming in Alzheimer disease patients at different stages of cognitive decline. *European Journal of Neurology*, *15*, 1286–1292.

Engelter, S. (2006). Aphasia in stroke patients: Frequency and significance. *Praxis*, *95*, 489–492.

Fertonani, A., Rosini, S., Cotelli, M., Rossini, P. M., & Miniussi, C. (2010). Naming facilitation induced by transcranial direct current stimulation. *Behavioural Brain Research*, *208*, 311–318.

Fiori, V., Coccia, M., Marinelli, C. V., Vecchi, V., Bonifazi, S., Ceravolo, M. G., et al. (2011). Transcranial direct current stimulation improves word retrieval in healthy and nonfluent aphasic subjects. *Journal of Cognitive Neuroscience*, *23*, 2309–2323.

Floel, A., Meinzer, M., Kirstein, R., Nijhof, S., Deppe, M., Knecht, S., et al. (2011). Short-term anomia training and electrical brain stimulation. *Stroke*, *42*, 2065–2067.

Fregni, F., Boggio, P. S., Nitsche, M., Bermpohl, F., Antal, A., Feredoes, E., et al. (2005). Anodal transcranial direct current stimulation of prefrontal cortex enhances working memory. *Experimental Brain Research*, *166*, 23–30.

Fridriksson, J. (2010). Preservation and modulation of specific left hemisphere regions is vital for treated recovery from anomia in stroke. *Journal of Neuroscience*, *30*, 11558–11564.

Fridriksson, J., Richardson, J. D., Baker, J. M., & Rorden, C. (2011). Transcranial direct current stimulation improves naming reaction time in fluent aphasia: A double-blind, sham-controlled study. *Stroke*, *42*, 819–821.

Galletta, E. E., Rao, P. R., & Barrett, A. M. (2011). Transcranial magnetic stimulation (TMS): Potential progress for language improvement in aphasia. *Topics in Stroke Rehabilitation*, *18*, 87–91.

Hamilton, R. H., Sanders, L., Benson, J., Faseyitan, O., Norise, C., Naeser, M., et al. (2010). Stimulating conversation: Enhancement of elicited propositional speech in a patient with chronic non-fluent aphasia following transcranial magnetic stimulation. *Brain & Language*, *113*, 45–50.

Heiss, W. D., Emunds, H. G., & Herholz, K. (1993). Cerebral glucose metabolism as a predictor of rehabilitation after ischemic stroke. *Stroke*, *24*, 1784–1788.

Iyer, M. B., Mattu, U., Grafman, J., Lomarev, M., Sato, S., & Wassermann, E. M. (2005). Safety and cognitive effect of frontal DC brain polarization in healthy individuals. *Neurology*, *64*, 872–875.

Jung, T. D., Kim, J. Y., Lee, Y. S., Kim, D. H., Lee, J. J., Seo, J. H., et al. (2010). Effect of repetitive transcranial magnetic stimulation in a patient with chronic crossed aphasia: fMRI study. *Journal of Rehabilitation Medicine*, *42*, 973–978.

Kakuda, W., Abo, M., Kaito, N., Watanabe, M., & Senoo, A. (2010). Functional MRI-based therapeutic rTMS strategy for aphasic stroke patients: A case series pilot study. International. *Journal of Neuroscience*, *120*, 60–66.

Kakuda, W., Abo, M., Uruma, G., Kaito, N., & Watanabe, M. (2010). Low-frequency rTMS with language therapy over a 3-month period for sensory-dominant aphasia: Case series of two post-stroke Japanese patients. *Brain Injury, 24,* 1113–1117.

Kang, E. K., Kim, Y. K., Sohn, H. M., Cohen, L. G., & Paik, N. J. (2011). Improved picture naming in aphasia patients treated with cathodal tDCS to inhibit the right Broca's homologue area. *Restorative Neurology and Neuroscience, 29,* 141–152.

Kelly, H., Brady, M. C., & Enderby, P. (2010). Speech and language therapy for aphasia following stroke. *Cochrane Database Systematic Reviews, 5,* CD000425.

Laska, A. C., Hellblom, A., Murray, V., Kahan, T., & Von Arbin, M. (2001). Aphasia in acute stroke and relation to outcome. *Journal of Internal Medicine, 249,* 413–422.

Lezak, M., Howieson, D., & Loring, D. W. (2004). *Neuropsychological assessment* (4th ed.). Oxford, UK: Oxford University Press.

Liebetanz, D., Nitsche, M. A., Tergau, F., & Paulus, W. (2002). Pharmacological approach to the mechanisms of transcranial DC-stimulation-induced after-effects of human motor cortex excitability. *Brain, 125,* 2238–2247.

Luzzatti, C., Willmes, K., De Bleser, R., Bianchi, A., Chiesa, G., De Tanti, A., et al. (1994). Nuovi dati normativi per la versione italiana dell'Aachener Aphasia test. *Archivio di Psicologia, Neurologia e Psichiatria, 55,* 1086–1131.

Martin, P. I., Naeser, M. A., Ho, M., Doron, K. W., Kurland, J., Kaplan, J., et al. (2009). Overt naming fMRI pre- and post-TMS: Two nonfluent aphasia patients, with and without improved naming post-TMS. *Brain & Language, 111,* 20–35.

Martin, P. I., Naeser, M. A., Ho, M., Treglia, E., Kaplan, E., Baker, E. H., et al. (2009). Research with transcranial magnetic stimulation in the treatment of aphasia. *Current Neurology and Neuroscience Reports, 9,* 451–458.

Martin, P. I., Naeser, M. A., Theoret, H., Tormos, J. M., Nicholas, M., Kurland, J., et al. (2004). Transcranial magnetic stimulation as a complementary treatment for aphasia. *Seminars in Speech and Language, 25,* 181–191.

Miceli, G., Amitrano, A., Capasso, R., & Caramazza, A. (1996). The treatment of anomia resulting from output lexical damage: Analysis of two cases. *Brain, & Language, 52,* 150–174.

Miceli, G., Laudanna, A., Burani, C., & Capasso, R. (1994). *Batteria per l'Analisi dei Deficit Afasici. B.A.D.A. (Battery for Analysis of Aphasic Deficits).* Milano: CEPSAG, Università Cattolica del Sacro Cuore.

Miniussi, C., Cappa, S. F., Cohen, L. G., Floel, A., Fregni, F., Nitsche, M. A., et al. (2008). Efficacy of repetitive transcranial magnetic stimulation/transcranial direct current stimulation in cognitive neurorehabilitation. *Brain Stimulation, 1,* 326–336.

Monti, A., Cogiamanian, F., Marceglia, S., Ferrucci, R., Mameli, F., Mrakic-Sposta, S., et al. (2008). Improved naming after transcranial direct current stimulation in aphasia. *Journal of Neurology, Neurosurgery, & Psychiatry, 79,* 451–453.

Naeser, M. A., Martin, P. I., Lundgren, K., Klein, R., Kaplan, J., Treglia, E., et al. (2010). Improved language in a chronic nonfluent aphasia patient after treatment with CPAP and TMS. *Cognitive and Behavioral Neurology, 23,* 29–38.

Naeser, M. A., Martin, P. I., Nicholas, M., Baker, E. H., Seekins, H., Helm-Estabrooks, N., et al. (2005). Improved naming after TMS treatments in a chronic, global aphasia patient – case report. *Neurocase, 11,* 182–193.

Naeser, M. A., Martin, P. I., Nicholas, M., Baker, E. H., Seekins, H., Kobayashi, M., et al. (2005). Improved picture naming in chronic aphasia after TMS to part of right Broca's area: An open-protocol study. *Brain & Language, 93,* 95–105.

Naeser, M. A., Martin, P. I., Treglia, E., Ho, M., Kaplan, E., Bashir, S., et al. (2010). Research with rTMS in the treatment of aphasia. *Restorative Neurology and Neuroscience, 28,* 511–529.

Nitsche, M. A., Schauenburg, A., Lang, N., Liebetanz, D., Exner, C., Paulus, W., et al. (2003). Facilitation of implicit motor learning by weak transcranial direct current stimulation of the primary motor cortex in the human. *Journal of Cognitive Neuroscience, 15,* 619–626.

Ohn, S. H., Park, C. I., Yoo, W. K., Ko, M. H., Choi, K. P., Kim, G. M., et al. (2008). Time-dependent effect of transcranial direct current stimulation on the enhancement of working memory. *Neuroreport, 19,* 43–47.

Paolucci, S., Antonucci, G., Pratesi, L., Traballesi, M., Lubich, S., & Grasso, M. G. (1998). Functional outcome in stroke inpatient rehabilitation: Predicting no, low and high response patients. *Cerebrovascular Diseases, 8,* 228–234.

Reis, J., Schambra, H. M., Cohen, L. G., Buch, E. R., Fritsch, B., Zarahn, E., et al. (2009). Non-invasive cortical stimulation enhances motor skill acquisition over multiple days through an effect on consolidation. *Proceedings of the National Academy of Sciences, 106,* 1590–1595.

Ridding, M. C., & Rothwell, J. C. (2007). Is there a future for therapeutic use of transcranial magnetic stimulation? *Nature Reviews Neuroscience, 8,* 559–567.

Rossi, S., Hallett, M., Rossini, P. M., Pascual-Leone, A., & Safety of TMS Consensus Group (2009). Safety, ethical considerations, and application guidelines for the use of transcranial magnetic stimulation in clinical practice and research. *Clinical Neurophysiology, 120,* 2008–2039.

Sparing, R., Dafotakis, M., Meister, I. G., Thirugnanasambandam, N., & Fink, G. R. (2008). Enhancing language performance with non-invasive brain stimulation – a transcranial direct current stimulation study in healthy humans. *Neuropsychologia, 46,* 261–268.

Szaflarski, J. P., Vannest, J., Wu, S. W., DiFrancesco, M. W., Banks, C., & Gilbert, D. L. (2011). Excitatory repetitive transcranial magnetic stimulation induces improvements in chronic post-stroke aphasia. *Medical Science Monitor, 17,* 132–139.

Thiel, A., Herholz, K., Koyuncu, A., Ghaemi, M., Kracht, L. W., Habedank, B., et al. (2001). Plasticity of language networks in patients with brain tumors: A positron emission tomography activation study. *Annals of Neurology, 50,* 620–629.

Thiel, A., Herholz, K., von Stockhausen, H. M., van Leyen-Pilgram, K., Pietrzyk, U., Kessler, J., et al. (1998). Localization of language-related cortex with 15O-labeled water PET in patients with gliomas. *NeuroImage, 7,* 284–295.

Thut, G., & Miniussi, C. (2009). New insights into rhythmic brain activity from TMS-EEG studies. *Trends in Cognitive Sciences, 13,* 182–189.

Tilling, K., Sterne, J. A., Rudd, A. G., Glass, T. A., Wityk, R. J., & Wolfe, C. D. (2001). A new method for predicting recovery after stroke. *Stroke, 32,* 2867–2873.

Turkeltaub, P. E., Messing, S., Norise, C., & Hamilton, R. H. (2011). Are networks for residual language function and recovery consistent across aphasic patients? *Neurology, 76,* 1726–1734.

Vines, B. W., Schnider, N. M., & Schlaug, G. (2006). Testing for causality with transcranial direct current stimulation: Pitch memory and the left supramarginal gyrus. *Neuroreport, 17,* 1047–1050.

Weiduschat, N., Thiel, A., Rubi-Fessen, I., Hartmann, A., Kessler, J., Merl, P., et al. (2011). Effects of repetitive transcranial magnetic stimulation in aphasic stroke: A randomized controlled pilot study. *Stroke, 42,* 409–415.

Winhuisen, L., Thiel, A., Schumacher, B., Kessler, J., Rudolf, J., Haupt, W. F., et al. (2005). Role of the contralateral inferior frontal gyrus in recovery of language function in poststroke aphasia: A combined repetitive transcranial magnetic stimulation and positron emission tomography study. *Stroke, 36,* 1759–1763.

Winhuisen, L., Thiel, A., Schumacher, B., Kessler, J., Rudolf, J., Haupt, W. F., et al. (2007). The right inferior frontal gyrus and poststroke aphasia: A follow-up investigation. *Stroke, 38,* 1286–1292.

You, D. S., Kim, D. Y., Chun, M. H., Jung, S. E., & Park, S. J. (2011). Cathodal transcranial direct current stimulation of the right Wernicke's area improves comprehension in subacute stroke patients. *Brain & Language, 119,* 1–5.

NEUROPSYCHOLOGICAL REHABILITATION
2011, 21 (5), 742–754

The neural basis of aphasia rehabilitation: Evidence from neuroimaging and neurostimulation

Stefano F. Cappa

Vita Salute University and Division of Neuroscience, San Raffaele Scientific Institute, Milan, Italy

This article is a selective review of functional imaging investigations and brain stimulation studies addressing the neural mechanisms of recovery of stroke-associated aphasia. The imaging results show that aphasia recovery is associated with a complex pattern of brain reorganisation, involving both ipsilateral and contralateral brain regions, which is modulated by lesion size and site, time post-onset, type of training, and language task. The information provided by the imaging investigations needs to be integrated with the results of brain stimulation studies, in order to specify the most effective protocols in term of modality, locus and timing of stimulation. Further studies, using multiple imaging and neuromodulation approaches, are required to reach sound conclusions about the potential usefulness of brain stimulation approaches as an adjunct to aphasia rehabilitation.

Keywords: Aphasia; Functional magnetic resonance; Recovery; Transcranial magnetic stimulation; Transcranial direct current stimulation.

INTRODUCTION

Disorders of language (aphasia) are a frequent consequence of stroke, associated with relevant disability and with a negative prognostic impact on long-term functional recovery (Paolucci et al., 2003). While behavioural interventions have been shown to be effective in improving recovery (Cappa et al., 2005; Cicerone et al., 2005; Kelly, Brady, & Enderby, 2010),

Correspondence should be addressed to Stefano F. Cappa, Vita Salute University and Division of Neuroscience, San Raffaele Scientific Institute, Milan, Italy. Email: cappa.stefano@hsr.it

© 2011 Psychology Press, an imprint of the Taylor & Francis Group, an Informa business
http://www.psypress.com/neurorehab   http://dx.doi.org/10.1080/09602011.2011.614724

there is no evidence supporting specific types of intervention, nor adequate knowledge of the neural foundations of aphasia therapy.

In recent years, functional imaging techniques have been increasingly applied to the investigation of the neural mechanisms subserving functional recovery after stroke, including both spontaneous and rehabilitation-associated recovery of aphasia. The results of these studies are providing important inputs to the field of brain stimulation techniques, which have also recently been applied to stroke patients with the aim of facilitating spontaneous and rehabilitation-induced recovery (Miniussi et al., 2008). This paper provides a selective review of the available evidence, with a main focus on the importance of developing a multimodal imaging approach to the investigation of aphasia recovery.

FUNCTIONAL IMAGING OF APHASIA REHABILITATION

The recovery of the consequences of acute stroke can be divided into temporal stages, associated with different physiological mechanisms responsible for clinical improvement (Mazzocchi & Vignolo, 1979). The early stage includes an acute phase of one to two weeks post-onset, and a subacute, "lesional" stage covering up to six months post-onset. This is followed by the chronic stage. During the early period, the likely mechanisms of clinical improvement are the disappearance of cerebral oedema and of intracranial hypertension, the reabsorption of blood, the normalisation of haemodynamics in ischaemic penumbra areas, and the resolution of local inflammation (Baldwin et al., 2010). Another crucial mechanism, which is probably at play mostly in the early stage, is the regression of diaschisis (functional suppression) effects in non-injured areas connected to the damaged region (Cappa et al., 1997; Feeney & Baron, 1986; von Monakow, 1914).

The mechanisms underlying recovery from cognitive impairment at later stages after an acute event are incompletely understood. One possibility is that recovery may be achieved by adopting novel cognitive strategies for performance, circumventing the damaged function. At the neural level, in the case of language this implies the recruitment of uninjured cerebral areas, which are not typically activated in normal subjects during linguistic tasks. More often, however, the recovery of impaired linguistic functions, such as naming or syntactic processing, has been attributed to the "reorganisation" of the cerebral substrate of language processing, The reorganisation may take place ipsilaterally, within the spared regions of the dominant hemisphere language areas, or contralaterally, in homotopic (i.e., homologous) regions of the right hemisphere. The latter hypothesis was originally put forward by Gowers (1895), and has been supported by the evidence of considerable right-hemispheric linguistic abilities, especially at the lexical-semantic level, in split-brain subjects (Gazzaniga, 1983). This potential for reorganisation within the language network may be due to the "degeneracy" of the neural systems, which, premorbidly, sustain the cognitive function of interest (Noppeney, Friston, & Price, 2004).

The application of this issue to neuroimaging techniques, i.e., positron emission tomography (PET) and functional magnetic resonance imaging (fMRI), allows a relatively direct testing of these competing hypotheses. There is now an extensive literature on this topic, which has been the subject of some excellent reviews (Crinion & Leff, 2007; Price & Crinion, 2005; Thompson & den Ouden, 2008). Only some of the available literature, which may have implications for the development of neurostimulation protocols, is summarised here.

The first issue to be addressed is the role of the right hemisphere. The presence of increased right hemispheric activity in recovered aphasics during language tasks has been replicated by many studies, starting from the early PET investigation of the correlates of word generation in recovered Wernicke's aphasics (Weiller et al., 1995). In the following years, however, several functional fMRI studies indicated that re-activation of spared left hemispheric areas is also frequently observed in recovered aphasics (Warburton, Price, Swinburn, & Wise, 1999; Perani et al., 2003). What then is the cause and functional role of increased right hemispheric activation? It has been hypothesised that a lesion of the language-dominant left hemisphere may result in a "release" of function of the contralateral hemisphere, via a reduction of transcallosal inhibition (Ferbert et al., 1992). In support of this hypothesis, Karbe et al. (1998) found that the application of inhibitory transcranial magnetic stimulation (TMS) to Broca's area results in a metabolic increase in the homologous right hemispheric areas (Thiel et al., 2006). An alternative interpretation is that right hemispheric activation may simply reflect the additional engagement of attentional and executive resources, dictated by the requirements of an inefficient strategy to cope with the task. A follow-up study reported that right hemispheric activation in Broca's and premotor regions predicted superior recovery in a sample of aphasic patients (Richter, Miltner, & Straube, 2008). At an individual level, improvement was associated with a reduction of right hemispheric activation. Several observations challenge the hypothesis of a "compensatory role" of right hemispheric activity. A PET study involved patients with chronic non-fluent aphasia, who had shown considerable improvement after the introduction of additional rehabilitation training with Melodic Intonation Therapy (MIT) (Belin et al., 1996). Patients were poor in repeating words with a natural intonation, but improved when they used a MIT-like intonation. The pattern of brain activation in comparison with the rest state indicated extensive right-sided involvement during single word repetition with natural intonation. However, in the other active task, which required repetition of words with MIT intonation, the right hemisphere was deactivated, and a significant increase was found in the left frontal areas. The authors argued that the right-sided activations might reflect a "maladaptive" functional reorganisation, due to the presence of the left lesion itself, while actual recovery mediated by MIT training might be associated with the reactivation of left-hemispheric undamaged structures. Important evidence has also been provided by the recent study by Postman-Caucheteux et al. (2010). Taking advantage of the event-related technique in order to analyse the activation pattern associated with correct and erroneous responses in a naming task, these authors found a robust association between errors and right hemispheric brain activity.

An additional crucial issue from the point of view of rehabilitation is the assessment of the neural changes associated with training-induced modifications of language performance. Again, an early study supported the role of the right hemisphere. Musso et al. (1999) investigated with PET the neural correlates of intensive verbal comprehension training in a group of aphasics. Intensive two-hour language comprehension training on a modified version of the Token Test (De Renzi & Vignolo, 1962) was carried out during the PET inter-scan intervals. Post-training performance on this test was positively correlated with the pattern of rCBF in the right homologues of Wernicke's area and of Broca's area. Additional evidence for a role of the right hemisphere in supporting lexical relearning has been reported by Raboyeau et al. (2008), who found that similar right hemispheric activations in the inferior frontal and insular regions were associated with lexical relearning in both control participants and aphasic patients.

Training-induced effects were prevalent in the right hemisphere also in the case of action-based "intentional" treatments (Crosson et al., 2005, 2009).

Anomia is a universal component of the aphasic syndrome, and it is thus not surprising that several studies have been dedicated to the neural correlates of anomia training. The role of perilesional areas was supported by a single case study of the effects of intensive phonological training in a patient with prominent phonological errors in speech production (Leger et al., 2002). The main difference between the pre- and post-treatment fMRI study was a re-activation of perilesional left hemispheric areas, in particular the Broca's region and the supramarginal gyrus. Subsequent studies indicate more complex patterns of results. Fridriksson et al. (2006) found bihemispheric increases in activation in two patients who improved their naming performance with anomia treatment. In a later study, the same group reported activations in non-language areas (precuneus, hippocampus) associated with anomia training in three additional patients (Fridriksson et al., 2007). Most recently, Fridriksson, Bonilha, Baker, Moser, and Rorden (2010) reported the results of a study of a large sample of aphasic patients. The main finding was reactivation of spared left hemispheric regions. Similarly, Meinzer et al. (2008) found a correlation between training-induced improvement in picture naming and reactivation of perilesional areas in the left hemisphere. A subsequent study by the same group assessed the pattern of brain activation associated with improvement immediately after intensive training and at follow-up several months later (Menke et al., 2009). The short-term effects were observed bilaterally in the hippocampal region, fusiform gyrus and precuneus, i.e., in non-language areas. Long-term effects were associated with activations in the language areas, both perilesionally and in the homologous right hemispheric regions.

Using event-related fMRI (er-fMRI) Vitali et al. (2007) monitored the neural correlates of naming performance in two anomic patients before and after specific language therapy for anomia (phonological cued naming training). A set of pictures that the patients could not name either spontaneously or after being phonologically cued was selected for intensive speech therapy. After acquisition of the first er-fMRI session, training was intensively administered on a daily basis by a speech pathologist, until a 50% correct naming performance (at least) on the training picture set was achieved. Before and after specific speech therapy, an er-fMRI acquisition was performed while patients had to overtly name the visually presented pictures of the experimental set, and items of a control set (that patients were able to name prior to admission to the study). In both patients naming was mainly associated with activations in the non-dominant hemisphere before starting speech therapy, while perilesional areas of the dominant hemisphere were mainly activated after speech therapy, supporting the role of the perilesional areas of the left hemisphere for effective recovery. However, in one of the patients, who had a lesion involving Broca's area, the right homologue was activated, indicating that the right hemisphere may mediate successful naming. A similar study included the additional control of repeated scanning of two untreated patients, and of a group of normal subjects (Rochon et al., 2010). The changes in brain activity associated to recovery in the two treated patients were mostly left-hemispheric. A bilateral change, with right-sided prevalence, was observed in one of the two untreated patients, who did not show any significant change at the behavioural level.

Several factors may be responsible for the observed variation in the extent of right hemispheric vs. perilesional involvement. Lesion size and site appear to play an important role. Right hemispheric involvement is typically found in association with large lesions (Cherney & Small, 2006; Crosson et al., 2005; Raboyeau et al., 2008; Vitali et al., 2007). In contrast, perilesional activity is prominent in the case of smaller lesions (Leger et al., 2002; Meinzer et al., 2008; Vitali et al., 2007). A crucial impact of lesion site is suggested by the study reported by Fridriksson et al. (2010), in which patients whose brain damage included regions associated with lexical retrieval and phonological processing (e.g., Brodmann's areas 37 and 39) were less likely to show treatment-related improvement in correct naming, compared with patients in which the same areas were spared. The role of time post-lesion onset in the balance between contra- and intrahemispheric activation should also be considered. In particular, follow-up studies with aphasic patients have revealed the existence of a temporal gradient in the enrolment of cerebral reorganisation mechanisms after stroke. The initial engagement of non-damaged homologous areas of the right hemisphere is followed over time by their gradual discarding, with a concomitant significant increase of activity in left hemispheric perilesional areas. The passage of functional competence from the right to the left hemisphere is associated with an improvement of linguistic performance (Karbe et al., 1998). A strong interpretation of post-stroke perilesional recruitment is that it may reflect the greatest improvement in language function over time (Belin et al., 1996; Saur et al., 2006; Winhuisen et al., 2007).

Finally, the role of task should also be taken into consideration. Calvert et al. (2000), for example, found task-specific differences in fMRI activation in a 28-year-old aphasic woman. Performing a semantic decision task recruited a network of brain areas that excluded the inferior frontal gyrus (in either hemisphere), whereas, a rhyming task activated this region in the right hemisphere. Blasi et al. (2002) found that the learning of a stem-completion task was associated with specific response decrements in the right frontal and occipital cortices, rather than in the left-sided network engaged by normal participants. Thompson et al. (2010) found that sentence comprehension training was associated with a bilateral recruitment of posterior cortical regions.

An important additional tool to explore functional imaging data is provided by functional connectivity analysis, which allows the assessment of functional integration in the normal and damaged brain. Increased functional connectivity between the left and right temporal lobes (Warren, Crinion, Lambon Ralph, & Wise, 2009) and between frontal and parietal areas (Sharp et al., 2010) has been observed in aphasics with good recovery of auditory comprehension. This approach has been applied to the investigation of training and generalisation effects in anomia rehabilitation (Vitali et al., 2010) and to the assessment of longitudinal changes associated with anomia treatment (Abutalebi, Rosa, Tettamanti, Green, & Cappa, 2009).

BRAIN STIMULATION AND APHASIA RECOVERY

The data summarised above provide the rationale for stimulation intervention in aphasia recovery. Transcranial magnetic stimulation (TMS) has been extensively applied in cognitive neuroscience with the aim of interfering with cognitive processing (Wassermann et al., 2008). The possibility of applying the method to improve function developed as a consequence of observations in motor recovery (see a review in Dimyan & Cohen, 2011). There is now considerable evidence that an enhancement of performance in specific cognitive tasks can be observed in patients with stroke or dementia submitted to non-invasive brain stimulation, i.e., repetitive TMS (rTMS) or transcranial direct current stimulation (tDCS), to specific cortical areas (Miniussi et al., 2008). These facilitation effects have been related to their possible impact on the recovery mechanisms revealed by functional imaging studies.

In principle, rTMS could be effective by stimulating the intact right hemisphere, or left hemispheric perilesional areas. An additional mechanism could be interference with transcallosal inhibitory activity from the right hemisphere (a mechanism that has been proposed to be responsible for the enhancement of motor recovery) or, more generally, suppression of maladaptive right hemispheric activation (Baron-Cohen, Leslie, & Frith, 1985; Fregni & Pascual-Leone, 2007).

There are now a handful of published studies based on rTMS stimulation. A series of case studies by the same group has suggested that the administration of rhythmic rTMS to the anterior portion of the right homologue of Broca's area results in improvements in the ability to name pictures in patients with non-fluent aphasia (Hamilton et al., 2010; Martin et al., 2004; Naeser et al., 2005, 2010). These studies have attempted to define on the basis of precise *in vivo* structural and functional information the most effective location of stimulation. In particular, the application of low frequency (1 Hz) rTMS over the right pars opercularis (Po) of Broca's area does not result in improvement, but rather in a decrease of naming performance. In contrast, the same inhibitory stimulation of the right pars triangularis (Pt) results in improved naming performance. How to explain this anatomical specificity? A diffusion tensor imaging study by the same group attempts to provide an answer (Kaplan et al., 2010). The main result is that the Po, together with the ventral premotor cortex, rather than the right Pt, is the origin/target of fibres forming the arcuate fasciculus, on both sides. The arcuate fasciculus is a major fibre tract connecting anterior and posterior language areas (see a review in Catani, Jones, & ffytche, 2005). Thus, while inhibitory TMS to the right Po might be expected to have extensive intra-hemispheric effects, the same stimulation applied to the right Pt, due to its limited intrahemispheric connectivity, can be expected to have relatively selective transcallosal effects on the left hemisphere.

Weak support for the prediction that right Pt inhibition may result in a "release" of compensatory left hemispheric activity was provided by an fMRI study during picture naming, in which a patient who had responded to rTMS showed an activation increase only in the left supplementary motor area (Martin, Naeser, Ho, Doron, et al., 2009). The same group has also investigated the effects of combined treatments in a pilot single-case study, in which rTMS sessions were immediately followed by constraint-induced language therapy (Martin, Naeser, Ho, Treglia, et al., 2009). The results suggest that a combined treatment may be more effective than its components.

The other brain stimulation technique that has been applied to aphasic subjects is tDCS. The method is based on the application of weak electrical currents directly to the head. These currents generate an electrical field that modulates neuronal activity, according to the modality of application. Anodal stimulation results in membrane depolarisation, i.e., to an activation effect, while cathodal stimulation results in hyperpolarisation and is thus expected to be inhibitory (Liebetanz, Nitsche, Tergau, & Paulus, 2002; Paulus, this issue). A handful of studies have also been published using this approach. Cathodal stimulation has been applied over the damaged left fronto-temporal areas in eight patients with chronic, non-fluent, post-stroke aphasia, resulting in naming facilitation (Monti et al., 2008). Baker, Rorden, and Fridriksson (2010) reported a study in 10 brain-damaged aphasic patients with chronic stroke who received five days of anodal tDCS over the left frontal cortex and five days of sham tDCS, while performing a computerised anomia treatment. Results indicated a significant improvement in naming accuracy for treated items after anodal tDCS, compared with sham tDCS. The positioning of tDCS was guided by fMRI during a naming task, in order to stimulate undamaged cortex. In addition, the treatment effect persisted at least 1 week after treatment. Finally, a recent study reports beneficial effects of combined anomia training and anodal tDCS (5 sessions, 1 mA f, 20 minutes) applied over Wernicke's area in three chronic left-brain-damaged aphasic patients. A two week follow-up in two of the patients provided evidence of persistent treatment effects (Fiori et al., 2011). The discrepancy between the positive effects of cathodal and anodal stimulation, which are supposed to have, respectively, inhibitory and excitatory effects on the same (left) hemisphere is puzzling, and deserves further investigation.

CONCLUSIONS: THE NEED FOR MULTIPLE IMAGING/ STIMULATION APPROACHES

The *in vivo* study of the neural mechanisms of recovery of aphasia has a short history, but has already provided a number of new insights into the underlying complexity of the research questions. The simplistic ideas about contralateral takeover of function have disappeared under the weight of new evidence, which indicates the interplay of multiple factors, such as lesion size and site, time post-onset and type of training, which probably interact with many more, of which we are still unaware. What is clear from the present status of our knowledge is that progress in this research area, which carries not only theoretical but also translational implications for patients' care, requires a multimodal imaging approach. The results from functional imaging studies, which provide invaluable information about the spatial patterns of brain activity associated with the performance of a language task, need to be combined with fine-grained anatomical information about the site and extent of grey and white matter damage, constraining the interpretation of functional data. This functional and anatomical information is required to guide the application of neuromodulatory procedures, providing information about the causal role of specific brain structures in mediating performance and training effects. There are still many methodological problems which limit the application of this approach to the large patient populations required to provide definitive answers to basic questions such as whether, where, when and how to apply brain stimulation procedures with the aim to facilitate functional improvement in aphasia. At this point, however, we are probably able to formulate the appropriate questions. Targeting the locus of stimulation on the basis of the results of structural imaging (including tractography) and/or of functional activation assessed with fMRI is one of the present challenges of this field. In particular, we need to test the impact of inhibitory or excitatory neuromodulation on specific ipsilateral and contralateral areas, on the basis of their hypothetic functional role in the individual subject. Given the huge variability among aphasic patients at the clinical and neurological level, it is highly unlikely that a single procedure may be universally effective. Tailored interventions, based on the combination of language training and neuromodulation, may be the most promising innovative approach to aphasia therapy.

REFERENCES

Abutalebi, J., Rosa, P. A., Tettamanti, M., Green, D. W., & Cappa, S. F. (2009). Bilingual aphasia and language control: A follow-up fMRI and intrinsic connectivity study. *Brain and Language, 109,* 141–156.

Baker, J. M., Rorden, C., & Fridriksson, J. (2010). Using transcranial direct-current stimulation to treat stroke patients with aphasia. *Stroke, 41,* 1229–1236.

Baldwin, K., Orr, S., Briand, M., Piazza, C., Veydt, A., & McCoy, S. (2010). Acute ischemic stroke update. *Pharmacotherapy, 30,* 493–514.

Baron-Cohen, S., Leslie, A. M., & Frith, U. (1985). Does the autistic child have a "theory of mind"? *Cognition, 21,* 37–46.

Belin, P., Van Eeckhout, P., Zilbovicius, M., Remy, P., François, C., Guillaume, S., Chain, F., Rancurel, G., & Samson, Y. (1996). Recovery from nonfluent aphasia after melodic intonation therapy: A PET study. *Neurology, 47,* 1504–1511.

Blasi, V., Young, A. C., Tansy, A. P., Petersen, S. E., Snyder, A. Z., & Corbetta, M. (2002). Word retrieval learning modulates right frontal cortex in patients with left frontal damage. *Neuron, 36,* 159–170.

Calvert, G. A., Brammer, M. J., Morris, R. G., Williams, S. C., King, N., & Matthews, P. M. (2000). Using fMRI to study recovery from acquired dysphasia. *Brain and Language, 71,* 391–399.

Cappa, S. F., Benke, T., Clarke, S., Rossi, B., Stemmer, B., & van Heugten, C. M. (2005). EFNS guidelines on cognitive rehabilitation: Report of an EFNS task force. *European Journal of Neurology, 12,* 665–680.

Cappa, S. F., Perani, D., Grassi, F., Bressi, S., Alberoni, M., Franceschi, M., Bettinardi, V., Todde, S., & Fazio, F. (1997). A PET follow-up study of recovery after stroke in acute aphasics. *Brain and Language, 56,* 55–67.

Catani, M., Jones, D. K., & Ffytche, D. H. (2005). Perisylvian language networks of the human-brain. *Annals of Neurology, 57,* 8–16.

Cherney, L. R., & Small, S. L. (2006). Task-dependent changes in brain activation following therapy for nonfluent aphasia: Discussion of two individual cases. *Journal of the International Neuropsychological Society, 12,* 828–842.

Cicerone, K. D., Dahlberg, C., Malec, J. F., & et al. (2005). Evidence-based cognitive rehabilitation: Updated review of the literature from 1998 through 2002. *Archives of Physical Medicine and Rehabilitation, 86,* 1681–1692.

Crinion, J. T., & Leff, A. P. (2007). Recovery and treatment of aphasia after stroke: Functional imaging studies. *Current Opinion in Neurology, 20,* 667–673.

Crosson, B., Moore, A. B., Gopinath, K., White, K. D., Wierenga, C. E., Gaiefsky, M. E., Fabrizio, K. S., Peck, K. K., Soltysik, D., Milsted, C., Briggs, R. W., Conway, T. W., & Gonzalez Rothi, L. J. (2005). Role of the right and left hemispheres in recovery of function during treatment of intention in aphasia. *Journal of Cognitive Neuroscience, 17,* 392–406.

Crosson, B., Moore, A. B., McGregor, K. M., Chang, Y. L., Benjamin, M., Gopinath, K., Sherod, M. E., Wierenga, C. E., Peck, K. K., Briggs, R. W., Rothi, L. J., & White, K. D. (2009). Regional changes in word-production laterality after a naming treatment designed to produce a rightward shift in frontal activity. *Brain and Language, 111,* 73–85

De Renzi, E., & Vignolo, L. A. (1962). The Token Test: A sensitive test to detect receptive disturbances in aphasia. *Brain, 85,* 665–678.

Dimyan, M. A., & Cohen, L. G. (2011). Neuroplasticity in the context of motor rehabilitation after stroke. *Nature Reviews Neurology, 7,* 76–85.

Feeney, D. M., & Baron, J. C. (1986). Diaschisis. *Stroke, 17,* 817–830.

Ferbert, A., Priori, A., Rothwell, J. C., Day, B. L., Colebatch, J. G., & Marsden, C. D. (1992). Interhemispheric inhibition of the human motor cortex. *Journal of Physiology, 453,* 525–546.

Fiori, V., Coccia, M., Marinelli, C. V., Vecchi, V., Bonifazi, S., Ceravolo, M. G., Provinciali, L., Tomaiuolo, F., & Marangolo, P. (2011). Transcranial direct current stimulation improves word retrieval in healthy and nonfluent aphasic subjects. *Journal of Cognitive Neuroscience, 23*(9), 2309–2323.

Fregni, F., & Pascual-Leone, A. (2007). Technology insight: Noninvasive brain stimulation in neurology – perspectives on the therapeutic potential of rTMS and tDCS. *Nature Clinical Practice Neurology, 3,* 383–393.

Fridriksson, J., Bonilha, L., Baker, J. M., Moser, D., & Rorden, C. (2010). Activity in preserved left hemisphere regions predicts anomia severity in aphasia. *Cerebral Cortex, 20,* 1013–1019.

Fridriksson, J., Morrow-Odom, L., Moser, D., Fridriksson, A., & Baylis, G. (2006). Neural recruitment associated with anomia treatment in aphasia. *NeuroImage, 32,* 1403–1412.

Fridriksson, J., Moser, D., Bonilha, L., Morrow-Odom, K. L., Shaw, H., Fridriksson, A., et al. (2007). Neural correlates of phonological and semantic-based anomia treatment in aphasia. *Neuropsychologia, 45,* 1812–1822.

Gazzaniga, M. S. (1983). Right hemisphere language following brain bisection. A 20 years perspective. *American Psychologist, 38,* 525–537.

Gowers, W. (1895). *Malattie del sistema nervoso.* Milan, Italy: Vallardi.

Hamilton, R. H., Sanders, L., Benson, J., Faseyitan, O., Norise, C., Naeser, M., Martin, P., & Coslett, H. B. (2010). Stimulating conversation: Enhancement of elicited propositional speech in a patient with chronic non-fluent aphasia following transcranial magnetic stimulation. *Brain and Language, 113,* 45–50.

Kaplan, E., Naeser, M. A., Martin, P. I., Ho, M., Wang, Y., Baker, E., & Pascual-Leone, A. (2010). Horizontal portion of arcuate fasciculus fibers track to pars opercularis, not pars triangularis, in right and left hemispheres: A DTI study. *NeuroImage, 52,* 436–444.

Karbe, H., Thiel, A., Weber-Luxenburger, G., Herholz, K., Kessler, J., & Heiss, W. D. (1998). Brain plasticity in poststroke aphasia: What is the contribution of the right hemisphere? *Brain and Language, 64,* 215–230.

Kelly, H., Brady, M. C., & Enderby, P. (2010). Speech and language therapy for aphasia following stroke (Review). *The Cochrane Library.*

Leger, A., Demonet, J. F., Ruff, S., Aithamon, B., Touyeras, B., Puel, M., Boulanouar, K., & Cardebat, D. (2002). Neural substrates of spoken language rehabilitation in an aphasic patient: An fMRI study. *NeuroImage, 17,* 174–183.

Liebetanz, D., Nitsche, M. A., Tergau, F., & Paulus, W. (2002). Pharmacological approach to the mechanisms of transcranial DC-stimulation-induced after-effects of human motor cortex excitability. *Brain, 125,* 2238–2247.

Martin, P. I., Naeser, M. A., Ho, M., Doron, K. W., Kurland, J., Kaplan, J., Wang, Y., Nicholas, M., Baker, E. H., Alonso, M., Fregni, F., & Pascual-Leone, A. (2009). Overt naming fMRI pre- and post-TMS: Two nonfluent aphasia patients, with and without improved naming post-TMS. *Brain and Language, 111,* 20–35.

Martin, P. I., Naeser, M. A., Ho, M., Treglia, E., Kaplan, E., Baker, E. H., & Pascual-Leone, A. (2009). Research with transcranial magnetic stimulation in the treatment of aphasia. *Current Neurology and Neuroscience Reports, 9,* 451–458.

Martin, P. I., Naeser, M. A., Theoret, H., Tormos, J. M., Nicholas, M., Kurland, J., Fregni, F., Seekins, H., Doron, K., & Pascual-Leone, A. (2004). Transcranial magnetic stimulation as a complementary treatment for aphasia. *Seminars in Speech and Language, 25,* 181–191.

Mazzocchi, F., & Vignolo, L. A. (1979). Localisation of lesions in aphasia: Clinical-CT scan correlations in stroke patients. *Cortex, 15,* 627–654.

Meinzer, M., Flaisch, T., Breitenstein, C., Wienbruch, C., Elbert, T., & Rockstroh, B. (2008). Functional re-recruitment of dysfunctional brain areas predicts language recovery in chronic aphasia. *NeuroImage, 39,* 2038–2046.

Menke, R., Meinzer, M., Kugel, H., Deppe, M., Baumgartner, A., Schiffbauer, H., Thomas, M., Kramer, K., Lohmann, H., Floel, A., Knecht, S., & Breitenstein, C. (2009). Imaging short- and long-term training success in chronic aphasia. *BMC Neuroscience, 10,* 118.

Miniussi, C., Cappa, S. F., Cohen, L. G., Floel, A., Fregni, F., Nitsche, M. A., Oliveri, M., Pascual-Leone, A., Paulus, W., Priori, A., & Walsh, V. (2008). Efficacy of repetitive transcranial magnetic stimulation/transcranial direct current stimulation in cognitive neurorehabilitation. *Brain Stimulation, 1,* 326–336.

Monti, A., Cogiamanian, F., Marceglia, S., Ferrucci, R., Mameli, F., Mrakic-Sposta, S., Vergari, M., Zago, S., & Priori, A. (2008). Improved naming after transcranial direct current stimulation in aphasia. *Journal of Neurology Neurosurgery Psychiatry, 79,* 451–453.

Musso, M., Weiller, C., Kiebel, S., Muller, S. P., Bulau, P., & Rijntjes, M. (1999). Training-induced brain plasticity in aphasia. *Brain, 122,* 1781–1790.

Naeser, M. A., Martin, P. I., Nicholas, M., Baker, E. H., Seekins, H., Kobayashi, M., Theoret, H., Fregni, F., Maria-Tormos, J., Kurland, J., Doron, K. W., & Pascual-Leone, A. (2005). Improved picture naming in chronic aphasia after TMS to part of right Broca's area: An open-protocol study. *Brain and Language, 93,* 95–105.

Naeser, M. A., Martin, P. I., Treglia, E., Ho, M., Kaplan, E., Bashir, S., Hamilton, R., Coslett, H. B., & Pascual-Leone, A. (2010). Research with rTMS in the treatment of aphasia. *Restorative Neurology and Neuroscience, 28,* 511–529.

Noppeney, U., Friston, K. J., & Price, C. J. (2004). Degenerate neuronal systems sustaining cognitive functions. *Journal of Anatomy, 205,* 433–442.

Paolucci, S., Antonucci, G., Grasso, M. G., Bragoni, M., Coiro, P., De Angelis, D., Fusco, F. R., Morelli, D., Venturiero, V., Troisi, E., & Pratesi, L. (2003). Functional outcome of ischemic and hemorrhagic stroke patients after inpatient rehabilitation: A matched comparison. *Stroke, 34,* 2861–2865.

Perani, D., Cappa, S. F., Tettamanti, M., Rosa, M., Scifo, P., Miozzo, A., Basso, A., & Fazio, F. (2003). A fMRI study of word retrieval in aphasia. *Brain and Language, 85,* 357–368.

Postman-Caucheteux, W. A., Birn, R. M., Pursley, R. H., Butman, J. A., Solomon, J. M., Picchioni, D., McArdle, J., & Braun, A. R. (2010). Single-trial fMRI shows contralesional activity linked to overt naming errors in chronic aphasic patients. *Journal of Cognitive Neuroscience, 22,* 1299–1318.

Price, C. J., & Crinion, J. (2005). The latest on functional imaging studies of aphasic stroke. *Current Opinion in Neurology, 18,* 429–434.

Raboyeau, G., De Boissezon, X., Marie, N., Balduyck, S., Puel, M., Bezy, C., Demonet, J. F., & Cardebat, D. (2008). Right hemisphere activation in recovery from aphasia: Lesion effect or function recruitment? *Neurology, 70,* 290–298.

Richter, M., Miltner, W. H., & Straube, T. (2008). Association between therapy outcome and right–hemispheric activation in chronic aphasia. *Brain, 131,* 1391–1401.

Rochon, E., Leonard, C., Burianova, H., Laird, L., Soros, P., Graham, S., & Grady, C. (2010). Neural changes after phonological treatment for anomia: An fMRI study. *Brain and Language, 114,* 164–179.

Saur, D., Lange, R., Baumgaertner, A., Schraknepper, V., Willmes, K., Rijntjes, M., & Weiller, C. (2006). Dynamics of language reorganization after stroke. *Brain, 129,* 1371–1384.

Sharp, D. J., Turkheimer, F. E., Bose, S. K., Scott, S. K., & Wise, R. J. (2010). Increased frontoparietal integration after stroke and cognitive recovery. *Annals of Neurology, 68,* 753–756.

Thiel, A., Schumacher, B., Wienhard, K., Gairing, S., Kracht, L. W., Wagner, R., Haupt, W. F., & Heiss, W. D. (2006). Direct demonstration of transcallosal disinhibition in language networks. *Journal of Cerebral Blood Flow and Metabolism, 26,* 1122–1127.

Thompson, C. K., & den Ouden, D. B. (2008). Neuroimaging and recovery of language in aphasia. *Current Neurology Neuroscience Reports, 8,* 475–483.

Thompson, C. K., den Ouden, D. B., Bonakdarpour, B., Garibaldi, K., & Parrish, T. B. (2010). Neural plasticity and treatment-induced recovery of sentence processing in agrammatism. *Neuropsychologia, 48,* 3211–3227.

Vitali, P., Abutalebi, J., Tettamanti, M., Danna, M., Ansaldo, A. I., Perani, D., Joanette, Y., & Cappa, S. F. (2007). Training-induced brain remapping in chronic aphasia: A pilot study. *Neurorehabilitation and Neural Repair, 21,* 152–160.

Vitali, P., Tettamanti, M., Abutalebi, J., Ansaldo, A. I., Perani, D., Cappa, S. F., & Joanette, Y. (2010). Generalization of the effects of phonological training for anomia using structural equation modelling: A multiple single-case study. *Neurocase, 16,* 93–105.

von Monakow, C. (1914). *Die Lokalisation in Grosshirn und der Abbau der Funktion durch Kortikale Herde.* Wiesbaden, Germany: Bergmann.

Warburton, E., Price, C. J., Swinburn, K., & Wise, R. J. (1999). Mechanisms of recovery from aphasia: Evidence from positron emission tomography studies. *Journal of Neurology, Neurosurgery & Psychiatry, 66,* 155–161.

Warren, J. E., Crinion, J. T., Lambon Ralph, M. A., & Wise, R. J. (2009). Anterior temporal lobe connectivity correlates with functional outcome after aphasic stroke. *Brain, 132,* 3428–3442.

Wassermann, E.M., Epstein, C.M., Ziemann, U., Walsh, V., Paus, T., & Lisanby, S.H. (Eds.). (2008). *The Oxford Handbook of Transcranial Stimulation.* Oxford: Oxford University Press.

Weiller, C., Isensee, C., Rijintjes, M., Huber, W., Mueller, S., Bier, D., Dutschka, K., Woods, R. P., Noth, J., & Diener, H. C. (1995). Recovery from Wernicke's aphasia – a PET study. *Annals of Neurology, 37,* 723–732.

Winhuisen, L., Thiel, A., Schumacher, B., Kessler, J., Rudolf, J., Haupt, W. F., & Heiss, W. D. (2007). The right inferior frontal gyrus and poststroke aphasia: A follow-up investigation. *Stroke, 38,* 1286–1292.

NEUROPSYCHOLOGICAL REHABILITATION
2011, 21 (5), 755–768

The future of cognitive neurorehabilitation

Donald T. Stuss

Ontario Brain Institute, Rotman Research Institute of Baycrest University of Toronto, Toronto, Canada

Cognitive neurorehabilitation is rooted both in the cognitive function being treated and the neural substrates underlying that ability. Recent progress in understanding both brain (in particular brain plasticity) and the complexities of behaviour imply a promising future for cognitive neurorehabilitation. The manuscripts in this issue focuse on advances in the use of non-invasive brain stimulation (NIBS) as a tool for cognitive neurorehabilitation. This paper presents a broader context in which to understand the importance and potential of this specific approach. Achieving the promise requires theoretical and experimental rigour including selection of relevant outcome measures, and understanding of the complexities of individual patients. Success will depend on our ability to integrate knowledge and approaches.

Keywords: Cognitive neurorehabilitation; Brain plasticity; Integrative approach; Patient factors; Best practices.

DEFINITION OF COGNITIVE NEUROREHABILITATION

Fitzpatrick and Robertson (2008) identified several elements of cognitive neurorehabilitation (hereafter identified as CR for sake of brevity), which helps differentiate CR from the more general concept of rehabilitation. Both have as a goal the improvement of daily functioning. However, CR is

Correspondence should be addressed to Donald T. Stuss, Ontario Brain Institute, MaRS Centre, Heritage Building, 101 College Street, Box 21, Toronto, Ontario M5G 1L7, Canada. Email: dstuss@braininstitute.ca

Several of the constructs are elaborated in an edited book on cognitive neurorehabilitation (Stuss, Winocur, & Robertson, 2008), and the contributors and co-editors are gratefully acknowledged. L. Fourie and S. Gillingham are thanked for comments on an earlier draft.

scientifically grounded in an understanding of how the brain works, and is targeted to treatment and improvement of cognitive impairment secondary to brain damage or dysfunction. Some change in brain functioning itself maybe a necessary mechanism of improvement. As such, CR demands an understanding of brain-behaviour relations – the theory underlying the particular cognitive function being rehabilitated, *and* the neural substrates related to that function.

Neurostimulation is obviously solidly grounded in the framework of CR and, as will be seen, appears to provide value above and beyond traditional CR.

FACTORS FOR SUCCESS IN COGNITIVE NEUROREHABILITATION

There is a burgeoning enthusiasm related to the efficacy of CR. The implementation of "best practices" and the knowledge that the brain indeed is "plastic" are two major reasons for this enthusiasm – but there are reasons for a cautious attitude.

The zeitgeist in clinical service is "best practices". This has as its lofty goal a critical review of the existing literature, and the extraction and implementation of experimentally validated methods. Although laudatory, there are potential landmines. Even if the practices represent the very best that exist at this moment, they may not be the best that can possibly be. This is problematic, since there is a strong possibility that this "gold standard" will ossify into a permanent practice that is not optimal. A continuing questioning, experimental attitude must exist. Some of the sections below are pertinent to this attitude.

A major principle underlying success in cognitive neurorehabilitation is the relatively new found capacity of the brain to recover from damage (e.g., Kolb, Teskey, & Gibb, 2010), and to re-organise in different ways (e.g., reconfigured neural networks) to maximise recovery. These findings have created excitement and hope. However, this capacity may not be maximised for the benefit of the individual patient. As indicated in several manuscripts in this issue, this capacity for brain plasticity is influenced by many different variables (see also Kolb & Gibb, 2008). Several of the most relevant factors are described below.

Theoretical foundations

Theory is the continuous spring from which flows the rationale for the development of CR techniques. However, both the theory and the methods need to be continuously validated, and updated as required. The history of neuropsychology in North America is an example of the importance of this. Neuropsychological assessments, and associated interventions, were dramatically altered by the theoretical position of Ward Halstead (1947). However, once methods were standardised, it was difficult to incorporate newer theories of brain functioning that evolved because of cognitive neuroscience and sophisticated functional and structural imaging methodologies (see also Stuss & Levine, 2002). How does one ensure practically that theory and practices are refreshed to ensure they are optimal, and then integrated into research and clinical practice? This is the challenge of translational research.

Another example, derived from my own research on executive functions and their relation to the frontal lobes and the application of this knowledge to the understanding and treatment of individuals with traumatic brain injury (TBI), illustrates how theories change, and how this impacts treatment. In the mid-1980s, my clinic was confronted by many moderately to severely injured (based on duration of loss of consciousness, Glasgow Coma Scale in early stages after injury, and/or duration of post-traumatic injury). At examination, months post-injury, these TBI patients appeared normal on then standard neuropsychological examination, but continued to complain of problems. A review of common neuropathology post-trauma (e.g., Courville, 1937) provided the anatomical basis for a hypothesis: the tests used in the standard examination were not sufficiently targeted or sensitive to the frontal/temporal damage, with the result that the patients appeared "normal". When more targeted tests tapping the functions of these regions were administered, significant impairment was noted (Stuss et al., 1985). We and others (Levin et al., 1985; Levin, Benton, & Grossman, 1982; Stuss & Gow, 1992) proposed a primarily "frontal" hypothesis of TBI, and an approach to rehabilitation based on current knowledge of frontal lobe functioning was proposed (Sohlberg, Mateer, & Stuss, 1993). However, once again, as knowledge of the functions of the frontal lobes evolved, and fractionation of these functions were revealed (e.g., Godefroy et al., 1999; Koechlin, Basso, Pietrini, Panzer, & Grafman, 1999; Shallice & Burgess, 1996; Stuss, 2007; Stuss & Alexander, 2007), it became obvious that development of CR for TBI could not be founded on a simple executive dysfunction hypothesis. This led to our ability to hypothesise a more targeted approach to CR in TBI patients, which was founded in this new knowledge (Cicerone, Levin, Malec, Stuss, & Whyte, 2006; Levine, Turner, & Stuss, 2008). This new knowledge also allows us to explain in a more theoretical manner the success one might have had with a rehabilitation technique, or to question the failures. For example, we (Stuss, Delgado, & Guzman, 1987) had proposed that self-talk could be a successful means of rehabilitating motor impersistence after right frontal lobe damage. Today one might describe the approach as the use of external task-setting through verbalisation (possible because of an intact left frontal lobe) to overcome a monitoring problem (secondary to right frontal lobe pathology) in sustaining goal-directed behaviour (Stuss & Alexander, 2007; Stuss, 2011).

The potential brain mechanisms underlying success in CR represent another theoretical foundation. This is aptly illustrated in the manuscript by Hesse, Sparing, and Fink (2011), demonstrating that theory related to the underlying mechanism of improvement is essential. Although most concepts underlying the efficacy of neurostimulation suggested the importance of inhibiting overactivation of the contralesional hemisphere to "rebalance" the system, they aptly pointed out the possibility of facilitation of ipsilesional circuitry. It may well be that the specific mechanism must be understood if the efficacy is to be maximised.

Scientific methodology

Real success in CR is dependent on the quality of the research. Although randomised control trials are the gold standard, the importance of stages of rehabilitation research should not be underestimated (Rodriquez & Rothi, 2008). This includes animal and basic human research to understand normal functioning (Craik et al., 2007; Levine et al., 2007; Stuss et al., 2007; Winocur, Craik, et al., 2007; Winocur, Moscovitch, Rosenbaum, & Sekeres, 2010; Winocur, Palmer, et al., 2007; Wojtowicz, Askew, & Winocur, 2008), observational studies (Cicerone, 2008), and exploratory Phase 1 research to establish the foundational knowledge necessary to support RCTs. Many of these approaches are illustrated in the papers of this issue.

Outcome measures

How we do measure success? Or, phrased experimentally, what should our outcome measures be? Outcome measurements that show effectiveness must become a priority for CR. These outcome measurements themselves must meet specific criteria, such as reliability, validity, practicality and so on (Lincoln & Nair, 2008). Moreover, not all measures are good outcome measures – some may be best for diagnostic, descriptive purposes.

Many of the papers in this issue discuss benefits that are targeted to a specific type of disorder (e.g., neglect), and could be described as being modular specific. Such modular specific reduction of impairment is of significant value. However, it is important to differentiate between reduced "impairment" in a specific cognitive ability and improvements in performance of more general daily life activities requiring that cognitive function. In addition, it is possible to examine if the improved performance post-CR is limited to the cognitive function being rehabilitated, or whether there is a corresponding alteration at a more general strategic level (e.g., fluid intelligence), the latter suggesting generalisation of improvement beyond the specific function, commonly labelled as far transfer. It is possible that rehabilitation may be effective in improving how one manages in daily life without necessarily reducing the fundamental impairment (Lincoln & Nair, 2008), or vice-versa – that there might be amelioration at the modular level without corresponding alteration in many aspects of daily life (Kagan et al., 2008). The clinicians who truly want to find and use "best practices" should know at what level of outcome the intervention, regardless of type, is successful.

The science of CR, including NIBS, certainly requires this behavioural level of evidence – do our interventions result in genuine improvement at some level of functioning? For CR to achieve its potential, however, grounded in the science and biology of the brain, additional evidence is required – what is happening *in* and *to* the brain (e.g., Miniussi & Rossini, 2011). This is where the research related to NIBS has played an exemplary role. Similarly, understanding of alterations at the neuronal or neurotransmitter level may be crucial to the development of pharmacological therapies.

Functional imaging perhaps deserves special mention as a biological outcome measure (see Corbetta, 2008). The use of functional imaging as an additional index of the efficacy of physiotherapeutic approaches to motor dysfunction led to a truly counter-intuitive approach to motor recovery – constraint-induced motor therapy (Morris & Taub, 2008; Taub et al., 1993; Taub, Crago, & Uswatte, 1998; Wolf, Lecraw, Barton, & Jann, 1989). This is an excellent example of how CR research, done properly, led to the realisation that the then current "best practices" were not only not the best, but perhaps somewhat detrimental to maximum recovery. Returning to pharmacological therapies, imaging could assist in the evaluation and specificity of targeted pharmacotherapeutics (McAllister & Arnsten, 2008). There are evolving new techniques of analysing neural networks (Grady et al., 2010; McIntosh & Grady, 2007) which allow assessment of specific aspects of brain plasticity: increased activity after CR in surrounding cortex, compensation by another region for damage to one area, and even brain network re-organisation. This approach is now being heralded as an important step in understanding and treating depression (e.g., Liotti & Mayberg, 2001), where it has been hypothesised that an appreciation of re-organisation of neural circuitry through neuroimaging may be the most important diagnostic and outcome measure (Williamson & Allman, 2011).

The success of an intervention may not be evident because variability may not have been considered. Group variability is defined as the variation among individuals within a group. There are many reasons for group variability to occur, and many of these are outlined in the section below on patient factors. Realisation that patients with frontal lobe damage were not all the same (that is, there was variability among these patients) led our research group to investigate the anatomical bases (see the following for descriptions of how group variability can be minimised: Stuss, Floden, Alexander, Levine, & Katz, 2001; Stuss, 2011; Stuss, Alexander, et al., 2002). The outcome led to our discovery of fractionation of functions within the frontal lobes (Alexander, Stuss, & Gillingham, 2009; Alexander, Stuss, Picton, Shallice, & Gillingham,

2007; Alexander, Stuss, Shallice, Picton, & Gillingham, 2005; Picton et al., 2007; Picton, Stuss, Shallice, Alexander, & Gillingham, 2006; Shallice, Stuss, Alexander, Picton, & Derkzen, 2008; Shallice, Stuss, Picton, Alexander, & Gillingham, 2008a, 2008b; Stuss et al., 2005; Stuss & Alexander, 2007; Stuss, Binns, Murphy, & Alexander, 2002; Stuss, Shallice, Alexander, & Picton, 1995), and this in turn is directing us to develop new methods of CR. As noted above, we now are able to describe some of our past interventions in more theoretical terms. The importance of searching for group variability in CR research cannot be underemphasised. In *any* study of CR, one should look for responders and non-responders, and then try to determine the reasons underlying the responses. Interventions should not be immediately rejected just because there is no overall group difference. TBI is so variable, for example, no single drug has proven effective for all forms of resultant cognitive impairment (Whyte, 2008). This approach is the door to "personalised" or "stratified" medicine, where treatments and interventions are targeted to those in whom they will be most effective.

There is one type of variability even more overlooked than group variability – and that is intra-individual variability (Stuss, Pogue, Buckle, & Bondar, 1994). Cognitively impaired patients can be extremely variable in the expression of their cognitive problems, and the causes of this variability are only partially known (Stuss & Binns, 2008). Aging is one factor (Hultsch & MacDonald, 2004). Another important variable is lesion location. Damage in primarily domain-specific regions can result in variability of performance in that specific function (Anderson, Mennemeier, & Chatterjee, 2000; Milberg, Blumstein, Giovanello, & Misiurski, 2003; Stuss, Murphy, Binns, & Alexander, 2003), while damage in the frontal regions cause more domain-general problems, resulting in variability in virtually all functions (Stuss et al., 2003; West, Murphy, Armilio, Craik, & Stuss, 2002). It follows that variability should be taken into account routinely in assessing recovery or the effects of cognitive rehabilitation (Stuss & Binns, 2008). What is most interesting, changes in variability can be an important outcome measure, either by its decrease behaviourally (Hetherington, Stuss, & Finlayson, 1996) or increase cortically (McIntosh, Kovacevic, & Itier, 2008).

Patient characteristics

Too often overlooked are the patient characteristics that might influence outcome. The patient factors are often a major contributor to increased group variability (Stuss & Binns, 2008) and therefore affect the outcome of an experiment. Hayman (2011) noted the importance of phenotyping in assisting gene discovery in mental health disorders. The awareness of these factors is relevant not only for experimental investigation but also for individual CR. Understanding the moderating factors that might influence outcome, from genetics to environmental differences, may provide clues as to why the techniques may be beneficial to some but not all. Inversely, paying attention to and discovering the behavioural phenotypes in our research provides a gateway to pursue further why this may be the case, and to reveal the relevant defining characteristics of the subgroups.

Lesion location, and possibly extent, are important variables. Our successes in fractionating frontal lobe functions, for example, only began once we started being more precise in measuring lesion location, limiting the extent of the lesion, controlling for chronicity, examining patients in sufficiently large numbers so that we could start to identify the importance of specific brain regions, and in developing methods of analysis (for examples and reviews, see Stuss et al., 1998, 2002; Stuss, 2011). Similarly, this precision enabled us to put to rest some of the misconceptions of the similarities between frontal lobe and cerebellar functioning (Alexander, Gillingham, Schweizer, & Stuss, 2011).

Differences in mood and motivation may impact patient's involvement on a psychological or on a physiological basis. There are likely different kinds of apathy (Stuss, van Reekum, & Murphy, 2000; van Reekum, Stuss, & Ostrander, 2005), related to damage in different brain regions and circuits (see Ghaffar & Feinstein, 2008). These concepts have to be integrated into the development of models of CR, particularly if one is interested in the mechanisms underling success or failure. Prigatano (2008, 2010) sees awareness of deficits as being closely allied with motivation. Winocur and colleagues (Dawson & Winocur, 2008; Winocur, Palmer, et al., 2007) stress the more general construct of psychosocial factors, such as environmental changes, and in particular perception of loss of control. The actual type of control itself appears to be relevant, suggesting finer differentiation of the mechanisms related to successful outcome (Krpan, Levine, Stuss, & Dawson, 2007; Krpan, Stuss, & Anderson, 2011).

Diet and exercise are now the source of many studies on their beneficial effect of cognitive abilities (e.g., Kramer, Erickson, & McAuley, 2008; Parrott & Greenwood, 2008; Scherder & Eggermont, 2008), but may not be considered when one looks at individual differences in recovery or in responding to interventions. Food is the major source of brain chemistry (Parrot & Greenwood, 2008). It feeds the engine on which CR is based. In a similar way, not only does exercise improve many aspects of physiological functioning, it is possible that certain cognitive and physical problems may result in diminished activity, which would have its own detrimental effect.

Summary

There are likely more factors which are important to success of CR. The important lesson is that such issues must be considered, and the type of factor may vary depending on the particular disorder and group being investigated and treated.

CONSIDERATIONS FOR THE FUTURE

There are significant challenges for the future of CR – or is there really only one challenge? How does one integrate the separate sources of information to maximise benefit for the individual patient? There are very few studies that integrate approaches. Miniussi and Rossini (2011), for example, suggest that brain stimulation is perhaps not a treatment on its own, but should be used in conjunction with behavioural neurorehabilitation to reduce treatment time and potentiate outcome. Another level of integration might occur with pharmacological and biological approaches. McAllister and Arnsten (2008) suggest that real progress in treating deficits pharmacologically in specific cognitive domains has been limited, although there are encouraging signs with drugs that have specific neurotransmitter targets (Arnsten, in press; Whyte, 2008). The possibility of using these drugs in conjunction with behavioural rehabilitation targeted to functions that are perhaps related to the same regions as the neurotransmitter targets is suggested if one considers the newer findings of frontal lobe functional specificity (e.g., Stuss, 2007) in light of the research from Arnsten's lab (Wang et al., 2007) on drugs with specific neurotransmitter targets. In other words, the most significant gains will likely result in a context where there are linkages from molecular to brain and behaviour, through stages of recovery, and from behaviour to brain mechanisms as demonstrated by imaging (Winocur, 2008, pp. 295–297).

Another beneficial linkage might occur by maximising brain plasticity through behavioural techniques that enhance neurogenesis, such as enriched environments, physical exercise, and new learning (Stickland, Weiss, & Kolb, 2008). NIBS might be especially important in increasing brain plasticity in individuals who are limited in engaging in such activities. However, in some the changes may be counter-productive (Kolb & Gibb, 2008).

Berlucchi (2011) provides a historical perspective, and paints a positive backdrop for the future of CR. He stresses the importance of a theoretical understanding at all levels of CR, and of the mechanisms underlying successful CR. Berlucchi (2011) also stresses integration. "It is now possible to couple traditional behavioural, cognitive and psychotherapeutic interventions of neuropsychological rehabilitation (e.g., Wilson, Herbert, & Shiel, 2003) with advanced neurological treatments such as direct invasive or non-invasive brain stimulation (e.g., Wassermann et al., 2008), transplantation of stem cells and neuronal precursors, gene therapies, computer-assisted learning, brain–machine interfaces, and so forth (e.g. Komitova, Johansson, & Eriksson, 2006)."

The papers in this Special Issue of *Neuropsychological Rehabilitation* demonstrate the potential of NIBS to provide an approach that is above and beyond traditional CR techniques. NIBS may provide a reversible "lesion", which may lead to theoretical support of imaging or lesion data. More importantly, however, it may result in positive modulation of human performance such as an increase of accuracy or decrease of response latencies (Vallar & Bolognini, 2011). The science of NIBS itself has developed to the point that one can start to think of selecting the type of NIBS, site, and intensity which would maximally interact with a behavioural and/or pharmacological intervention, all related to the targeted cognitive disorder. Integrating these different approaches, which may work on different mechanisms, may lead to faster, longer-lasting, and more beneficial therapeutic impact.

Fitzpatrick and Robertson (2008) felt that such an attempt at integration would not only be beneficial clinically but that "the science of cognitive neurorehabilitation, precisely because it requires serious attempts at such integration, could actually lead the field of neuroscience in this effort".

The future of CR with an increasing armamentarium of approaches is indeed bright.

REFERENCES

Alexander, M. P, Gillingham, S., Schweizer, T. A., & Stuss, D. T. (2011). Cognitive impairments due to focal cerebellar injuries in adults. *Cortex*. Advance online publication. doi: 10.1016/j.cortex.2011.03.012.

Alexander, M. P., Stuss, D. T., & Gillingham, S. (2009). Impaired list learning is not a general property of frontal lesions. *Journal of Cognitive Neuroscience, 21,* 1422–1434.

Alexander, M. P., Stuss, D. T., Picton, T., Shallice, T., & Gillingham, S. (2007). Regional frontal injuries cause distinct impairments in cognitive control. *Neurology, 68,* 1515–1523.

Alexander, M. P., Stuss, D. T., Shallice, T., Picton, T. W., & Gillingham, S. (2005). Impaired concentration due to frontal lobe damage from two distinct lesion sites. *Neurology, 65,* 572–579.

Anderson, B., Mennemeier, M., & Chatterjee, A. (2000). Variability not ability: Another basis for performance decrements in neglect. *Neuropsychologia, 38,* 785–796.

Arnsten, A. F. T. (in press). Fleeting thoughts: Molecular vulnerabilities in prefrontal cortical circuits. In D. T. Stuss & R. T. Knight (Eds.), *Principles of frontal lobe function, 2nd edition.* New York, NY: Oxford University Press.

Berlucchi, G. (2011). Brain plasticity and cognitive neurorehabilitation. *Neuropsychological Rehabilitation, 21*(5), 560–578.

Cicerone, K. D. (2008). Principles in evaluating cognitive rehabilitation research. In D. T. Stuss, G. Winocur, & I. H. Robertson (Eds.), *Cognitive neurorehabilitation: Evidence and application, 2nd edition* (pp. 106–118). Cambridge, UK: Cambridge University Press.

Cicerone, K., Levin, H., Malec, J., Stuss, D., & Whyte, J. (2006). Cognitive rehabilitation interventions for executive function: Moving from bench to bedside in patients with traumatic brain injury. *Journal of Cognitive Neuroscience, 18,* 1212–1222.

Corbetta, M. (2008). Functional brain imaging and neurological recovery. In D. T. Stuss, G. Winocur, & I. H. Robertson (Eds.), *Cognitive neurorehabilitation: Evidence and application, 2nd edition* (pp. 162–181). Cambridge, UK: Cambridge University Press.

Courville, C. B. (1937). *Pathology of the central nervous system, Part 4*. Moutain View, CA: Pacific Publishers.

Craik, F. I. M., Winocur, G., Palmer, H., Binns, M. A., Edwards, M., Bridges, K., et al. (2007). Cognitive rehabilitation in the elderly: Effects on memory. *Journal of the International Neuropsychological Society, 13,* 132–142.

Dawson, D. R., & Winocur, G. (2008). Psychosocial considerations in cognitive rehabilitation. In D. T. Stuss, G. Winocur, & I. H. Robertson (Eds.), *Cognitive neurorehabilitation: Evidence and application, 2nd edition* (pp. 232–249). Cambridge, UK: Cambridge University Press.

Fitzpatrick, S. M., & Robertson, I. H. (2008). The future of cognitive neurorehabilitation. In D. T. Stuss, G. Winocur, & I. H. Robertson (Eds.), *Cognitive neurorehabilitation: Evidence and application, 2nd edition* (pp. 565–574). Cambridge, UK: Cambridge University Press.

Ghaffar, O., & Feinstein, A. (2008). Mood, affect and motivation in rehabilitation. In D. T. Stuss, G. Winocur, & I. H. Robertson (Eds.), *Cognitive neurorehabilitation: Evidence and application, 2nd edition* (pp. 205–217). Cambridge, UK: Cambridge University Press.

Godefroy, O., Cabaret, M., Petit-Chenal, V., Pruvo, J.-P., & Rousseaux, M. (1999). Control functions of the frontal lobes. Modularity of the central-supervisory system? *Cortex, 35*(1), 20.

Grady, C. L., Protzner, A. B., Kovacevic, N., Strother, S. C., Afshin-Pour, B., Wojtowicz, M., et al. (2010). A multivariate analysis of age-related differences in default mode and task-positive networks across multiple cognitive domains. *Cerebral Cortex, 20,* 1432–1447.

Halstead, W. C. (1947). *Brain and intelligence: A quantitative study of the frontal lobes.* Chicago: Chicago University Press.

Hayman, S. E. (2011). The meaning of the human genome project for neuropsychiatric disorders. *Science, 331,* 1026.

Hesse, M. D., Sparing, R., & Fink, G. R. (2011). Ameliorating spatial neglect with non-invasive brain stimulation: From pathophysiological concepts to novel treatment strategies. *Neuropsychological Rehabilitation, 21*(5), 676–702.

Hetherington, C. R., Stuss, D. T., & Finlayson, M.A.J. (1996). Reaction time and variability 5 and 10 years after traumatic brain injury. *Brain Injury, 10,* 473–486.

Hultsch, D. F., & MacDonald, S.W.S. (2004). Intraindividual variability in performance as a theoretical window onto cognitive aging. In R. A. Dixon, L. Backman, & L.-G. Nilsson (Eds.), *New frontiers in cognitive aging* (pp. 65–88). New York, NY: Oxford University Press.

Kagan, A., Simmons-Mackie, N., Rowland, A., Huijbregts, M., Shumway, E., McEwen, S., et al. (2008). Counting what counts: A framework for capturing real-life outcomes of aphasia intervention. *Aphasiology, 22,* 258–280.

Koechlin, E., Basso, G., Pietrini, P., Panzer, S., & Grafman, J. (1999). The role of the anterior prefrontal cortex in human cognition. *Nature, 399,* 148–151.

Kolb, B., & Gibb, R. (2008). Principles of neuroplasticity and behavior. In D. T. Stuss, G. Winocur, & I. H. Robertson (Eds.), *Cognitive neurorehabilitation: Evidence and application, 2nd edition* (pp. 6–21). Cambridge, UK: Cambridge University Press.

Kolb, B., Teskey, G. C., & Gibb, R. (2010). Factors influencing cerebral plasticity in the normal and injured brain. *Frontiers in Human Neuroscience, 4,* 1–12.

Komitova, M., Johansson, B. B., & Eriksson, P. S. (2006). On neural plasticity, new neurons and the postischemic milieu: An integrated view on experimental rehabilitation. *Experimental Neurology, 199,* 43–55.

Kramer, A. F., Erickson, K. I., & McAuley, E. (2008). Effects of physical activity on cognition and brain. In D. T. Stuss, G. Winocur, & I. H. Robertson (Eds.), *Cognitive neurorehabilitation: Evidence and application, 2nd edition* (pp. 417–434). Cambridge, UK: Cambridge University Press.

Krpan, K. M., Levine, B., Stuss, D. T., & Dawson, D. R. (2007). Executive function and coping at 1-year-post traumatic brain injury. *Journal of Clinical and Experimental Neuropsychology, 29,* 36–46.

Krpan, K. M., Stuss, D. T., & Anderson, N. (2011). Planful versus avoidant coping: Behaviour of individuals with moderate-to-severe traumatic brain injury during a psychosocial stress test. *Journal of the International Neuropsychological Society, 17,* 248–255.

Levin, H. S., Benton, A. L., & Grossman, R. G. (1982). *Neurobehavioral consequences of closed head injury.* New York, NY: Oxford University Press.

Levin, H. S., Kalisky, Z., Handel, S. F., Goldman, A. M., Eisenberg, H. M., Morrison, D., & Vonlaufen, A. (1985). Magnetic resonance imaging in relation to the sequelae and rehabilitation of diffuse closed head injury: Preliminary findings. *Seminars in Neurology, 5,* 221–232.

Levine, B., Stuss, D. T., Winocur, G., Binns, M. A., Fahy, L., Mandic, M., et al. (2007). Cognitive rehabilitation in the elderly: Effects on strategic behavior in relation to goal management. *Journal of the International Neuropsychological Society, 13,* 143–152.

Levine, B., Turner, G. R., & Stuss, D. T. (2008). Rehabilitation of frontal lobe functions. In D. T. Stuss, G. Winocur, & I. H. Robertson (Eds.), *Cognitive neurorehabilitation: Evidence and application, 2nd edition* (pp. 464–486). Cambridge: Cambridge University Press.

Lincoln, N., & Nair, R. D. (2008). Outcome measurement in cognitive neurorehabilitation. In D. T. Stuss, G. Winocur, & I. H. Robertson (Eds.), *Cognitive neurorehabilitation: Evidence and application, 2nd edition* (pp. 91–105). Cambridge, UK: Cambridge University Press.

Liotti, M., & Mayberg, H. S. (2001). The role of functional neuroimaging in the neuropsychology of depression. *Journal of Clinical and Experimental Neuropsychology, 23,* 121–136.

McAllister, T. W., & Arnsten, A.F.T. (2008). Pharmacologic approaches to cognitive rehabilitation. D. T. Stuss, G. Winocur, & I. H. Robertson (Eds.), *Cognitive neurorehabilitation: Evidence and application, 2nd edition* (pp. 298–320). Cambridge, UK: Cambridge University Press.

McIntosh, A. R., & Grady, C. L. (2007). Network analysis of the human brain: Applications to understanding normal and abnormal neural system operations. In F. G. Hillary & J. Deluca (Eds.), *Functional neuroimaging in clinical populations* (pp. 117–144). New York, NY: The Guilford Press.

McIntosh, A. R., Kovacevic, N., & Itier, R. J. (2008). Increased brain signal variability accompanies lower behavioral variability in development. *PLOS Computational Biology, 4,* 1–9.

Milberg, W., Blumstein, S., Giovanello, K. S., & Misiurski, C. (2003). Summation priming in aphasia: Evidence for alterations in semantic integration and activation. *Brain and Cognition, 51,* 31–47.

Miniussi, C., & Rossini, P. M. (2011). Transcranial magnetic stimulation in cognitive rehabilitation. *Neuropsychological Rehabilitation, 21*(5), 579–601.

Morris, D. M., & Taub, E. (2008). The use of constraint-induced movement therapy (CI therapy) to promote motor recovery following stroke. In D. T. Stuss, G. Winocur, & I. H. Robertson (Eds.), *Cognitive neurorehabilitation: Evidence and application, 2nd edition* (pp. 401–416). Cambridge, UK: Cambridge University Press.

Parrott, M., & Greenwood, C. (2008). Is there a role for diet in cognitive rehabilitation? In D. T. Stuss, G. Winocur, & I. H. Robertson (Eds.), *Cognitive neurorehabilitation: Evidence and application, 2nd edition* (pp. 272–291). Cambridge, UK: Cambridge University Press.

Picton, T. W., Stuss, D. T., Alexander, M. P., Shallice, T., Binns, M. A., & Gillingham, S. (2007). Effects of focal frontal lesions on response inhibition. *Cerebral Cortex, 17,* 826–838.

Picton, T. W., Stuss, D. T., Shallice, T., Alexander, M. P., & Gillingham, S. (2006). Keeping time: Effects of focal frontal lesions. *Neuropsychologia, 44,* 1195–1209.

Prigatano, G. P. (2008). Anosognosia and the process and outcome of neurorehabilitation. In D. T. Stuss, G. Winocur, & I. H. Robertson (Eds.), *Cognitive neurorehabilitation: Evidence and application, 2nd edition* (pp. 218–231). Cambridge, UK: Cambridge University Press.

Prigatano, G. P. (2010). *The study of anosognosia.* New York, NY: Oxford University Press.

Rodriguez, A. D., & Rothi, L.J.G. (2008). Principles in conducting rehabilitation research. In D. T. Stuss, G. Winocur, & I. H. Robertson (Eds.), *Cognitive neurorehabilitation: Evidence and application, 2nd edition* (pp. 79–90). Cambridge, UK: Cambridge University Press.

Scherder, E., & Eggermont, L. (2008). Exercise, cognition and dementia. In D. T. Stuss, G. Winocur, & I. H. Robertson (Eds.), *Cognitive neurorehabilitation: Evidence and application, 2nd edition* (pp. 250–271). Cambridge, UK: Cambridge University Press.

Shallice, T., & Burgess, P. W. (1996). Domains of supervisory control and the temporal organisation of behaviour. *Philosophical Transactions of the Royal Society of London, B: Biological Sciences, 351,* 1405–1412.

Shallice, T., Stuss, D. T., Alexander, M. P., Picton, T. W., & Derkzen, D. (2008). The multiple dimensions of sustained attention. *Cortex, 44,* 794–805.

Shallice, T., Stuss, D. T., Picton, T. W., Alexander, M. P., & Gillingham, S. (2008a). Multiple effects of prefrontal lesions on task-switching. *Frontiers in Human Neuroscience, 1,* 1–12.

Shallice, T., Stuss, D. T., Picton, T. W., Alexander, M. P., & Gillingham, S. (2008b). Mapping task switching in frontal cortex through neuropsychological group studies. *Frontiers in Neuroscience, 2,* 79–85.

Sohlberg, M. M., Mateer, C. A., & Stuss, D. T. (1993). Contemporary approaches to the management of executive control dysfunction. *Journal of Head Trauma Rehabilitation, 8,* 45–58.

Stickland, T., Weiss, S., & Kolb, B. (2008). Intrinsic and extrinsic neural stem cell treatment of central nervous system injury and disease. In D. T. Stuss, G. Winocur, & I. H. Robertson (Eds.), *Cognitive neurorehabilitation: Evidence and application, 2nd edition* (pp. 376–393). Cambridge, UK: Cambridge University Press.

Stuss, D. T. (2007). New approaches to prefrontal lobe testing. In B. Miller & J. Cummings (Eds.), *The human frontal lobes: Functions and disorders, 2nd edition* (pp. 292–305). New York, NY: Guilford Press.

Stuss, D. T. (2011). Functions of the frontal lobes: Relation to executive functions. *Journal of the International Neuropsychological Society, 17*(5), 759–765.

Stuss, D. T., & Alexander, M. P. (2007). Is there a dysexecutive syndrome? *Philosophical Transactions of the Royal Society of London, Series B: Biological Sciences, 362,* 901–915.

Stuss, D. T., Alexander, M. P., Floden, D., Binns, M. A., Levine, B., McIntosh, A. R., et al. (2002). Fractionation and localization of distinct frontal lobe processes: Evidence from focal lesions in humans. In D. T. Stuss & R. T. Knight (Eds.), *Principles of frontal lobe function* (pp. 392–407). New York, NY: Oxford University Press.

Stuss, D. T., Alexander, M. P., Hamer, L., Palumbo, C., Dempster, R., Binns, M., Levine, B., & Izukawa, D. (1998). The effects of focal anterior and posterior brain lesions on verbal fluency. *Journal of the International Neuropsychological Society, 4,* 265–278.

Stuss, D. T., Alexander, M. P., Shallice, T., Picton, T. W., Binns, M. A., MacDonald, R., et al. (2005). Multiple frontal systems controlling response speed. *Neuropsychologia, 43,* 396–417.

Stuss, D. T., & Binns, M. A. (2008). The patient as a moving target: The importance to rehabilitation of understanding variability. In D. T. Stuss, G. Winocur, & I. H. Robertson (Eds.),

Cognitive neurorehabilitation: Evidence and application, 2nd edition (pp. 39–61). Cambridge, UK: Cambridge University Press.

Stuss, D. T., Binns, M. A., Murphy, K. J., & Alexander, M. P. (2002). Dissociations within the anterior attentional system: Effects of task complexity and irrelevant information on reaction time speed and accuracy. *Neuropsychology, 16,* 500–513.

Stuss, D. T., Delgado, M., & Guzman, D. A. (1987). Verbal regulation in the control of motor impersistence: A proposed rehabilitation procedure. *Journal of Neurologic Rehabilitation, 1,* 19–24.

Stuss, D. T., Ely, P., Hugenholtz, H., Richard, M. T., LaRochelle, S., Poirier, C. A., & Bell, I. (1985). Subtle neuropsychological deficits in patients with good recovery after closed head injury. *Neurosurgery, 17,* 41–47.

Stuss, D. T., Floden, D., Alexander, M. P., Levine, B., & Katz, D. (2001). Stroop performance in focal lesion patients: Dissociation of processes and frontal lobe lesion location. *Neuropsychologia, 39,* 771–786.

Stuss, D. T., & Gow, C. A. (1992). "Frontal dysfunction" after traumatic brain injury. *Neuropsychiatry, Neuropsychology, and Behavioral Neurology, 5,* 272–282.

Stuss, D. T., & Levine, B. (2002). Adult clinical neuropsychology: Lessons from studies of the frontal lobes. *Annual Review of Psychology, 53,* 401–433.

Stuss, D. T., Murphy, K. J., Binns, M. A., & Alexander, M. P. (2003). Staying on the job: The frontal lobes control individual performance variability. *Brain, 126,* 2363–2380.

Stuss, D. T., Pogue, J., Buckle, L., & Bondar, J. (1994). Characterization of stability of performance in patients with traumatic brain injury: Variability and consistency on reaction time tests. *Neuropsychology, 8,* 316–324.

Stuss, D. T., Robertson, I., Craik, F. I. M., Levine, B., Alexander, M. P., Black, S., et al. (2007). Cognitive rehabilitation in the elderly: A randomized trial to evaluate a new protocol. *Journal of the International Neuropsychological Society, 13,* 120–131.

Stuss, D. T., Shallice, T., Alexander, M. P., & Picton, T. W. (1995). A multidisciplinary approach to anterior attentional functions. *Annals of the New York Academy of Sciences, 769,* 191–212.

Stuss, D. T., van Reekum, R., & Murphy, K. J. (2000). Differentiation of states and causes of apathy. In J. Borod (Ed.), *The neuropsychology of emotion* (pp. 340–363). New York, NY: Oxford University Press.

Stuss, D. T., Winocur, G., & Robertson, I. H. (Eds.). (2008). *Cognitive neurorehabilitation: Evidence and application, 2nd edition.* Cambridge, UK: Cambridge University Press.

Taub, E., Crago, J. E., & Uswatte, G. (1998). Constraint-induced movement therapy: A new approach to treatment in physical rehabilitation. *Rehabilitation Psychology, 43,* 152–170.

Taub, E., Miller, N. E., Novack, T. A., Cook, E. W.I., Fleming, W. C., Nepomuceno, C. S., et al. (1993). Technique to improve chronic motor deficit after stroke. *Archives of Physical Medicine and Rehabilitation, 74,* 347–354.

Vallar, G., & Bolognini, N. (2011). Behavioural facilitation following brain stimulation: Implications for neurorehabilitation. *Neuropsychological Rehabilitation, 21*(5), 618–649.

van Reekum, R., Stuss, D. T., & Ostrander, R. N. (2005). Apathy: Why care? *Journal of Neuropsychiatry and Clinical Neurosciences, 17,* 7–19.

Wang, M., Ramos, B. P., Paspalas, C. D., Shu, Y., Simen, A., Duque, A., et al. (2007). A2A-adrenoceptors strengthen working memory networks by inhibiting cAMP-HCN channel signaling in prefrontal cortex. *Cell, 129,* 397–410.

Wassermann, E. M., Epstei, C. M., Ziemann, U., Walsh, V., Paul, T., & Lisanby, S. H. (2008). *The Oxford handbook of transcranial stimulation.* New York, NY: Oxford University Press.

West, R., Murphy, K. J., Armilio, M. L., Craik, F. I. M., & Stuss, D. T. (2002). Lapses of intention and performance variability reveal age-related increases in fluctuations of executive control. *Brain and Cognition, 49,* 402–419.

Whyte, J. (2008). Pharmacologic treatment of cognitive impairment after traumatic brain injury. In D. T. Stuss, G. Winocur, & I. H. Robertson (Eds.), *Cognitive neurorehabilitation: Evidence and application, 2nd edition* (pp. 321–333). Cambridge, UK: Cambridge University Press.

Williamsom, P. C., & Allman, J. M. (2011). *The human illnesses. Neuropsychiatric disorders and the nature of the human brain.* New York, NY: Oxford University Press.

Wilson, B. A., Herbert, C. M., & Shiel, A. (2003). *Behavioural approaches in neuropsychological rehabilitation: Optimising rehabilitation procedures.* Hove, UK: Psychology Press.

Winocur, G. (2008). Introduction to Section 4. In D. T. Stuss, G. Winocur, & I. H. Robertson (Eds.), *Cognitive neurorehabilitation: Evidence and application, 2nd edition* (pp. 295–297). Cambridge, UK: Cambridge University Press.

Winocur, G., Craik, F. I.M., Levine, B., Robertson, I. H., Binns, M., Alexander, M. P., et al. (2007). Cognitive rehabilitation in the elderly: Overview and future directions. *Journal of the International Neuropsychological Society, 13,* 166–171.

Winocur, G., Moscovitch, M., Rosenbaum, R. S., & Sekeres, M. (2010). A study of remote spatial memory in aged rats. *Neurobiology of Aging, 31,* 143–150.

Winocur, G., Palmer, H., Dawson, D., Binns, M. A., Bridges, K., & Stuss, D. T. (2007). Cognitive rehabilitation in the elderly: An evaluation of psychosocial factors. *Journal of the International Neuropsychological Society, 13,* 153–165.

Wojtowicz, J. M., Askew, M. L., & Winocur, G. (2008). The effects of running and of inhibiting adult neurogenesis on learning and memory in rats. *European Journal of Neuroscience, 27,* 1494–1502.

Wolf, S. L., Lecraw, D. E., Barton, L. A., & Jann, B. B. (1989). Forced use of hemiplegic upper extremities to reverse the effect of learned nonuse among chronic stroke and head-injured patients. *Experimental Neurology, 104,* 104–132.

Subject Index

SUBJECT INDEX

SUBJECT INDEX